WRITING WRONGS

WRITING WRONGS:

COMMON ERRORS IN ENGLISH

ROBERT M. MARTIN

broadview press

BROADVIEW PRESS – www.broadviewpress.com
Peterborough, Ontario, Canada

Founded in 1985, Broadview Press remains a wholly independent publishing house. Broadview's focus is on academic publishing; our titles are accessible to university and college students as well as scholars and general readers. With over 600 titles in print, Broadview has become a leading international publisher in the humanities, with world-wide distribution. Broadview is committed to environmentally responsible publishing and fair business practices.

The interior of this book is printed on 100% recycled paper.

Library and Archives Canada Cataloguing in Publication

Martin, Robert M., author
      Writing wrongs : common errors in English / Robert M. Martin.

Includes bibliographical references and index.
ISBN 978-1-55481-391-9 (softcover)

      1. English language—Errors of usage. I. Title.

PE1460.M37 2017   428   C2017-907048-7

Broadview Press handles its own distribution in North America:
PO Box 1243, Peterborough, Ontario K9J 7H5, Canada
555 Riverwalk Parkway, Tonawanda, NY 14150, USA
Tel: (705) 743-8990; Fax: (705) 743-8353
email: customerservice@broadviewpress.com

Distribution is handled by Eurospan Group in the UK, Europe, Central Asia, Middle East, Africa, India, Southeast Asia, Central America, South America, and the Caribbean. Distribution is handled by Footprint Books in Australia and New Zealand.

Broadview Press acknowledges the financial support of the Government of Canada through the Canada Book Fund for our publishing activities.

Edited by Martin R. Boyne
Cover and interior design by George Kirkpatrick
Interior typeset by Eileen Eckert and George Kirkpatrick

PRINTED IN CANADA

CONTENTS

FOREWORD

THIS BOOK GREW FROM some notes I was writing in my copy of the fifth edition (2003) of *The Broadview Book of Common Errors in English*, by Don LePan. I wrote Don telling him that I could send him the notes, in case any were useful for a new edition. After he told me that he was too busy with other projects to revise, I offered to do it, and he and Marjorie Mather, Broadview's English Studies Editor, accepted. So I began making some small additions, changes, and re-organizations, but I couldn't stop; and what eventually grew was a revision that was substantial enough that Don felt it should be a book on its own, with a different title, and listing me as sole author.

Those familiar with Don's *Common Errors* book will recognize that it forms the solid backbone of this one. Don and I have rather different writing styles, and some friendly disagreements about matters of content. My footprints are all over this book, but a great deal of Don's splendid book survives in here, with his very generous permission, for which I'm enormously grateful.

Books of advice on grammar and usage are often outstandingly dull — so dry that bits of them flake off and eventually get vacuumed up from under the furniture. But by contrast Don's book, like its classic predecessor Fowler's *A Dictionary of Modern English Usage* (1926), is full of vigorous, interesting writing; one could (and I did) read each of them strictly for pleasure. I have kept this tradition firmly in mind and have done my best to make the present book readable, even occasionally enjoyable. Among all the minutiae about usage rules and so on, I have sprinkled some quirky bits that I hope you'll discover and find entertaining.

My daughter Erica Martin, a grammar nerd and (at times) an ESL teacher, gave a great deal of enormously useful advice in response to an early draft. And the sharp eyes and linguistic smarts of Martin Boyne, Broadview's copy editor, are responsible for fixing what must have been (I shamefacedly admit) a thousand mistakes of all sorts in the penultimate version.

Thanks also go to Maureen Okun and Nora Ruddock, the authors of *The Broadview Pocket Guide to Citation and Documentation*, and to the always helpful Broadview Press, for permission to reprint sections on attribution styles here.

Robert M. Martin

PART I:

WAIT! STOP! MAKE SURE YOU READ THIS!

How to Use This Book

I'M GLAD YOU HAVEN'T skipped this part of the book.

The ordinary way to use a book — start with the beginning and go on reading (if you can stand it) till the end — won't work here. For this book, here's my advice:

(1) Part II, mysteriously titled **WHAT AND WHY**, responds to these questions:

+ What exactly is the difference between a bit of correct English and an error?
+ Why (if at all) is correct English worth learning?

These questions, and the answers I propose, may interest you. Give it a try and see. But reading this part will not help you actually to learn correct English. So if you're not interested in these questions (and if your instructor doesn't assign this part), I'd advise you to skip it, except for the first section of Part II, titled "What's Going On." This discusses the two kinds of good English this book is about: Standard Written English (SWE) and Informal Educated English (IEE) — good *spoken*

English. A particular bit of language might be an error in both, or okay in both, or okay in one but not the other. I'll indicate which of these is the case using a system of symbols; you'll find these translated inside the front cover of this book.

(2) In Parts III, IV, V, and VI we get down to the real business of the book: separating good English from mistakes. You can use these parts as a reference source, when you have a question about a particular bit of the language, or you can read them through. If you read these parts, don't do this the way you'd read a novel or a science textbook, for example. There will be many items telling you things you already know; just skim through these. Find things you didn't already know, and read about them carefully. There are in these parts, as little prizes to keep you going, occasional silly bits, jokes, and the like.

The long first section of Part III, "Meanings, Uses, and Idioms" is a dictionary of English words and phrases, correcting mistakes in meanings and spellings, and other matters. It's too long (and in parts too boring) to go through all in one sitting; I'd suggest you tackle it in small doses at different times. The entries are alphabetized here, so it can be used as a reference dictionary if you have a particular question. But not all the words and phrases dealt with in here are in alphabetical order. For example, if you forget what the difference between the words **affect** and **effect** is, you can find this in the entry headed **affect/effect**. But if you look up **effect** in the **e**'s, you won't find it. This is where the index at the end of the book is useful. **Effect** there will direct you to the entry for **affect/effect**.

The rest of Part III is in much smaller chunks, organized by topics. These are of readable length and can be read sequentially or by skipping around. You can locate discussion of particular topics by checking subject headings in the index, or by looking in the Table of Contents.

3) Parts IV, V, and VI have to do with constructing sentences, and with topics such as organization, style, form, and so on. Again, a miscellany of topics is dealt with here, in readable chunks. Look at the Table of Contents and index.

4) Part VII is not for reading sequentially. It's a summary of proper form (footnotes, bibliography, etc.) for writing papers or books, as prescribed (sometimes differently) by the three authoritative style guides (MLA, Chicago, and APA). Use this as a reference if you need to make your writing adhere to one particular style or another.

NOTE on SYMBOLS: You'll find little pictorial symbols in almost all parts of this book. What they mean is given in the Key to Symbols printed inside the front cover of this book.

PART II:
WHAT AND WHY

ive never seen such a waste of breathe in my life. any professor that tells his class there all going to fail roght before you take a test is nuts! dont believe me take his class and waste a semester
— critical review of teacher at Macomb Community Junior College, on *Rate My Professors* website

What's Going On?

YOU HAVE THIS BOOK in your hands, so somebody — you or the instructor who made you get it — thinks that there is a difference between good and bad English, and that it's a good idea for you to learn how to speak and write the good kind. But what makes something bad English? And what's the point in learning how to speak or write good English? These are questions that aren't often asked, and when they are, they don't often get good answers. I'll try to do better.

The first important point to consider is that English is not one language. It's a collection of dialects — of linguistic systems differing from one another in vocabulary (what words are in it, relative frequency of their use, what they mean), idiomatic combinations, grammar, spellings, and pronunciations.[1] Different dialects are often associated with different regions. The three main regional dialects of English, broadly speaking, are North American, British, and Australasian. Within each of these areas, all sorts of regional and class- and education-related dialects can be distinguished. Each dialect has its own conventional rules, in some

---

1 Linguists sometimes distinguish *dialects* and *registers*. Dialects are linguistic patterns peculiar to particular groups; registers are different patterns individuals switch between depending on who they're communicating with. This distinction is fuzzy and sometimes hard to make. Often in this book I'll be (I guess) talking about registers of English, not dialects; but for simplicity I'll call every different pattern a dialect.

ways different from the others. This means that there isn't any one thing that's good English, that follows *the* conventional rules of the language. There are instead several good Englishes — one for each dialect.

But in this book I'm going to concentrate on two dialects. One of them I'll call **Standard Written English (SWE).** This is the form of language you're supposed to write in, if you're writing a paper for a university class, or for the more formal sorts of publication. There are regional differences among SWEs, but these are minor; to a large extent, it's the same the world over. So, for example, you wouldn't be able to identify the first language of authors of articles in academic journals: they're all written in, or translated or edited into, SWE. Maybe standardization is a good thing, but the bad news is that SWE is like a *second* language for everyone who knows it. I mean *everyone*. SWE has to be learned in school, or later. The dialect every child learns at home — the child's *first* language — is what's spoken there, but, amazingly, SWE is exclusively restricted to writing. Nobody speaks it.[2] You'll notice the difference when somebody reads something written in SWE: it doesn't sound like anybody's normal talk, although SWE writing has admittedly become slightly more informal over the years.

The other dialect we'll concentrate on is a spoken one, associated with educated English speakers. You learned this as your first language if you grew up in a household where this was spoken. It's also found written in less formal contexts — in personal letters, for example (but not emails and certainly not text messages, which typically have their own different dialects), on some websites, and in some popular journalism. It's also sometimes tolerated by book publishers.[3] We'll call this **Informal Educated English (IEE).**

So this book won't simply classify bits of language as acceptable or unacceptable in English as a whole, since that is almost impossible to do. Its major categories will be:

+ Acceptable/unacceptable in SWE
+ Acceptable/unacceptable in IEE

Obviously, what is an error — an unacceptable bit of language — in one of these categories might not be an error in another. **I couldn't believe it was him** is as an error in SWE, partly because of the contraction **couldn't**, which is unacceptable in very formal SWE, but mainly because of the objective case form **him**; the acceptable replacement in SWE would be **I could not believe it was he.** But that SWE sentence would be very odd if spoken in IEE and should be avoided

---

2   I exaggerate slightly. There are some people who can speak it, but extremely few. You can hear them sometimes on the radio or TV being interviewed. Almost all of them were expensively educated in England and they speak like a book. How did they learn how to do it?

3   For example, Broadview Press, who tolerated my language in this book.

there.[4] Here's another example: **It's awfully good of you to remember my birthday.** The use of **awfully** to mean *very* is an error in SWE. But there's no problem with that use in IEE.

The sentence **You don't want to, but do it anyways** is unacceptable in both SWE and in IEE because of its last word (which should be **anyway**), but that word is firmly established in some other informal English dialects and is not an error there. Another example is **I tried to ignore that insult as best as I could**, which should be **I tried to ignore that insult in the best way I could**, or **to the best of my ability.** If you're a language snob and get offended when people say **anyways** or **as best as I could**, try to remember that the coexistence of different dialects is often thought of as a good thing. People get upset when a dialect spoken in some remote area of the world is becoming extinct. The dialects of English containing **anyways** are healthy, and isn't that a good thing?

So this book is designed to help you with the two dialects of Standard English: SWE and IEE. (Other dialects will just have to look after themselves.) What you should understand, when you read the judgement here that a certain bit of language is unacceptable, is that this means that it's unacceptable-in-SWE or unacceptable-in-IEE, or both. That does not mean that it's unacceptable everywhere. Maybe it's at home in other dialects.

It's assumed, of course, that you already have some familiarity with SWE and IEE; otherwise, you wouldn't have understood what's already been said in this section. This book will help you *polish up* your SWE and IEE.

Why?

Okay, but why might it be a good idea for you to make the effort to do this?

First, let's lay to rest the idea that SWE and IEE are *better* than the other English dialects. There is absolutely no basis for this idea. The two are not superior to the others in any way. There's nothing that you can say in either that you can't say in any other English dialect. They may have more vocabulary than other dialects (maybe!), but that doesn't make them better: it just means that you might have to use a few more words in another dialect to say the same thing. Their emotional expressivity is not greater. In fact, it may be more limited, because SWE and IEE are both quite prudish about excluding expletives and colourful slang expressions that pep up other dialects considerably.

Sometimes people claim that good written or spoken English is necessary for your audience to understand what you write or say. This claim is hardly ever true.

---

4   Don't train your children to say things like this. It's the kind of thing that will get them exiled to the nerds' table in the school cafeteria.

Consider these bits of language, each of which contains (what's often, at least, supposed to be[5]) a mistake in English:

+ And it ain't a fit night out for man nor beast. — W.C. Fields, *The Fatal Glass of Beer* (1933)
+ I never heard nothing about none of that.
+ I seen it
+ where she's at
+ not too good of a
+ growed
+ irregardless
+ alright
+ who would of thought
+ a ways to go
+ besides the point
+ I'm presently out of the office
+ that's how come it doesn't work
+ flaunt convention
+ rather unique; most unique
+ Then she's like, "Jaden is sooo gross!"
+ this begs the question [*when taken to mean: this raises the question*]
+ For now, she wants to enjoy the enormity of the moment. — *Newsweek*
+ US was reticent to help, Taliban says — headline, the *Toronto Globe and Mail*
+ Do you mean not use the Conrad quote or simply not put Conrad's name to it? — T.S. Eliot, letter to Ezra Pound (1951)
+ Charlie had never fallen in love, but was anxious to do so on the first opportunity. — Kipling, "The Finest Story in the World" (1891)
+ the youngest of the two daughters. — Jane Austen, *Emma* (1816)
+ All debts are cleerd between you and I. — Shakespeare, *The Merchant of Venice* (1600)
+ I will lift up mine eyes unto the hills, from whence cometh my help. — King James Bible, Psalm 121 (*This sentence is my candidate for the most beautiful in the history of English.*)
+ *Pronunciations:* liberry, heighth, excape, acrost, Febuary, nuculer, mischievious

---

5   Information about what's supposed to be wrong in some of these cases can be found in the section below called Meanings, Uses, and Idioms (pp. 29–135), in the entries for **not too good of a, irregardless, all right, have/of, as best as, beside, presently, how come, flaunt, unique, like, beg the question, enormity, reticent, quote, anxious, hence**. In some cases, the judgement that there's a mistake is questionable, and will be discussed.

Everyone understands all of these perfectly. There is *absolutely* zero difference in intelligibility between the first of the following sentences, written in perfect SWE, and the second, which is not:

+ Rosenberg and I went to the seminar.
+ Me and Ashley went to the mall.

Sometimes the weaker claim is made: that SWE and IEE are more clearly understandable than other dialects. Would you find any of the defective items on the list above more difficult to understand than the corresponding corrected version? (In fact, sometimes you might find the SWE or IEE version *more* difficult to comprehend.) SWE and IEE are not inherently clearer, more precise, or more communicative than the other English dialects.

Grammar teachers and advisors often exaggerate the importance of learning SWE. Humourist Dave Barry writes:

I cannot overemphasize the importance of good grammar. What a crock. I could easily overemphasize the importance of good grammar. For example, I could say: "Bad grammar is the leading cause of slow, painful death in North America," or "Without good grammar, the United States would have lost World War II." The truth is that grammar is not the most important thing in the world. The Super Bowl is the most important thing in the world. But grammar is still important.— "What Is and Ain't Grammatical" (1985)

There must be some other good reasons why you should learn facility with SWE and IEE.

Admission to some academic programs might require some facility with those dialects, and once in, your written work will often be evaluated, in part, on how closely it approximates SWE. But some university teachers won't require it, either because they've given up in the face of growing SWE incompetence among their students, or because they themselves don't know the language, having been taught by teachers who didn't require it or didn't know it.

If you want to have something published, it might have to be written in SWE, or in a language somewhere between SWE and IEE. What you submit need not be perfect — publishers all employ sharp-eyed, expert, and hugely underpaid copy editors to fix things up once a manuscript has been accepted — but if what you submit is too far from SWE, it will be rejected, no matter how wonderful it is otherwise. (I'm not talking about internet publication, of course. A huge amount of what you see there shows no familiarity with SWE or IEE at all.)

17

Okay, but what about when you've left academia for the real world, and you're not interested in having something published?

Sometimes some degree of competence with SWE and IEE will help you get a government or corporate job, and succeed in it. Not invariably, however. I've heard corporate hiring officers say that they look for "people skills," not language skills. And if your boss has no idea about how to use an apostrophe, then you might not need to know that either. It has to be admitted that the necessity and expectation of knowing SWE have diminished somewhat in recent years, but they are far from gone.

But let's look at these matters in a more general way. To have interaction with, not to mention acceptance by, any social group, it helps to have some facility with their dialect, and the more facility you have, the more advantage that confers. Speaking their language is like knowing the secret handshake of a club. People with very little facility with the dialect used in important interactions of a community will be at a disadvantage; and, to some extent, educated people, those who speak IEE and write SWE, are the ones who participate in important political and financial interactions. Educated people may think less of the content of what you write or speak in another dialect — indeed, of you personally. Putting it bluntly: you run the risk that *you* and *what you say* will be thought uneducated, and thus stupid. That's really too bad. Un- or under-educated does not equal stupid. And it's regrettable that people prejudge the content of written or spoken material merely on the basis that it's not in the approved dialect.[6] But that's the way things often are, like it or not, and that makes it in your interest to learn what's in this book.

But here's a different reason for gaining facility with these dialects — a reason you'll feel more comfortable with. As you'll see as you wander around in this book, many judgements about what's right and wrong have to do with how language treats the reader (or listener). Bad English will put off, or annoy, or exasperate, or jar, or trip up, or bore, or offend, or temporarily confuse the reader. Good English is smoother and will be easier and more pleasant to read. It's also easier to understand — not (again) because SWE and IEE are inherently clearer than other dialects, but because skill in SWE and IEE, or in any dialect, the ability to manage any dialect *well*, consists, in part, of the ability to be clear and comprehensible in that dialect.

Good English is *kinder on the reader.* Even if you didn't have any feelings of benevolence toward your readership (but I know you do), it would still be in your self-interest to be nice to them. You're writing for a purpose — maybe to amuse, or convince, or request, or inform, or whatever — and you stand a better chance of success if you write prose that's kind to the reader. And your readers will be

---

6   On the other hand, from another perspective, this attitude isn't so awful. It shows that intelligence and education still get some respect. Isn't that good news?

more favourably inclined to the content of what you write when they notice that you respect them enough to have taken some care in its production. Good English, then, is *effective* English — it accomplishes what you want it to do.

And here's another good reason. A well-written bit of prose is *beautiful*. It's a work of art, of grace and harmony. Not many people can turn out a really beautiful piece of writing — I can't, certainly. But we should still try to make our writing as beautiful as we can. At least then we'll be able to save it from being ugly. When we try, every little bit we do very slightly alters the ugly/beautiful balance in the universe for the better. That's a good thing to aim at.

What Makes for Acceptability?

Acceptability in a dialect is a moving target, because dialects mutate. Bits of a dialect that were once acceptable become strange and archaic. More importantly for our purposes, linguistic objects that crop up in a dialect, newborn or migrating from another dialect, at first count as errors; but if these become frequent and solidly embedded, they may therefore become acceptable. The connection between frequent use and correctness in this case is unusual and worth thinking about. Take a very simple case: why is it correct to use the word **dog** to refer to dogs rather than to cats or lakes or peanut-butter sandwiches? The only possible reason is that that's the way English speakers use the word. You *should* use the word that way because that's what people *do*.

The facts about every language show the pervasiveness of linguistic change of this sort. This is shown in the etymology of words — the history of how each word evolved in meaning and in spelling from earlier ones. Here's a typical example. The word **endeavour** derives from a Middle English phrase **put in dever**, which is a slightly garbled import from the Old French phrase *metter en deveir*, literally, **put in duty**, meaning *make it one's duty to do something*. *Deveir* comes from Latin *debere*, owe. Each new use was at first an error, running contrary to established usage, spelling, or pronunciation; and each became itself established. Similar changes happened in grammar. For example: Whereas we use **you** to address one or more than one, in both subject and object forms, in earlier periods of English, as sentence subjects, **thou** was singular and **ye** was plural, with corresponding objects **thee** and **you**. Between the twelfth and fifteenth centuries, the mistaken additional use of **ye** and **you** as polite singular forms became more common, and then acceptable. Later the mistaken substitution of **you** for **ye** gained frequency and, in Early Modern English, acceptability. By 1700, the similar mistaken replacement of **thou** by **you** became correct.

Sometimes the conclusion drawn from all of this is that the so-called *correctness* of any bit of language amounts to nothing but its common use. What that would mean, then, is that there can be no such thing as a common error in usage, because any usage that's common must be correct. If that's right, then, the job of an arbiter of linguistic correctness would be nothing but statistical research: finding out how people actually talk and write. A dictionary with this approach to language, called *descriptivism*, might report that **ain't** is frequently heard (though often found substandard).[7] A prescriptive dictionary, on the other hand, would simply tell readers that it's unacceptable.

Comparison of these two passages, one in Old English, the other a translation, shows just how much change has happened:

An. M.LXVI. On þyssum geare man halgode þet mynster æt Westmynstre on Cyldamæsse dæg 7 se cyng Eadward forðferde on Twelfts mæsse æfen 7 hine mann bebyrgede on Twelftan mæssedæg innan þære niwa halgodre circean on Westmyntre 7 Harold eorl feng to Englalandes cynerice swa swa se cyng hit him geuðe 7 eac men hine þærto gecuron 7 wæs gebletsod to cynge on Twelftan mæssedæg 7 þa ylcan geare þe he cyng wæs he for ut mid sciphere togeanes Willelme ...

1066 In this year the monastery at Westminster was hallowed on Childermas day (28 December). And king Eadward died on Twelfth-mass eve (5 January) and he was buried on Twelfth-mass day, in the newly hallowed church at Westminster. And earl Harold succeeded to the Kingdom of England, as the king had granted it to him and men had also chosen him thereto and he was blessed as king on Twelfth-mass day. And in the same year that he was king he went out with a naval force against William ...

This is the beginning of *The Anglo-Saxon Chronicle*, the "Peterborough Version," copied from an earlier Old English manuscript during the twelfth century. Text and translation provided by Elly van Gelderen in the website "A History of the English Language" (http://www.public.asu.edu/~gelderen/hel/chron.html). You can figure out much of this by comparing it with its translation, and by understanding that what looks like the numeral **7** is the abbreviation for **and**, and that the letters þ and ð are both roughly equivalent to the modern **th**.

But what is "common usage"? The division of English into separate dialects means that what is very common in English in general need not be very common in a particular dialect. **I ain't got none** shows up frequently in the language production of English speakers as a whole, but not, of course, in the SWE and IEE

---

7 The publication of Webster's Third New International Dictionary (1961) was a landmark of the new movement toward descriptivism. Its (in)famous entry on **ain't** said "though disapproved by many and more common in less educated speech, used orally in most parts of the US by many cultivated speakers esp. in the phrase *ain't I*."

dialects. So even if *frequently used = correct*, it doesn't follow that **I ain't got none** is correct in SWE or IEE. And that's what this book is about.

Whether a usage is common or not, *frequently used* is a matter of degree. What characteristically happens when a bit of language gradually works its way into acceptability is that it is used more and more frequently. When a usage that was previously clearly deemed an "error" has achieved a frequency in the language of 1% of that of the old accepted usage, that's probably not enough to grant it acceptability. But what frequency does some previously incorrect usage have to attain before a case can be made for its acceptability? That's a question for which there is nothing but a very vague answer: *a good deal of frequency.*

Let's look at some actual cases.

For a long time, usage arbiters have been telling whoever would listen that the phrase **identical with** was correct, and **identical to** was not. Here's a graph showing actual usage of those two phrases in books since 1940:[8]

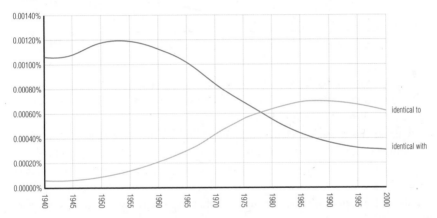

Before 1945, according to the graph, **identical with** showed up in books about fifteen times more often than **identical to**. At that point, there was no problem in agreeing with the grammarians. But the latter started to replace the former, and in 1978, when they were equally frequent, the grammarians' advice, presumably backed up with tradition, more or less won the day. But in 2000, **identical to** appeared more than twice as often as **identical with**, and it seems that most grammarians have become convinced by its frequency that it's now a legitimate part of SWE. But when, during that 55-year period, did it become acceptable? The

---

8   This graph is the product of a website called Ngram Viewer (https://books.google.com/ngrams/); you insert one or more words or phrases, and it tells you about their occurrence in books over the years. It's an amazing service provided by the big-data people at Google. The numbers on the vertical scale represent the percentage (in this case) of these two-word combinations among all two-word combinations in a large number of books. The horizontal scale is year of publication of the books.

cross-over point, 1978, doesn't mark acceptability. And it's clear that a considerable advantage in frequency is not a necessary or sufficient condition for acceptability. **Disorient** occurs almost six times as often as **disorientate**, but because the usage of the latter is still substantial, and has actually remained steady or even grown over time, it's usually still judged acceptable, along with its shorter cousin, in SWE.

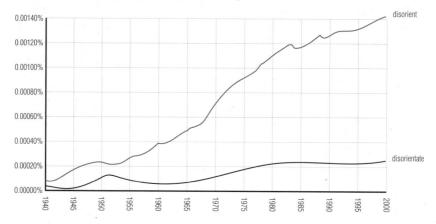

While actual usage by educated speakers and writers is a very important consideration for correctness, it's clear that there is a variety of other considerations. I now survey some of the main ones.

A usage has a weaker claim on acceptability when it expresses a concept or performs a function already exactly covered by another one. Needless proliferation in language is undesirable in one person's linguistic repertoire and in the language culture as a whole — a waste of energy and resources. So if you already know and use the verb **disorient**, it's pointless to insist that you also recognize and use the verb **disorientate**.

That example also illustrates another criterion. While both **disorient** and **disorientate** are deemed acceptable, the former is generally preferable just because it's shorter and easier, without the apparently useless extra syllable of the latter. So we'll be making judgements not only about acceptability or non-acceptability but also about relative desirability.

An additional criterion for acceptability is how recently the linguistic object has arrived in the language.[9] The fact that a phrase has come from nowhere only a few decades ago can count against it, especially if it's in competition with another one that's been around for centuries. This conservatism in linguistic prescription is not just stick-in-the-mud old-fogeyism. There are a couple of good reasons why

---

9   The term for a new word is *neologism*. In case you want to impress people by inserting this word into your conversation, you should know that it's pronounced *nee-AH-luh-jizm*, not *nee-oh-LOW-jizm*.

older usages ought to be favoured, everything else being equal. One is that there is some value in linguistic continuity: sticking with the older forms allows us to read and appreciate older literature. It's impossible, of course, to prevent linguistic evolution, but someone whose linguistic repertoire has narrowed to exclude somewhat older terms has a poorer cultural heritage available. A second reason is that the older terms might have clearer and more settled uses and meanings. The exact meaning of a very new term, if it has one, is more likely to be unknown to some of one's audience.

Among the newest arrivals in language behaviour are vogue words, trendy buzzwords, and jargon. Sometimes these are harmless changes in what was arbitrary to start off with — for example, the sudden ubiquity of **No problem!** as a replacement for **You're welcome**, as a response to **Thanks!**

But for your own good, you should be warned against sprinkling your speech and writing with language-du-jour. While you might think that doing this shows your audience just how cool and hip you are, it can have the opposite effect: suggesting that maybe you're a bit insecure and overly concerned with making a good impression. Speech infested with trend-words, psychobabble, socialworkisms, and business and bureaucrat jargon is a pretty good sign of a mouth disconnected from its brain. You're trying to sound smart, but you wind up sounding foolish. It also means a great deal of work for you: constant effort to keep up. Fad expressions often depart as quickly as they arrive, and you're likely to be left saying something uncool because it has become passé or standard or hackneyed, or has just disappeared.

Much the same is true regarding language that is complicated, pompous, pedantic, pretentious, or over-intellectual. Again this is motivated by the desire to impress, and again it often has the opposite result. Remember this important motto:

An ounce of pretension is worth a pound of manure. — *Steel Magnolias* (1989)

Oddly, the simpler your language, the smarter it makes you seem. Contorted, overblown language has an additional bad effect: it makes things more difficult for the audience, and this is always a mistake, making writing and talk less effective. You're always better off making your writing and speaking easy and pleasant. Good English is easy to follow.

A consideration that has grown increasingly important for writers is making sure that terms expressing bias, or found insulting, should be avoided. A section of this book (pp. 240–47) will be devoted to problems and techniques involved with this.

But sometimes irrelevant considerations are raised regarding linguistic correctness. One of them is logic.

+ Consider the phrases **centre around** and **centre on**. It's sometimes complained that the first is illogical: a centre is a point, so something can't **centre around**. Another example: the slang phrase **I could care less**. What's meant here is clearly *I don't care*, but to express that logically, it's claimed, what should be said is: caring less than I do is impossible: **I *couldn't* care less**.[10]
+ What's a **meteoric rise?** Meteors *fall*.
+ **The eye of the storm** is often used to refer to the point where something is the most intense, but the only storms with eyes are hurricanes, and the eye of a hurricane is the point in the middle where things are briefly calm.
+ How can it be that **a near miss** is a miss, not a hit that nearly misses?
+ How can it be that **a slim chance** and **a fat chance** are the same things?

In each of these examples, a case might be made for logical peculiarity. Each might have been considered an error when it first appeared, but by now they all have solidly established idiomatic meanings that everyone knows. So there's usually no point in raising "logical" objections. These are amusing to people who are amused by this sort of thing, but they aren't serious considerations.

Another irrelevant consideration is that a word is being used in a way contrary to its original meaning. Consider the word **tremendous** (see box). In the 1600s, that word was still closely related to its Latin origin, ***tremendus***, meaning *what excites trembling*, thus *something horrible*. Mistakes in using that word accumulated, and by the mid-1800s the word had broadened out to mean *great, astounding, immense*. Later, its central sense became merely *huge*. Now it often is used merely to mean *really great*.[11]

Donald Trump used the word **tremendous** thirteen times during his 26 September 2016 debate with Hillary Clinton. Hinting that Clinton was medically unfit, he said, "To be president of this country you need tremendous stamina." He also referred to his "tremendous income" and the "tremendous problems" America faces. He said he would "be reducing taxes tremendously" and that this would "create tremendous numbers of new jobs." He's not exactly a virtuoso language-user, but were these actual mistakes?

Does **tremendous** really mean *horrible?* Of course not. Each of these historical changes was a mistake for a while, until it became so solidly embedded in English that it was no longer a mistake. It's called a semantic change and is a normal part of the evolution of a language.

---

10 Linguist Steven Pinker argues that there's nothing wrong with this phrase because it's uttered ironically (*The Language Instinct*, p. 377).
11 Compare a similar migration in the word **terrific**, which started out meaning *terror-producing*.

Usage advice should not fight battles lost long ago. Word-wranglers should recall the advice of the wise ancients: "You've gotta know when to hold 'em, know when to fold 'em."

Last in this category of the irrelevant is what the groundbreaking usage expert H.W. Fowler called *superstitions*. These are pointless language rules that somebody made up. They had no basis in real usage and no connection with effective writing. People kept ignoring these in their real talking and writing, and they are rejected by most contemporary writers on good English. Yet they have been relentlessly drilled into students learning to write (see box).

Here are some examples of superstitions:

- Never split an infinitive. An infinitive is a noun formed from a verb by prefixing **to**, e.g. **to run**, **to carry**, **to be**. Splitting an infinitive is inserting a word, usually an adverb, between **to** and the verb: **to quickly run, to always carry, to hardly be.**
- You should never use the pronoun **I** in formal writing, or refer to the reader as **you**.
- Prepositions are never words to end a sentence with.
- The passive voice should never be used.
- Don't use contractions in formal writing.
- No sentence fragments.
- And never begin a sentence with **And** or **But**.
- Never use **hopefully** to mean *I hope* (as in **Hopefully, it won't snow tomorrow.**)
- **None** must take a singular verb.

You have already seen violations of some of these rules in this book, and you'll see many more. In fact, there are dozens of other superstitions. Trying to remember and follow these rules imposes extra effort on writers and often results in distorted, unnatural-sounding language, impeding your meaning.

Sticklers

This word will be used often in this book to identify people who were taught a huge collection of old rules for English, including a large number of superstitions, and who often point out — and always get upset about — others' violations of them. Should you just ignore their objections? NO! If you're writing something that a Stickler will read, it may be in your interest not to violate those old rules (especially if the Stickler is marking your paper, or considering it for publication, or evaluating you for a job). KNOW YOUR AUDIENCE. If it includes Sticklers, and you don't want to upset them, you should pay attention to the old rules. You'll be told, throughout this book, when violations of useless old rules might get you in trouble with Sticklers.

A Surprising Note on Rules

Do you know the infield-fly rule in baseball? It's fairly obscure, and it has nothing to do with informal games, but it's known by all professional players and enforced in their games. Here it is:

> An Infield Fly is a fair fly ball (not a line drive or bunt) that, in the judgment of the umpire, can be caught by an infielder, pitcher, or catcher with ordinary effort and when there are runners on first and second or first, second, and third, and fewer than two outs. When the umpire calls "infield fly" the batter is out, regardless of whether the ball is subsequently caught or dropped. The ball is live, and runners already on base may advance (at their own risk) if the ball is not caught or tag up and advance if it is caught.[12]

This rule is so complicated, and is brought to bear so rarely, that new players couldn't just pick it up in the course of play. They have to be told it, explicitly, and they must memorize it and be prepared to deal with it on the rare occasions when it arises. First-language users of English, however, almost never learn the rules of the language that way. There are a few exceptions — the rules you have to learn in grammar class — but these are the ones that are very rarely followed in ordinary speech, and mistakes are rarely corrected outside the schoolroom. If they had been more commonly obeyed, then you'd just learn them the same way you learned most of the others: by imitating what people do and don't do, and by observing when things are understood, misunderstood, and corrected.

The interesting thing about learning rules this way is that people who have done it sometimes can't even state the rule they've learned. To demonstrate this, try this experiment. Read these two sentences out loud:

+ This bicycle no longer is of any use to me.
+ I can't use this bicycle any longer.

If you're a native speaker of English, or a very competent ESL speaker, you pronounced **use** in the first sentence with a final hissing -**s** (an *unvoiced* sound), but **use** in the second with a final buzzing -**z** (a *voiced* sound). You weren't even thinking about parts of speech, but the unvoiced version went with the noun (a word referring to a thing), and the voiced went with the verb (a word referring to an action).

---

12 This statement of the rule is widely reprinted on the internet; however, the real rule—the one in the official rulebook of Major League Baseball, is even more complicated. (See http://m.mlb.com/news/article/39516960//). Unless you're after a career in baseball, you should forget this rule right now. You'll have plenty of other more useful things to pack into your brain before you get very far into this book.

Don't believe this is a fairly general rule? Pronounce these:

*   When I was a little kid I lived in a house just like that one.
*   The empty building on this army base will house new immigrants temporarily

See? In the first sentence, **house**, a noun, ends with an unvoiced, hissing -**s**. In the second, **house**, a verb, ends with a voiced, buzzing -**z**.

Many other examples show that there's a rule here. Sometimes spelling changes reflect the change from an unvoiced final consonant in the noun to a voiced final consonant in the verb: noun: **advice**; verb: **advise.** And this unvoiced/voiced difference works with other consonants too: a final **th**, and a final **f**. Here are some other examples, with the unvoiced-consonant noun first and the voiced-consonant verb second:

Final S		Final Th		Final F	
noun	**verb**	**noun**	**verb**	**noun**	**verb**
use	use	bath	bathe	shelf	shelve
house	house	teeth	teethe	life	live
excuse	excuse	mouth	mouth	half	halve
abuse	abuse	cloth	clothe	safe	save
loss	lose			belief	believe
spouse	espouse			relief	relieve
advice	advise			proof	prove
choice	choose				

You've been following this rule, but you probably didn't even know it existed. So there's something very strange about language: its rules are followed by language users who very often nevertheless can't state them. Every native English speaker follows this rule, even though some of them don't know what a "verb" or a "noun" is. (They've stopped teaching this in many schools.)

It's up to linguists to *discover* rules such as this. And sometimes there's disagreement, or puzzlement, among linguists about exactly what these rules are. That's amazing, given that every 10-year-old native speaker of the language can apply most of these rules just fine.

In this book you'll see attempts to state linguistic rules where there are common mistakes. What these rules are is sometimes controversial. Sometimes it's not clear if there really is a general rule that accounts for a correct/incorrect judgement — maybe it's just a random particular custom. A second major source of disagreement is whether an old rule everyone used to be taught has been swept away by widespread actual usage. I'll try to make sensible judgements, but there will be plenty of room for argument with these.

One Last Word

English is a hugely complicated language, often said to be more complicated than most others. It has an enormous vocabulary, with many words referring to the same thing but differing subtly in flavour. It has a great pile of idioms — arbitrary, somewhat irregular ways of expressing things that don't make any sense; these have to be learned one by one. Its grammar is stupendously complex. Correct spelling is haphazard; unlike many other languages, you can't tell spelling from pronunciation, or pronunciation from spelling.

So what? If you're a native speaker of English, congratulate yourself on having achieved substantial competence at a hugely complex skill, and don't feel ashamed that there's a large amount remaining for you to learn. If you're learning English as a second language, my heart goes out to you. It's an enormous job learning any second language, and maybe an even bigger one learning English. You're a hero! Don't feel overawed, or reluctant to speak or write. You'll find that a lot of English speakers are sympathetic to the linguistic problems of second-language speakers.

There's a huge amount of linguistic instruction in this book. As a first- or second-language speaker you shouldn't feel worried if you can't master all of it, or even a lot of it. Take what you can from this book: any improvement in your language will be a benefit. Nobody — I mean *nobody* — ever gets it perfect.

PART III:
WORDS

Meanings, Uses, and Idioms: A Dictionary

REMINDER: YOU'LL FIND THE meanings of all those little symbols inside the front cover of this book.

a/an The article **an** goes before words that *sound like* they start with a vowel. Thus, of course, **an artichoke, an elephant, an orchid** ... but also **an hour, an MBA, an x-ray.** The article **a** goes before the rest: **a bank, a cat, a dollar** ... but also **a one, a use.** The **h** beginning some words is silent, so **an hour, an honest.** But when the **h** is aspirated (spoken with an outflow of breath), the appropriate article is **a: a homage, a hotel, a heater.** Sometimes you read **an historian, an hypothesis, an hereditary,** but given that these words all start with an aspirated **h,** this is a mistake, and a pomposity as well. See herb for a peculiar case

a bit/abit The second one is not a word.
🖙 **Wait abit. I'll be there soon.**
☑ **Wait a bit. I'll be there soon.**

a capella/a cappella It means *without instrumental accompaniment,* and the second spelling is correct.
🖙 **Dartmouth A Capella Resource Guide** — Dartmouth College Alumni Magazine

accede/exceed To **accede** to something is to agree to it; to **exceed** something is to go beyond it.
☑ **Canada acceded to the treaty demands of the US.**
☑ **Canada exceeded its previous annual oil production in 2016.**

accept something (not 'accept to do something):

🖙 The Committee accepted to try to improve the quality of the postal service.

☑ The Committee accepted the task of trying to improve the postal service.

☑ The Committee agreed to try to improve the postal service.

accept/except **Accept** is a verb meaning *to receive something favourably (or at least without complaining)*. **Except**, on the other hand, is a conjunction (or preposition) which means *not including* or *but*.

🖙 We excepted the invitation to his party.

☑ We accepted the invitation to his party.

🖙 All the permanent members of the Security Council accept China voted to authorize the use of force.

☑ All the permanent members of the Security Council except China voted to authorize the use of force.

☑ I wanted to order onion soup, except it wasn't on the menu.

accompanied by not with.

🖙 Trump attended the party accompanied with his trophy wife.

☑ ... accompanied by....

according to This expression normally is used only when one is referring to a person or to a group of people.

🖙 According to geography, Congo is larger than all of Western Europe.

☑ As we learn in geography, Congo is larger than all of Western Europe.

🖙 According to the story of *Cry the Beloved Country*, Stephen Kumalo has a quick temper.

☑ The events of the story show that Stephen Kumalo has a quick temper.

☑ According to Nixon, he was not a crook.

☑ According to researchers, most people eat too much salt.

accuse someone of doing something (not to do)

🖙 Socrates mentions Plato as one of the youths he was accused to have corrupted.... — "Plato," Philosophers.co.uk website

☑ ... he was accused of having corrupted....

acute/chronic/habitual The core meaning of **chronic** describes a medical condition that persists or recurs, but the word is also commonly extended to describe any problem that is long-lasting or difficult to solve. An **acute** medical problem is a brief or sudden one, but the word, especially when used of other difficulties, sometimes implies severity. (However, an **acute** person is a smart one). A **habitual** action is one done as a habit, or just regularly or often.

☑ Dylan's asthma is chronic — it just keeps showing up.

☑ Abagail's acute knee problem came on suddenly after the hike and was gone two days later.

☑ Donald is a habitual liar.

adapt/adopt To **adapt** something is to alter or modify it; to **adopt** something is to approve it or accept responsibility for it.

👎 The Board adapted the resolution unanimously.

☑ The Board adopted the resolution....

☑ Mozart adapted *The Messiah* for classical orchestra.

☑ We're going to adopt a Bulgarian orphan.

adapter/adaptor Some usage writers imagine a distinction between these words, and the former is more widely used, but they're really interchangeable.

☑ An adapter is needed to connect this device to the computer.

☑ An adaptor is needed to connect this device to the computer.

address as in

☹ The Addressing Tobacco Through Organizational Change (ATTOC) Approach is guided by a 10-Step model designed to help an organization systematically improve their tobacco addiction treatment for patients/clients and change their culture to better address tobacco use. — Ziedonis et al., Article Abstract, *Journal of Psychoactive Drugs*

What exactly does this word mean? Perhaps *to raise as a topic for discussion or as a problem to be solved? to deal with? to confront?* Buzzwords like this are a sign of a mind on auto-pilot.

adduce/deduce To **adduce** something is to cite it as evidence, or to bring it forth for consideration. To **deduce** something is to arrive at or confirm a conclusion by reasoning.

☑ At this point, the prosecution adduced a blood-stained glove.

☑ From the fact that OJ couldn't get his hand into the glove, the defense deduced that it was not his.

adverse/averse **Adverse** means *unfavourable* or *opposed to;* **averse** means *reluctant* or *unwilling.*

👎 Technology and training were on the U-M team's side, despite some averse weather conditions and rain. — "MichiganToday," University of Michigan website

☑ The pilot was averse to the idea of landing in the fog.

31

advice/advise **Advice** is the noun, **advise** is the verb.

🖐 **They refused to take our advise.**

☑ **They refused to take our advice.**

🖐 **They adviced me not to buy that brand of car.**

☑ **They advised me not to buy that brand of car.**

affect/effect In their most common uses, **effect** is a noun meaning *result* and **affect** is a verb meaning *cause a result*.

🖐 **These genes have no visible affect in one sex because the necessary machinery to express them is not present.** — Northern Arizona University website

☑ **... no visible effect....**

🖐 **"The issues that effect us here on the reserve are the same issues that effect the whole constituency," Mr. Littlechild said.** — the *Toronto Globe and Mail*

☑ **... the same issues that affect the whole constituency....**

Confusingly, however, **effect** can also be used as a verb meaning *put into effect:*

☑ **The changes were effected by the Committee.)**

and **affect** as a noun meaning *a feeling or emotion*, or its outward display:

☑ **Meursault showed no affect when told of the death of his mother.**

afflict/inflict A person **inflicts** pain or hardship on someone else, who is **afflicted** by the pain and hardship.

🖐 **These human rights abuses afflict terrible suffering on individuals while tearing at the fabric of entire societies.** — from a speech by Asha-Rose Migiro, Deputy Secretary-General of the UN

☑ **... abuses inflict terrible suffering....**

age/aged Only the second can be an adjective:

🖐 **A woman age 35 was struck and killed by the car.**

☑ **... woman aged 35....**

aggravate/annoy/irritate The Standard-English meaning of **aggravate** is *make worse*. In formal English **aggravate** should not be used to mean *annoy* or *irritate*; however, this use is common enough in informal language to be acceptable there.

☑ **The injury was aggravated by the bumpy ride in the ambulance.**

✊ **She found his constant complaints very aggravating.**

☑ **She found his constant complaints very irritating.**

agree <u>with</u> someone, <u>with</u> what someone says; agree <u>to do</u> something, <u>to</u> something; agree <u>on</u> a plan, proposal, etc.

👎 The union representatives did not agree with the proposed wage increase.

☑ The union representatives did not agree to the proposed wage increase.

☑ The union representatives did not agree with management about the proposed wage increase.

ahold/a hold The first is a quite informal variant of **hold**. The second is a noun phrase meaning *a grip*.

👎 Tennis needs to get ahold of Nick Kyrgios and shut him down — headline, ESPN website

☑ ... get hold of ...

☑ You should get a hold on that rope before you jump.

aid/aide Both terms can mean *a person whose job it is to provide help*. The second one avoids the ambiguity possibly caused by the first.

☹ A teacher's aid is what's needed in this classroom.

☑ A teacher's helper is what's needed in this classroom.

☑ A teacher's aide is what's needed in this classroom.

☑ A teacher's assistant is what's needed in this classroom.

all/both Use **both** to refer to two, and **all** to refer to more than two.

👎 Anna and Kaia were the chief speakers in the debate yesterday. They all spoke very well.

☑ .... They both spoke very well.

allege/contend To **allege** that X is to make a formal statement without proof that X is true. To **contend** that X is also to state that X is true, but the emphasis here is on adversarial argument.

👎 Justin contended that he's not bright enough to pass the logic class, and everyone believed him.

☑ Fred's attorney contended that the prosecution had the facts all wrong.

allegory/fable/myth/parable All of these are stories with moral points. **Allegories** are stories of any length with a clear double structure: the apparent story and the deeper unspoken one. **Fables** are very short tales often involving talking animals; they usually have a clear and simple moral, often explicitly presented at the end. **Myths** are traditional stories, often with ancient origins and often dealing with supernatural beings or heroes. **Parables** are very brief stories illustrating a moral or religious lesson; the primary examples are the stories told by Jesus in the Bible.

alliterate/illiterate **Alliterate** is a verb meaning *to use multiple words that begin with the same sound*, for example in this sentence: "The big, burly brute was frighteningly fat." **Illiterate** is an adjective meaning either *unable to read* or *unable to read and write well.*

🖅 More than forty per cent of the population of Zambia is functionally alliterate.

☑ More than forty per cent of the population of Zambia is functionally illiterate.

all of On the principle that shorter is better, **all the cake** is better than **all of the cake**. But the second is not terrible, and sometimes leaving **of** in improves the rhythm of the sentence, as in:

☑ **You can not fool all the people all of the time.** — attributed to Abraham Lincoln

allot/alot/a lot **Alot** is not a word. **A lot** means *a large quantity*, or, as an adverb, *frequently*, and is often considered unacceptable in formal writing. (But you'll find both uses in this book.) The great frequency of this term in student writing drives teachers crazy. Be kind to your teachers, and try to minimize its use. And don't confuse **a lot** with **allot**, a verb meaning to *distribute* or *allocate*.

🖅 I eat grapefruit alot. (adverb)

🖅 I eat alot of grapefruit. (noun)

⚠ I eat grapefruit a lot. (adverbial phrase)

⚠ I eat a lot of grapefruit. (noun phrase)

☑ Allot three weeks for this project.

allow/make To **make** people do something is to force them to do it (against their wishes); to **allow** people to do something is to permit them or make it possible for them to do something that they want to do.

🖅 **A new hospital wing is being built; this will make many more people come for treatment.**

☑ ... this will allow many more people to come....

all right/alright To say that something is acceptable, you can acceptably say **It is all right**. And of course, **all right** can also mean *totally correct*. Experts still insist that **alright** is not a word, even though its use is growing, and it now occurs in books about fifty times as often as the two-word version. It's only a matter of time before this word is considered acceptable.

☑ It turns out to be all right to go swimming immediately after eating.

🖅 Progress might have been alright once, but it has gone on too long. — Ogden Nash

☑ She got the answers all right on the test.

all together/altogether The first means *as a group,* or *at the same place or time.* The second means *totally.*

☑ We sang the national anthem all together.

☑ The graduates were all together for the last time.

☑ It's altogether finished.

allude/elude To **allude** to something is to refer to it indirectly. To **elude** something is to escape or avoid it cleverly.

☑ **Andrew alluded to the fact that he'd be home before dinner.** (But a mistake if what Andrew had said was "I'll be home before dinner.")

🖑 **Andrew eluded to the fact that he'd be home before dinner.**

allusion/illusion An allusion is a statement that refers to something indirectly. An illusion is a distorted sense-perception in which things are represented falsely; or more generally, a false idea that seems to be true.

☑ **Freud wrote that religious belief is illusion.**

☑ **Freud's allusion to the biblical Joseph was buried in a footnote.**

along/a long Both are legitimate: the first as a preposition or sometimes an adverb, the second as an adjective phrase. Don't confuse them.

☑ **Willow trees were growing along the riverbank.**

☑ **I've waited for this for a long time.**

already/all ready The first is the adverb; the second is an adjective phrase meaning *completely prepared.*

☑ **It's dark already.**

☑ **The bus had already left.**

🖑 **I am already for the exam.**

☑ **I am all ready for the exam.**

altar/alter An **altar** is a table or other structure where religious rites are performed. **Alter** is a verb, meaning *change.*

☑ **Walter, Walter, lead me to the altar / I'll make a better man of you.**

☑ **The test results convinced the physician to alter his diagnosis.**

alternate/alternative **Alternative,** not **alternate,** is the adjective meaning providing a choice:

🖑 *Looking for a Third Option: An Alternate Solution in the Gun Debate* — title of a book by Richard Miyasaki.

☑ *... Alternative Solution ...*

Sticklers sometimes object to **alternative** used when more than two objects are involved, as in the fix for the book title above, or in:

⚠ **The alternatives for side dishes are baked potato, green salad, and coleslaw.**

⚠ **The steak comes with fries, but alternatively you can have baked potato or salad.**

But almost everyone these days finds these uses acceptable.

always/never The phrases **generally always, generally never, usually always, and usually never** are self-contradictory.

🖝 **The fee-free parks days generally always include Martin Luther King, Jr., Day, National Public Lands Day (September 24), and Veterans Day....**
— "Money" website of Time.com.

🖝 **The popular TV vet generally never speaks about his personal life....**
— *Sydney Daily Telegraph* website

🖝 **Passengers are usually never responsible for their injuries and thus passengers usually always get car accident money for their injuries.**
— Stan Kooner Law Corporation website

a.m./p.m./noon/midnight The abbreviations (which can also be written with small capital letters and no periods: AM, PM), distinguish midnight till noon (Latin *ante meridiem*, before noon) from noon till midnight (Latin *post meridiem*, after noon), respectively. But is noon 12:00 a.m. or 12:00 p.m.? It's illogical either way, because noon is neither after noon nor before noon. It would seem that since **12:00** looks like the end of the numerical series ..., **11:58 a.m, 11:59 a.m.**, it should be **12:00 a.m.**, but by official convention, noon is **12:00 p.m.** Midnight is **12:00 a.m.**, and is officially part of the following, not the previous, day. Nobody will ever remember any of that. A lunch invitation for **12:00 p.m.** won't confuse, but when there is the possibility of ambiguity, you should write **noon** or **midnight**. And if you say

☹ **Entries must be received before midnight, September 15,**

nobody will be able to figure out whether you mean the middle of the night before or after the rest of September 15. So to prevent ambiguity, people choose a time one minute before or after midnight:

☑ **Entries must be received before 11:59 p.m., September 14.**

☑ **Entries must be received before 12:01 a.m., September 15.**

ambiguity Occasionally there's a real lack of clarity about how an ambiguous sentence should be understood. But more often, context or obvious good sense supply the correct reading, though the alternative interpretations are sometimes amusing (see box).

Here are some samples of this sort of ambiguity in newspaper headlines, culled from one of the countless internet collections:

- EYE DROPS OFF SHELF IN PHARMACY
- PROSTITUTES APPEAL TO POPE
- KIDS MAKE NUTRITIOUS SNACKS
- STOLEN PAINTING FOUND BY TREE
- DEALERS WILL HEAR CAR TALK AT NOON
- MINERS REFUSE TO WORK AFTER DEATH
- MAN HELD OVER GIANT L.A. BRUSH FIRE
- RED TAPE HOLDS UP NEW BRIDGE
- SQUAD HELPS DOG BITE VICTIM

A splendid World War II headline announced

- BRITISH PUSH BOTTLES UP GERMANS

This famous advertising slogan

- MORE DOCTORS RECOMMEND THE INGREDIENTS IN ANACIN THAN ANY OTHER PAIN RELIEVER

can be read to mean that among pain relievers (that is, doctors, nurses, acupuncturists, etc.) doctors recommend those ingredients more often than the others do.

A similar possibility of ambiguity can be found in this advertising slogan:

- CANADA POST DELIVERS MORE PARCELS TO CANADIANS THAN ANYONE.

No doubt they mean that they deliver more parcels in Canada than their competition. But this can also be read to make the unsurprising statement that they deliver more parcels to Canadians than to any other nationality.

amiable/amicable **Amiable** is used to describe someone's personality; **amicable** describes the state of relations between people.

☞ **Geri Halliwell and the Spice Girls will apparently square off and rehash Ginger Spice's less-than-amiable split from the group in two new books set for release this fall.** — MTV News website

☑ **... less-than-amicable split....**

among/between You might have been told to use **between** only when two things are involved, but when there are three or more, use **among**:

☑ Choose between green salad and coleslaw.

? Choose between green salad, coleslaw, and peas.

Somebody invented this rule because the **tween** part of **between** is connected with the word **two**. It is, but so what? The OED says "In all senses, *between* has been, from its earliest appearance, extended to more than two." So you may use it that way also if you like, and sometimes that way is much better.

☑ Negotiations have concluded on a trade agreement between Canada, the US, and Mexico.

☹ Negotiations have concluded on a trade agreement among Canada, the US, and Mexico.

Perhaps the most important difference is that **between** involves particular individual things, whereas **among** involves a collection with no particular number of individual things. Thus

☑ The ball fell among the hollyhocks.

👎 The ball fell between the hollyhocks.

So it's sometimes okay to say **between** when there are three or more individual things:

☑ For the curious dynamic of this spring election is that it is more a battle between the three opposition unionist parties than it is about taking on the SNP. — *Scotland Independent* website

☑ First Debate Highlights Early Divisions Between Republican Candidates for Governor — headline, New Hampshire Public Radio website. (There were four candidates.)

amoral/immoral Amoral means *not based on moral standards*; **immoral** means *wrong according to moral standards.*

👎 Infants are immoral.

☑ Infants are amoral.

amount/number Amount should be used only with things that are uncountable (sugar, goodwill, etc.). For countable things use **number**. (See "Mass Nouns and Count Nouns" in the "Singular and Plural" section below.)

👎 John Worthing and Austin Lamb had a large amount of goals for the postseason. — *The Towanda and Troy PA Daily Review.*

☑ ... a large number of goals....

☑ A large amount of beer was consumed by the students.

amuse/bemuse To **amuse** means *to entertain or make laugh*. To **bemuse** means *to confuse.*

☑ The famous graffiti artist Banksy has built an absurdist parody of the Disneyland amusement park in England. It's called Dismaland, and he says it's "a bemusement park."

and In most cases, **or** rather than **and** should be used as a connective if the statement is negative.

👎 Moose are not found in South America, Africa, and Australia.

☑ Moose are not found in South America, Africa, or Australia.

angry/mad **Mad** can mean either *insane* or *angry*. Despite the fact that the second sense had been legitimate since 1400, around the beginning of the twentieth century it was decided that using the word that way was unacceptable. But people keep doing it. Beware of ambiguous uses.

☹ Constant abuse from his parents made him mad. (insane or angry?)

⚠ The way he treats his children makes me mad.

☑ The way he treats his children makes me angry.

annoyed with/by You're annoyed <u>with</u> someone, and <u>by</u> something.

👎 The professor is often annoyed with the attitude of the class.

☑ The professor is often annoyed by the attitude of the class.

☑ The professor is often annoyed with the class.

an other/another As a rule, the phrase **an other** should be replaced by **another**.

👎 I'll have an other cookie please.

☑ I'll have another cookie please.

☑ I'll have another, please.

anti-/ante-: If you remember that **anti-** means *against* and **ante-** means *before*, you are less likely to misspell the many words that have one or the other as a prefix.

👎 The game appears to have antecedents from India and China.... — "Nyout," website of Univ. of Waterloo Elliott Avedon Virtual Museum of Games.

☑ ... appears to have antecedents....

anxious/eager: The adjective **anxious** has two senses: (1) *uneasy, nervous, worried,* and (2) *eager.* The OED traces the second sense back to 1570, but this is another case in which, for some reason, it has been decided that a longstanding sense is illegitimate.

⚠ Anxious to help, they come as builders and end up as porters in the morgues — headline, the UK *Guardian*

☑ Eager to help....

☑ He was anxious about his upcoming exam.

any/either Use **either** for two, **any** for more than two.

🖐 Ethan has six sisters, but he hasn't seen either of them since Christmas.

☑ ... he hasn't seen any of them....

any/some/anyone/someone With negatives (**not**, **never**, etc.) **any** is used in place of some.

🖐 He never gives me some help with my work.

☑ He never gives me any help with my work.

🖐 She didn't see someone there.

☑ She didn't see anyone there.

any body/anybody The second is a common pronoun. The first, a noun phrase, is much rarer.

☑ Anybody want some ice cream?

☑ I didn't see anybody in the house.

🖐 I didn't see any body in the house. (If this means that the speaker saw no one.)

☑ I didn't see any body in the house. (Suppose the speaker is a detective looking for dead bodies in the house.)

☑ We sell clothes to fit any body.

The same goes for **every body/everybody**, **no body/nobody**, and **some body/somebody**.

any day/anyday The first is legitimate; the second isn't.

🖐 Same Day Parcel Delivery 7 Days A Week, Anyday...Everyday! — Maritime Bus (NS) Courier Express website ad (See also **everyday**, and notes on the ellipsis and the exclamation mark, below.)

☑ Any day — every day.

☑ Any day you choose is fine with me.

anyhow This is legitimate to use meaning *in any way*, but not for formal use meaning *anyway* or *nevertheless*.

✊ My car broke down, but I got here anyhow.

☑ Anyhow they do it is acceptable to me.

any more/anymore The first should be used for quantity, and the second for time.

☑ I don't want any more cake.

🖐 I don't want anymore cake.

🖐 It's not enough to just feed and clothe them any more. — Margaret Wente in the *Toronto Globe and Mail*. (Worried about that split infinitive? Read the section about that below.)

☑ ... just to feed and clothe them anymore.

any one/anyone When you mean *anybody*, use the second. When you mean *any single one*, use the first.

🕮 **Any one who has common sense will remember that the bewilderments of the eyes are of two kinds, and arise from two causes...** — Plato, *The Republic*, book VII, translated by Benjamin Jowett. (Unfair! The translation by this eminent scholar was published in 1871, when the two-word version was preferred.)

☑ **Anyone who has common sense....**

☑ **If any one of you has borrowed my book, please give it back.**

any place/anyplace The second isn't standard as an adverb; substitute **anywhere**.

🕮 or 🖐☹ **We were unable to find him anyplace.**

☑ **We were unable to find him anywhere.**

☑ **Any place I hang my hat is home.**

any thing/anything The second is the ordinary word; the first can be found rarely, in the plural or contrasting with **any person**.

☑ **Is there anything you'd like for dinner?**

☑ **Are there any things you'd like me to put in my car?**

☑ **I didn't see any person or any thing in that room.**

The same is true for **every thing/everything**.

any time/anytime The second is an adverb that used to be considered unacceptable in formal English but is often seen there now. The first can be used adverbially, or as a noun phrase.

⚠ **Anytime you want to drop in, that's fine.**

☑ **Any time you want to drop in, that's fine.**

☑ **Do you have any time for a chat this evening?**

any way/anyway/anyways The first two are acceptable, as a noun phrase and an adverb, respectively. The third is not a word.

☑ **Do it any way you can.**

🕮 **There isn't anyway I can get to the party.**

☑ **You don't want to, but do it anyway.**

🕮 **You don't want to, but do it anyways.**

any where/anywhere/anywheres The first doesn't occur; substitute the second. The third is not a word.

🕮 **We were unable to find him any where.**

☑ **We were unable to find him anywhere.**

🕮 **We were unable to find him anywheres.**

appeal <u>to</u> someone <u>for</u> something, not for someone to do something.

🖐 The Premier appealed for the residents to help.

☑ The Premier appealed to the residents for help.

appraise/apprise: To **appraise** something is *to estimate its value*; to **apprise** someone of something is *to inform him or her of it.*

🖐 The house has been apprised at $160,000.

☑ The house has been appraised at $160,000.

☑ The real estate agent apprised her of the house's jump in value.

appreciate means *to understand the worth of something,* or *to be grateful to someone for something.* Without an object, it means *to increase in value.*

🖐 I would appreciate if you would reply by July 1.

☑ I would appreciate your replying by July 1.

☑ I would appreciate it if you could reply by July 1.

☑ I would appreciate a reply by July 1.

But better than any of these is:

☑ Please reply by July 1.

archaic/obsolete/obsolescent Archaic means *old-fashioned.* Obsolete means *so old-fashioned that it is no longer used.* Obsolescent means *becoming obsolete.*

☑ The rotary phone is archaic.

☑ The steam locomotive is obsolete.

☑ The cathode-ray-tube computer monitor is obsolescent.

arrive <u>in</u> a place, <u>at</u> a place (<u>not</u> arrive a place, <u>except</u> arrive home). Airlines are perhaps to blame for the error of using both **arrive** and **depart** without prepositions.

🖐 He won't join the Yankees until tomorrow night when they arrive Milwaukee.

☑ He won't join the Yankees until tomorrow night when they arrive in Milwaukee.

as In this sentence:

☑ As I got out of bed, I heard the sound of gunfire,

the word **as** indicates that the two events happened at the same time. But **as** can also mean *because:*

☑ As I was hungry, I made myself a peanut butter and banana sandwich.

When the two events are simultaneous, this can result in an ambiguity:

☹ As I heard the telephone ringing, I realized that I hadn't called mom in days.

Does this sentence mean that the speaker came to that realization *because* the telephone was ringing, or merely *when* the telephone was ringing? It's better to prevent this ambiguity by avoiding **as**:

☑ **When I heard the telephone ringing, I realized that I hadn't called mom in days.**

☑ **Because I heard the telephone ringing, I realized that I hadn't called mom in days.**

When the two events are not simultaneous, it's clear that **as** means *because*:

☑ **As I had studied hard the day before, I did well on the exam.**

as best as is highly informal.

✊☹ **I tried to make up for the insult as best as I could.**

☑ **I tried to make up for the insult as well as I could.**

🎓 **I tried to make up for the insult as best I could.**

assist in doing something (<u>not</u> to do)

👎 **He assisted me to solve the problem.**

☑ **He assisted me in solving the problem.**

☑ **He helped me to solve the problem.**

assume/presume Both words can mean *to take something for granted.* **Assume** also means *to take on duties;* **presume** also means *to be audacious enough to do something.*

☑ **He assumed I was coming to the party.**

☑ **He presumed I was coming to the party.**

☑ **He assumed command of the battalion.**

☑ **He presumed to invite himself to dinner.**

assure/ensure/insure To **assure** someone of something is to tell them with confidence or certainty. To **insure** something is to purchase insurance on it to protect yourself in case of loss. **Ensure** is generally considered much better than **insure** when what you mean is *make sure.*

👎 **Our inventory is ensured for $10,000,000.**

☑ **Our inventory is insured for $10,000,000.**

☑ **I assure you that it will never happen again.**

☹ **I will insure that it never happens again.**

☑ **I will ensure that it never happens again.**

atheist/agnostic The first is someone who believes that God does not exist. The second is someone who thinks that we cannot know whether God exists. Watch out for the spelling on the first word. Be aware it's not a superlative (**-est**) form.

👎 **Martin, you're the athiest person I've ever known.**

Bertrand Russell wrote about going to prison for his pacifist activities during World War I: "I was much cheered on my arrival by the warden at the gate, who had to take particulars about me. He asked my religion, and I replied 'agnostic.' He asked how to spell it, and remarked with a sigh: 'Well, there are many religions, but I suppose they all worship the same God.' This remark kept me cheerful for about a week."

— *Portraits from Memory and Other Essays*

attain/obtain To **attain** something is to achieve a goal. To **obtain** something is merely to get it. So sometimes one can substitute **obtain** for **attain**, but not vice versa.

☑ **To obtain your maximum fitness level, daily exercise is required.**

☑ **To attain your maximum fitness level, daily exercise is required.**

🖐 **No one may apply for a driver's license before obtaining the age of 18.**

🖐 **I went to the supermarket to attain some pickled peppers.**

Both words are, however, rather formal and pompous. Why not just say **get** or **get to**?

attitude In uses such as this:

☹ **I'm taking a wait-and-see attitude,**

it should be replaced by a leaner equivalent:

☑ **I'm going to wait and see.**

Colloquially,

✊ **She's got attitude**

means that she's uncooperative or antagonistic. Don't use the word that way in formal writing.

auger/augur The first is a drill. The second is a verb meaning *foretell* (or more rarely a noun, meaning *something/someone that foretells*).

aural/oral **Aural** means *having to do with the ear or hearing*. **Oral** means *having to do with the mouth*, or spoken as opposed to written.

☑ **Aural problems prevented me from hearing your oral presentation.**

author Unnecessary as a verb; there is no need to find a substitute for **write**.

☹ **Bruce Armstrong, aka Uncle Max, enchanted kids, authored several books** — headline, obituary, *Halifax Chronicle-Herald*

☑ **... author of several books.**

☑ **... wrote several books.**

44

avenge/revenge: Both verbs apply to actions of inflicting pain or harm in return for the same; **avenging** suggests that this is done in accord with justice, but **revenge** is done as mere retaliation.

☑ The judge gave him the maximum sentence, to avenge his string of horrible crimes.

☑ As revenge for his numerous insults, they started false damaging rumours about him.

aviary/apiary The former is a birdcage; the latter is a place for keeping bees.

avocation/vocation A **vocation** is an employment, with the suggestion that one is dedicated to it or finds it worthwhile or fulfilling. An **avocation** is what one does when not working, for enjoyment. Teaching is a **vocation**; drinking when you get home from teaching is an **avocation**.

a way/away/aways The difference between the first, a noun phrase, and the second, an adverb, is clear. Just make sure you write the right one. The third, and its spelling variant **a ways**, are too colloquial even for informal talk (except in phrases such as **take-aways**, **come-from-aways**).

☑ She has gone away.

☑ She has found a way to get there.

🕬 I spotted a moose off the road aways

awesome This word, unlike those in the next entry, does retain some connection with awe, so you can get away with saying, in formal contexts,

☑ The Grand Canyon is an awesome sight.

But that word has been overcome with extremely informal use as a term of enthusiastic praise:

✊☹ That group is like totally awesome.

The opposite evaluation is **sucks**:

✊☹ That other group sucks.

Don't talk this way if you're over 18.

awful You might still run across a language pedant who insists that this adjective has something to do with **awe**, which properly speaking means *reverential dread or wonder inspired by something huge or powerful* such as the Grand Canyon or God. Those meanings are long dead. Its only use these days is rather informal, meaning *very bad*. **Awfully** has also receded into exclusively informal use, sometimes meaning *very badly*, but often just meaning *very*.

45

✊ That's an awful mess.
✊ He behaved awfully at dinner.
✊ It's awfully nice of you to remember my birthday.

Compare the change in **terrific**, which (as was mentioned earlier) was changing in the opposite direction: from *terror-inspiring* to *really good*.

a while/awhile Use the first as a noun phrase and the second as an adverb.
☑ I sat there awhile.
☞ I sat there a while.
☑ I needed a while to sit down.
☞ I needed awhile to sit down.

axel/axle: An **axel** is a manoeuvre in figure skating; an **axle** is a rod connecting two wheels of a vehicle.

back up/backup The first is a verb:
☑ He backed up the truck out of the driveway.
☑ The lawyer backed up her assertion with some strong evidence.
☑ The traffic was backed up for miles.
☞ The police told me to backup my pickup truck.

The second is a noun or adjective:
☑ The accident caused a huge traffic backup.
☞ In case my hard disk fails, I have stored my files in the cloud as a back up.
☑ He was backup quarterback for the Saskatchewan Roughriders.

There are many pairs in which a two-word verb phrase is pushed together and thus transformed into a noun or adjective that (roughly speaking) refers to the outcome of the verb's action. Some more examples: **pay back/payback; run away/runaway; set up/setup; wake up/wakeup; work out/workout.**

bail/bale You **bail** water out of a boat; **bail** is the release from prison prior to trial. You **bale** hay, putting it into a bundle called a **bale.**

baloney/bologna Bologna, upper-case **B**, is the name of the Italian city where **bologna**, the nasty food-like sausage, is supposed to have originated. The city is pronounced *bo-LOAN-ya*, but the sausage is called *buh-LOW-nee*. **Baloney** is nonsense. (That word may derive from the name of the meat.)

bare/bear The first as an adjective means *without covering*, and as a verb means *to uncover*. The second names the big hairy beast or its toy cousin Teddy; as a verb it means *to carry or endure*.

46

Cafes across the world, during the 2016 election, were serving a very topical lunch — the Donald Trump sandwich. On boards outside the venues, they advertise it as having "white bread, full of baloney, with Russian dressing and a small pickle"

— *UK Telegraph* website.

bath room/bathroom. The second is correct.

be/become: The difference between the two is that **to be** simply indicates existence, while **to become** indicates a process of change. Whenever you are talking about a change, use **become** instead of **be**.

🖙 I had been quite contented, but as time went by I was unhappy.

☑ ... I became unhappy.

🖙 After years of struggle, East Timor finally was independent in 2002.

☑ ... East Timor finally became independent....

begrudging/grudging The central meaning of the verb **to begrudge** is *to envy someone the possession of something*, so **begrudgingly** means *enviously*. But that word has become confused with **grudging**, which means *reluctant and grumbling*. That use is common enough but still may be found undesirable.

? She begrudgingly agreed to invite her son's sleazy roommate to Thanksgiving dinner.

☑ She grudgingly agreed to invite her son's sleazy roommate to Thanksgiving dinner.

? Jennings begrudged Rodgers for being disloyal — headline, ESPN News website

☑ She begrudged her stupid co-worker his huge raise.

beg the question: The original meaning of **beg the question** is *take for granted the very thing to be argued about* — <u>not</u> *invite the question*. But the second use has become so extensive that it's useless to fight it. However, you'll embarrass yourself if you use it that way when talking to a philosopher or logician.

⚠ The Josh Norman Bowl begs the question: What's an elite CB worth?
— headline, the *Washington Post* website.

☑ The Josh Norman Bowl raises the question: ...

☑ Calling abortion "murder of unborn babies" begs the question of its moral status.

behalf (in/on behalf of): There used to be a distinction here: **in behalf of** meant *for the benefit of*, while **on behalf of** meant *as an agent of*; so you could say:

☑ My lawyer acted on my behalf, but not in my behalf.

But that distinction is now gone, and only the most strenuous Stickler would object if you used them interchangeably.

beneficent/benevolent Beneficent means *good-doing*. **Benevolent** means *good-wishing* — having good intentions.

☑ Someone who does you a favour purely selfishly, hoping for something in return, is beneficent but not benevolent.

But this distinction is disappearing, and one often hears them being used interchangeably.

beside/besides The first is a preposition; the second is an adverb. So:

☑ That's her husband standing beside her.

👎 That's her husband standing besides her.

☑ I'm not going to bed; I'm not sleepy, and besides, I'm hungry.

better/bettor Better is the comparative form of **good** — *more good*. A **bettor** is a person who bets.

biannual, biennial, semiannual, -weekly, -monthly, etc. The prefixes **bi-** and **semi-** produce a great deal of confusion. **Bi-** means *two*, so **bimonthly** means *every two months*. **Semi-** means half, so **semimonthly** means *every half-month*, i.e., *every two weeks*. Unfortunately, **bimonthly** is also legitimately used to mean *twice a month*. **Biennial** means *every two years*, so a **biennially** flowering plant flowers every other year. But **biannual** means *twice a year*. Isn't that awful? For clarity it's best to avoid all these terms. If you want to say that your work gets reviewed every two years, say so.

☹ My work gets reviewed biennially.

👎 My work gets reviewed biannually.

☑ My work gets reviewed every two years.

Bible/bible Used as the name of the Judeo-Christian holy text, this starts with an upper-case **B**, but lower-case when meaning any sort of definitive text. The adjective **biblical** always has a lower-case **b**.

blackmail/bribery/extortion These are sometimes confused. **Bribery** is offering or giving something of value in order to influence the actions of someone with public or legal duties. **Extortion** is obtaining something of value from somebody through threats of harm. **Blackmail** is extortion in which the threat is to reveal information potentially harmful to that person.

blatant/flagrant Both adjectives are applicable to bad acts, but there the clarity ends, and the subtle distinction between these words is disappearing. One authority says that **blatant** means *offensively conspicuous*, but **flagrant** means *conspicuously offensive*. Get it? Neither do I. If there's a difference here, it's that **flagrant** emphasizes the negative intentions behind an obvious act, while **blatant** emphasizes the obvious nature of a negative act.

To say that a murder was especially bad:

☑ **a flagrant murder**

⚠ **a blatant murder**

To say that it was especially obvious:

⚠ **a flagrant murder**

☑ **a blatant murder**

bloc/block A **bloc** is a group (especially of nations) with common interests, working together. A **block** is a solid piece of something — of wood, of words, etc.

☞ **Professor Helps Former Soviet Block Nation Develop Police Regulations**

— headline, "WSU Today" website published by Weber State University.

☑ **... Soviet Bloc Nation....**

boned/deboned/boneless Do you think that **boned** chicken breasts have bone in them or not? The answer is no, but **boned** is a confusing term; use a substitute.

☹ **boned chicken**

☑ **deboned chicken**

☑ **boneless chicken**

See also a similar difficulty with pitted and shelled. See also another ambiguous word: sanction.

Words that can mean both something and its opposite are called **contronyms**. Unlike **boned**, **pitted**, and **shelled**, most others are quite unlikely to cause any confusion when they're encountered in context. Here are a few:

- Clip these papers *(fasten together)*
- Clip your toenails *(cut)*

- Dust the cake with powdered sugar *(cover with fine particles)*
- Dust the lampshade *(remove fine particles)*

- Rent my apartment to her while I'm away *(get paid for use of what you own)*
- Rent an apartment during my month's stay *(pay for use of what you don't own)*

- Sanction the proposal *(authorize it)*
- Sanction the treaty violation *(punish it)*

- Seed the lawn *(put seeds in)*
- Seed the tomatoes *(take seeds out)*

- It's all downhill from here on *(are things getting better or worse?)*

born/borne To be born is to be given birth to. To be borne is to be carried or put up with. (Both words are past participles of bear, meaning to carry [a baby or something else]).

☑ **Bores are borne.**

☑ **Babies are born.**

borrow something <u>from</u> someone

🖅 **I borrowed him a pair of trousers.**

☑ **I borrowed a pair of trousers from him.**

boss Informal. Substitute **manager** or **supervisor** for more formal use.

bravado/bravery **Bravado** is a show of courage, designed to impress. **Bravery** is genuine courage.

breach/breech: To **breach** a wall or a contract is to break or break through it, and the breach is the breaking. **Breech** originally was the part of the body covered by the breeches — the buttocks — whence **breech birth**, in which the buttocks (or feet) emerge before the head, and whence **the breech** is the rear, thick end of a cannon or rifle.

🖅 **... while [NLR Board] is usually not the proper forum to remedy an alleged breech of contract, failure to remit dues in breech of contract is [an unfair labor practise] because ...** — *Classified Index of the National Labor Relations Board Decisions and Related Court Cases* V. 340–344.

☑ **... breach of contract ...** (twice)

breath/breathe: **Breath** is the noun, **breathe** the verb.

🖅 **... begin to focus on the feeling of your chest expanding when you breath in, and contracting when you breath out.** — Kevin David Arnold, *Passing the Ohio Ninth Grade Proficiency Test* (1996)

☑ **... when you breathe in ... when you breathe out.**

bridal/bridle The first is an adjective meaning *having to do with a bride*. The second is the straps that go around a horse's head.

bring/take Use **bring** about actions conveying things toward you or your reader/hearer; and **take** about actions conveying things away from there. This is a distinction that may be disappearing.

☑ **I'm going to take the cake to her house before the party.**

☑ **She's going to bring the cake here before the party.**

☑ **Take this book with you when you go to class.**

But it's not clear which to use when the direction involves neither speaker nor audience:

☑ **Noah used to bring pizza to Chloe's every Friday.**
☑ **Noah used to take pizza to Chloe's every Friday.**

Context might make only one of these correct. If the speaker is in the habit of being at Chloe's every Friday, then the first is correct. If the speaker is describing a situation in which he wasn't involved, then the second is preferable.

Britain/British Isles/Great Britain/United Kingdom. There's a difference here that residents of none of these tend to ignore (see box). **Great Britain** and the **British Isles** are geographical terms. The former names a large island including England, Scotland, and Wales; the latter refers to a large group of islands including Great Britain, Ireland (Northern Ireland and the Irish Republic), the Isle of Man, the Hebrides, the Orkneys, the Shetlands, and thousands of others. The **United Kingdom** is the name of a country including Northern Ireland, England, Scotland, and Wales. **Britain** sometimes just means Great Britain, but sometimes it's used rather loosely

---

The name **Great Britain** did not arise as a term of superlative praise. It just meant *big*, distinguishing the island from places at times called **Little** or **Lesser Britain**.

Beware of confusing the terms **British** and **English**. Scots will not appreciate being called English, nor does British exclude them. The **British Isles** is an official geographical designation including Ireland, but the Irish in the Republic might object to that name, as well as to calling the Northern Irish **British**. The official name of the second-largest city in Northern Ireland is **Londonderry**, but in the Irish Republic its official name is **Derry**.

Place names mean something. Here are some changes, made mostly for political reasons:

East Pakistan → Bangladesh

Gold Coast → Ghana

Ceylon → Sri Lanka

Rhodesia → Zimbabwe

Burma → Myanmar

Bombay → Mumbai

Saigon → Ho Chi Minh City

Tsaritsyn → Stalingrad → Volgograd (**Tsaritsa** = female tsar, or tsar's wife; **Volgograd** = city on the Volga River)

St. Petersburg → Leningrad → St. Petersburg

Topeka, Kansas, renamed itself **Google** for the month of March 2010. Google responded by temporarily changing its name to **Topeka** on April Fool's Day in 2010.

to mean the United Kingdom, as when the residents of Northern Ireland are called British.

bunch Unless you're talking about grapes or bananas, substitute **group** in formal contexts.

Beating around the Bush?

Anyone who speaks a good deal in public on an impromptu basis will utter the odd absurdity, but George W. Bush has had more problems with meaning than most. A few examples:

- "The future will be better tomorrow."
- "I believe we are on an irreversible trend toward more freedom and democracy — but that could change."
- "It isn't pollution that's harming our environment. It's the impurities in our air and water that are doing it."
- "A low voter turnout is an indication of fewer people going to the polls."
- "Republicans understand the importance of bondage between a mother and child."
- "I am not part of the problem. I am a Republican."
- "I stand by all the misstatements that I've made."

In 2016, researchers at Carnegie Mellon University analyzed the vocabulary size and grammaticality of the (then) five presidential candidates (Ted Cruz, Hillary Clinton, Marco Rubio, Bernie Sanders, and Donald Trump) and added comparisons with presidents Barack Obama, George W. Bush, Bill Clinton, Ronald Reagan, and Abraham Lincoln. Trump scored the lowest of the eleven for vocabulary size, but G.W. Bush's grammar was the worst, slightly below Trump's. (Google *A Readability Analysis of Campaign Speeches from the 2016 US Presidential Campaign.*)

---

burglary/larceny/robbery/stealing/theft **Stealing**, **theft**, and **larceny** are synonymous; all three are acts of illicitly taking away somebody's property, intending to permanently deprive the owner of it. **Theft** accomplished through unlawful entry is **burglary.** **Theft** accomplished through force or the threat of force is **robbery** (see box).

And so I quit the police department
And got myself a steady job
And though she tried her best to help me
She could steal but she could not rob.
— "She Came In Through the Bathroom Window," song by The Beatles (1969)

business man/businessman The second is the standard term, but see the section on biased language for why you might not want to use that term either.

calendar/calender The first is a display of dates and months; the second is a machine with rollers to press paper or cloth. Hardly anyone ever talks about these machines, but people frequently misspell **calendar** that way.
  📢 **2016–17 Academic Calender** — Delaware Academy Central School District at Delhi (NY) website

callous/callus The first is an adjective, meaning (of skin) *hardened and thickened by friction*, or by extension, *insensitive*. The second is a noun referring to that kind of thickened skin.
  👎 **Woman angry with sister's callus attitude.** — headline, *Yuma Sun*
  ✓ **... sister's callous attitude.**
  ✓ **Guitarists can get callous fingers.**
  👎 **Guitarists can get callouses on their fingers.**
  ✓ **... calluses on their fingers.**

can/may In formal writing **can** should be used to refer to ability, **may** to refer to permission; but this distinction has disappeared in informal talk.
  👎 **Can I leave the room?** (In formal English, this would make sense if you are an injured person conversing with your doctor, or if you're wondering if the door is locked.)
  ✓ **May I leave the room?**

cancel something (<u>not</u> **cancel out**, except when used to mean *counterbalance* or *neutralize*)
  👎 **She cancelled out all her appointments.**
  ✓ **She cancelled all her appointments.**
  ✓ **The advantages and disadvantages cancel each other out.**

cannot help but: One too many negatives in this very informal phrase; use **cannot help.**
  👎 **He couldn't help but think he had made a mistake.**
  ✓ **He couldn't help thinking he had made a mistake.**

canon/cannon A **cannon** is a very large piece of artillery; a **canon** is a general rule, or a collection or list of sacred books. (Sometimes the Great Books that everyone is supposed to have read is, by extension, known as the **canon.**)

canvas/canvass The first is the heavy cotton cloth. The second is a verb meaning *to collect opinions.*

capable <u>of doing</u> something (not <u>to do</u>)

🖐 He is capable to run 1500 metres in under four minutes.

☑ He is capable of running 1500 metres in under four minutes.

☑ He is able to run 1500 metres in under four minutes.

☑ He can run 1500 metres in under four minutes.

capital/capitol As a noun, **capital** can refer to *wealth*, to *the city from which the government operates*, to *an upper case letter*, or to *the top of a pillar*. It can also be used as an adjective to mean *most important* or *principal*. **Capital punishment** is the most severe form of punishment. **Capital letters** are bigger. A **capital city** is the governmental headquarters. **Capitol** is much more restricted in its meaning, almost always *an American legislative building*.

☑ When we were in the capital, we toured the Capitol.

carat/caret/karat These are often confused. The first is a unit of weight for gems; the third is the unit for fineness of gold; the second is a wedge-shaped mark pointing up or down, used to show where to insert something in writing. (But don't confuse any of these words with **carrot**: that orange root vegetable.)

☑ A 1-carat diamond is a very big one.

☑ 24 karat gold is pure gold.

🖐 Rabbits are very fond of carets.

care

✊ I could care less

produces a lot of complaints. People argue that it should mean *I care a substantial amount*, but doesn't. In fact, it means the same thing as

☑ I couldn't care less.

That is, *I don't care at all*. **I could care less** came to have this meaning, apparently, through ironic use, but that's not important. There are three important considerations here: (1) in real use, it always means *I don't care*, and everybody knows this. (2) This is a *very* colloquial bit of language. Never say/write it in an even slightly formal context. (3) It *really* annoys a lot of people. If the person you're talking to is over 30, the wisest choice is not to say it.

care <u>about</u> something (meaning *to think it worthwhile or important to you*).

? George does not care for what happened to his sister.

is incorrect if used to mean that George doesn't care about what happened. But **not care for** also means *(mildly) dislike*; so it is correct (but mildly informal) used to mean that George is unhappy about what happened.

54

careen/career As a verb, **career** means *to swerve wildly*. **Careen** originally meant *to tilt or lean*, but now in North America especially is often treated as a synonym for **career**. Since **careen** has other specifically nautical meanings, some authorities resist the conflation of the two verbs.

careless/uncaring **Careless** means *negligent* or *thoughtless*; you can be careless about your work, for example, or careless about your appearance. Do not use **careless**, however, when you want to talk about not caring enough about other people.

🐦 He was very careless toward his mother when she was sick.

☑ He acted in an uncaring way toward his mother when she was sick.

catalog/catalogue The first spelling started from nowhere around 1900, and was ahead of the second since 1970 in US usage; but it's now in rapid decline in the US, and was always unpopular in the rest of the English-speaking world.

cede/concede/secede To **cede** something is to surrender it formally. To **concede** is to admit the truth of something, or to end a game by admitting defeat. To **secede** is to withdraw formally from membership.

celibate/chaste A **chaste** person is one who refrains from unsanctioned sex, and by extension, one who is morally pure. So a person having sex within marriage is not therefore unchaste. A **celibate** person is simply one who is unmarried (perhaps because of a religious vow). But due to the pious assumption that unmarried people won't have any sexual activity, **celibacy** has often — incorrectly — been used to mean *without sexual activity*.

Celsius/centigrade Both of these name the temperature scale used everywhere except in non-scientific contexts in the US (where Fahrenheit still holds on). **Celsius** became the official international name of the scale when things were standardized in 1948, so don't use the word **centigrade**. Capitalize the initial letters of **Celsius** and **Fahrenheit**, because both are the names of people.

☑ On the Celsius scale, water freezes at 0° and boils at 100°.

censer/censor/censure/sensor A **censer** is a container for burning incense in some churches. **To censor** a movie, book, etc., is to ban it or to have parts removed, usually on grounds of obscenity or political unacceptability; and **a censor** is the person who decides these matters. **Censure** (noun and verb) is strong, often official, disapproval. A **sensor** is something that senses — detects or measures a physical property.

🐦 The Senate censored the Attorney General for his part in the scandal.

☑ The Senate censured the Attorney General for his part in the scandal.

centre around/on something. Word-nerds object to **centre around**, claiming this is illogical: for a centre is a point, and can't be around something else. You should, they say, substitute **centre on**. But **centre around** has long been recognized as an acceptable idiom, and idioms don't have to be logical. And everybody knows what **centre around** means.

⚠ The novel centres around the conflict between British imperialism and Native aspirations.

☑ The novel centres on the conflict between British imperialism and Native aspirations.

centrifugal/centripetal The first is a force pulling away from the center of a circle, the latter, pulling toward. A common misspelling of the second is **centripedal**.

☑ When you swing a weight around in a circle, you can feel the centrifugal force pulling the weight outward; and you keep it from flying off by exerting a counterbalancing centripetal force on it.

certainty/certitude **Certainty** is unshakable confidence in a belief; **a certainty** is one of those beliefs. **Certitude** is the state of feeling certain. It's a rare and probably unnecessary word.

challenge Around 1950, people decided that because it was so negative to call something a **problem**, they should call it a **challenge** instead. The word **challenge** is now used twelve times more frequently than pre-1950, almost always with that use, which the OED delicately calls "weakened"; but, not constrained by British understated politeness, we can call it bureaucrat/social-work/psychobabble; the sign of a mealy mouth and a mushy brain. (Compare **issue**: same contemporary use, same diagnosis.)

change You <u>make</u> a change (not <u>do</u> a change).

🕮 The manager did several changes to the roster before the match with Russia.

☑ The manager made several changes to the roster before the match with Russia.

cheap/cheep The first is an adjective meaning *inexpensive* or *shoddy*; the second is the sound a bird makes. Sometimes a spelling confusion.

childlike/childish Both words mean *like a child*; but **childlike** suggests positive qualities (simplicity, trustfulness, innocence), whereas **childish** suggests negative ones (foolishness, immaturity).

chord/cord A **chord** is a harmonious combination of musical notes, or a line joining two points on a circle. A **cord** is a piece of rope or a measure of firewood. **Vocal cords**

(not **chords**) are so-called because they resemble thin rope. Be careful about these spellings.

cite/sight/site These sound-alikes make for spelling confusion. The first is a verb meaning *to quote*; the second is what eyes provide; the third is an area of ground.
- ☞ **The campus was the sight of noisy demonstrations.** — the *Toronto Globe and Mail*[1]
- ☑ **The campus was the site of noisy demonstrations.**
- ☑ **In an essay, it's often useful to cite authorities.**

civil rights/civil liberties The difference here is subtle and often ignored but is some-times thought of as follows: **Civil rights** traditionally protect people from unequal treatment. **Civil liberties** guarantee that people can vote, have a fair trial, have rea-sonable degrees of privacy and free speech, etc.

classic/classical As an adjective **classic** means *of such a high quality that it has lasted or is likely to last for a very long time.* **Classical** is used to refer to a former culture considered important. Classical music is, loosely and popularly, Western non-pop, non-folk, non-jazz music. Those familiar with the history of this music restrict the term to what was produced 1750 to 1830, including works by Mozart, Haydn, and early Beethoven, after Bach and Handel, and before late Beethoven, Brahms, Chopin, and Tchaikovsky.
- ☞ **Sophocles was one of the greatest classic authors; his plays are classical.**
- ☑ **Sophocles was one of the greatest classical authors; his plays are acknowledged classics.**
- ☑ **Early Beethoven is classical; late Beethoven is Romantic.**

climatic/climactic The first is the adjective from **climate**; the second is the adjective from **climax**. Confusing them can sometimes lead to embarrassment.
- ☞ **Difficulties in predicting long-term trends are inherent in any climactic projections.**
- ☑ **Difficulties in predicting long-term trends are inherent in any climatic projections.**
- ☑ **The climactic point of her childhood was her visit to Disneyland.**

coarse/course Another frequent spelling confusion. The first is an adjective mean-ing *rough textured*; the second is a noun meaning *a route, a division of a dinner, or a series of educational sessions.* And in the phrase **of course**, of course.

collaborate/corroborate To **collaborate** is to work together, whereas to **corroborate** is to give supporting evidence. **Collaborate together** is redundant.

---

1 Admirably candid (and linguistically sophisticated) columns by Sylvia Stead, the *Toronto Globe and Mail*'s Public Editor, pointed out and corrected this and several other errors I mention that the paper had let slip through.

👎 He collaborated her claim that the Americans had corroborated with the head of the Gestapo, Klaus Barbie.

☑ He corroborated her claim that the Americans had collaborated with....

collide Some (just some) authorities want you to say **collide with** when two moving objects are involved, and **collide against** when what's hit is stationary:

☑ The bus left the road and collided against a tree.

👎 The bus left the road and collided with a tree.

☑ The bus crossed the divider and collided with a van.

Does that distinction sound right to you? Maybe not. What's clear is the use of **collide with** is over 100 times more frequent, and that when the object is stationary you can't say

👎 The bus and the tree collided.

comic/comical Comic means *intentionally funny*, **comical** *unintentionally*.

☑ Monty Python produced well-known comic sketches.

☑ George W. Bush produced well-known comical language muddles.

comment We <u>make</u> comments (not <u>say</u> or <u>do</u> them).

👎 Anyone who wishes to say any comments will have a chance to speak after the lecture.

☑ Anyone who wishes to make any comments will have a chance to speak after the lecture.

compare to/with: To compare X <u>to</u> Y is to liken X to Y. To compare X <u>with</u> Y is to judge how the two are similar or different. This is a difference not often noted in casual English.:

☑ Shall I compare thee to a summer's day? — Shakespeare, Sonnet 18

☑ If you compare one brand with another you will notice little difference.

✋☹ February saw a hike in real estate values in Maine compared to the year before, but a decline in the number of homes sold. — MainePublic.com, website of Maine Public Radio & TV.

complement/compliment To **complement** something is to add to it to make it better or complete, and a **complement** is the number or amount needed to make it complete; two things are **complementary** when one completes or supplements the other. To **compliment** someone is to praise that person, and a **compliment** is the praise; something is **complimentary** when it expresses praise, but also when it is supplied free of charge.

👎 **None of the divisions had its full compliment of troops.**

✓ **... full complement of troops.**

👎 **Gretzky's mission in New York will be to compliment Mark Messier, the team's captain and franchise player.** — Associated Press. (This would mean that Gretzky's job was to keep saying "Nice work, Mark.")

✓ **... to complement Mark Messier ...**

👎 **None of the reviews of Noam's book were complementary.** (Assuming this is trying to say that none of them were positive.)

✓ **... were complimentary.**

✓ **When you buy strawberries you get complimentary whipping cream.**

✓ **It became clear that Benjamin and Beatrice were a complementary couple, each having the qualities the other lacked.**

compound One of the many words for which pronunciation makes a difference. The first syllable is accented if it's a noun, the second if it's a verb.

comprise/compose The whole **comprises** or includes the various parts; the parts **compose** the whole.

👎 **The MedLinks program is comprised of students like you.** — website, Medlinks, MIT

✓ **The MedLinks program comprises students like you.** (But this sounds weird.)

✓ **The MedLinks program is composed of students like you.**

concerned <u>with</u> something (meaning *having some connection with it, having something to do with it*) and concerned <u>about</u> something (meaning *being interested in it or worried about it*).

👎 **I'm concerned with the predicted ice-storm.**

✓ **I'm concerned about the predicted ice storm.**

✓ **The study is concerned with improving traffic flow downtown.**

✓ **The study concerns improving traffic flow downtown.**

But this is ambiguous:

☹ **The visit by the police did not concern her.**

This should be rewritten to make it clear what is meant:

✓ **The visit by the police did not worry her.**

✓ **The visit by the police was not about her.**

conduct One of the many words for which pronunciation makes a difference. The first syllable is accented if it's a noun, the second if it's a verb.

conference Used to mean *have a meeting with* or *talk to*, this is a buzzword easily and properly avoided.

confident of doing something (not to do)
- 🖙 She is confident to be able to finish the job before dusk.
- ☑ She is confident of being able to finish the job before dusk.
- ☑ She is confident that she will finish the job before dusk.

conflict One of the many words for which pronunciation makes a difference. The first syllable is accented if it's a noun, the second if it's a verb.

conform to/with: Some Sticklers insist that **conform with** is mistaken. It is, in fact, used far less frequently than **conform to**, but is not considered wrong by most modern authorities.

congratulate Here is a widely ignored finnicky distinction: You congratulate people on their good fortune, but you congratulate people for their achievements.
- ☑ Congratulations to Michael on winning the lottery!
- ⚠ Congratulations to Michael for winning the lottery!
- ☑ Everyone congratulated Emma for getting A+ in philosophy.
- ⚠ Everyone congratulated Emma on getting A+ in philosophy.

connect up Sometimes **connect up** seems a bit more appropriate than merely **connect**, as in:
- ☑ As soon as the plumber connects up the dishwasher, we're ready to go.

Though it's perhaps never wrong to substitute the shorter (and therefore better) **connect**.

connote/denote; connotation/denotation These words have technical senses in the philosophy of language, but the meanings usually encountered are these: the denotation of a bit of language is its direct, explicit, definitional meaning, whereas its connotation is what's indirectly suggested.
- ☑ The denotation of "Wall Street" is the financial centre in New York.
- ☑ The connotation of "Wall Street" is wealth and power.

conscience/conscious To be **conscious** is to be awake and aware of what is happening, whereas **conscience** is the part of our mind that tells us what's right or wrong.
- 🖙 She was tempted to steal the chocolate bar, but her conscious told her not to.
- ☑ ... but her conscience told her not to.

60

consider It's usually better to drop the **to be** from **consider to be**, and to drop the **as** from **consider as**.

☑ Sally considered her house a splendid work of architecture.

☹ Sally considered her house to be a splendid work of architecture.

☹ Sally considered her house as a splendid work of architecture.

consist in/of **Consist in** means *to exist in, to have as the essential feature*; **consist of** means *to be made up of*. But this distinction is disappearing, except perhaps in philosophical writing.

? Success consists of hard work. (i.e., The essence of success is hard work.)

☑ Success consists in hard work.

? The US Congress consists in two houses — the House of Representatives and the Senate.

☑ The US Congress consists of two houses....

consult someone is formal English, not the frequently heard but trendy and informal **consult with** someone.

✊ She will have to consult with the Board of Directors before giving us an answer.

☑ She will have to consult the Board of Directors before giving us an answer.

☑ She will have to talk to the Board of Directors before giving us an answer.

contemptuous/contemptible We are **contemptuous** of anyone or anything we find **contemptible**.

☞ The judge called the crime utterly contemptuous.

☑ The judge called the crime utterly contemptible.

contest One of the many words for which pronunciation makes a difference. The first syllable is accented if it's a noun, the second if it's a verb.

continual/continuous If something is **continuous** it never stops; something **continual** is frequently repeated but not unceasing. The same distinction holds for the adverbs **continually** and **continuously**.

☞ Thank you for the lovely carving set. I'm sure we'll use it continuously.

☑ He has been phoning me continually for the past two weeks.

contract One of the many words for which pronunciation makes a difference. The first syllable is accented if it's a noun, the second if it's a verb.

contrast Another of the many words for which pronunciation makes a difference. The first syllable is accented if it's a noun, the second if it's a verb.

contributing Pronounced *con-TRIB-you-ting*, not *CON-truh-byou-ting*.

convenient <u>for</u> someone, <u>for</u> a purpose; convenient <u>to</u> a place

🖎 This house is very convenient to me; it is only a short walk to work.

☑ This house is very convenient for me; it is very convenient to my work.

convince/persuade: According to a traditional usage distinction, one is **persuaded** to do something, but **convinced** that something is true. But speaking of convincing somebody to do something is now so common as to be considered acceptable just about anywhere.

☑ I persuaded Benjamin to get the lock fixed.

⚠ I convinced Benjamin to get the lock fixed.

☑ I convinced Benjamin that he should get the lock fixed.

⚠ I persuaded Benjamin that he should get the lock fixed.

What is not acceptable, however, is using **persuade** or **convince** to refer to the attempt to persuade or convince. If one does not succeed in making people believe or do what one wants, then one has not persuaded or convinced them, but only tried to.

🖎 No matter how seriously I convinced her, she would not believe me.

🖎 After all of Portia's persuasion, Shylock still refuses to change his mind.

☑ After all of Portia's attempts to persuade him, Shylock still refuses to change his mind.

(See deny/refute for a parallel mistake.)

copyright is the right to make copies of something. Two frequent misspellings: **copywrite, copywright**, but note that a copywriter is one who writes copy, usually for a newspaper, magazine or other publication.

correspond <u>to</u> (be in agreement with); correspond <u>with</u> (exchange letters with)

🖎 The fingerprints at the scene of the crime corresponded with those of the suspect.

☑ The fingerprints at the scene of the crime corresponded to those of the suspect.

could have/could of see have/of.

council/counsel; councillor/counsellor A **council** is an assembled group of officials, and a **councillor** is a member of that group. **Counsel** is advice, or in the special case of a lawyer, the person offering advice. In other situations, the person offering **counsel** is a **counsellor**.

🖎 The city counsel met to discuss the proposed bylaw.

☑ The city council....

🖎 The lawyer offered sound council as to the advisability of launching a suit.

☑ The lawyer offered sound counsel …

🖋 Ask Sally Yates, under oath, if she knows how classified information got into the newspapers soon after she explained it to W.H. [White House] Council. — Donald Trump, tweet. (He meant the lawyer who advises the President.)

🖋 Overall, she enjoyed summer camp, but she did not like her councillor.

☑ … she did not like her counsellor.

couple **A couple** means *two*, so

✊ The school is only a couple of miles from here (meaning a few).

But

✊ The school is only a couple of miles from here (meaning two)

is still somewhat casual, probably unacceptable in formal writing. It's a good idea to substitute **two** or **about two** if that's what you mean.

☑ The school is only two miles from here.

☑ The school is only about two miles from here.

One sometimes hears it without **of**, as in

✊☹ The boat drifted a couple hundred feet down the river.

This is quite informal, and unacceptable in writing.

credible/credulous Someone **credulous** (*believing*) is likely to believe anything, even if it is not **credible** (*believable*). Corresponding terms are **credibility/credulity**.

🖋 "Maybe I'm too credible," she said. "I believe everything my husband tells me."

☑ "Maybe I'm too credulous," ….

credit Saying that someone is credited with an action should be restricted to cases in which the action is a good thing. Thus:

🖋 No group is credited as yet with the stadium bombing.

But

☑ ISIS claims credit for the stadium bombing.

Because in that group's eyes, this was a good thing.

crevasse/crevice The second is a narrow split; the first a wider or deeper one, especially in a glacier. The first is pronounced *cruh-VASS*, the second, *CREV-is*.

criticism of something or somebody (not against)

🖋 His criticisms against her were completely unfounded.

☑ His criticisms of her were completely unfounded.

dearth This means *scarcity*, but it's sometimes mistakenly used to mean *complete absence*.

deceptively Consider:
☹ **The test was deceptively easy.**
Does that mean that it appeared easy, but was actually difficult? Or that it was actually easy, even though it did not appear that way? It's best to rephrase for clarity:
☑ **Deceptively, the test was easy.** (actually easy but it didn't seem that way)
☑ **The test seemed easy, but was actually difficult.**
☑ **The test was easy, but didn't seem to be.**

decimate This originally meant *kill one of every ten*. It has come to be used more loosely to mean *destroy a considerable number of,* but in formal writing, you shouldn't use it in a way that some authorities think, as H.W. Fowler puts it, "expressly contradicts the proper sense."
✊ **The regiment was decimated; fewer than 40 per cent of the troops survived.**
☑ **The regiment suffered extreme losses; fewer than 40 per cent of the troops survived.**

decrease One of the many words for which pronunciation makes a difference. The first syllable is accented if it's a noun, the second if it's a verb.

deduce/deduct **Deduction** is the noun stemming from both these verbs, which is perhaps why they are sometimes confused. To **deduce** means *to draw a conclusion*, whereas to **deduct** means *to subtract*.
✊ **Sherlock Holmes deducted that Moriarty had committed the crime.**
☑ **Sherlock Holmes deduced that Moriarty had committed the crime.** (This was his deduction.)
☑ **Your employer will deduct taxes from your monthly pay.** (This is called a deduction.)

definite/definitive If something is **definite** then there is no uncertainty about it; a **definitive** version of something fixes it in its final or permanent form — just as a dictionary definition attempts to fix the meaning of a word.
✊ **Glenn Gould's recording of Bach's Goldberg Variations is often thought of as the definite modern version.**
☑ **… the definitive modern version.**
✊ **"It is too early to reach any definitive conclusions on the success of the Prevent Duty in schools."** — UK Parliament Committee on Human Rights Statement on Counter-Extremism
☑ **It is too early to reach any definite conclusions….**

defuse/diffuse Another spelling trap. **Defuse** = *remove the fuse from, make safe*; **diffuse** = *spread out.*

☑ **The police acted quickly to defuse the dangerous situation.**

☑ **Light bulbs are frosted to diffuse what would otherwise be glaring light.**

deny/refute To **deny** something is to assert that it is not true; to **refute** it is to <u>prove</u> that it is not true.

✊ **During yesterday's press conference the President angrily refuted the allegations: "There has been no improper relationship," he said.**

☑ **... the President angrily denied the allegations: ....**

(See convince/persuade for a parallel distinction.)

depart <u>from</u> a place

🕮 **One woman was heard saying to a friend as they departed the SkyDome ...**

☑ **One woman was heard saying to a friend as they departed from the SkyDome ...**

But why not substitute a simpler alternative:

☑ **One woman was heard saying to a friend as they left the SkyDome ...**

dependent/dependant The first is the adjective, the second the noun. You are **dependent** on someone or something, and your young children are your **dependants**; they are **dependent** on you.

deprecate/depreciate To **deprecate** something means *to suggest that it is not valuable or worthy of praise*; something that **depreciates** loses its value.

🕮 **When I mess up, I say self-depreciating things....** — "Emotional Intelligence Test," *Psychology Today* website.

☑ **... self-deprecating ...**

desert/dessert Another potential spelling problem. The first means either *a very dry or relatively lifeless place* (*DEH-zurt*) or *what is deserved* (*duh-ZERT*); the second (also *duh-ZERT*) is the sweet or fruit at the end of a meal.

☑ **In the hot desert, ice cream is a welcome dessert.**

☑ **He thinks that a good job is only his just desert.**

detail Another word for which pronunciation makes a difference. The first syllable is accented if it's a noun, the second if it's a verb.

determine if/whether These are just about equivalent, though **determine whether** is more common.

diagnosis/prognosis The first is the process or result of determining the nature of something, especially of a disease. The second involves its future course.

dialogue As a verb, **talk** or **discuss** is less trendy but far better.
- ☹ The two department heads should dialogue with each other more frequently.
- ☑ The two department heads should talk to each other more frequently.

die <u>of</u> a disease, <u>of</u> old age; <u>from</u> injuries, wounds
- 📖 My grandfather died from cancer when he was only forty-two years old.
- ☑ My grandfather died of cancer when he was only forty-two years old.

die/dye The first means *to cease living*; the second means *to colour*, usually fabric or hair. Watch the spelling. (The first is also the singular form of **dice**, as in *The die is cast*.)

different from/to/than. **Different to** and **different from** are both acceptable British usage; **different from** is the preferred form in Canada; **different than** is a common and entirely acceptable form in the United States. Sometimes Sticklers tell you that one or the other (**different than**, usually) is unacceptable, but good writers have been using all three for a long time.
- ? These results are different than those we obtained when we did the same experiment yesterday. (Mostly US)
- ? These results are different to those…. (Mostly UK)
- ☑ These results are different from those….

dilemma Strictly speaking (as the prefix **di-** indicates), this is a choice between two problematic possibilities; but very often it refers to more than two.
- ☑ The dilemma we face is that we must choose between failing to protect against terrorism and abridging civil liberties.
- ⚠ My dilemma is that I can either go for a dead-end job, or go back to my awful school, or do nothing and get completely bored.

disc/disk CDs and DVDs are **discs**. The storage in your computer is a **disk**. In medical use, e.g., what you slip in your spine, spell it **disk**. But in other contexts, there's no real consensus.

discomfit/discomfort To **discomfit** means *to defeat or frustrate or make puzzled or uneasy or embarrassed*; but centuries of confusion have produced a legitimate use of this verb to mean *discomfort*. **Discomfort** as a noun means *annoyance* or *irritation* or *minor pain*, but it's also a medical euphemism for pain that's not so minor.

☑ Having to lie so much caused him a good deal of discomfort.
☑ When I remove these stitches you may feel some discomfort.
☑ She was discomfited by her mother's bad manners.

discount One of the many words for which pronunciation makes a difference. The first syllable is accented if it's a noun, the second if it's a verb.

discourage someone <u>from doing</u> something (not <u>to do</u>)
🖎 The new Immigration Act is intended to discourage anyone who wants to come to Canada to enter the country illegally.
☑ ... from entering the country illegally.

discrete/discreet **Discrete** means *separate* or *distinct*, whereas **discreet** means *prudent and tactful; unwilling to give away secrets.*
🖎 David Letterman is not renowned for being discrete.
☑ ... for being discreet.
🖎 The work is divided into discreet sections.
☑ ... into discrete sections.

dis-/un- **Dis-** is a prefix conveying (among other things) negativity or deprivation or rejection. **Un-** by contrast simply means *not*. See entries for these often-confused pairs: disbelief/unbelief; disinterested/uninterested; disorganized/unorganized; disquali-fied/unqualified; dissatisfied/unsatisfied.

disbelief/unbelief If you **disbelieve** something you actively reject; **unbelief** means you merely don't believe it.

discuss something, not discuss <u>about</u> something
🖎 They discussed about what to do to ease tensions in the Middle East.
☑ They discussed what to do to ease tensions in the Middle East.

disinterested/uninterested A **disinterested** person is unbiased, with nothing to gain by taking a stand. If one is **uninterested** in something, on the other hand, one is bored by it. It is thus quite possible for a person who is entirely **disinterested** in a particular matter to be completely fascinated by it. **Disinterested** has in recent years been routinely misused to mean *uninterested*. The distinction is well on the way to becoming erased. Too bad, because there's an important and useful difference in meaning here.
✍☹ Sloppy, pedestrian and disinterested, several players not only wrote themselves out of City's crucial Champions League return in Madrid next Wednesday, but out of a place in next season's squad. — ESPN website

67

WRITING WRONGS: COMMON ERRORS IN ENGLISH

☑ **Sloppy, pedestrian and uninterested, ...**

☑ **Judges must truly be disinterested in the cases that come before them.**

disorganized/unorganized The first pejoratively suggests that things are in confusion, a bad mess; the second merely that they haven't been organized, perhaps not yet, or perhaps without need of organization.

disorient/disorientate Both are considered correct, and the same goes for **orient/orientate**. The shorter terms are much more frequent in the US and somewhat more frequent in the UK. Shorter is better.

disqualified/unqualified The first applies to somebody who is actively rendered ineligible, the second to somebody who merely lacks the necessary qualifications.

dissatisfied/unsatisfied A person who is dissatisfied is one who is bothered, displeased or unhappy; but an unsatisfied person may merely be neutral, without positive satisfaction. A rather subtle distinction that's often ignored.

dissemble/disassemble To **dissemble** means *to disguise your feelings* — a mild form of lying. To **disassemble** means *to take apart.*

📖 **For the test, we are required to first assemble and then dissemble a six-cylinder engine.**

☑ **... and then disassemble....**

☑ **Louis smiled, but he was dissembling.**

dissociate/disassociate The shorter word is four times more frequent. Why go for the extra syllable?

☺ **T.S. Eliot speaks of the disassociation of sensibility that began in the seventeenth century.**

☑ **... of the dissociation of sensibility....**

distinct/distinctive **Distinct** means *able to be seen or perceived clearly; easily distinguishable from those around it.* **Distinctive** means *unusual; not commonly found.* There is a similar contrast between the adverbs **distinctly** and **distinctively**, and the nouns **distinction** and **distinctiveness**.

📖 **I distinctively heard the sound of a car engine.**

☑ **I distinctly heard the sound of a car engine.**

do something <u>for</u> someone (meaning something that will help); do something <u>to</u> someone (meaning something that will hurt)

🖐 Norman Bethune did a lot to the people of China.
☑ Norman Bethune did a lot for the people of China.

Down syndrome has now replaced the older possessive form **Down's syndrome**. It is named after a British physician, so the **D** should be capitalized.

drier/dryer **Drier** is an adjective meaning *more dry*. A **dryer** is a laundry or hair appliance. Older dictionaries might count these spellings as interchangeable, but the difference has recently become well established.

each other/one another Use **each other** for two, **one another** for more than two.
🖐 The three brothers always tell stories to each other before going to sleep.
☑ ... to one another....
🖐 The two men had long since begun to get on one another's nerves. — Alan Moorehead, *The White Nile*
☑ ... to get on each other's nerves.

economic/economical **Economic** means *pertaining to economics*, or *sufficient to allow a reasonable benefit for the amount of money or effort put in*. **Economical** means *thrifty*. The difference applies as well to **uneconomic** and **uneconomical**.
✋ Controversy over whether it would be economical to develop the vast Hibernia oilfield continued for many years.
☑ ... whether it would be economic....

effete/effeminate The old meaning of **effete** was *worn out* or *barren*. More recently, maybe due to Nixon's vice-president Spiro Agnew's rant against intellectuals as "effete corps of impudent snobs," people came to think of the word as meaning *sophisticated, snobby, pretentious*. The word is also misused to mean the same as **effeminate**. Avoid **effete**, and **effeminate** as well, which is usually applied in a derogatory way to men, meaning that they are not manly, that they have (stereotyped) womanly characteristics.
🖐 But who, exactly, are the Effete Elite? For starters, "effete" means affected and pretentious and "elite" means "superior" people, or in this case those who think they are. — Mike Strobel, *Toronto Sun*

e.g./i.e. The abbreviation **e.g.** is short for *exempli gratia* ("for the sake of example"). It is sometimes confused with the abbreviation **i.e.**, which is short for *id est* ("that is"). Use the second only if what follows describes what precedes it; use the first to provide one or more examples.

🗣 Those citizens of India who speak Hindi (e.g., the vast majority of the population) are being encouraged by the government to learn a second language.

☑ Those citizens of India who speak Hindi (i.e., the vast majority of the population)....

☑ Crustaceans (e.g., crabs, lobsters, shrimp) have a hard outer shell.

egoist/egotist The first term carries the suggestion of one who talks too much about him- or herself. The second suggests selfishness. But these terms are really interchangeable.

either See any/either

elder/older **Elder** can act as an adjective (**my elder son**) or a noun (**the elder of the two**). **Older** can act only as an adjective. If using **than**, use **older**.

🗣 She is four years elder than her sister.

☑ She is four years older than her sister.

elemental/elementary A thing is **elemental** if it forms *an important or essential or basic element of the whole*; it is **elementary** if it is *easy to understand*, or *at a relatively simple level*.

🗣 He lacked even the most elemental understanding of the problem.

☑ He lacked even the most elementary understanding of the problem.

☑ The Golden Rule is an elemental directive of morality.

elicit/illicit **Elicit** is a verb; one **elicits** information about something. **Illicit** is an adjective meaning *illegal* or *not approved*.

🗣 Attempts to recognize the early signs of substance abuse and identify those athletes "at risk" of experimenting with elicit drugs are paramount to the optimal treatment response program. — Article abstract, *Clinical Sports Medicine*

☑ ... with illicit drugs....

☑ The police elicited details about her drug use.

eligible/illegible One is **eligible** for a job or for membership in an organization if one meets the standard set for applicants. **Illegible** means *unreadable*.

🗣 He regretted that I was not illegible to join his club.

☑ He regretted that I was not eligible to join his club.

emigrant/immigrant To **migrate** is to move from one place to another. The prefix **ex-**, shortened to **e-**, means *out of*, so an **emigrant** from a country is someone who is moving out of it. The prefix **in-** or **im-** means *in* or *into*, so an **immigrant** to a country is someone moving into it. Similarly, **emigration** means *the movement of people out of*

70

a country, while **immigration** means *the movement of people into a country.* Notice the spelling in both cases; e-migrant (one **m**), im-migrant (two **m**s).

👎 More than 100,000 emigrants entered America last year.

☑ More than 100,000 immigrants entered America last year.

☑ More than 100,000 emigrants left America to move to Canada last year.

eminent/imminent/immanent An **eminent** person is one who is well known and well respected; an event is **imminent** if it is about to happen; a quality (or a god) is **immanent** if it pervades everything.

👎 Even those working for the party in the campaign did not believe that a majority victory was eminent.

👎 ... a majority victory was immanent.

☑ ... a majority victory was imminent.

☑ Those who believe in God's immanence think that God is present in all of creation.

☑ Alexander Hamilton was an eminent graduate of Columbia University.

empathy/sympathy **Empathy** is putting yourself in someone else's place, feeling what they feel, and understanding it. **Sympathy** is feeling compassion, sorrow, or pity for someone in a bad situation.

end at the end of something; in the end (no additional preposition). **In the end** is used alone when what's meant is *eventually* or *ultimately.* **At the end of** is used when the particular thing whose end is referred to is mentioned.

👎 In the end of *Things Fall Apart,* we both admire and pity Okonkwo.

☑ At the end of *Things Fall Apart,* we both admire and pity Okonkwo.

☑ In the end, we both admire and pity Okonkwo.

enervate/invigorate Because of the similarity in sound between **enervate** and **energy**, it is often thought to mean *make more energetic.* In fact, it means just the opposite — *to lessen the strength of.* If something makes you more energetic it *invigorates* you.

👎 I have seen the trailers for this movie and it is going to be a lot of FUN and will get you off to an enervating and laughing start to 2017.

☑ ... get you off to an invigorating and laughing start to 2017.

enormity/enormousness Originally the adjective **enormous** simply meant *deviating from the norm,* but by the early nineteenth century it had also come to mean *abnormal, monstrous,* or *extraordinarily wicked.* Today the only meaning is of course *very large,* but the connotation of wickedness is preserved in the noun **enormity.** We may speak of the **enormity** of a person's crime, but if we want a noun to express vast size

71

we should use **enormousness** or **vastness**. It's very common, but still an error, to use **enormity** to mean *very large size.*

🖐 **Given the enormity of this moment, the United States stands ready to help, as you help yourselves.** — George Bush, Address to the Polish Parliament. (He means enormousness.)

🖐 **What most impresses visitors to the Grand Canyon is usually its sheer enormity.**

☹ **What most impresses visitors to the Grand Canyon is its sheer enormousness.**

☑ **What most impresses visitors to the Grand Canyon is its vastness.**

enquire/inquire Some authorities try to find a difference in meaning, but there probably isn't any in North America, though the second is the preferred spelling. In the UK an **inquiry** used to mean an official investigation, and an **enquiry** just a question, but this distinction is dying.

enthuse/enthusiastic **Enthuse** is a verb, but not one appreciated in formal English. **Enthused** is its past participle. The fully acceptable adjective is **enthusiastic.**

✋ **Are Canadians that enthused about clean energy?** — headline, the *Ottawa Citizen*

☑ **Are Canadians that enthusiastic about clean energy?**

✋ **In 2002 millions were enthused about South Korea's World Cup performance.**

✋ **In 2002 millions enthused over South Korea's World Cup performance.**

☑ **In 2002 millions were enthusiastic about South Korea's World Cup performance.**

entitled/titled **Is entitled to** means *has a right (to something),* but **is entitled** is a somewhat old-fashioned and pompous way of saying *has the title;* substitute **is titled.**

☑ **We are entitled to a magnificent 1½ days off at Christmas.**

☹ **The book is entitled *Treasure Island*.**

☑ **The book is titled *Treasure Island*.**

entomology/etymology The first is the study of insects, the second of word origins.

enumerable/innumerable The central meaning of **innumerable** is *too many to be counted,* but an astoundingly large number, with a bit of exaggeration, can be called that also. **Enumerable** has the reverse meaning: *countable.*

🖐 **Scholars have advanced enumerable explanations for the dinosaurs' disappearance.**

☹ **Scholars have advanced innumerable explanations for the dinosaurs' disappearance.**
(Many but not an extraordinary large number.)

☑ **Scholars have advanced numerous explanations for the dinosaurs' disappearance.**

⚠ **There are innumerable species of butterfly in Manu National Park in Peru.** (Well, there are about 1,300; that's a huge number, but countable. With exaggeration for effect, this might be called innumerable, but literal-minded pedants will object.)

envelop/envelope **Envelop:** a verb, *en-VEL-up,* to surround completely. **Envelope:** a noun, *EN-vuh-lope,* or *ON-vuh-lope,* what you seal a letter in. Watch the spelling.

epicure/gourmand/gourmet All three are lovers of fine food. **Epicure** is derived from the philosophical movement called Epicureanism (which decidedly did *not* advocate developing a refined taste in food). It's a snobbier term than **gourmet**, which now is applied by its producer to just about anything food-related and expensive. The word **gourmand** however is derogatory, implying gluttony.

epigram/epigraph/epitaph/epithet four words often confused. **Epigram** = a short, witty, or pointed saying. **Epigraph** = an inscription placed upon a building, tomb, or statue; or a short quotation at the beginning of a written work. **Epitaph** = words describing a dead person, often the words inscribed on the tomb. **Epithet** = an adjective or short phrase describing someone; currently, what are called **epithets** are often terms of abuse.

- ☜ His epigram will read, "A good man lies here."
- ☑ His epitaph will read, "A good man lies here."
- ☑ "The First Lady of Song" is Ella Fitzgerald's epithet.
- ☑ "Liberal" is Rush Limbaugh's favourite abusive epithet.
- ☑ Groucho Marx was famous for epigrams, including "No one is completely unhappy at the failure of his best friend."

equal/equitable/equable Things that are **equal** have the same value. Arrangements that are **equitable** are fair and just. An **equable** person is one who is moderate and even-tempered.

- ☜ ... gradual abolition of the distinction between town and country, by a more equable distribution of population over the country.... — Bertell Ollman, "Marx's Vision of Communism: The First Stage," NYU website (Does he mean more equal or more equitable?)

escort One of the many words for which pronunciation makes a difference. The first syllable is accented if it's a noun, the second if it's a verb.

especially/specially There are subtle differences here, easily and forgivably ignored. Use **specially** to emphasize that something is out of the ordinary or particular:

- ☑ Our programmers are specially trained.
- ☑ These shoes are specially for running.

Use **especially** to emphasize individuality, or an unusual high degree of something:

- ☑ Sydney is especially to blame.
- ☑ Watch for children in the crosswalks, especially now that school is open.

73

espresso Spelled and pronounced that way, not **expresso**, although the latter is becoming more widely heard and reluctantly accepted.

🖐 **PREPARE AND SERVE EXPRESSO COFFEE** — course listing, Boxhill Institute, Australia

every body/everybody See **any body/anybody**

every day/everyday These are frequently confused, and you'll risk being thought to be language-incompetent if you use one for the other. **Everyday** is an adjective meaning *ordinary*. **Every day** is an adverb phrase meaning *daily, each day*.

🖐 I try to get some exercise everyday.

☑ I try to get some exercise every day.

🖐 **Same Day Parcel Delivery 7 Days A Week, Anyday...Everyday!** — Maritime Bus (NS) Courier Express website ad (See also **anyday**, and notes on the ellipisis, below. Yes, I know, it's just an ad, but.)

☑ **Any day — every day!**

☑ **These are my everyday shoes.**

🖐 **These are my every day shoes.**

every one/everyone The way to tell which one of these is proper is to try substituting **everybody**. If what you get is okay, then **everyone** is okay.

☑ **Everyone is happy that you're here.**

Substitution works:

☑ **Everybody is happy that you're here.**

☑ **Every one of those people are drunk.**

Substitution doesn't work:

🖐 **Everybody of those people are drunk.**

everyplace Not an acceptable word. Substitute **everywhere**.

every thing/everything See **any thing/anything**

explicit/implicit If something is **explicit** it is stated outright, not merely suggested or implied. (A growing use of this is to refer euphemistically to direct representation or description of sexual activity, but you should try to be more explicit.) Something that is **implicit** is not stated overtly. By extension **implicit** has also come to mean *complete* or *absolute* in expressions such as **implicit trust** (i.e., trust so unquestionable and unquestioning that it does not have to be put into words).

🖐 I told you implicitly to have the report on my desk first thing this morning.

☑ I told you explicitly to have the report on my desk first thing in the morning.

☑ When she thanked him for doing the dishes, in her words there was implicit criticism that he hadn't done them on other days.

☹ *Fifty Shades of Grey* is very explicit.
☑ *Fifty Shades of Grey* is sexually very explicit.

exponential The word has a special meaning in mathematics, but in everyday talk the only place it occurs is in the phrase **exponential growth**. That does not mean *fast growth*. It means *growing at an increasing rate*.

export One of the many words for which pronunciation makes a difference. The first syllable is accented if it's a noun, the second if it's a verb.

family values refers to the values supposedly upheld and transmitted by the family: honesty, loyalty, hard work, religious faith. While you might be in favour of these things, you should be careful using this term, which clearly suggests a conservative social and political standpoint you might not want to endorse.

farther/further **Farther** refers only to physical distance, but **further** can refer to physical or metaphorical distance. (Sometimes the pickiest US usage critics will object to **further** for physical distance.)
👎 **A farther study including more number of subjects and influence nutrition and non-nutrition factors on blood pressure in adults are necessary.**
  — Article abstract, US Library of Medicine, NIH (Note three other errors.)
☑ **The gas station was farther down the street.**
⚠ US **The gas station was further down the street.**

February Pronounce (and include in the spelling) the first **r**.
👎 **Febuary's Terrific Kids** — website link, Popp's Ferry Elementary School, Biloxi, MS.

feel good/well/bad/badly/poorly In an effort to be grammatically correct, some people say "I feel well/poorly/badly," but this is a mistake. Substitute "I feel good/bad." **Feel** here takes an adjective; that is, the word after **feel** describes the subject, not the action. **Feel poorly** is almost never encountered in writing, and **feel good** is written seven times as often as **feel well**. Don't be afraid of **feel good**.

Here are some other cases that are parallel, but more obvious:

👎 It appears soundly.	☑ It appears sound.
👎 It looks correctly.	☑ It looks correct.
👎 It sounds strangely.	☑ It sounds strangely
👎 It became lately.	☑ It became late.
👎 It smells rottenly.	☑ It smells rotten.
👎 It tastes well.	☑ It tastes good.
👎 Chop carrots finely.	☑ Chop carrots fine.
👎 Slice beef thinly.	☑ Slice beef thin.

75

feel (like/as if) See **like**.

feel/think/believe "I feel that …" is a weak way of introducing your assertions. Substitute "I think that…." or "I believe that …" or, best of all, just leave the initial phrase out and make the assertion you believe.

fewer/less The rule (frequently ignored, perhaps on the way out) is: when something can be counted (e.g., people, books, trees), use **fewer**. Use **less** only with uncountable nouns (e.g., sugar, meat, equipment). (See the section "Mass Nouns and Count Nouns" in the "Singular and Plural" section below.)

☞ **As the modern economy spreads through the countryside, less people will die of tropical diseases or infected wounds.** — *The New York Times*

☑ **… fewer people will die….**

☞ **Myopia is on a dramatic rise. Can outdoors and less devices for children be a solution?** — headline, the *Toronto Globe and Mail* (Did you notice the second problem? If not, see **rise**. And there's more wrong here in this dreadful headline.)

Anyway, when a quantity of money, or distance, or weight, etc., is being talked about as a singular whole, not as a plural bunch of individual things, then use **less**:

☑ **Fifteen dollars is less than I expected to pay for that.**

☞ **Fifteen dollars are fewer than I expected to pay for that.**

☑ **It's less than twenty miles from here.**

☞ **It's fewer than twenty miles from here.**

(See section on singular/plural matters for more on this.)

financial/fiscal/monetary/economic Financial = *having to do with finance or the handling of money*. **Fiscal** = *having to do with public revenue*. **Monetary** = *having to do with the currency of a country*. (Only in very limited circumstances, such as the expression **monetary value**, can monetary have the more general meaning of *having to do with money*.) **Economic** = *having to do with the economy*. Thus a government's **economic** program embraces both **fiscal** and **monetary** policies.

☞ **My brother is a nice person, but he has no monetary ability.**

☑ **My brother is a nice person, but he has no financial ability.**

first/firstly, second/secondly … **Firstly** goes in and out of fashion, and these days is out, generally thought of as archaic; and things get awkward when you get to **thirteenthly**. Do avoid inconsistency, however.

☹ **There were several reasons for France's reluctance to commit more resources to the New World. First, she was consumed with the battle for supremacy in Europe. Secondly, the returns on previous investments had been minimal.** (Inconsistent)

☹ There were several reasons for France's reluctance to commit more resources to the New World. Firstly, the country was consumed with the battle for supremacy in Europe. Secondly, the returns on previous investments had been minimal. (Archaic)

☑ There were several reasons for France's reluctance to commit more resources to the New World. First, the country was consumed with the battle for supremacy in Europe. Second, the returns on previous investments had been minimal.

flack/flak A **flack** is a public-relations agent. **Flak** is what's fired by an anti-aircraft gun, so, by extension, *harsh criticism*. (The word, by the way, is an abbreviation of the German term *Fliegerabwehrkanone*, *aircraft-defence gun*. It's a good thing that word was abbreviated.)

🗫 **Men get a lot of flack for their behavior.** — the *Toronto Globe and Mail*

flair/flare **Flair** is talent or ability or style. A **flare** is a flame or bright light.

🗫 **Pageau has always had a flare for the dramatic.** — TSN website.

flammable/inflammable The two words have the same meaning, but the second one may confuse people because it looks like a negative; avoid it. **Non-flammable** should be used to mean *difficult or impossible to burn*.

🗫 **Asbestos is an inflammable material.**

☑ **Asbestos is a non-flammable material.**

flaunt/flout To **flaunt** is to display very openly, to show off; to **flout** is to contemptuously disobey or show disrespect for. These two words are so widely confused that it's nearing the time when insisting on the difference would be useless (sigh!).

🗫 or maybe **The Government of Iran must realize that it cannot flaunt with impunity the expressed will and law of the world community.** — Jimmy Carter

☑ **They flouted the rules to supply performance-enhancing drugs.**

for/since Both these words can be used to indicate length (or duration) of time, but they are used in slightly different ways. **Since** is used to mention the point at which a period of time began (**since 6 o'clock, since last Christmas**, etc.). **For** is used to mention the amount of time that has passed (**for two years, for centuries**, etc.).

🗫 **Haley has been staying with us since three weeks.**

☑ **Haley has been staying with us for three weeks.**

☑ **Haley has been staying with us since three weeks ago.**

forego/forgo These are almost always considered to be different spellings of the same verb, meaning *to relinquish* or *do without*; but occasionally it's insisted that **forego** still has only its old different meaning: *to precede*.

77

☑ I'm going to forgo dessert tonight.

⚠ I'm going to forego dessert tonight.

☑ That's a foregone conclusion (i.e., already come to)

for ever/forever The two-word version is infrequent in the US, but it's used in the UK about as often as the one-word version.

forget To **forget** something means *to fail to remember it*. Informally, however, it has also come to mean *to leave something somewhere*.

✊ I forgot my textbook at home.

☑ I left my textbook at home.

☑ I forgot to bring my textbook from home.

formerly/formally The similarity of sound sometimes leads to confusion. The first means *in the past*; the second means *in accordance with the rules*.

☞ In August, Mr. Laurel formerly broke with Mrs. Aquino.

☑ In August, Mr. Laurel formally broke with Mrs. Aquino.

forte Have language snobs ever told you that this word (in the phrase **not my forte**, meaning *not my strong point*) comes from French, not Italian, so it should be pronounced *fort*, not *FOR-tay*? Yes, it does come from French, but other than that, this is wrong all over the place. First, the French phrase with that meaning, from which this English word derives, is *pas mon fort*. So if we really wanted to use correct French, it would be spelled without a final **e**, and the final **t** would be silent, so it would be pronounced *for*. But that's irrelevant. In English, which is what I understood we were talking about, it has a final **e** and is pronounced *FOR-tay*. If you said either "not my *fort*," or "not my *for*," nobody would understand you. Don't do it.

fortuitous/fortunate **Fortunate** means *lucky*; **fortuitous** means *happening by chance*. This is a dying distinction, as **fortuitous** has come to be used much more often to mean *a fortunate chance happening*.

☞ Setting out with a nasty storm in the forecast, my decision to depart early was looking like a fortuitous one. — *The Toronto Star*.

☑ ... a fortunate one.

☑ A fortuitous sighting of him in the supermarket told me that, unfortunately, Alex was back in town.

forward/foreword/foreward You find a **foreword** before the other words in a book. **Forward** means (among other things) toward the future. And **foreward** doesn't exist.

☞ **Ernst Robert Curtius in the author's foreward to the English translation of his landmark study ...** — *Proceedings of the IXth Congress of the International Comparative Literature Association: Classical Models in Literature*

☑ **I'm looking forward to finishing this term.**

founder/flounder To **founder** means *to get into difficulty, to stumble or fall, to sink* (when speaking of a ship), or *to fail* (when speaking of a plan). To **flounder** means *to move clumsily or with difficulty or awkwardly,* or *to become confused* in an effort to do something. Because many things that are foundering are also floundering, it's hard to find definite mistakes. But ships founder, never flounder.

frightened <u>by</u> something (when it has just frightened you); frightened <u>of</u> something (when talking about a constant condition or a particular sort of thing)

☞ **He was suddenly frightened of the sound of a door slamming.**

☑ **He was suddenly frightened by the sound of a door slamming.**

☑ **He was frightened of big dogs.**

☑ **He was frightened by a big dog.**

fulsome The only formally acceptable use of this word is to mean *offensive*, especially when that offensiveness is because of excessiveness. But it has a long history of being used to mean *abundant* or *comprehensive*, and that's the intention behind the majority of uses now. Should Sticklers give up on this one? Some dictionaries have. Anyway, because of the ambiguity here, this word is best avoided.

✊☹ **A fulsome meal (meaning abundant)**

✊☹ **A fulsome meal (meaning disgustingly overloaded)**

✊☹☹ **Business should provide a fulsome answer in a timely basis.** — the *Toronto Globe and Mail* (Note also the unidiomatic **in a timely basis.**)

☑ **... a comprehensive answer in a timely manner.**

fun As an adjective, as in

✊☹ **That was a fun thing to do.**

✊☹☹ **Apple once again getting ahead of the game, offering something cuter and funner and more Appley than anyone else.** — *The New York Times* (They know better but they're just being cute.)

The word, and even more so its comparative and superlative forms, are too informal for serious writing, and maybe even too valley-girl for adult informal talk.

further more/furthermore The familiar adverb is one word. It's hard to imagine the two-word phrase in a sentence.

gamut/gantlet/gauntlet The second and third are interchangeable spellings, meaning either *glove* or *ordeal*. For some reason, authorities used to insist that only **run the gantlet** is an acceptable way to say *undergo an ordeal*. But **run the gauntlet** has always been more common, and nobody should object to it. **Throw down** (or **take up**) **the gantlet/gauntlet** is what used to be done to a glove to issue (or take up) a challenge. Don't confuse any of this with **run the gamut. Gamut** means *complete range*.

☑ **Miss Hepburn ran the whole gamut of emotions from A to B.** — Dorothy Parker, on seeing Katharine Hepburn in a play.

gay It's ridiculous to insist (as some dinosaurs used to) that this only means *carefree*. Of course its primary meaning has been *homosexual* for decades. But the question is whether it refers to male and females alike; if so, then **gay and lesbian** would be redundant. It appears, however, that its use for males only is now solidly established.

gentleman The use of this word to refer to a man of superior social position is dead. Now (with a rather old-fashioned flavour nevertheless) it means *a man who is polite or considerate*. But you hear this word increasingly just as a replacement for **man**, when the speaker is trying to sound smart or cultured or formal or official (sometimes with bizarre results):

☹ **The gentleman in question had tortured, beheaded, and buried all eight of his victims.**
(See also individual)

get There are over a hundred familiar phrases that this word is part of: **get lost, get along, get up, get to, get dressed, get married, get over, get through, get the point**.... Some grammarians object to these, preferring more formal substitutes (**become lost, arrive at, understand the point** ...); but there's no reason for that. There's nothing wrong with most **get** phrases, and they are almost always more vigorous than the alternatives. So they mostly get a △. There are, however, some slangy or informal idioms:

✊ **I didn't get your name.**
✊ **That punch got him on the chin.**
✊ **The catcher got him sliding into home.**
✊ **Her attitude gets me.**
✊ **I'll get him for that.**
✊ **You've got to hear this album.**
✊ **Get going!**
✊ **He got away with plagiarizing that paper.**
✊ **I don't get it.**
But:
🖐 **You got to try this.**
☑ **You have to try this.**

God/god This word is capitalized when it's the proper name of the deity of a monotheistic religion, but not when it refers to a deity otherwise. The rule now is not to capitalize mid-sentence uses of pronouns (**he, his, him**) referring to God.

goodbye/good-bye/good-by/goodby The first spelling replaced the second as the most common fifty years ago; but both are still acceptable. The third and fourth are much rarer and should be avoided.

gorilla/guerrilla A **gorilla** is a large ape; a **guerrilla** (or **guerilla**) is a member of a small band of military raiders.

government If you really want to impress people, pronounce the **n** in the middle of this word: *GUV-urn-ment.*

graduate <u>from</u> + name of school, not **graduate** + name of school, though it appears that the second way of speaking is now more common than the first. Try to remember to insert **from**, because you don't want to sound as if you didn't graduate from anywhere.

✋☹ **Vitko is now in her second year of Ryerson's Collaborative Nursing Degree Program, having already graduated McGill with a bachelor of science.** — Ryerson University website

☑ **... graduated from McGill ...**

grammar/grammer The first is the correct spelling.

👎 **Grammer for Writing Professionals ... aims to provide students with a thorough knowledge of the editing and proofreading process.** — Confederation College (Ontario) website course description

gristly/grisly/grizzled/grizzly **Gristly** means *containing a good deal of gristle* (unpleasant cartilage in meat). **Grisly** means *horrifying.* **Grizzly** appears now only in the name of the **grizzly bear**. The explorers Lewis and Clark gave it that name, probably not because it's horrifying, but rather because of the silvery-grey tips of its hair; the word **grizzly** means *greyish,* though that use is very rare. You may see the related word **grizzled,** meaning *turned grey.* (The bear, by the way, was given the scientific name *Ursus horribilis,* meaning in Latin *terrifying bear.*)

👎 **However, if you are attacked by a grizly bear, curl into a fetal position, covering up your neck and head, and be quiet.** — *Salt Lake City Deseret News*

☑ **... a grizzly bear ...**

👎 **When I hear about a grizzly murder, I instinctively blame the killer for having done such a terrible thing. What can this mean if Spinoza's naturalism is correct?** — Daniel Frank and Jason Waller, *Routledge Philosophy GuideBook to Spinoza on Politics*

☑ **... a grisly murder ...**

☑ **"A Grizzly Murder"** — title of Season 5 Episode 17 of *CSI Miami* (What looks like a mistake here is actually a pun. A grizzly bear did the killing.)

grow When what's growing is a living thing, using this word is fine:

☑ **I'm growing a beard.**

☑ **The farmer is going to grow kale next year.**

But the following sentences are not:

✊☹ **You cannot grow this economy from the top down. You grow this economy from the middle class up.** — Barack Obama

✊☹ **I'm reading the dictionary in order to grow my vocabulary.**

This sort of use, which appears to have emerged in the 1970s, has grown (ha!) more common, but it still makes many people cringe.

had ought/hadn't ought Not okay. Find a substitute.

👎 **[Billy] Graham has gone off the beam. He's ... well, I hadn't ought to say this, but he's one of those "counterfeits" I was telling you about. He claims he's a friend of all the presidents, but he was never a friend of mine when I was president.** — Harry S. Truman

👎 **He hadn't ought to have risked everything at once.**

🎓 **He ought not to have risked everything at once.**

☑ **He shouldn't have risked everything at once.**

hanged/hung An often-ignored rule of standard English is that the first applies only to a method of executing criminals.

✊ **Saddam Hussein was hung at dawn December 30, 2006, for crimes against humanity....** — SourceWatch website

☑ **Saddam Hussein was hanged at dawn....**

hardly *Hardly* acts as a negative, meaning *almost not*, so it's a mistake to add a second negative.

👎 **The advertisers claim that you can't hardly tell the difference.**

☑ **The advertisers claim that you can hardly tell the difference.**

have/of The similarity of sound results in the common mistake of writing (more often saying) **should of** for **should have**. Similarly mistaken are **would of, could of, may of, might of**, and **must of**. The contractions, acceptable colloquialisms, are written **would've**, not **woulda**, and similarly **could've, may've, might've, must've**.

👎 **The experiment would of succeeded if the solution had been prepared correctly.**

☑ **The experiment would have succeeded if the solution had been prepared correctly.**

👋 I would've if I could've.
🤟 I woulda if I coulda.

heads-up As a noun this came to mean *advance warning of some sort of danger or problem*; but nowadays the use has extended to any kind of update or information. In either case, this is inappropriate in formal contexts.

healthful/healthy It's frequently insisted that it's proper to call certain foods or exercise **healthful** (= *health-productive*) not **healthy**, which is what you are if you eat/do it. For centuries, this distinction was not made; it was invented during the 1800s and has been widely ignored, except by Sticklers, ever since.
⚠ **Healthy Food for Healthy Schools Act, 2008** — Title of Law, Province of Ontario
☑ **Healthful Food....**

heighth Not a word. It's **height**.
🤟 **Bulldogs return experience, heighth and athletic ability** — headline, *Washington (KS) County News*

help doing something:
🤟 **Every summer since 1978, her extended family had gone to the beach at Oak Island. What, she could not help from wondering, was he doing there?** — "Not Love at First Sight," *University of North Carolina Gazette.*
🎓 **... What, she could not but wonder, ...**
☑ **... What, she could not help wondering, ...**

hence, thence, whence **From** preceding any of these words is sometimes officially considered a mistake, because they all are thought to include this word in their definitions: (**hence** = *from here*; **thence** = *from there*; **whence** = *from where*); so adding **from** is redundant. Well, sure enough, **from** isn't necessary:
☑ **He is but even now gone hence** — Shakespeare, *As You Like It*

But there's a long history of its inclusion, without serious objection.
☑ **Let him walk from whence he came** — Shakespeare, *The Comedy of Errors*

So maybe this is just another superstition. Anyway, all three words are so antique that you'll probably never wind up using them. Sorry I brought this up.

herb, herbal, herbicide, herbivore Most speakers of US English pronounce **herb** and **herbal** with a silent **h**, but **herbicide** and **herbivore** with an aspirated **h** (i.e., with outward expression of breath). Thus:

83

☑ **US** **What is an herb?** — University of Virginia Health Sciences Library website

☑ **UK** **Is a banana a fruit or a herb?** — Oxford Dictionaries online

☑ **There is a concentration in the soil at which a herbicide will inhibit weed growth.** — Oregon State University website

☑ **A herbivore is an animal that gets its energy from eating plants, and only plants.** — Northwestern University website

Most English-speakers in the rest of the world pronounce all four words with an aspirated **h**, thus using the article **a** in front of all. (See a/an)

heterogeneous/heterogenous homogeneous/homogenous **Heterogeneous,** pronounced *het-ur-oh-JEE-nee-us* means *containing different sorts of things.* **Heterogenous,** pronounced *het-ur-AH-jen-us,* is a less common word meaning the same thing. (Look carefully to see the spelling difference.) The first version is preferred. The opposites to these words, meaning *uniform in content,* are **homogeneous** and **homogenous.**

☑ **A heterogeneous group of people arrived at the civic celebration for the free lunch.**

☹ **A heterogenous group of people …**

☑ **Despite what Westerners often think, the Arab world is not at all homogeneous.**

☹ **… not at all homogenous.**

(There are also senses of both words and other words that are very close to them that have technical uses in biology and medicine, and we'll just ignore all these here.)

historic/historical **Historic** means *of sufficient importance that it is likely to become famous in history;* **historical** means *having to do with history* (historical research, historical scholarship, etc.).

✊ **Honored to witness the historical Inauguration and swearing-in ceremony for the 45th President of the United States!** — Betsy DeVos, Trump's Secretary of Education, tweet

For **a/an historical**, see a/an.

hoard/horde A **hoard** is a hidden or stored fund. A **horde** is a large group of people.

hopefully This word is one of the greatest causes of nagging by grammarians. Traditionalists argue that the correct meaning of the adverb **hopefully** is *filled with hope,* and that the use of the word to mean *it is to be hoped that* is therefore incorrect. But most contemporary grammar writers point out that many adverbs can function as independent comments at the beginning of a sentence:

☑ **Finally, let me point out … ;**

☑ **Clearly, we have much to do if … ;**

☑ **Obviously, it will not be possible to….**

Why should **hopefully** be treated differently? Why indeed? But this use of **hopefully** will be found objectionable by Sticklers, so it's best avoided in formal writing.

⚠ **Hopefully, it will be possible to finish before tomorrow.**

☑ **We hope we can finish before tomorrow.**

☹ **Hopefully, we will arrive before dusk.** (This sentence, which probably means "It's hoped that we will arrive …" should be rewritten to rule out the interpretation "We will arrive filled with hope …")

☑ **I hope we will arrive before dusk.**

how come This very colloquial phrase must be avoided in even slightly formal writing.

✊ **How come Jasmine didn't show up at the party?**

☑ **Why didn't Jasmine show up at the party?**

human/humane Until the eighteenth century there was no distinction made between the two in either meaning or pronunciation; they were simply alternative ways of spelling the same word. More recently, **humane** has come to be used to refer exclusively to the more attractive human qualities — kindness, compassion, and so forth.

🐸 **Their group is campaigning for the human treatment of animals.**

☑ **… the humane treatment of animals.**

identical with/to Until about 1940, **identical with** was the only form used. Since then, **identical to** has been gaining on it. Today, either may be used, despite the protests of old-fashioned purists.

☑ **This motel room is completely identical to the one in Albuquerque.**

☑ **… completely identical with….**

impact As a trendy verb it's best kept out of formal language

☺☹ **"Issues which Impact upon Marketing in the Small Firm"** — article by Danielle Mc Cartan-Quinn and David Carson, *Small Business Economics.* (Another issue here is the word **issues**, an inferior buzzword replacement for **problems** or **difficulties**.)

☹ **"Issues which Affect Marketing …**

☹ **"Issues which Influence Marketing …**

☑ **"Marketing Problems for the Small Firm"**

Have an impact is okay, but **impactful** is not.

☹ **"The Most Impactful Inventions in Each State"** — article in the website of Nazarene University (www.mnu.edu).

☑ **"The Most Influential Inventions …"**

imply/infer To **imply** something is to suggest it without stating it directly; the other person will have to **infer** your meaning.

📢 I implied from his tone that he disliked our plan.

☑ He implied by his tone that ...

📢 He inferred from his tone that ...

☑ I inferred from his tone that ...

(*These words have other technical meanings in the study of logic.*)

import One of the many words for which pronunciation makes a difference. The first syllable is accented if it's a noun, the second if it's a verb.

in Do not use **in** where **throughout** is meant.

📢 Political repression is common in the whole world.

☑ Political repression is common throughout the world.

incidents/incidence **Incidents** is the plural of **incident** (*something that is happening*), whereas **incidence** is a singular noun meaning *the rate at which something occurs.*

📢 A comprehensive cancer report released Wednesday by Algoma Public Health reveals that cancer mortality rates and incidents of most cancers are higher in the Algoma District ... compared to provincial rates. — SaultStar (Sault Ste. Marie, Ontario) website.

☑ ... incidence of most cancers is higher ...

incredible/incredulous **Incredulous** means *unbelieving.* A person can be incredulous. **Incredible** means *unbelievable.* A statement can be incredible.

☑ Hunter was incredulous when Alyssa said she'd be joining the army.

☑ Hunter found it incredible that Alyssa was going to join the army.

It's very slangy to call something **incredible** as merely a strong term of praise. In formal English, only claims can be incredible (or credible).

✊ I had an incredible onion soup at that restaurant yesterday.

The same goes for unbelievable.

in deed/indeed The second word, with a basic meaning of *in truth*, is sometimes the expression of surprise or affirmation. The first is a rarely encountered prepositional phrase:

☑ He is honest in talk and in deed.

independent of something or someone (not from)

📢 I would like to live independent from my parents.

☑ I would like to live independent of my parents.

indicate This word has a legitimate use, meaning *show*; but it's found as a pompous replacement for **say** in Bureaucrat-speak. See the following item for more on this language.

individual/person The word **individual** has a use when a person is contrasted with a group or organization, or when the emphasis is on singularity rather than group:

☑ **Capital gains taxes must be paid by corporations and individuals.**

☑ **Those little plastic containers of Kraft jams are individual servings.**

But when somebody uses that word without that contrast:

☹ **The individual who applied for clearance from the agency this morning was turned away.**

what you're hearing is BureaucratSpeak. a language that somewhat resembles English but has less meaning. (See the section on overblown speech, below.) The speaker is trying to sound smart and official. If you're tempted to use **individual** that way, remember that people will actually respect you less as a result. Substitute **person** or **somebody**:

☑ **The person who applied for clearance from the agency this morning was turned away.**

(See also gentleman)

Individual sometimes means somebody who is distinctive, striking, original, or unusual, but it is better to use one of those four words instead, for greater precision. (Is that what the company in Winnipeg called "Tattoos for the Individual" had in mind? If this interests you, pay them a visit, but bear in mind that all the other individualistic bikers have tattoos of skulls also.)

in fact/infact The second is not a word.

information You give information (not tell it).

🗣 **He told me all the information I wanted about how to apply.**

☑ **He gave me all the information....**

in front/infront You might be tempted to write this the second way, as one word, thinking of expressions such as 🗣 **out infront.** But that's not a word.

ingenious/ingenuous **Ingenious** means *clever;* **ingenuous** means *pleasantly open and unsophisticated.* Note the pronunciation difference: *in-JEEN-yus, in-JEN-you-us.*

🗣 **Her manner was completely ingenious; I cannot imagine she was trying to deceive us.**

☑ **Her manner was completely ingenuous; I cannot imagine she was trying to deceive us.**

☑ **Her solution of the problem was completely ingenious.**

87

The most frequently encountered relative of **ingenuous** is **disingenuous**, a fancy word that means *insincere*.

inferior to someone or something, not than. (**Inferior** and **superior** are the only two comparative adjectives which are not followed by **than**.)
- ☞ Most people think that margarine is inferior than butter.
- ☑ Most people think that margarine is inferior to butter.

in order/inorder Again, the one-word version does not exist.

insert One of the many words for which pronunciation makes a difference. The first syllable is accented if it's a noun, the second if it's a verb.

insist on doing something *or* that something be done (but not to do)
- ☞ The customer has insisted to wait in the front office until he receives a refund.
- ☑ The customer has insisted on waiting....
- ☑ I insisted that she accept the gift.

insist/persist To **insist** (that something be done, or on doing something) is to express yourself very forcefully. To **persist in** doing something is to keep on doing it, usually despite some difficulty or opposition.
- ☞ Even after he had been convicted of the crime, he persisted that he was innocent.
- ☑ ... he insisted that he was innocent.
- ☑ He persisted in calling me, even though I said he should go away.

in spite of/in spiteof **Spiteof** is not a word.

instinctive/instinctual There is no difference in meaning; it is thus better to stay with the more common, and more pleasant sounding, **instinctive**.
- ☹ Biologists disagree about which behaviors are instinctual.
- ☑ Biologists disagree about which behaviors are instinctive.

in store/instore **Instore** is a word born in about 1950. It's an adverb or adjective, meaning *in the store*. To have something in store means to have saved for the future.
- ☑ Our Walmart has an instore McDonald's.
- ☑ I have a surprise in store for your birthday.

insult One of the many words for which pronunciation makes a difference. The first syllable is accented if it's a noun, the second if it's a verb.

in tact/intact The second is an adjective meaning whole. The first is a rare prepositional phrase.
- 👎 Bobani said the coalition was still in tact. — the *South Africa Herald* website
- ☑ What he lacked in tact he made up for in charm.

intention of/to/that You have an intention <u>of doing</u> something, <u>to do</u> something, <u>that</u> something be the case.
- 👎 Hitler had no intention to keep his word.
- ☑ Hitler had no intention of keeping his word.
- ☑ Hitler did not intend to keep his word.
- ☑ Hitler's intention was to break the treaty.
- ☑ Hitler intended that the treaty be broken.

in to/into
- 👎 Is the United States caving into Iranian interests? — headline, CNN website
- ☑ Is the United States caving in to Iranian interests?
- ☑ I'm looking into the matter now.

investigation We <u>make</u>, <u>carry out</u>, or <u>hold</u> an investigation (not <u>do</u> one).
- 👎 The manager did a thorough investigation into the disappearance of funds from his department.
- ☑ The manager made a thorough investigation....

invitation, invite The first word is a noun, the second a verb sometimes mistakenly used as a noun.
- 👎 Did you get an invite to the party?
- ☑ Did you get an invitation to the party?
- ☑ She didn't invite me to the party.

irony/sarcasm **Irony** comes in two main forms: something said that expresses the opposite of its literal meaning: (e.g., "Lovely day isn't it?" said during a hurricane); or the incongruity of an event — the last thing one would expect (e.g., the police station is robbed). Sarcasm is irony of the first kind but expressed in a mocking, contemptuous, or sneering tone (e.g., "That's very smart," said to somebody who's just done something stupid.)

irregardless Not a word; it's the result of confusion between **regardless** and **irrespective**. Substitute **regardless**.
- 👎 She told us to come for a picnic, irregardless of whether it is rainy or sunny.
- ☑ She told us to come for a picnic, regardless of whether it is rainy or sunny.

> **is** The surprising claim that this word is ambiguous was made by President Clinton when questioned by a grand jury concerning the truthfulness of his earlier statement about his (then ongoing) relationship with Monica Lewinski, "There's nothing going on between us." Clinton explained his statement to the grand jury this way:
>
> > It depends upon what the meaning of the word "is" is. If the — if he — if "is" means is and never has been, that is not — that is one thing. If it means there is none, that was a completely true statement.

is when/where: Sometimes these phrases are used in definitions. There is always a better way.

- ☜ **Osmosis is when a fluid moves through a porous partition into another fluid.**
- ☑ **Osmosis occurs when a fluid moves through a porous partition into another fluid.**
- ☑ **Osmosis is the movement of a fluid through a porous partition into another fluid.**
- ☑! **Poetry is when an emotion has found its thought and the thought has found words.** — Robert Frost (He's breaking the rule on purpose. Poetry is where you're allowed to do this.)

it's/its: **Its** is a possessive adjective meaning *belonging to it*. **It's** is a contraction of **it is** or **it has** — a pronoun plus a verb. (Compare **who's/whose**.) Confusing these two, while common, will make you seem linguistically incompetent. Try not to.

- ☜ **% of residents who feel its important for them to feel part of their local community** — title, report by City of York (UK) Council
- ☑ **... it's important....** (contraction of **it is**)
- ☜ **Its been confirmed that the suspects were not guests at the hotel....** — "Hotel Thieves Being Sought by Barrie Police," website of radio station KICX News (http://kicx106.com)
- ☑ **It's been confirmed ...** (contraction of **it has**)
- ☜ **Another report found that Vancouver's "green brand"' is worth about $31-billion and it's economy could suffer a $1.2-billion loss.** — the *Toronto Globe and Mail*[2]
- ☑ **... its economy....**

See the section below on the correct use of the apostrophe.

journey You <u>make</u> or <u>complete</u> a journey (not <u>do</u> one).

- ☜ **If we do not stop along the way, we can do the journey in an hour.**
- ☑ **If we do not stop along the way, we can make the journey in an hour.**

judicial/judicious **Judicial** means *having to do with law courts and the administration of justice*. **Judicious** means *having good judgement*.

---

2   This is one of the *Globe*'s previous errors discussed in the column mentioned above.

🖐 He made one or two judicial comments about her new dress.

☑ He made one or two judicious comments about her new dress.

☑ A judicial inquiry will be made into the matter.

jump (not **jump up**)

🖐 Unemployment has jumped up to record levels recently.

☑ Unemployment has jumped to record levels recently.

justified <u>in doing</u> something (not <u>to do</u> something)

🖐 He is not justified to make these allegations.

☑ He is not justified in making these allegations.

keep Unacceptable in formal writing as a substitute for **stay**:

✊ Keep calm and carry on.

kid Unless you're talking about a baby goat, antelope, etc., substitute **child**, **girl**, or **boy** in formal contexts.

kind of Using this to mean *rather*, *somewhat*, or *partially* is very casual:

✊ Fred is kind of unpredictable.

☑ Fred is rather unpredictable.

And this:

✊ Erica is the kind of teacher this department needs.

is also non-standard. A kind of thing is a category: an individual in that category is not the category. So:

☑ Erica is an example of the kind of teacher this department needs.

The same goes for **sort of.**

know **Knowing** something is not an event, it's a continuing state; so when referring to the event of the arrival of knowledge, say **I discovered** or **I came to know**.

🖐 Although I talked to the new employee on Monday, I knew her name on Tuesday when I saw it on the bulletin board.

☑ Although I talked to the new employee on Monday, I discovered her name on Tuesday when I saw it on the bulletin board.

knowledge is not just any belief — no matter how sincerely it's believed, and no matter how basic to one's culture it is. It's a belief that's true, and that the person is rationally entitled to believe. (But see section on bias-free language.)

lama/llama The first is a Buddhist spiritual leader; the second a domesticated South American hoofed animal. When you're speaking English, pronouncing **llama** the Spanish way (roughly *YA-ma*) is pretentious.

> The one-l lama,
> He's a priest.
> The two-l llama,
> He's a beast.
> And I will bet
> A silk pajama
> There isn't any
> Three-l lllama.*
> *The author's attention has been called to a type of conflagration known as a three-alarmer. Pooh.
>
> — Ogden Nash

later/latter **Later** means *afterwards in time*, whereas **the latter** is the second of two things mentioned.

- 🗣 I looked up the Battle of Stalingrad in both the *World Book* and the *Encyclopaedia Britannica*. The later provided much more information.
- ☑ I looked up the Battle of Stalingrad in both the *World Book* and the *Encyclopaedia Britannica*. The latter provided much more information.
- ☑ The Battle of Stalingrad took place later than the Battle of Britain.

laudable/laudatory **Laudable** means *worthy of praise*; **laudatory** means *expressing praise*.

- 🗣 His efforts to combat poverty are very laudatory.
- ☑ His efforts to combat poverty are very laudable.
- ☑ The speech was extremely laudatory.

learned/learnt The proper form is **learned** in North America; this variant is preferred 5:1 in the UK. The adjective **learned** (pronounced with two syllables: *LURN-ed*) means *knowledgeable*.

lend/loan Usage authorities in the nineteenth century decided for some reason that the use of **loan** as a verb was illegitimate, despite its having been standard for a very long time. Sticklers for formal English will think that it is a mistake.

- ⚠ He was unwilling to loan his sister any money.
- ☑ He was unwilling to lend his sister any money.
- ☑ The bank wouldn't give her the loan she asked for.

let's us

👈 Let's us go to the restaurant now.

🎓 Let us go to the restaurant now.

☑ Let's go to the restaurant now.

liable/likely The central meanings of **liable** are *obliged by law*, and *likely in danger of an undesirable change*; but there's a long history of using this to mean *likely to undergo a change (of any sort)*. Using it to mean merely *likely* is sometimes considered mistaken or informal.

☑ You will be liable for any damage caused when you are driving the vehicle.

☑ That chimney is liable to fall.

⚠ The snow is liable to continue past midnight.

☑ The snow is likely to continue past midnight.

libel/slander Both are communication damaging to someone, and false or unproven: **libel** is *written* (and *published*); **slander** is *oral*.

👈 He was careful in his speech to avoid libel.

☑ He was careful in his speech to avoid slander.

☑ The newspaper had been sued several times for libel.

An underappreciated but interesting literary genre is the official licence-plate slogan. As advertising designed to make you visit the state or province, or at least to think highly of it, some slogans are a bit odd.

Idaho had a plate that simply stated **Potatoes**. And South Carolina's was **The Iodine State**. Decades ago, Indiana's choice caused some controversy, when residents didn't understand the single-word slogan **Wander**. Later plates boasted **Hoosier Hospitality**. Nobody really knows why Indianans are called Hoosiers, but Dave Barry somewhere suggested that it was the sound of a pig sneezing. DC's plate offers the complaint **Taxation Without Representation**, and New Hampshire's what Bill Bryson calls the "strange and pugnacious" **Live Free or Die**. But the prize for the most idiotic slogan surely goes to the Canadian province of New Brunswick. A $229,000 study came up with **Be ... in this place**, complete with the inexplicable ellipsis, followed (because New Brunswick is officially bilingual) by the equally bizarre French version, **Être ... ici on le peut**. Widespread public mockery caused the province to stop printing plates with those messages.

---

lie (meaning *speak falsely*): You **lie** <u>about</u> something, not <u>that</u> something.

👈 He lied that he was eighteen years old.

☑ He lied about his age, stating that he was eighteen.

☑ He lied when he said he was eighteen years old.

lie/lay **Lay** takes an object — something that is put down; **lie** doesn't. So:

☑ **I'm going to lay the book down on the table.**

☞ **I'm going to lie the book down on the table.**

☞ **Another protestor lays on the ground.** — the *Toronto Globe and Mail.*

☑ **Another protestor lies on the ground.**

Except when talking to your dog, who doesn't care about grammar:

🐶 **Lay down, Rover!**

It's been claimed that the use of **lay** without an object, as in the third sentence, is the most common error in English. But it's hard to find anyone who thinks that this use of **lay** is now so common that it must be accepted — promoted, perhaps from ☞ to ☺. It's still a sign of language incompetence, and you should try hard to avoid it, even in casual conversation.

One very confusing thing about these words is that the past tense of **lie** is also **lay**. Here's how the different tenses of these verbs work:

	LIE	LAY
Present tense	I lie down	I now lay the book down.
Past tense	I lay down earlier.	I laid the book down earlier.
Past perfect tense	I have lain down often.	I have laid the book down often.

lifestyle This word hardly existed before 1970, and it has shown a strong increase in usage ever since. Derided by language traditionalists, it nevertheless is a handy term meaning *the mode of living of a person or group*, and it's here to stay.

lightening/lightning The first is the action of getting lighter; the second is the flash seen during a thunderstorm.

☞ **Three of the men were severely injured by the lightening.**

☑ **Three of the men were severely injured by the lightning.**

☑ **You're unlikely to see the sky lightening until after the thunder and lightning are over.**

light year Despite the word **year**, this is a measure of distance, not of time. It means *the distance light travels in a year.*

like There are two widespread and very informal **like**s. One is as a substitute for the verb **to say**, as in

☺ **So she's like, "Eew that's soooo gross!"**

This is the way you apparently have to talk if you're younger than sixteen. If you're saying things like this, find your birth certificate and calculate your age to see if you should be worried. Another use of **like** is as a space-filler:

94

👋😖 So I'm, like, walking to school, and it's so cold that, like, I couldn't breathe.

The use of this expression appears to be to slow down speech to give a not very speedy mind a chance to catch up. It's not clear that this is an improvement over the older space-fillers **um** and **er.** For another popular space-filler, see y'know. For another annoying valley-girl-ism, see uptalk.

like/as Still an important distinction for formal writing. **Like** introduces the name of something, but **as** introduces a clause — words that could stand on their own in the form of an independent sentence.
✊ Like I said before, smoking is forbidden.
☑ As I said before, smoking is forbidden.
✊ He runs like I do — with short, choppy strides.
☑🎓 He runs as I do — with short, choppy strides.
☑ He runs like me. We both take short, choppy strides.
✊ Baby Doc ran Haiti like his father had done.
☑ Baby Doc ran Haiti the way his father had.
✊ Winston tastes good, like a cigarette should.

A second rather informal use of **like** is to introduce examples:
✊ Very small birds, like hummingbirds and chickadees, need to eat constantly.
☑ Very small birds, such as hummingbirds and chickadees, need to eat constantly.

But respected writers have routinely violated these rules, and the substitutes using **as** and **such as** sometimes sound stuffy or awkward. It's very close to the time at which the ✊s in the sentences above should be replaced by ⚠s.

Like what is worse than **like** in place of **as.** This is bad form even in casual talk.
👉 Bush wanted to appear tough, like what Reagan did when he ordered the invasion of Grenada.
☑ Bush wanted to appear tough, as Reagan did when he ordered the invasion of Grenada.

lion's share This idiom started out meaning *all of something* (based on one of Aesop's fables in which that's what the lion got); but more recently it has come to mean *most of something* (based on the idea that a lion eats most of the prey, and bits are left for jackals and vultures). The second understanding predominates now, but the ambiguity means it's best to avoid this phrase.

literally **Literal** means *by the letter* — the most basic meaning of words, as contrasted with their figurative or metaphorical meaning. It is sloppy to use the adverb **literally** simply to emphasize something:

95

✊☹ **It was literally the worst storm to hit the Outer Banks in a century.**

☑ **It was definitely the worst storm to hit the Outer Banks in a century.**

But it's even worse to use the word to emphasize some exaggerated or metaphorical description — one that is not literal at all:

☞ **And the direction we turn is not figuratively, is literally in your hands.** — V.P. Joe Biden, nominating speech, Democratic National Convention.

☞ **I literally died laughing.**

☑ **I died laughing.**

This use has unfortunately increased to the point where soon it might be issued a ✊☹.

loath/loathe **Loath** is the (rare) adjective; **loathe** is the verb.

☞ **He told me he is beginning to loath his job.**

☑ **He told me he is beginning to loathe his job.**

☑ **He is loath to return to his former job.**

look forward <u>to doing</u> something (not <u>to do</u> something)

☞ **I am looking forward to receive your reply.**

☑ **I am looking forward to receiving your reply.**

---

lorem ipsum Ever seen this passage before?

Lorem ipsum dolor sit amet, consectetur adipiscing elit, sed do eiusmod tempor incididunt ut labore et dolore magna aliqua. Ut enim ad minim veniam, quis nostrud exercitation ullamco laboris nisi ut aliquip ex ea commodo consequat. Duis aute irure dolor in reprehenderit in voluptate velit esse cillum dolore eu fugiat nulla pariatur. Excepteur sint occaecat cupidatat non proident, sunt in culpa qui officia deserunt mollit anim id est laborum.

You may recognize the first few words, even if you don't know Latin — even if you don't recognize this as Latin. This passage, known as **lorem ipsum**, is a linguistic curiosity. It's used by graphic designers as dummy text — a bunch of writing that doesn't mean anything, inserted as a non-distracting filler in a preliminary design for a page containing some text and some other elements, to be replaced later by the appropriate meaningful text. So you may have seen such a preliminary version with some of this in it. It's been used as dummy text for a *long* time — since the 1500s. So what does it mean in Latin? Well, nothing. It's closely related to a passage written by Cicero in 45 BCE, intentionally somewhat garbled by the sixteenth-century typesetter who needed some nonsense. If you're interested, you can find and compare Cicero's text on the internet.

looking **Looking to find** is post-1980 colloquial and very grating. Substitute **looking for**. **Looking to** plus a verb other than **find** sounds just as bad, but it has the additional problem of being extremely vague: it can mean all sorts of things including *expecting to, hoping to, planning to, investigating into*. You should always use other words instead.

👎🙁 I spent all week looking to find an apartment I could afford.

☑ I spent all week looking for an apartment I could afford.

👎🙁🙁 Is Trump looking to start a war with China, or is his team just not being clear? — headline, the *Washington Post*

👎🙁🙁 I'm looking to visit my parents for Thanksgiving. (= inquiring about? expecting to? hoping to? investigating possibilities regarding? planning to? trying to arrange? thinking about?)

loose/lose **Loose** as a verb means *make something less tight*; as an adjective, it means *not tightly fixed*. To **lose** something is to cease to have it, or be unable to find it.

🗨 Ted Cruz is totally unelectable, if he even gets to run (born in Canada). Will loose big to Hillary. — Donald Trump, tweet.

☑ … will lose …

☑ Jayden has a loose tooth.

make up/makeup The noun **makeup** (or less frequently, **make-up**) refers to cosmetics worn to transform appearance. It also can mean *replacement* (**makeup test**), or the way in which something is constructed or composed (**the post-election makeup of the Senate**). The two-word form is a verb meaning *to put on makeup, to reconcile, to put in order, to compensate for something missed*, etc.

🗨 After that fight, I kept phoning her to makeup.

☑ … to make up.

☑ The clown arrived early to put on his makeup.

mantel/mantle The most common use of the first refers to a fireplace structure or shelf; the second spelling is also acceptable for this. But the second alone names a loose robe, or by extension, something that envelops.

☑ Over the ground lay a mantle of white.

☑ We left cookies for Santa on the mantel.

marital/martial

🗨 Mixed Marital Arts 8pm — the *Toronto Globe and Mail*

Martial means *pertaining to marriage*; **marital** means *pertaining to war or fighting*. Martial arts are codified combat traditions such as judo. What are marital arts? Don't answer that.

masterful/masterly **Masterful** means *domineering* or *powerful*; **masterly** means *exhibiting mastery* or *great skill*. This is a distinction that has almost disappeared in casual language and probably won't be noticed in formal language.

⚠ When not on drugs, Elvis could give a masterful performance.

☑ … a masterly performance.

☑ You always expect heads of big companies to be masterful, but Schmidlap was a sweetheart.

maybe/may be: **Maybe** is a word that expresses tentativeness. It should be replaced by **perhaps** in formal writing. **May be** is a tentative substitute for **is**, indicating that something is possible, not actual.

✊ May be he will come, but I doubt it.

⚠ Maybe he will come, but I doubt it.

☑ Perhaps he will come, but I doubt it.

👎 The prototype maybe ready by 2007.

☑ The prototype may be ready by 2007.

may have/of see have/of

meantime/meanwhile **Meantime** is a noun, used most frequently in the phrase **in the meantime**. **Meanwhile** is an adverb.

👎 The Germans were preparing for an attack near Calais. Meantime, the Allies were readying themselves for the invasion of Normandy.

☑ … Meanwhile, the Allies were readying themselves….

☑ … In the meantime, the Allies were readying themselves….

meet/meet with **Meet with** meaning *attend a meeting with* is a recent addition to the language with a strong odour of bureaucratic jargon, but it seems to be here to stay, as a short and clear alternative. When all that's meant is *come face to face with*, don't say **with**.

⚠ I'm going to meet with the curriculum committee on Tuesday.

👎 I met with my sister in the supermarket.

☹ I met my sister in the supermarket.

The problem with that last sentence is that it seems to say that the speaker hadn't been introduced to his sister before that. The best thing to do here is rephrase.

memento/momento The first word names something kept as a souvenir or reminder. The root word here is **memory** with an **e** in it. The second word means *moment* in Spanish, but in English people who say that are always aiming at **memento** and missing.

🗯 **Woman begs thief to bring back her childhood momentoes** — headline, *UK Evening Standard* website.

☑ **... her childhood mementos**

might have/of see have/of

minuscule/miniscule The first is the correct spelling. The correct pronunciation, therefore, has an *uh* in the middle, not an *ih*.

🗯 **Miniscule & Meteoric Research Travel to Space Station on SpaceX-7 Mission**
— headline, NASA website

mistake **Mistakes** are made (not done).

🗯 **He did seven mistakes in that short spelling exercise.**

☑ **He made seven mistakes in that short spelling exercise.**

mitigate/militate To **mitigate** something is to make it less harsh or severe; thus **mitigating circumstances** are those that make a criminal offence less serious. To **militate** against something is to act as a strong influence against it.

☑ **What we need to concentrate on is mitigating the risk of wildfires in the area.**

🗯 **The natural history orientation of early anthropology also mitigated against studies of change.** — Bruce. G. Trigger, *Natives and Newcomers.*

☑ **... militated against studies of change.**

momentarily Usage experts sometimes insist that **momentarily** means *lasting only a moment* (**He was momentarily confused**). But the use of the word to mean *in a moment* or *soon* has become so common that opposition to it is crumbling, and it's widely found acceptable except in the most formal writing contexts.

✊ or ⚠ **Ms. Billings has informed me that she will join us momentarily.**

☑ **Ms. Billings told me that she will join us soon.**

☑ **While driving to the office, I stopped momentarily to have a look at the new construction.**

more/most The first word compares two things, the second three or more. You can compare two things by adding the word **more**, or adding **er** to a word; compare three things by adding **most** before the word, or **-est**.

✊☹ **Smith was the most accomplished of the two.**

☑ **Smith was the more accomplished of the two.**

☑ **Smith was the most accomplished of the three.**

☑ **Smith was faster than the other runner.**

☑ **Smith was the fastest of the three runners.**

But the idiom

☑ **Put one's best foot forward**

is so deeply ingrained that you can get away with it anywhere, the ordinary number of feet per person notwithstanding.

To use **more** with a comparative **-er** adjective, or **most** with a superlative **-est** adjective is to repeat oneself.

🗣 **Copenhagen in Denmark, one of the most happiest countries in the EU**
  — photo caption, the *UK Independent* website

☑ **… one of the happiest countries.…**

☑ **… one of the most happy countries.…**

🗣 **Gandalf is much more wiser than Frodo.**

☑ **Gandalf is much wiser than Frodo.**

more than/over Somebody once made up the rule that **over** plus a number is wrong, apparently because **over** has a central meaning of *physically above*. But the OED calls this use legitimate, tracing it back to Old English (i.e., earlier than 1150), in sentences you will be fully familiar with such as **Gyf þær byð an ofer þa seofon.** Okay? So most contemporary usage experts find this use quite acceptable.

⚠ **She owed me over $20.**

☑ **She owed me more than $20.**

must have/of see have/of.

nauseous/nauseated/nauseating We used to be told that **nauseous** means *causing nausea*, not *experiencing nausea*, and that the way to express *experiencing nausea* is **nauseated**. Almost all contemporary experts agree that the attempt to get people to talk this way is a lost cause. Using **nauseous** to mean *experiencing nausea* won't bother anyone but the dyed-in-the-wool Stickler.

☑ **I'm feeling nauseated.**

⚠ **I'm feeling nauseous.**

But **nauseating** is preferred to **nauseous** for *causing nausea*.

☹ **I find the smell of sardines nauseous.**

☑ **I find the smell of sardines nauseating.**

naval/navel The first is an adjective meaning *having to do with a navy*; the second is the official name of your bellybutton, and of the variety of orange that looks like it.

near by/nearby Should be one word.

👎 **We went to the near by park.**

👎 **I live near by.**

✓ **I live nearby.**

near miss Is there something wrong with this expression? It's objected that what should be said instead is **near hit**, but why? Everyone knows that it means *a miss that was near to a hit*, not *a hit that was near to a miss*.

✓ **Brazil finally won the World Cup after several near misses.**

need/want **Need** is often used to mean *want very much*; but strictly speaking it conveys the idea that it would be difficult or impossible for you to do without the needed thing. Everyone **needs** water and food, but no one really **needs** a smartphone.

☹ **I need to marry someone who is very beautiful, very intelligent, very kind, and very rich.**

✓ **I want to marry someone who is very beautiful, very intelligent, very kind, and very rich.**

The use of **need to** for **should** is definitely quite informal.

✊ **The government needs to improve the roads in this area.**

✓ **The government should improve the roads in this area.**

neither/none Use **neither** for two, **none** for more than two.

👎 **Shirley has three sisters, but she has seen neither of them since Christmas.**

✓ **Shirley has three sisters, but she has seen none of them since Christmas.**

✓ **Aiden has two brothers, but he has seen neither of them since Christmas.**

never mind/nevermind The two-word spelling is standard, but the one-word version now occurs in writing eight times more frequently.

✓ **Never mind the weather.**

⚠ **Nevermind the weather.**

no body/nobody See **any body/anybody**

non sequitur A **non sequitur** (Latin, *it does not follow*) is a statement that has no clear relationship with what has preceded it. There may be some connection within the mind of the speaker or writer, but it has not been expressed in words. The passage below contains two non sequiturs.

☹ **Probably in terms of the applying for the job of president, a weakness would be not really seeing myself in that position until hundreds of thousands of people began to tell me that I needed to do it. I do, however, believe in Reagan's 11th commandment, and**

101

will not be engaging in awful things about my compatriots here. And recognizing that it's so important, this election, because we're talking about America for the people versus America for the government. — Dr. Ben Carson, Republican Presidential Nomination debate 2015

none See **neither/none**

no one/no-one/noone **No one** has remained two words (unlike **anyone, someone, anybody**), perhaps because the word **noone** looks like it rhymes with **soon**, and thus is confusing. In British English, however, **no-one** is frequent and acceptable. In the US and Canada, however, stick with two words.

noplace Not a word. Substitute **nowhere**.

nor This word is usually used with **neither**. Don't use it with **not**; when using **not**, use **or** instead of **nor**.
- 🖝 She does not drink nor smoke.
- ☑ She does not drink or smoke.
- ☑ She neither drinks nor smokes.

nothing/nobody/nowhere These words should not be used with another negative word such as **not**. If one uses **not**, then one should use **anything** instead of **nothing**, **anybody** instead of **nobody, anywhere** instead of **nowhere**.
- 🖝 He could not do nothing while he was in prison.
- ☑ He could not do anything while he was in prison.
- ☑ He could do nothing while he was in prison.

not too good of a This sounds illiterate even in informal contexts. Substitute **not a very good**:
- 🖝 What is your child's concept of herself? Is she a very important person in her own eyes? Or does she think she's not too good of a person?
  — Newsletter of Growing Child Inc.
- ☑ … she's not a very good person?

not un- As for example in:
- 🖝 It is not uncommon to have squirrels damage trees when food supplies are short. — University of Nebraska Lincoln Extension education program.

This is acceptable when it's said in contrast to a preceding positive, for example, in this context:

☑ **It's uncommon to have squirrels gnaw at non-food substances such as electric wires. But it's not uncommon to have them damage trees when food supplies are short.**

or else to convey very faint praise:

☑ **The decoration in the room was not unattractive.**

or else to find a middle-ground between positive and negative:

☑ **I'm not unproud of it.** — Donald Trump, presidential candidates' debate, about his use of social media.

Otherwise, it's just a useless complication.

> **George Orwell**, in his essay "Politics and the English Language," commented on the use of **not un-** by producing this sentence: "A not unblack dog was chasing a not unsmall rabbit across a not ungreen field."

nuclear Among those who mispronounced this word *NOO-kyuh-lur* have been George W. Bush, Sarah Palin, and Homer Simpson. This pronunciation is widely found cringe-worthy. Try to say *NOO-klee-ur* or *NYOO-klee-ur*.

object <u>to</u> something (not <u>against</u>)

🖙 **Some people have objected against being required to wear a seat belt.**

☑ **Some people have objected to being required to wear a seat belt.**

Note that this is one of the many words for which pronunciation makes a difference. The first syllable is accented if it's a noun, the second if it's a verb.

observance/observation The first is *participation in a ritual or custom*; the second is *using the senses.*

☑ **Christmas has become more a secular holiday than a religious observance.**

☑ **Observation of customer behaviour is one duty of a salesperson.**

octopi/octopuses The first word is a try at the Latin plural of **octopus**, but that isn't a Latin-origin word (or Greek either). Stick to **octopuses**. The same is true for **platypuses.**

off The Section on Bloated Language recommends **off** instead of **off of**, because shorter is better. It is, but **off of** is widely used in the US, and it will get you into trouble there only in quite formal contexts. **Off** with no **of** is the standard usage in the UK.

✊ **Get down off of that refrigerator!**

☑ **Get down off that refrigerator!**

often Don't pronounce the **t**: *OFF-ten*. That pronunciation came about during the nineteenth-century rise in literacy, when people decided that every letter in a word should be pronounced. It's an *overcorrection* — a failed attempt to talk smart — and it will be a mistake until its growing prevalence forces its acceptability. The silent **t** in the word is quite regular; compare **soften, glisten, fasten, christen, moisten, hasten, listen, whistle, wrestle, bristle, bustle, rustle, trestle, hustle, castle, nestle, epistle, apostle, jostle,** and **Christmas.** It's consistent. (!)

one

☞ **It is one of Canada's only marine biology programs.** — the *Toronto Globe and Mail*[3]

Only means that there's just one. So what has to follow **only** has to be singular:

☑ **It is Canada's only marine biology program.**

But that's not what's meant. There are other such programs. The sentence should be:

☑ **It is one of Canada's few marine biology programs.**

one another See each other/one another

on to/onto The one-word version is a preposition meaning *to the top of*, or, informally, *understand*.

☑ **The dog jumped onto the bed.**

✋ **I'm onto your secret.**

The two-word version should be reserved for uses when the **on** is an adverb connected to the verb, for example, **go on, move on, hold on.**

☑ **Shawn will not be going on to university.**

☞ **Shawn will not be going onto university.**

The reason why this is confusing is that we can sometimes understand a use in both ways. For example, **jump on** can also be seen as a verb-adverb combination like **go on,** etc.; in that case, this is acceptable also:

☑ **The dog jumped on to the bed.**

opposed <u>to</u> something or someone (not <u>with</u> or <u>against</u>)

☞ **Charles Darwin was opposed against the literal interpretation of the story of Creation, as found in Genesis.**

☑ **Charles Darwin was opposed to....**

---

3   Another mistake corrected in the *Globe* column referred to in a footnote above.

opposite When used as a noun, **opposite** is followed by **of**; when used as an adjective, it is followed by **to** or **from**, or by no preposition.

🖎 His conclusion was the opposite to mine.

☑ His conclusion was the opposite of mine. (In these two, opposite is a noun.)

☑ His conclusion was opposite to mine. (Here, opposite is an adjective.)

optimistic/pessimistic Attitudes toward the future: the first positive and hopeful, the second negative and hopeless.

oral/verbal **Oral** means *spoken* (rather than *written*), whereas **verbal** means *having to do with words*.

🖎 I can write well enough, but I have difficulty in expressing ideas verbally.

☑ … expressing ideas orally.

organize something (not <u>to do</u> something)

🖎 We organized to meet at ten the next morning.

☑ We organized a meeting for ten the next morning.

☑ We arranged to meet at ten the next morning.

orient/orientate See **disorient/disorientate**.

other **The other** suggests that what is mentioned is the <u>only</u> other one. If there are several others to be mentioned, **another** is the word to choose. In the first passage below, the use of **the other** in the second sentence leads the reader to believe this is the <u>only</u> other reason. When a third reason is mentioned in the next sentence, the reader is taken by surprise.

🖎 One reason Germany lost the Second World War was that it underestimated the importance of keeping the United States out of the conflict. The other reason was that its intelligence network was inferior to that of the Allies. Moreover, Hitler's decision to invade Russia was a disastrous mistake.

☑ One reason Germany lost the Second World War was that it underestimated the importance of keeping the United States out of the conflict. Another reason was that its intelligence network was inferior to that of the Allies. Moreover, Hitler's decision to invade Russia was a disastrous mistake.

our/are Like the substitution of **of** for **have** (see **have/of**) the confusion of **our** and **are** should never survive the rough draft stage.

🖎 Almost all are time is spent together.

☑ Almost all our time is spent together.

☑ Our dog has fleas.

105

our selves/ourselves The second has familiar, acceptable uses such as the following:
- ☑ We will not be going there ourselves.
- ☑ We are congratulating ourselves on that victory.

But as a substitute for **we**, this is a reliable sign of language incompetence:
- ☞ The Hendersons and ourselves are renting a cottage together this summer.

This may be the same sort of error that is often heard in the use of **myself**. (See the discussion of **me**, **myself**, and **I** in the section called The Cases of Pronouns, below.) Or perhaps it's a reaction to the old rule of mentioning **I** (and **we**) second to someone else:
- ☞ The Hendersons and we are renting a cottage together this summer.

is terrible. Never mind that rule in this case.

- ☑ We and the Hendersons are renting a cottage together this summer.

The two-word version, **our selves**, is much rarer:
- ☑ We should think of preserving not just our reputations, but also our selves.

over time/overtime The second is the familiar way of referring to time for working, playing, parking, etc., above the normal time limit. The first, meaning *gradually during an extended period*, will be rarer, occurring in sentences like
- ☑ Over time, I'll forget about that embarrassing incident.

palate/palette/pallet Your **palate** is in your mouth. An artist uses a **palette** to mix paint on. (By extension a painter's palette is the range of colours that painter typically uses.) A **pallet** (or **skid**) is a wooden frame designed for transporting goods.
- ☞ In his later work Matisse's pallet was more limited; much of his work was in unmodulated, primary colours.
- ☑ In his later work Matisse's palette....
- ☑ I burned my palate with the soup right out of the stove.

parameter This word was used exclusively with technical meaning in mathematics and some sciences until it was picked up as a fancy vogue word in general use, where it often seems to mean (if anything) merely a *boundary* or *limit*, and is avoided by careful writers.

partake in/of Partake in means *to participate in*; **partake of** means *to receive or share a portion of*.
- ☞ Dudley Farm Partake of the Past is a partnership between the Florida State Park and Girl Scouts of Gateway Council to provide a living history opportunity for girls in our 16 counties. — Gateway Girl Scouts website

☑ ... Partake in the Past....
☑ The Governor General made a brief appearance but did not partake in the festivities.
☑ The Governor General made a brief appearance but did not partake of the wine and cheese.

partially/partly Is there a difference here? A couple of experts claim to have found this very subtle distinction: **Partly** has to do with something true of only a part of a whole thing, but **partially** has to do with something that's incompletely true of a whole thing. Got that? No? Well: **I partly read the book** means *I read only a part of it.* **I partially cooked the chicken** means *I cooked the whole chicken, but only part-way.* If that's right, then there's a difference between that second sentence and **I partly cooked the chicken**, which should mean *I cut off a part of the chicken and cooked it, leaving the rest uncooked.* Is that right? Language is amazing. Everyone can more-or-less do it, but there are subtleties that nobody has noticed and we're not even sure are really there.

pay back/payback The first is the two-word verb; the second is the noun. For other examples of this sort of pair, see back up/backup.

per cent/percentage If you don't give a number, use **percentage**. If you do, you can say **percent** or **per cent**. (The one word version is much more common in the US, and somewhat more common in the UK.) But with a numeral, the percentage sign **%** is easier to read.
✊ The percent of people surveyed who reported any change of opinion was very small.
☑ The percentage of people surveyed who reported any change of opinion was very small.
☑ Only six per cent of the people surveyed reported any change of opinion.
☹ As many as 78 percent of the voters rejected the proposal.
☑ As many as 78% of the voters rejected the proposal.

perfume One of the many words for which pronunciation makes a difference. The first syllable is accented if it's a noun, the second if it's a verb.

permit Another of the many words for which pronunciation makes a difference. The first syllable is accented if it's a noun, the second if it's a verb.

perpetrate/perpetuate The first verb, occurring mostly in the phrase **perpetrate a crime**, means *to carry out.* (A **perpetrator**, or in cop-slang a **perp**, is the criminal). To **perpetuate** means *to prolong the existence of something, or its memory.*

🖐 **He and unidentified others helped Mr. Madoff perpetuate the crime.** — "Madoff Aide Reveals Details of Ponzi Scheme," *The New York Times.*

☑ **... perpetrate the crime.**

☑ **The zoning laws perpetuate the economic segregation of our city.**

perquisite/prerequisite A **perquisite**, informally a **perk**, is a tip or a benefit in addition to salary. A **prerequisite** is a prior requirement for something.

🖐 **Senator Duffy expected to have his private travel reimbursed as a prerequisite.**

☑ **... as a perquisite.**

✋ **... as a perk.**

☑ **Philosophy 1000 is a prerequisite for Philosophy 3520.**

persecute/prosecute **Persecution** is treatment in a harsh and unfair manner, often because of one's political or religious beliefs. **Prosecution** is legal action against someone believed to have committed a crime.

🖐 **The tax amounts to prosecution of the poor.**

☑ **... persecution of the poor.**

☑ **The prosecution of OJ did not result in conviction.**

personify This does not mean merely *to represent or symbolize.* This word has two different meanings: *to think of or represent an inanimate object as having human qualities,* or *to represent a quality or idea in a human figure.*

🖐 **Their lyrics personify Canada.** — CBC radio news reporter, of a disbanding Canadian rock group.

☑ **The ancient Greeks personified forces of nature as gods and goddesses.**

☑ **People sometimes personify their cars by giving them human names and imagining their personalities.**

peruse This is just a pompous synonym for **read**. It's sometimes thought mistakenly to mean *skim over lightly.*

phthisic This is a good word to drop into your conversation. So is **syzygy**.

pick up/pickup The first is a two-word verb, meaning *to take up something by hand* (plus a variety of slang or informal uses). The second is a noun referring to a small truck or to something or someone that's picked up. There are very many pairs that work this way; see back up/backup for a list of more.

pitted Do you think that the bags labelled **pitted prunes** in the supermarket contain prunes with pits or without? (Turns out that means *without.*) Next to those bags are ones labeled **whole prunes** (as opposed to *cut into pieces?* no: meaning *with pits*). Neither is a good label. Be cleverer in your language.

☹ **pitted prunes**
☑ **prunes — pits removed**
☹ **whole prunes**
☑ **prunes with pits**

See also a similar difficult with boned/deboned and shelled. See also another ambiguous word, sanction.

platypi/platypuses See octopi/octopuses

plenitude/plentitude The second spelling, originally a typographical or pronunciation error, now appears about one-tenth as often as the first and is found in some dictionaries. The word means *abundance*.

✋ *or maybe* ⚠ **Bruins share Thanksgiving plentitude with others** — headline, UCLA website.

plethora This word is a fancy way to say *too many*. It's sometimes misused to mean *very many*. It's fun to say, but the ambiguity means it should be avoided.

pore/pour Only the first means to read or study with attention, though it could be that the student mentioned below prefers his books wet:

☞ **For academic inspiration, the dorm is outfitted with paintings of a student pouring over a book and the shields of the world's great universities.**
— Morressy Hall web page, Division of Student Affairs, University of Notre Dame.
☑ **... poring over a book....**

position/theory Positions and theories are **held** or **argued**; they do not **hold** or **argue** themselves.

☞ **This position holds that a particular form, such as the English spatial particle** over, **is conventionally associated with a number of distinct but related meanings.** — *The Semantics of English Prepositions* by Andrea Tyler & Vyvyan Evans.
☑ **This position is that ...**

practical/practicable **Practical** means *suitable for use,* or *involving activity rather than theory.* **Practicable** means *able to be done.* In most cases **practical** is the word the writer wants; excessive use of **practicable** will make writing sound pretentious rather than important.

109

🔊 We do not feel that the construction of a new facility would be practicable at this time.

☑ It would not be practical to construct a new facility now.

☑ Changing the railway system back to steam locomotives would be practicable but extremely impractical.

practice/practise In Canada and Britain, **practise** (verb) and **practice** (noun) should be distinguished; in the US, **practice** serves as both noun and verb.

☑US   The team will practice on Thursday.

☑UK/CDA   The team will practise on Thursday.

predominant/predominate **Predominate** is the verb, **predominant** the adjective. (Either **predominately** or **predominantly** may be used as adverbs.) Meaning: *strongest or greatest in number or amount.*

🔊 Also, regardless of which partner type was predominate, the target students and partners engaged in a high degree of interactive behavior. — Kenneth Oliver Simpson, Dissertation Abstract, University of Nebraska, Lincoln.

☑ ... which partner type was predominant....

☑ ... which partner type predominated....

prefer one thing or person <u>to</u> another (not <u>more than</u> another)

🔊 They both prefer tennis more than squash.

☑ They both prefer tennis to squash.

prescribe/proscribe To **prescribe** something is to recommend or order its use; to **proscribe** something is to forbid its use. Related nouns: **prescription/proscription**

🔊 While state officials had previously indicated the medical marijuana program would launch in January, they had not provided an exact date or released any information on the number of doctors certified to proscribe the drug. — *New York Daily News*

☑ ... certified to prescribe the drug.

☑ The new regulations proscribe street parking after a snowstorm.

present One of the many words for which pronunciation makes a difference. The first syllable is accented if it's a noun, the second if it's a verb.

presently The subject of much disagreement among grammarians. The traditional view is that **presently** should be restricted to its original meaning of *soon*; some contemporary experts are willing to accept the now common meaning *at present* — i.e., *now*. The argument against this is that it permits ambiguity, but context will usually clear up which meaning is intended. Do not use it to mean *now* in the most formal writing, however. Perhaps the best solution is to avoid the rather pompous **presently** altogether, and stick to those fine Anglo-Saxon words **soon** and **now**.

⚠ **I am presently between jobs.**

☞ **I am seeing Mr. Jones presently. (Ambiguous: now or soon?)**

☑ **I am seeing Mr. Jones now.**

☑ **I will be seeing Mr. Jones soon.**

pretty This is a very informal word meaning *somewhat*.

☿☹ **It's pretty ugly and a little big.**

principal/principle **Principal** can be either a noun or an adjective. As a noun it can mean *the person in the highest position of authority in an organization* (e.g., a school **principal** — remember the old mnemonic: "The **principal** is your **pal**.") It can also mean *an amount of money*, as distinguished from the interest on it. As an adjective, it means *first in rank or importance*. **Principle** is always a noun, and is never used to describe a person; a **principle** is a *basic truth or doctrine*, a *code of conduct*, or a *law describing how something works*.

☑ **The principal city of northern Nigeria is Kano**

☞ **LAPD Stance on Immigration 'A Matter of Principal, Chief Beck Says**
— headline, *North Hollywood Patch* website. (Note also the lack of a second quotation mark.)

☑ **... A Matter of Principle....**

☞ **The radii of these two circular fragments, R1 and R2, are called the principle radii of curvature, and their inverse values, c1 = 1/R1 and c2 = 1/R2, are referred to as the two principle curvatures.** — "Nature Reviews" at nature.com

☑ **... the principal radii ... the two principal curvatures.**

proactive Like many buzzwords, it's often unclear what this is supposed to mean: *making things happen? taking the initiative? ready to do something?* It's somewhat useful, however, in contrast with **reactive**.

project One of the many words for which pronunciation makes a difference. The first syllable is accented if it's a noun, the second if it's a verb.

prophecy/prophesy **Prophecy** (pronounced *PROF-uh-see*) is the noun, meaning *a prediction*, **prophesy** (pronounced *PROF-uh-sigh*) the verb, meaning *to predict*.

☞ **The point is that there must be a clear distinction between genuine predictions and prophesy.** — "Philosophy of Science Portal" website

☑ **... predictions and prophecy.**

proposition/proposal There is some overlap here, and both can mean *a suggested plan or offer*. But only **proposal** can mean *offer to marry*; only **proposition** can mean *request for sexual favours*; only **proposition** can mean a statement in mathematics or logic.

☞ In the old days, when they wanted to marry, men were supposed to have gone down on their knees to make a proposition.

☑ ... make a proposal.

protest One of the many words for which pronunciation makes a difference. The first syllable is accented if it's a noun, the second if it's a verb.

prove To **prove** something is to demonstrate that it is true. Don't overstate things: when something is shown to be plausible or fairly likely, that does not constitute **proof.** It's still more of a mistake to say that somebody proved something when what you mean is simply that it was asserted.

☹ It has been proven that eating kale reduces the effects of aging.

☑ There is some evidence that eating kale reduces the effects of aging.

purposefully/purposely A subtle difference here: the second adjective means *on purpose* (as opposed to *accidentally*); the first means *with determination or meaning* (as opposed to *aimlessly or meaninglessly*).

☑ **Victoria weeded her garden purposefully** (= with determination and concentration).

☑ **Christian arrived late purposely** (= he intended to be late).

quality Although in colloquial English **quality** is frequently used as a replacement for **good** or **worthwhile**, in formal writing it should be used as a noun, not an adjective.

✊ **What constitutes a quality education?** — World Economic Forum website

☑ ... an education of good quality?

☑ ... a good education?

In the phrase **quality time**, it has a special meaning and is not easily replaceable; but this use is nevertheless informal.

quote/quotation There's a widely ignored old rule that **quote** is the verb, **quotation** the noun.

⚠ The following quote shows just how determined she is to change the Constitution.

☑ The following quotation....

? **William Shakespeare Quotes and Quotations** — www.williamshakespeare.info

rain/reign/rein A monarch **reigns** over a territory; to control a horse you **rein** it in (using the reins); by extension, **reining in** means any sort of restraining. **Free reign**

makes sense, but the real phrase is **free rein**. **Rain** is, of course, water drops falling from the clouds.

👎 **Megawati has so far shown no signs of reigning in the armed forces.** — *The Economist*

👎 **... no signs of raining in the armed forces.**

✅ **... no signs of reining in the armed forces.**

👎 **But you need not be an anti-Semite to give anti-Semitism criminally free reign, and this Trump has done.** — *Time Magazine*

raise/raze/rise **Raise** means *to lift*; the past tense of **raise** is **raised**, not **rose**. To **raze** something is to destroy it completely. **Rise** means *to come up*. The idiom is **on the rise**, not **on a rise**.

👎 **I felt all of the hairs on my neck raise.** — the *Toronto Globe and Mail*

✅ **I felt all of the hairs on my neck rise.**

👎 **Yet I knew our cast would rally, and when we rose the curtain again, we went right back to young Will's line: "What the hell was that?"** — Playwright John August, interviewed in *Newsweek*.

✅ **... when we raised the curtain again.**

✅ **The curtain rose at 8 o'clock.**

👎 **As yet no one has been injured, but many properties have been raised to the ground or were in flames.** — the (UK) *Sun* website

✅ **... razed to the ground....**

👎 **Myopia is on a dramatic rise. Can outdoors and less devices for children be a solution?** — headline, the *Toronto Globe and Mail* (Did you notice the second problem in this headline? If not, see **fewer/less**.)

✅ **The rate of occurrence of myopia is increasing dramatically....**

rational/rationale **Rational** (pronounced *RASH-un-ul*) is an adjective meaning *logical* or *sensible*. A **rationale** (pronounced *rash-un-AL*) is *an explanation* for something.

👎 **Many marketing professionals are not aware of the origin and underlying rational behind the diffusion concept....** — George P. Boretos, "S-curves and their Applications in Marketing, Business, and the Economy"

✅ **... the underlying rationale behind ...**

✅ **Gambling is not rational economic behaviour.**

ravish/ravage To say that something is **ravishing** means that it is enchanting. As a verb, **ravish**, meaning *delight*, sounds quite old-fashioned and literary. To **ravage** means *to damage or destroy*.

👎 **The Outer Banks were fully ravished by the storm....** — ESPN website

✅ **... ravaged by the storm ...**

reach out There's a long history of the figurative use of this phrase to mean *contact somebody with help*; but recently its use has mushroomed and now means ... what? Merely *contact*? Why does its use inspire such revulsion?

🖐☹ **We outreached to the CBSA who reconfirmed and provided us clear instructions not to accept travellers with expired permanent resident cards....** — Isabelle Arthur, an Air Canada spokesperson, explaining the airline's bizarre mistreatment of a passenger; quoted on CBC News website. (Do you like that verb **outreached**?)

Unfortunately, it's not easy to find an all-purpose synonym. What's going on when your newspaper says **Trump reached out to Republicans regarding the health insurance bill**? Did he telephone or tweet or what? Merely substituting **contacted** does not convey the force or urgency of things. You wouldn't say **I reached out to my friends to give them my new telephone number.**

real The basic sense of this adjective is supposed to be *existing*, as opposed to *imaginary* or *fictitious* or *illusory*. It is also commonly used to mean *genuine, authentic*, as opposed to *fake* or *forged*, and only the most picky Stickler would object to that.

☑ **The movie is based on real events.** (i.e., not fictitious)

⚠ **This is real fur.** (i.e., not fake)

The use of this word to mean *very* is too informal for just about any context. Substitution of the adverbial form **really** makes things a bit better, but still inappropriate for formal writing.

🖐 **I'm real sorry.**

🖐 **I'm really sorry.**

☑ **I'm very sorry.**

reason: The reason ... is because repeats itself; so does **the reason why**. Even worse is **the reason why ... is because**. Substitute **the reason ... is that** or just eliminate the whole phrase and reword.

🖐 **The reason ice floats is because it is lighter than water.**

🖐🖐 **The reason why ice floats is because it is lighter than water.**

☑ **The reason ice floats is that it is lighter than water.**

☑ **Ice floats because it is lighter than water.**

🖐 **The reason I have come is because I want to apply for a job.**

rebel One of the many words for which pronunciation makes a difference. The first syllable is accented if it's a noun, the second if it's a verb.

record Another of the many words for which pronunciation makes a difference. The first syllable is accented if it's a noun, the second if it's a verb.

114

recoup/recuperate The first means *to get back the equivalent of a loss* (and rarely, *to reimburse*); the second *to recover from an illness*.

☑ Higher stock prices allow us to recoup our last-year's losses.

☑ I'll go back to work as soon as I've recuperated from the flu.

reek/wreak/wreck To **reek** is to *smell bad*. To **wreak** is to *inflict* (e.g., *damage*); just about the only place you see this word is in the phrase **wreak havoc**. **Wreak** is pronounced just like **reek**, and its past tense is **wreaked**, not **wrought**.[4] And keep both distinguished from **wreck**, a noun meaning *something damaged or destroyed*, or *a damaging or destructive event*, or a verb meaning *to damage*.

🖐 Strong winds reek havoc in Montreal — Global News website

🖐 Winds wreck havoc on Wyoming roads — NBC News Nebraska website

☑ ... wreak havoc....

☑ After the flood, the reek of sewage was awful.

☑ His car was a wreck.

refund One of the many words for which pronunciation makes a difference. The first syllable is accented if it's a noun, the second if it's a verb.

refuse Another of the many words for which pronunciation makes a difference. The first syllable is accented if it's a noun, the second if it's a verb. (The noun form means *garbage*.)

regard With **regard** to something, or in **regard** to. But never **regards**. Anyway, these are pompous formalism. Substitute **about**.

🖐 What work is the USGS doing in regards to Burmese Pythons? — US Geological Survey website

🖐 ... with regards to ...

☹ ... in regard to ...

☹ ... with regard to ...

☑ ... about ...

regarded as (not **regarded** to be)

🖐 You may rip into your parcel's many layers of packaging with a feeling of guilt, but despite the extra wastage it is still widely regarded to be more eco-friendly overall.
 — Article about online shopping, *The Phoenix News*

☑ ... regarded as ...

---

4   **Wrought** (as in **wrought iron** or **What hath God wrought?**) is a past participle, but of what verb? You'll never guess. Should I tell you? Nah. If this bothers you enough, you can do a little research. Here's another question to torture yourself with. The English live in England; the Germans live in Germany; what's the name of the region where the Flemish live? No, it's not **Flemland**, and the answer is not **Belgium**.

reject One of the many words for which pronunciation makes a difference. The first syllable is accented if it's a noun, the second if it's a verb.

rejoice <u>at</u> something (not <u>for</u> something)

🖐 He rejoiced for his good fortune when he won the lottery.

☑ ... at his good fortune....

respectively/respectfully **Respectively** means *in the order mentioned*; **respectfully** means *done with respect.*

🖐 Toronto, Cleveland, and Texas were leaders in the East, Central, and West divisions, respectfully.

☑ Toronto, Cleveland, and Texas were leaders in the East, Central, and West divisions, respectively.

☑ I tried to indicate very respectfully that smoking was not allowed in the building.

responsible <u>for doing</u> (not <u>to do</u>)

🖐 Mr. Dumpty is responsible to market the full line of the company's pharmaceutical products.

☑ Mr. Dumpty is responsible for marketing the full line of the company's pharmaceutical products.

restaurateurs, not **restauranteurs**, is correct. The mistaken use hit a small peak in 1990, and has been declining since. Maybe spell-check is the reason for this decline — it's hard to notice the difference in spelling.

🖐 **The Mouthful: Who's Who Among Seattle Restauranteurs** — headline, University of Seattle Spectator website.

☑ ... **Restaurateurs**

reticent/reluctant **Reticent** means *reluctant to speak; reserved about speaking.* But its use to mean just plain *reluctant* has grown so common that it might be nearing acceptability; it's still unusable, however, in formal contexts, and a sign of language ineptness in everyday talk.

✊☹ Some are reticent to go right back to a pitcher after he tossed 113 pitches but research published at Baseball HQ concludes there's no concern.
— ESPN website

☑ Some are reluctant to go ...

☑ She was reticent when she met the Queen, and later regretted not having expressed her life-long devotion.

retroactive <u>to</u> a date (not <u>from</u>)

🖎 **Pensions offered by the Commonwealth of Massachusetts are retroactive from the time you apply for them.** — Massachusetts Department of Unemployment Insurance online FAC sheet.

☑ **... retroactive to the time....**

review/revue The first means *general survey*; the second is the word for a theatrical event.

🖎 **Spring Musical Review to showcase music, drama talent** — Texas State University website

☑ **Spring Musical Revue....**

☑ **The last day of classes will be devoted to a review of the term's work.**

rewrite One of the many words for which pronunciation makes a difference. The first syllable is accented if it's a noun, the second if it's a verb.

right/rite A **right** is something you're allowed to do; a **rite** is a ceremony. A **rite of passage** is a ceremony marking an important change. But a **right of passage** is a legal permission to travel over some area.

🖎 **Freshman Orientation: A Right of Passage** — University Libraries website, Washington University in St. Louis

☑ **... Rite of Passage**

☑ **International law grants a right of passage to ships through these straits.**

righteous/rightful **Righteous** means *law abiding or morally upright*, with the hint that a bit of sanctimonious smugness might be involved. A **rightful** action is simply one that's right.

☑ **Lucy always acts righteous when returning from church.**

☑ **It's rightful for someone who steps on your toe to apologize.**

run away/runaway The first is a two-word verb; the second is a noun. For other examples of this sort of pair, see **back up/backup**.

sanction This word can mean opposite things. It can mean either *punish* or *provide official permission for*. Sometimes the meaning is obvious from context, but sometimes it isn't.

🖎 **Your teacher will not sanction late assignments.**

What does that mean? But there's no problem about what's meant in

☑ **The UN will impose sanctions on Iran for nuclear violations.**

If you're going to use this word, make sure it's clear what you mean.

Compare **boned, pitted,** and **shelled**; and see the text box on contronyms under **boned**.

117

scan/skim For centuries, **to scan** meant *to examine closely*, but in the twentieth century it evolved into its opposite: to look through quickly, a synonym for **skim**. In case your reader insists on the old and almost dead meaning, avoid the first word when you mean *skim*; though there's no trouble with its use to refer to what the computer gadget does when it digitizes something on paper.

⚠ **Sam scanned the printer manual very quickly.**

☑ **Sam skimmed the printer manual very quickly.**

☑ **Sam scanned the photo of his grandmother to email to his sister.**

scarce/short If a person or place is **short** of something, that thing is **scarce**.

🖑 **It is not uncommon to have squirrels damage trees when food supplies are short.** — University of Nebraska Lincoln Extension education program. (See also: **not un-**)

☑ **Food is now extremely scarce throughout the country.**

☑ **The country is now desperately short of food.**

seeing as/as how/that **Seeing that** is often the beginning of a dangling participial phrase (see the section on danglers, below) but it also has correct uses:

✋☹ **Seeing that it's past noon, it's too late to make a reservation for today.**

☑ **Because it's past noon, it's too late to make a reservation for today.**

☑ **Seeing that it was past noon, Arnold hurried off to the doctor's office.** (= **When he saw that it was past noon, Arnold …**)

☑ **It seems to me most strange that men should fear; / Seeing that death, a necessary end, / Will come when it will come.** — Shakespeare, *Julius Caesar*

Seeing as how and **seeing as to how** are just unacceptable.

🖑 **I graduated with a degree in Mass Communications, majoring in Persuasive Communications. Seeing as to how I'm in Public Relations now, the course I studied prepared me completely for this role.** — Alumni Interview, Taylor's University (Malaysia) website

seek something or someone (not seek <u>for</u> something)

🖑 **Recreational marijuana advocates seek for 'yes' votes in eastern US states.** — headline, the *Toronto Star*

☑ **… seek 'yes' votes …**

set/sit: **Set** means *to place something somewhere*. Compare **lie/lay**.

🖑 **He asked me to set down on the couch.**

☑ **He asked me to sit down on the couch.**

☑ **Please set that package down over there.**

🖑 **Please sit that package down over there.**

sesquipedalianism is a somewhat jocular self-referential word meaning *the tendency to use long words*. It was derived from the Latin word **sesquipedalis**, meaning *a foot and a half long*. Isn't that great?

The longest word in any English dictionary is a forty-five letter medical term referring to a lung disease caused by inhalation of silica or quartz dust:

Pneumonoultramicroscopicsilicovolcanoconiosis.

There's a chemical name for the titin protein found in humans which has 189,819 letters. Its name starts with **Methionylthreonylthreonylglutaminylarginy**, and is about 57 pages long. No, it is not found in dictionaries, but there is a gripping 1 hr. 11 mins. video of the whole thing being pronounced rather quickly by a Mac OS voice simulator. (https://www.youtube.com/watch?v=7F0JWhHRa8s). It's got a heavy computer accent, and this may give you trouble when you want learn how to pronounce the word.

set up/setup The first is a two-word verb; the second is a noun. For other examples of this sort of pair, see back up/backup.
- ☑ **My roadies will arrive early to set up the amplifiers.**
- ☑ **That auditorium is a horrible setup for a class.**

sharing When somebody tells you something in private, it's social-work psychobabble to call this **sharing it with you**. If you're interested in maintaining the integrity of your language, say, "Thanks for telling me," not "Thanks for sharing that with me."

shelled Do you think that the bags labelled **shelled walnuts** in the supermarket contain walnuts with shells or without? (Turns out that means *without*.) Be cleverer in your language.

See also a similar difficulty with boned and pitted. See also another ambiguous word, sanction.

should have/should of See have/of.

sight in sight (near enough to be seen); <u>out of</u> sight (too far away to be seen); <u>on</u> sight (immediately after being seen)
- 👎 **The colonel ordered that deserters be shot in sight.**
- ☑ **... be shot on sight.**
- ☑ **The colonel reported that the enemy was out of sight.**
- ☑ **The colonel ordered us to hold our fire till the enemy was in sight.**

See also **cite/sight/site**.

simple/simplistic Simplistic is a derogatory word meaning *too simple* or *excessively simplified*.

✊ The questions were so simplistic that I was able to answer all but one correctly.

☑ The questions were so simple that I was able to answer all but one correctly.

☑ The advice that those who failed the test should try harder next time is simplistic.

since see for

Sir Form of address used for (among others) men receiving a knighthood in Britain. The proper usage is to add to this either the whole name or the first name only.

✊ If there's anyone on the planet qualified to write such a guide, it's Sir Evans – he was knighted in 2004. — "Author Harold Evans offers a knight's guide to writing well" by Mark Medley, the *Toronto Globe and Mail*

☑ ... Sir Harold — he ...

☑ ... Sir Harold Evans — he ...,

so When used to show degree or extent, **so** is normally used with **that: so big that** ... , **so hungry that** ... , etc. **So** should not be used as an intensifier in the way that **very** is used.

✊ That movie was so funny.

☑ That movie was very funny.

☑ That movie was so funny that I laughed all the way home.

some body/somebody See any body/anybody

some day/someday These terms are used interchangeably a good deal, but this is sloppy, and for more careful writing they should be distinguished. **Someday** is an adverb meaning *at some time in the indefinite future*. **Some day** is a noun phrase meaning *some particular day or other*.

☑ Someday he'll come along: the man I love.

✊☹ Some day he'll come along: the man I love.

☑ Let's go to the museum together some day next week.

✊☹ Let's go to the museum together someday next week.

somehow means *by some method*. It does not mean *in some ways, to some extent*, or *somewhat*.

☑ Somehow I must repair my car so that I can arrive in time for my appointment.

✊ His brother is somehow mentally disturbed.

☑ His brother is mentally disturbed in some way.

☑ His brother is somewhat disturbed mentally.

some one/someone The second is the familiar pronoun. The first is rare and awkward. If what's meant by **some one** is *one*, say **one** instead.

🖐 Some one in the department will meet you at the airport.

☑ Someone in the department will meet you at the airport.

☹ I know that some one of my cousins is going to attend, but I don't know who.

☑ I know that one of my cousins is going to attend, but I don't know who.

someplace Considered inappropriate in formal writing, where you should substitute **somewhere**.

somersault That's how it's spelled, not **somerset, summersault, somersaut, somersalt, or summerset.**

🖐 And Mr. H will demonstrate / Ten summersets he'll undertake on solid ground — The Beatles, "Being for the Benefit of Mr. Kite!," *Sgt. Pepper's Lonely Hearts Club Band*

some time/sometime/sometimes All three are acceptable and have different uses. **Some time** is a noun phrase meaning, roughly, *a long time*:

☑ I've wanted to visit here for some time.

☑ They will need some time to finish.

Sometime is an adverb, equivalent to **someday**, meaning *at a future unspecified time*:

☑ Let's get together sometime soon.

Sometimes is an adverb, meaning *occasionally*:

☑ Sometimes I wish I had a different job.

sort of Using this to mean *rather, somewhat*, or *partially* is very casual:

✋ Fred is sort of stupid.

☑ Fred is rather stupid.

And this:

✋ Erica is the sort of teacher this department needs.

is also non-standard. A sort of thing is a category: an individual in that category is not the category. So:

☑ Erica is an example of the sort of teacher this department needs.

The same goes for **kind of**.

sour grapes This means *the tendency to disparage something that's unobtainable*, as the fox did in Aesop's fable. Sometimes people mistakenly think the phrase means *envy* or *jealousy*, since the fox had those feelings. Or that it means this:

121

☞ **If you describe someone's behaviour or opinion as sour grapes, you mean that that person is angry because they have not got or achieved something that they wanted** — Cambridge Dictionary online.

which must be the meaning in here:

☞ **SOUR GRAPES? Hundreds of people turn out in London to protest against Brexit referendum result.** — headline, the (UK) *Sun* website.

These understandings of the phrase are so common that they're probably becoming acceptable.

spate A **spate** of things is not just many of them. It's a sudden onslaught of them, especially of floodwater or rainwater. The word is fancy, rare, and often misunderstood. Avoid it.

speak to someone (when one speaker is giving information to a listener); speak with someone (when the two are having a discussion)

☞ **She spoke with her class about their next assignment.**

☑ **She spoke to her class....**

☞ **She spoke to her reading group about the novel.** (If this is a discussion)

☑ **She spoke with her reading group about the novel.**

But the use of **speak to** meaning *show, demonstrate, express, relate to, address,* or *speak about* is sure to annoy everyone but your fellow bureaucrats.

☞ **Developed initially for the early grades (kindergarten through third grade) and primarily in the area of reading, many — although not all — of these issues speak to the expansion of RTI to address a broader set of academic content areas and the full range of grade levels.** — Article abstract, *Journal of Learning Disabilities*

☑ **... many — although not all — of these issues are connected to the expansion ....**

speech You make a speech or give a speech (not do a speech).

☞ **If I were to do a speech about any one of these topics, I know that I may not have to explain who or what to an audience of my own age.** — Stacy DeGeer, Monmouth College website

☑ **... give a speech ...**

start If both the time at which an event begins and the time at which it finishes are mentioned, it is not enough to use only the verb **start**.

☞ **The dance started from 9 p.m. till midnight.**

☑ **The dance started at 9 p.m. and finished at midnight.**

☑ **The dance continued from 9 p.m. until midnight.**

☑ **The dance lasted from 9 p.m. until midnight.**

stationary/stationery **Stationary** means *not moving*; **stationery** is what you write on.

🖅 **Office Depot has the Personalized Stationary and Personalized Note Cards you're looking for!** — their website (Why the capital letters?)

☑ **… personalized stationery….**

☑ **The train stopped inside the tunnel and was stationary for an hour.**

> Peculiarly, the words **stationary** and **stationery** are related. In medieval England, merchants in markets used mostly moveable carts, but booksellers had permanent stalls which did not move — thus they were stationary shops. Later these shops sold writing supplies as well.

stimulant/stimulus **Stimulus** (plural **stimuli**, never **stimuluses**) is the more general word for *anything that produces a reaction*; **stimulant** also has that meaning, but it's better than the other term to use for a stimulating substance.

☹ **Nervous people should avoid stimuli such as coffee.**

☑ **Nervous people should avoid stimulants such as coffee.**

☑ **Lowering taxes is intended to be a stimulus for business.**

straight/strait The first means *without curvature*, or *directly*. The second means *narrow*, especially referring to a narrow passage of water.

☑ **When we get home, I want you to go straight to bed.**

☑ **Vancouver Island is separated from the mainland by straits in the north and northeast.**

Be careful to use the second in these phrases:

☑ **strait jacket**

☑ **strait-laced**

☑ **dire straits**

☑ **straitened circumstances**

> The phrase **straight and narrow** arose from a confusion about a biblical passage in Matthew 7:14: "Because strait is the gate, and narrow is the way, which leadeth unto life…." The surrounding passages in the King James translation make it clear that *narrow*, rather than *direct*, is what's meant: "Enter ye in at the strait gate: for wide is the gate, and broad is the way, that leadeth to destruction, and many there be which go in thereat: Because strait is the gate, and narrow is the way, which leadeth unto life, and few there be that find it."

straight forward/straightforward The second is the common adjective, meaning *honest* or *direct*. The first means *proceeding without turning*, and is rarer.

🖾 You can trust what Sally says: she's very straight forward.

☑ You can trust what Sally says: she's very straightforward.

☑ Turn the steering wheel back, and drive straight forward into the space.

strata This word means *layers* or *levels*. It's the plural of **stratum**, but often misused as singular.

🖾 It's not just happening in the Philippines. It's happening here, in every strata. —
  lawyer David Boies, quoted in *The New Yorker*

🎓 ... here, in every stratum.

Stratum sounds pedantic and stuffy. Rephrase:

☑ ... here, at every social level.

subject One of the many words for which pronunciation makes a difference. The first syllable is accented if it's a noun, the second if it's a verb.

suck **It sucks** has *extremely* informal use as a term of enthusiastic condemnation:

👋☹ That group like totally sucks.

The corresponding opposite evaluation is **awesome**:

👋☹ That other group is awesome.

Don't talk this way if you're over 18.

suffer <u>from</u> something (not <u>with</u>)

🖾 He told me that he was suffering with the flu.

☑ He told me that he was suffering from the flu.

superior <u>to</u> someone or something (not <u>than</u> someone or something)

🖾 The advertisements claim that this detergent is superior than the others.

☑ The advertisements claim that this detergent is superior to the others.

suppose/supposed Be sure to add the **d** in the expression **supposed to.**

🖾 Wired glass is suppose to offer superior protection but does it? — Global News website.

☑ ... supposed to....

supposed to This is an expression with a variety of uses. Compare these sentences:

☑ Their new album is supposed to be very good. (= said to be)

☑ I am supposed to get to work by eight. (= required to)

☑ You're not supposed to park there. (= required not to)

☑ I was supposed to be at work by eight. (= ought to have been, but wasn't)

☑ **That plant was supposed to have flowered by now.** (= expected to, but didn't)

☑ **Suppose he doesn't get here? Then what?** (= imagine that)

☑ **Suppose we have dinner now.** (= I suggest that)

Sometimes there is ambiguity. Which of the two sentences below expresses what the first one means?

☹ **He was supposed to have been finished by now.**

☑ **The plan was that he be finished by now.**

☑ **He was required to have been finished by now.**

To avoid ambiguity, it's best to reword **supposed to** constructions to make the meaning clear.

sure and/to: After **sure** use **to**, not **and**:

🖅 **Be sure and discuss your need for this accommodation with a DPRC specialist....**
— San Francisco State University Disability and Resource Center brochure.

☑ **Be sure to discuss....**

(For a parallel error, see **try and/to**)

survey One of the many words for which pronunciation makes a difference. The first syllable is accented if it's a noun, the second if it's a verb.

suspect someone of doing something (not <u>to do</u>)

🖅 **His wife suspected him to have committed adultery.**

☑ **His wife suspected him of committing adultery.**

☑ **His wife suspected that he had committed adultery.**

Note that this is another of the many words for which pronunciation makes a difference. The first syllable is accented if it's a noun, the second if it's a verb.

syzygy See **phthisic.**

tack/tact A **tack** is a small nail; **tack** is a term for sailing equipment, and also has to do with sailing or changing directions relative to the wind, and derivatively, to the direction taken. **Tact** is skill in saying or doing the right or polite thing.

🖅 **Ability to exercise tack and diplomacy** — job description, Disabled Living Foundation (UK) website

☑ **... exercise tact....**

🖅 **Do Not put tape, staples, post-it-notes, thumb tacts or any other adhesive items to the walls, ceiling, tables, fans, or any other item belonging to the community.** — Leicester (NC) Community Center rental agreement. (Notice other language problems.)

☑ … thumb tacks.…

☑ Tacking is necessary when sailing into the wind.

☑ Now we're on the right tack.

tendency <u>to do</u> something (not <u>of doing</u>)

☜ Some Buick engines have a tendency of over-revving.

☑ Some Buick engines have a tendency to over-rev.

☑ The Buick engine has a habit of over-revving.

that/which/who An old and dying grammar rule tells you to use **who** as the relative pronoun for a person, not **that**:

☑ The person who wanted to see me phoned me again last night.

⚠ The person that wanted to see me phoned me again last night.

As indicated by the symbol, the use of **that** here will be found objectionable by some readers in formal prose; but it's by and large acceptable these days.

But **which** must not be used with people:

☜ My dad, which is coming to see me next week, wants to meet you.

Although it's fine with objects:

☑ My jacket, which I bought only last February, has already lost one of its buttons.

(About whether to use **which** or **that** as a relative pronoun, see the discussion of non-essential identification in the section on the use of the comma, below).

But what about animals? Must **who** be restricted to humans?

• The dog who lives next door likes me.

seems acceptable; but compare

• The fly who was buzzing around my head is now smashed.

If **the dog who** is okay, but **the fly who** is not, is this a matter of which animals we feel fond of or connected with?*

* See "Humans and Other Animals," a chapter of *How to Be Good with Words* by Don LePan, Laura Buzzard, and Maureen Okun for a very interesting discussion of this.

their/there/they're Three words that are frequently confused. **There** can be used to mean *in* (or *at*) *that place*, or can be used as an introductory word before various forms of the verb **to be** (**there is, there had been,** etc.). **Their** is a possessive adjective meaning *belonging to them*. **They're** is a contraction of **they are**.

🖋 **Teen army recruits end up in tears as they're are pushed to their limits in new Channel 5 documentary** — headline, UK *Mirror* website

☑ **... they are pushed ...**

🖋 **Their are times when children hit periods of rapid growth.** — Medicine.net online newsletter

☑ **There are times....**

🖋 **I've met many Scottish nationalists with portraits of the Queen in there living room.** — the *Toronto Globe and Mail.*

☑ **... their living rooms.** (Note plural of rooms. Is the singular room here a mistake? See the discussion of this kind of thing at the end of the section called "Other Agreement Problems.")

🖋🖋 **Looks to me like the Bernie people will fight. If not, there blood, sweat and tears was a total waist of time.** — Donald Trump, tweet. (Note other language problems.)

their/them/they/theirselves/them selves/themselves/themself **Theirselves** and **themself** are not words, and the two-word phrases **their selves** and **them selves** are highly unlikely to be correctly used in a sentence.

There's increasing use of these words as substitutes for the gendered pronouns him, her, himself, and herself. But this is a grammar mistake when these pronouns refer back to a singular noun. So each of the following sentences has its problems:

☹ **Each person in the group should introduce himself.** (can be taken to exclude females in the group)

☹ **Each person in the group should introduce herself.** (can be taken to exclude males in the group)

☹ **Each person in the group should introduce him- or herself.** (wordy and awkward)

☹ **Each person in the group should introduce theirself.** (not a word)

☹ **Each person in the group should introduce themselves.** (Each is singular, so this is a grammar mistake.)

For further discussion of this problem, see the entry for gendered pronouns in Biased or Insulting Language, subsection: Replacement, below.

tic/tick The first word means *involuntary muscle contraction*. The second is a small blood-sucking creature, or the noise a clock makes.

☑ **The tic on his face looked like a very brief smile.**

☑ **The tick on his dog had to be removed carefully.**

tiring/tiresome Something that is **tiring** makes you feel tired, though you may have enjoyed it very much. Something that is **tiresome** is tedious and unpleasant.

🖋 **Although it is tiresome for him, my father likes to play tennis at least twice a week.**

☑ **Although it is tiring for him, my father likes to play tennis at least twice a week.**

☑ **My teacher's monotone boring lectures are hugely tiresome.**

127

to/too/two **To** appears in phrases such as **a lot to do**, and **going to the park. Two** is, of course, the number. **Too** can mean *also* or be used to indicate excess (**too many, too heavy**); but don't use it just for emphasis.

- ☞ She seemed to feel that there was to much to do.
- ☑ She seemed to feel that there was too much to do.
- ☞ She looked too beautiful in her new dress.
- ☑ She looked very beautiful in her new dress.

told/tolled The first is the past tense of **tell**; the second is the past tense of **toll** (= *what bells do*, or *tax for driving on a road or across a bridge*).

- ☞ All tolled, she has about $3,000,000 in savings. — the *Toronto Globe and Mail*
- ☑ All told....
- ☑ Do not ask for whom the bell tolls.
- ☑ The new highway they're building is to be a toll road.

tortuous/torturous The first means *having many turns*; don't confuse it with the second, meaning *involving torture* or (by extension) *great pain or suffering*.

translucent/transparent **Transparent** means you can see clearly through it. **Translucent** means you can't see thought it, but it allows light to pass through. Frosted glass is translucent.

try and/to Opinions differ on this. Some experts report that in the US, **try and** is thought inappropriate for formal contexts, but it's accepted and far more common in the UK.

- ✊ (☑ in UK) He's going to try and stop that sale.
- ☑ He's going to try to stop that sale.

But the two are not interchangeable in some contexts, for example:

- ☑ Try and try again.
- ☞ Try to try again.

(See also sure and/to)

type of person/thing, not **type** person/thing.

- ☞ This type carburetor is no longer produced.
- ☑ This type of carburetor is no longer produced.

unbelievable It's very slangy to call something **unbelievable** as merely a strong term of praise. In formal English, only claims can be unbelievable (or believable).

👋 I had an unbelievable onion soup at that restaurant yesterday.

☑ ... a wonderful onion soup ...

The same goes for **incredible**.

underneath something, not **underneath of**

👎 When we looked underneath of the table, we found what we had been looking for.

☑ When we looked underneath the table, we found what we had been looking for.

under way/underway Older sources sometimes do not recognize the one-word term at all, or allow that it exists, but only as an adjective, as in

☑ Mechanical troubles in the ship necessitated mid-Atlantic underway repairs.

and the two-word version only as an adverb, as in

☑ The ship got under way at noon.

But this subtlety is outdated, and modern usage experts tend to treat them as interchangeable, appearing with about the same frequency.

unexceptional/unexceptionable **Unexceptional** means *ordinary, not an exception*; **unexceptionable** means *not open to objection*.

👎 One way the President pays for this is in the confusion and controversy that surround the unexceptional White House plan to reflag 11 Kuwaiti tankers with the Stars and Stripes.

☑ ... the unexceptionable White House plan....

☑ Woody Allen's latest movie was unexceptional.

unique Using **unique** in a comparative context always horrifies Sticklers.

👎 I am in the rather unique position of being the son, the grandson, and the great grandson of preachers. — Rev. Martin Luther King, *Letter from a Birmingham Jail*

👎 Each case is very unique. — Dr. Brenda Whiteside, Guelph University's Associate Vice-President of Student Affairs, quoted in the *Toronto Globe and Mail*

👎 I don't know that the critics who may say that of me, if they found themselves in this very unique and unprecedented situation that I am now in, would do any differently than I'm doing. — Ivanka Trump in a TV interview.

The problem here is that **unique** is supposed to be a noncomparable adjective: either something is unique (that is, there's nothing like it) or it isn't. So there aren't any degrees of uniqueness. There are many noncomparative adjectives, including **absolute, complete, false, fatal, perfect, uniform, unprecedented,** and **pregnant**.

👎 We the People of the United States, in Order to form a more perfect Union.... — Preamble, US Constitution.

129

Anyone can see that the following sentences are no good:

🤛 **Felix's gunshot wound was more fatal than Sam's.**

🤛 **Sally was more pregnant than Sheila.**

But how about **more** or **very** or **quite unique**? Steven Pinker writes that these are acceptable, because "Calling something 'quite unique' or 'very unique' implies that the item differs from the others in an unusual number of qualities, that it differs from them to an unusual degree, or both." Pinker does, however, warn that this "grates on enough readers that it's wise to avoid it."[5] He's right about this, anyway. So perhaps the three ratings above should be changed to ⚠.

until a time or an event; though **up until** is common in informal speech.

✊ **Up until 1967 the National Hockey League was made up of only six teams.**

☑ **Until 1967 the National Hockey League was made up of only six teams.**

upset One of the many words for which pronunciation makes a difference. The first syllable is accented if it's a noun, the second if it's a verb.

uptalk This is a speech mannerism that, like, really annoys people over thirty? Y'know, it's when like every sentence goes up at the end, like a question? It makes you sound, y'know, like you're, like, twelve? So don't? See also **like** and **y'know**?

up to/upto The first can mean *as far as*, or can introduce an upper limit. The second is not a word.

☑ **I can stay in my apartment up to the end of the month.**

☑ **You may take up to three donuts.**

urban/urbane **Urban** means *in or relating to a city*. **Urbane** (pronounced *ur-BAIN*) means *refined, elegant*.

☑ **The candidate is popular in urban, not rural, areas.**

☑ **These sunglasses make me look urbane.**

use/used Be sure to add the **d** in the expression **used to**.

🤛 **New Brunswick enterprise isn't what it use to be; it might even be better.**
   — headline, *Atlantic Business* website.

☑ **... used to be ...**

---

5 "10 'Grammar Rules' it's OK to Break [Sometimes]." The UK *Guardian* website.

valet Is this word pronounced *VAL-it* or *vah-LAY*? Well, that depends on whether you're talking about your manservant in Downton Abbey, or having your car parked in Los Angeles. The French word was adopted centuries ago by the English, with the anglicized pronunciation *VAL-it*, but the Americans, perhaps hoping to show some Continental class, re-Frenchified it to *vah-LAY*.

valid This word has a precise technical meaning in philosophical logic, and when talking about insurance, but it's quite vague (and often heard) in ordinary usage. Instead of calling an opinion **valid**, it would be more informative to say that it's well grounded, or true.
- ☹ **Churchill's fear that the Nazis would become a threat to the rest of Europe turned out to be valid.**
- ☑ **... turned out to be well-founded.**
- ☑ **... turned out to be true.**

vein/vain **Veins** are tubes in your body for blood; to be **vain** is to be conceited; an effort that fails to brings any of the desired results has been **in vain**.
- ☞ **Shakespeare portrays Sir John Oldcastle — or Falstaff, as he is usually known — as vein and irresponsible but immensely amusing and likeable.**
- ☑ **... as vain and irresponsible....**
- ☑ **They tried in vain to put out the fire.**

viable This word once meant *capable of living*; now it has become a trendy word meaning *feasible, capable of working successfully*. It's a good idea to replace it with something more specific.
- ☹ **She outlined a viable alternative.**
- ☑ **... a practical alternative....**
- ☑ **... a feasible alternative....**
- ☑ **... a satisfactory alternative....**

vibrant You can be sure that whenever somebody talks on the radio about the "cultural scene" somewhere it will be described as **vibrant**. What exactly does it mean to call something **vibrant**? Clearly it doesn't mean moving rapidly to and fro. Does it mean *vigorous, energetic, lively, vital*? Be more specific.

vicious/viscous The first means *cruel or immoral*. The second means *thick and oily, between solid and liquid*.

WRITING WRONGS: COMMON ERRORS IN ENGLISH

vomit Sorry, but there are two matters of (very slight) linguistic interest here.

(1) Dr. Brian Deady reports* that the most frequently misspelled word on medical charts is **vomitting** (should be one **t**). He suggests that the correct spelling here is not another of those countless random facts of the language that have to be memorized one-by-one; rather, it's governed by a general rule:

Double the last consonant when adding a vowel suffix to words ending in one vowel followed by one consonant, only if the syllable before the suffix is accented. This is always true for one-syllable words.

There! isn't that easy? No, so maybe we just have to memorize the spelling of **vomiting**. But in addition, unfortunately it's not at all clear that the double/single **t** matter is rule-governed at all. Responses to Dr. Deady's article point out that another supposed rule is this:

- The **t** is doubled when the preceding vowel is pronounced long (a preceding **i**, for example, is pronounced *eye*); but a **t** for a short vowel (short **i** pronounced *ih*).

Examples:

- Double consonant for short **i**: **bitten, written**
- Single consonant for long **i**: **biting, writing**

But the short **i** should make the word in question be spelled **vomitting**. So what is the rule that applies here? Consider stress; compare **debiting**, **crediting**, etc. English is complicated.

(2) **Vomitorium** is a word I'll bet you've never seen before, and will never see again. On the rare occasions this word is mentioned, it is almost always explained that this is a room where the ancient Romans could go during an obscenely overdone banquet to vomit up all the food and wine they had consumed, to prepare themselves for eating and drinking way more. The degenerates! Well, no. This word does come from the Latin, meaning *to spew forth*, but it was in fact the name of the passageway under the seats for exiting from Roman stadiums. When the entertainment was finished (and presumably the last Christian eaten by a lion) the crowd would rapidly spew forth out of this exit.

---

* "Grammar doc," the *Toronto Globe and Mail*, 16 Feb. 2017

waist is the body-part between ribs and hips. Waste is something discarded or expended carelessly.

👎 **These pants are too tight around my waste.**

☑ **... around my waist.**

👎👎 **Looks to me like the Bernie people will fight. If not, there blood, sweat and tears was a total waist of time.** — Donald Trump, tweet. (Note also **there**, and singular **was**.)

☑ **... a total waste of time.**

wait on meaning *wait for*, as in

⚠️☹ **"Many Conservatives are said to be waiting on former cabinet minister and purported front-runner Peter MacKay to make his decision on whether to run, which is expected soon."** — the *Toronto Globe and Mail*

☑ **... waiting for ...**

This is still considered non-standard, associated with some regional dialects. Despite the fact that it has spread to all sorts of contexts, it will annoy some readers.

waive/wave To **waive** something is to refrain from using, applying, or enforcing it. Beware of spelling confusion with **wave**, which is a water or hand movement.

🖐 **Mother-of-two Esther waved her right to anonymity after the case to tell of her ordeal.**
  — UK *Sun*

☑ **... waived her right ...**

wake up/wakeup The first is the verb phrase; the second is the adjective. For other examples of this sort of pair, see **back up/backup**.

war time/wartime The second is a standard-English adjective. The first probably doesn't have a legitimate use.

weather/whether The first is a noun meaning *the state of the atmosphere*. The second is a conjunction, meaning *if*. A potential spelling confusion.

🖐 **He was unsure weather to go by bus or train.**
☑ **He was unsure whether to go by bus or train.**
🖐 **Listen to the whether report.**
☑ **Listen to the weather report.**

were/where/we're **Were** is a past tense form of the verb **to be**, while **where** refers to a place. **We're** is the contraction of **we are**. Spell-check will not tell you if you have used the wrong word.

🖐 **The place were awkwardness happens** — "Scratch," an educational website for children published by MIT.
☑ **the place where ...**
🖐 **Were all going to the party.**
☑ **We're all going to the party.**
☑ **All my friends were at the party.**

what ever/whatever The first is legitimate, but rare; here's one way it might be used:
✊ **What ever do you want?**

The second is the common version.

☑ **You can have whatever you want.**

(Similarly for **when ever/whenever**.)

whatever!, apparently short for **Whatever you say!**, is valley-girl slang that should stay out of formal contexts, and it may be too annoying for informal conversation.

when ever/whenever See what ever/whatever

where Do not use **where** to mean *that*.

👎 **I read in the paper where the parties are now tied in popularity.**

☑ **I read in the paper that the parties are now tied in popularity.**

In which is better to use than **where** when location is not precisely involved:

✊☹ **This is a situation where everyone must be careful.**

☑ **This is a situation in which everyone must be careful**

☑ **This is a coffee-house where students like to go.**

But be careful not to write **in which** when simply **which** would do:

👎 **This is something in which I should do.**

☑ **... which I should do.**

who's/whose **Whose** means *belonging to whom*; **who's** is a contraction of **who is** or **who has.** (Compare **it's/its.**)

👎 **Who's plan uses the most number of food items?** — Sarah Joubert, *Daily Life Skills Big Book Gr. 6-12.* (Note also **the most number**)

☑ **Whose plan uses the largest number of food items?**

☑ **Who's going to lunch today?** (Contraction of **Who is**)

☑ **Who's had lunch?** (Contraction of **Who has**)

work out/workout The first is the verb phrase; the second is the noun. For other examples of this sort of pair, see back up/backup.

worry <u>about</u> something (not <u>at</u> something or <u>for</u> something)

👎 **He is always worried at what will happen if he loses his job.**

👎 **... worried for what will happen....**

☑ **... worried about what will happen....**

would have/of See have/of.

y'know This is a space-filler: Like **like**, this is a verbal tic that's very annoying to some people. If you want to get people to run the other way when they see you, say "I don't know" whenever they say "y'know."

134

🗣 So, y'know, I'm like "What's goin on?" y'know, and she, y'know, doesn't even, like, hear me.

For another annoying speech mannerism, see uptalk.

yo A linguistic tidbit apparently popularized by the 1976 movie *Rocky*, and frequently heard in the speech of very cool young people. I haven't any idea what it means.

🗣 Yo, I'm afraid to not be a teen-ager in two years. No one takes you seriously as an adult. — software developer Isaiah Turner, quoted in *The New Yorker.*

Singular and Plural

Plurals not Made with -S

Most plurals are made by adding **-s** to the end of the word, of course. But when the word already ends with s, or with other letters making a hissing or buzzing sound (usually **z**, **x**, **ch**, **sh**), add **-es**. These rules go for proper names too:

🗣 There are two Mary's in my class.
☑ There are two Marys in my class.
☑ The Hendersons will all be there.
☑ I'm going to spend the weekend with the Schwartzes.
☑ Sherlock Holmes and his brother Mycroft — the Holmeses — were both described as brilliant.
☑ The Rushes are hosting Thanksgiving dinner this year. (i.e., the Rush family)

However, if the word has a silent **s** on the end — because it comes from French — then the plural is the same as the singular, except pronounced differently in English. For example, the plural of the singular term **corps** (pronounced *kor*) is **corps** (pronounced *kors*). Similarly, if you want to talk about the parents of René Descartes (pronounced *day-cart*), you can call them **the Descartes**, pronounced *day-carts*.

The rule for pluralizing nouns ending in a **y** preceded by a consonant — *drop the* **-y** *and add* **-ies** — is not followed for proper names:

☑ The kids at the party were treated with rides on two ponies.
🗣 Dorothy's friend has the same name, so they're known as the two Dorothies.
☑ Dorothy's friend has the same name, so they're known as the two Dorothys.

Nouns ending in -f are a problem. Some just add -s: **dwarfs, roofs, proofs**. Some end with -ves: **halves, loaves, selves**. If in doubt, consult a dictionary. Spell-checkers sometimes don't get -f plurals right. Mine accepts **loafs**, but that's because it's correct as a verb (**Seymour loafs around all day**). It also accepts 🖓 **dwarves** and 🖓 **rooves**. (Those are gaining in usage, but will widely be found unacceptable.) Occasionally both forms are acceptable: **hoofs** and **hooves**.

And there are other irregular ways of making plurals, for example:

man	►	men
woman	►	women
child	►	children
mouse	►	mice
louse	►	lice
foot	►	feet
goose	►	geese
tooth	►	teeth
ox	►	oxen

Some words are the same when singular or plural. Examples are **moose, sheep** (and many other animal-type names), **youth, means, offspring, species, aircraft, series**. Thus:

☑ **I cooked one fish.**
☑ **I caught two fish.**
🖓 **I caught two fishes.**

Rarely, when referring to *types* of things, these come in plural form, so

☑ **Three Asian fishes have recently turned up in the Great Lakes.** (meaning *three different species of Asian fish have turned up*)

These singular -s words have no plural form: **billiards, cards, darts, diabetes, measles, mumps, rabies**.

These -ics words are odd: **acoustics, aerobics, aerodynamics, aeronautics, athletics, classics, economics, electronics, genetics, linguistics, logistics, mathematics, mechanics, obstetrics, physics, politics, statistics, thermodynamics**.

When referring to a field of study, they are singular:

☑ **Economics is correctly called "the dismal science."**
☑ **Physics tells us that space is warped in a gravitational field.**

136

And as well when they are linked to a singular noun:
- ☑ **Politics is a funny game.**

But otherwise the plural sounds right.
- ☑ **The acoustics in this auditorium are great.**
- ☑ **The statistics in this study are misleading.**
- ☑ **Electronics are cheaper at big box stores.**

Singular or Plural?

bacteria is the traditional plural form of **bacterium**. Growing mistaken use of **bacteria** as singular, with the generated plural 📖 **bacterias**, is still unacceptable in all contexts.

biceps is, strictly speaking, singular, the name of a muscle in your arm, but it looks like it's plural. Because of this, there has been growing use of ✊☹**bicep** as a singular form. That's almost common enough to be acceptable at this point, but avoid it in formal language. So if **biceps** is singular, what's its plural? ☹**bicepses**? You'll find that word listed as plural in some dictionaries, but it's almost never used. Or, because **biceps** is a Latin word, an adjective meaning *two-headed*, should we be using its Latin plural 📖 **bicipites**? Never. Common acceptable practice now is to use **biceps** as both singular and plural:
- ☑ **She's exercising to increase the strength of her left biceps.**
- ☑ **She's exercising to increase the strength of both her biceps.**

buses is the plural of **bus**, not **busses**. Busses are kisses.

gases works the same way.

cognoscenti, tympani, and graffiti are all Italian plurals, but in English they're all often treated as singular nouns. The real Italian singulars are hardly, if ever, heard in English.

criteria is the plural form of **criterion**, but it's frequently mistaken for singular, and a false plural 📖 **criterias** has developed. 📖 **Criteria** as singular and 📖 **criterias** as its plural are not yet common enough to be acceptable, even in quite informal uses.

phenomena works the same way.

data is another word in flux. Traditionally, **data** is the plural of **datum**, so use of **data** as a singular noun, as in

⚠ **This data is misleading.**

will be found objectionable in formal contexts. The problem with this use, which is about half-way along toward acceptability, is that the traditional correct use

☛ or ☑ **These data are misleading.**

may sound awkward. You're in trouble both ways. The best thing to do is to avoid the word altogether; but if you must use it, use it as singular in informal and oral contexts, and as plural in more formal writing.

media and **strata** work the same way.

⚠ **Social media controls her life.**

⚠ **Table-manners differ in various social stratas.**

fungi is the only acceptable plural of fungus. It's pronounced *fun-ji* not *fun-guy*.

headquarters is plural except when referring to a building.

☑ **Their headquarters are in Brazil.**

☑ **Their headquarters was raided by the police.**

brain People can have at most only one of them. Therefore

✊ **He used his brains to solve the problem.**

police is almost always a plural noun:

☑ **Police are investigating this killing.**

For singular uses, substitute **a police officer** (not ☹ **a policeman** — see section on biased writing).

Words Borrowed from Other Languages

Some words coming from other languages form their plurals the way their home languages do. Sometimes this is the only acceptable plural; sometimes the English **-s** version is acceptable as well; and sometimes the word has become so well embedded in English that the home-language plural is never used (or sounds impossibly pretentious).

Your spell-checker may help you figure out which plural to use of such words. In case of doubt, your best bet is probably to use the English plural. That way you'll avoid the pitfalls of trying to use foreign-language plurals: sounding stuffy and pedantic, or (worse) being mistaken about what the plural in the other language is.

138

In the following table of adopted nouns from other languages, the plural in the word's home language, when acceptable in English, is in the middle-column, and the acceptable anglicized plural (if any) in the right column.

LATIN: -a ➤ -ae Never mind how the Romans pronounced these plurals. You're speaking English, so pronounce **larvae** *lar-vee*, not *lar-vay* or *lar-vI*, and similarly for the other plurals here. This is odd, because it will seem more natural to many English speakers to pronounce the **ae** as *ay*.

alga	☑ algae	
alumna	☑ alumnae	
ameba (US)	☑ amebae	☑ amebas
amoeba (UK)	☑ amoebae	☑ amoebas
antenna	☑ antennae	☑ antennas
formula	☑ formulae	☑ formulas
larva	☑ larvae	☹ larvas
vertebra	☑ vertebrae	

LATIN: -is ➤ -es Pronounce the last syllable *eez*: *ba-seez*, not *ba-sez*. Here, in contrast to the previously listed Latin plurals, the Latin pronunciation is preferred. There's no logic to this. Sorry.

analysis	☑ analyses
axis	☑ axes
basis	☑ bases
crisis	☑ crises
diagnosis	☑ diagnoses
ellipsis	☑ ellipses
emphasis	☑ emphases
hypothesis	☑ hypotheses
neurosis	☑ neuroses
oasis	☑ oases
parenthesis	☑ parentheses
synopsis	☑ synopses
synthesis	☑ syntheses
thesis	☑ theses

LATIN: -um ➤ -a

addendum	☑ addenda	☑ addendums
aquarium	☑ aquariums	
auditorium	☑ auditoriums	
bacterium	☑ bacteria	
curriculum	☑ curricula	☑ curriculums
datum	☑ data*	
erratum		☑ errata
honorarium	🎓 honoraria	☑ honorariums
medium	☑ media*	
memorandum	☑ memoranda	☑ memorandums
millennium	☑ millennia	☑ millenniums
pendulum		☑ pendulums
referendum	🎓 referenda	☑ referendums
stratum	☑ strata*	
symposium	☑ symposia	☑ symposiums

*see items in the previous section. **Media** here is the plural when you mean *a method of communication*; but people who relay messages from the dead are **spirit mediums**.

LATIN: -us ➤ -i Pronounce, e.g., *a-lum-nI*, not *a-lum-nee*. **Foci** is is pronounced *fo-sI*.

alumnus	☑ alumni	
cactus	☑ cacti	☑ cactuses
focus	🎓 foci	☑ focuses
hippopotamus	🎓 hippopotami	☑ hippopotamuses
stimulus	☑ stimuli	
syllabus	🎓 syllabi	☑ syllabuses

LATIN: other transformations

appendix*	🎓 appendices	☑ appendixes
index	🎓 indices	☑ indexes
matrix	🎓 matrices	☑ matrixes
genus	☑ genera	

***Appendices** are parts of books. **Appendixes** are surgically removed. **Indexes** are parts of books. **Indices** are indications. Again, no consistent logic.

OTHER LANGUAGES

FRENCH

bête noire	☑ bêtes noires	
chargé d'affaires	☑ chargés d'affaires	
fait accompli	☑ faits accomplis	
nouveau riche	☑ nouveaux riches	
cul-de-sac		☑ cul-de-sacs
filet mignon		☑ filet mignons
hors d'oeuvre		☑ hors d'oeuvres
chateau	☑ chateaux	

GREEK

criterion	☑ criteria
phenomenon	☑ phenomena

ITALIAN

🕮 cognoscente*	☒ cognoscenti	
soprano		☑ sopranos
alto		☑ altos
allegro		☑ allegros
virtuoso	☑ virtuosi	☑ virtuosos
solo		☑ solos
🕮 tympano*	☑ tympani	
🕮 graffito*	☑ graffiti	

*See entry on **cognoscenti** in section above about these three.

Don't even try for the real non-English plural on the following words. Some of them don't have proper non-English plurals, and some you won't guess right about unless you have studied their home languages. Stick to the regular English **-es** plurals.

apparatus	virus
status	ignoramus
prospectus	octopus
campus	platypus

Compound Words

You can see in the table below how these work in formal language. Your spell-checker may not be helpful here; mine objects to some incorrect hyphenated plurals (e.g., **father-in-laws**) but does not suggest the correct plural form.

aide-de-camp	☑ aides-de-camp
battle royal	☑ battles royal
(brother/sister/father/mother /son/daughter)-in-law	☑ (brothers/sisters etc.)-in-law
(commander/editor)-in-chief	☑ (commanders/editors)-in-chief
(consul/governor/postmaster /surgeon/attorney) general	☑ (consuls/governors etc) general
court-martial	☑ courts-martial
hanger-on	☑ hangers-on
hole in one	☑ holes in one
maid of honour	☑ maids of honour
man-of-war	☑ men-of-war
notary-public	☑ 🎓? notaries public
passer-by	☑ passers-by
poet laureate	☑ poets laureate
right-of-way	☑ 🎓? rights-of-way
runner-up	☑ runners-up
sergeant-at-arms	☑ sergeants-at-arms

Some of these plurals sound rather stilted and 🎓. Use them if you must, but consider rewriting to avoid them.

Note that terms constructed from a noun + **ful** do not make their plural by pluralizing the noun. Instead they add **s** at the end. So, for example, the plural of **teaspoonful** is ☑**teaspoonfuls** not 👎**teaspoonsful**. Similarly **cupfuls**, **handfuls**, **mouthfuls**.

Abbreviations and Acronyms

There is some variation here about what's recommended, but the best practice usually is this: simply add an **-s** (not an **-'s**; this preserves the **-'s** for its main home: in contractions and possessives.) So:

☑ **PINs**
👎 **PIN's**

But in some cases, just adding s would result in something confusing. Most experts recommend using the dreaded apostrophe for a plural of abbreviations made of capital letters with a period at the end:

👎 **M.D.s**

☑ **M.D.'s**

Opinion is divided about **'s** for plurals of single letters, because it's confusing without:

☑?   **Mind your p's and q's.**

☹?   **Mind your ps and qs.**

☹☹?   **All the entries in Volume 1 start with as.**

An irregular case is abbreviations not composed of capitals: then the **s** goes before the period:

☑   **Fred Schmidlap and Assocs.**

Mass Nouns and Count Nouns

Count nouns are nouns that refer to things that can be counted: **book, idea, month, toe,** etc. The contrast is with mass nouns, which refer to things that cannot be counted: **knowledge, music, news, courage, scenery, milk, homework, electricity, money, confusion,** etc. Mass nouns are always singular and have no plural form. Thus

👎 **three musics,** 👎**two news (newses?),** 👎**55 courages;**

👎 **Reading that book did not produce even one knowledge.**

But ways of quantifying these things often exist: **a lot of music, one news item, more knowledge, three glasses of milk,** etc.

A few nouns can function both as count nouns and as mass nouns: normally mass, but sometimes count when they refer to types of things:

- 👎**three cheeses** referring to the amount of cheese you ate; but ☑**three cheeses** referring to the different kinds of cheese sold in a store.
- **Behaviour** is normally a mass noun, but psychologists sometimes talk about (types of) **behaviours.**
- **Money** is normally a mass noun with no plural. Some people seem to think that **monies** has a more official ring to it when they are talking of business affairs, but this is just usually pomposity. But it's acceptable in the jargon of financial writing, referring to discrete sums of money or funds: ☑ **Monies from several sources will fund the new project.**

- **Beer** is normally a mass noun, but since it usually arrives in standard containers, it has become colloquial to say ✊**I had eight beers** (= bottles/cans/glasses/pints of beer) **last night.**

There are many problems involving agreement in number (i.e., singular or plural) between subjects and their verbs. See the section called "Subject-Verb Agreement" below.

Irregular Verbs

Regular verbs add **-ed** for past forms, like this:
☑ **I want to go to Tuscany.** (present)
☑ **I wanted to go to Tuscany last year.** (past)
☑ **I have always wanted to go to Tuscany.** (past participle)

The *past participle* form is the one that goes with **have**. So simple past: **wanted**; past participle [have] **wanted**.

Irregular verbs form their past and past participle otherwise. So, for example:
☑ **I arise at 6 am every day.**
☑ **During the summer I arose at 6 am.**
☑ **After I have arisen, I let the cat in.**

There are some general patterns you might notice by looking through the following list, but I'm afraid that, aside from looking up the occasional instance, the way to learn these is just to get used to them through practice and exposure to the language.

On this list there is sometimes more than one acceptable form. In general, the first on the list is the more common. Former US/UK differences have mostly disappeared, with what used to be prevalent only in the US now having taken over in the UK.

Present	Past	Past Participle
arise	arose	arisen
awake	awoke	awoke or awoken
be	(I/he/she/it) was (we/you/they) were	been
bear	bore	borne
beat	beat	beaten
become	became	become
begin	began	begun

behold	beheld	beheld
bend	bent	bent
bet	bet	bet
bid (express)	bade	bidden
bid (offer)	bid	bid
bind	bound	bound
bite	bit	bitten
bleed	bled	bled
blow	blew	blown
break	broke	broken
breed	bred	bred
bring	brought	brought
broadcast	broadcast	broadcast
build	built	built
burn	burned/burnt	burned/burnt
burst	burst	burst
buy	bought	bought
can	could	been able to
cast	cast	cast
catch	caught	caught
choose	chose	chosen
cling	clung	clung
come	came	come
cost	cost	cost
creep	crept	crept
cut	cut	cut
deal	dealt	dealt
dig	dug	dug
dive	dived/ ⚠ dove	dived
do	did	done
drag	dragged	dragged
draw	drew	drawn
dream	dreamed/dreamt	dreamed/dreamt
drink	drank	drunk
drive	drove	driven
eat	ate	eaten
fall	fell	fallen
feed	fed	fed
feel	felt	felt
fight	fought	fought

145

find	found	found
fit	fitted/fit	fitted
flee	fled	fled
fling	flung	flung
fly	flew	flown
forbid	forbade	forbidden
forecast	forecast	forecast
forget	forgot	forgotten
forgive	forgave	forgiven
freeze	froze	frozen
get	got	(UK)got/(US)gotten
give	gave	given
go	went	gone
grind	ground	ground
grow	grew	grown
hang (a picture)	hung	hung
hang (execution)	hanged	hanged
have	had	had
hear	heard	heard
hide	hid	hidden
hit	hit	hit
hold	held	held
hurt	hurt	hurt
keep	kept	kept
kneel	knelt	knelt
know	knew	known
lay	laid	laid
lead	led	led
lean	leaned/leant	leaned/leant
leap	leaped/leapt	leaped/leapt
learn	learned/learnt	learned/learnt
leave	left	left
lend	lent	lent
let	let	let
lie (= to rest)	lay	lain
light	lit/lighted	lit/lighted
lose	lost	lost
make	made	made
may	might	
mean	meant	meant

meet	met	met
mistake	mistook	mistaken
overcome	overcame	overcome
overtake	overtook	overtaken
pay	paid	paid
put	put	put
quit	quit	quit
read	read (but pronounced red)	read (but pronounced red)
rid	rid	rid
ride	rode	ridden
ring	rang	rung
rise	rose	risen
run	ran	run
saw (= cut)	sawed	sawed/sawn
say	said	said
see	saw	seen
seek	sought	sought
sell	sold	sold
send	sent	sent
set	set	set
sew	sewed	sewn
shake	shook	shaken
shall	should	
shed	shed	shed
shine	shone	shone
shoot	shot	shot
show	showed	showed/shown
shrink	shrank	shrunk
shut	shut	shut
sing	sang	sung
sink	sank	sunk
sit	sat	sat
sleep	slept	slept
slide	slid	slid
sling	slung	slung
slink	slunk	slunk
slit	slit	slit
smell	smelled/smelt	smelled/smelt
sneak	sneaked	sneaked
	⚠ snuck	⚠ snuck

147

sow	sowed	sowed/sown
speak	spoke	spoken
speed	speeded/sped	speeded/sped
spell	spelled/spelt	spelled/spelt
spend	spent	spent
spill	spilled/spilt	spilled/spilt
spin	spun	spun
spit	spat	spat
split	split	split
spread	spread	spread
spring	sprang	sprung
stand	stood	stood
steal	stole	stolen
stick	stuck	stuck
sting	stung	stung
stink	stank	stunk
strew	strewed	strewn
stride	strode	strode
strike	struck	struck
string	strung	strung
strive	strove	striven
swear	swore	sworn
sweep	swept	swept
swim	swam	swum
swing	swung	swung
take	took	taken
teach	taught	taught
tear	tore	torn
tell	told	told
think	thought	thought
throw	threw	thrown
thrust	thrust	thrust
tread	trod	trodden
understand	understood	understood
undertake	undertook	undertaken
undo	undid	undone
uphold	upheld	upheld
upset	upset	upset
wake	woke	woken or woke
wear	wore	worn

weave	wove	woven
weep	wept	wept
win	won	won
wind	wound	wound
withdraw	withdrew	withdrawn
withhold	withheld	withheld
withstand	withstood	withstood
wring	wrung	wrung
write	wrote	written

Homophones or Nearly

Homophones are words that sound alike but have different meanings. Some of them are also homonyms, i.e., spelled alike (**bank** = financial institution; **bank** = land next to a lake or river). But the ones that give writers trouble are not spelled alike: (**poll** = voting; **pole** = long piece of wood or metal): you mean one, but write the other. This sort of error, of course, will not be caught by your spell-checker. I'm not able to give a comprehensive list of all such pairs, but I can give a longish list of the more common ones. Also included in this list are near-homophones — words not exactly pronounced alike, but close enough to confuse some writers. You should look through this list and locate those that you think you might be confusing. Some entries include a brief clue about their meaning. Some pairs are explained in greater detail in the MEANING AND USAGE section.

absence [*noun*] — absent [*adjective*]
accept — except
access [entry] — excess [too much]
adapt — adopt
adieu — ado
advice [*noun*] — advise [*verb*]
affect [to influence] — effect [result]
allowed [permitted] — aloud
allusion [reference] — illusion [unreal image]
alter [change] — altar [in a church]
alternate — alternative
anecdote — antidote
appraise [value] — apprise [inform]
attain — obtain
auger [drill] — augur [foretell]
averse — adverse
base [foundation] — bass [in music]
bath [*noun*] — bathe [*verb*]

bear — bare
berry [fruit] — bury [the dead]
beside [by the side of] — besides [as well as]
better — bettor
birth — berth [bed]
bizarre [strange] — bazaar [market]
bloc [political grouping] — block
brassiere — brazier
breach — broach — breech
breath [*noun*] — breathe [*verb*]
buoy [in the water] — boy
buy [purchase] — by
Calvary [biblical place] — cavalry [mounted troops]
carat [weight for jewels] — karat [purity of gold] — caret [insertion mark] — carrot
cash — cache [hiding place]

149

casual [informal] — causal [to do with causes]

ceased [stopped] — seized [grabbed]

ceiling [above you] — sealing

censor [*noun*: person who bans, *verb*: to ban] — censer [incense carrier] — sensor [detector] — censure [criticize]

chose [past tense] — choose [present tense]

cite [make reference to] — sight [vision] — site [location]

climatic [climate] — climactic [climax]

cloths [fabric] — clothes

coma [unconscious] — comma [punctuation]

compliment [praise] — complement [make complete]

comprise [consist of] — compose [constitute]

conscious [aware] — conscience [moral sense]

constructive — constructional

contemptuous [scornful] — contemptible [deserving contempt]

continuous [without interruption] — continual [frequent or constant]

contract — construct

contravene — controvert

conventional [usual] — convectional [transfer of heat]

convinced — convicted [of a crime]

cord [rope] — chord [music]

corollary — correlation

council [group] — counsel [advice]

course — coarse [rough]

credible [believable] — creditable [deserving credit]

credulity — credibility

crevice [narrow opening] — crevasse [deep crack]

critic [one who criticizes] — critique [piece of criticism]

cue [signal to begin] — queue [lineup]

cypress — Cyprus

defer [show respect] — differ

deference [respect] — difference

definite — definitive

demure [*adjective*: modest, shy] — demur [*verb*: raise doubts]

dependent — dependant

deprecate [criticize] — depreciate [reduce in value]

desert [dry place] — dessert [sweet]

device [thing] — devise [to plan]

dialectal — dialectical — dialectic

die — dye

dissent [protest] — descent [downward motion]

drier [*adjective*: more dry] — dryer [*noun*: laundry appliance]

edition [of a book, etc.] — addition [something added]

emigrant [leaving a country] — immigrant [coming in]

emigrate [leave a country] — immigrate [enter a country]

emulate [imitate] — immolate [sacrifice by burning]

envelop [*verb*] — envelope [*noun*]

expedient — expeditious

fair — fare [payment]

faze [*verb*: disconcert] — phase [*noun*: period]

flagrant [blatant] — fragrant [pleasant smelling]

flaunt [display] — flout [disobey]

floes [*noun*: floating ice chunks] — flows [*verb*: moves smoothly]

forbear [*verb*: refrain] — forebear [*noun*: ancestor]

formally — formerly [previously]

forth [forward] — fourth [after third]

foreword [in a book] — forward

foul — fowl [birds]

fryer [cooker] — friar [monk]

funeral [ceremony] — funereal [somber]

gait [manner of walking] — gate [hinged opening]

genus [biological type] — genius [creative

150

intelligence]

grate [*verb*: scrape; *noun*: barred opening]
— great

guerrillas [fighters] — gorillas [animals]

heed — he'd

heir [inheritor] — air

homophobe — homophone

human — humane [kind]

illicit [not permitted] — elicit [bring forth]

incredulous — incredible

independence [*noun*] — independent
[*adjective*]

inflammable — inflammatory

inhabit [live in] — inhibit [retard]

instance [occurrence] — instants [moments]

intense [strong] — intents [purposes]

invest — infest

isle [island] — aisle [to walk in] — I'll

its — it's

kernel [nut or corn bit] — colonel [officer]

knave [dishonest person] — nave [church
area]

know — no — now

later — latter

lath [piece of wood] — lathe [machine]

laudatory [expressing praise] — laudable
[praiseworthy]

lead [heavy element] — led

leave — leaf

lessen [reduce] — lesson

lightning [from clouds] — lightening
[becoming lighter]

loathe — loath

loose [not tight] — lose [be unable to find]

luxurious — luxuriant [lush]

mad [insane or angry] — maid [servant]

mantel [shelf over fireplace] — mantle [robe]

martial [to do with fighting] — marshal

masterful [powerful] — masterly [expert]

medley [mixture] — melody [musical
sequence]

merry — marry — Mary

minor [underage] — miner [underground]

mist [light fog] — missed

moral [ethical] — morale [spirit]

mourning [after death] — morning

mute [quiet] — moot [subject to debate]

new — knew

observance [obeying, respecting] — observation [watching]

one — won — worn

ones — once

ought [should] — aught [anything]

pain — pane [of glass]

patients [sick people] — patience [ability to
wait]

peer [look closely] — pier [wharf]

perpetrate [be guilty of] — perpetuate
[cause to continue]

perquisite [privilege] — prerequisite
[requirement]

personal [private] — personnel [employees]

perspective [vision] — prospective
[anticipated]

poor — pour [liquid] — pore [*noun*: tiny
opening; *verb*: pore over = examine
carefully]

populace — populous

practice — practise

precede [go before] — proceed [continue]

precedent [earlier guide] — president [chief
executive]

precipitous — precipitate

predominate — predominant

price [cost] — prize [reward]

principle — principal

prophecy — prophesy

propagate — promulgate

prescription [authorization] — proscription
[banning]

prostate [gland] — prostrate [lying down]

quay [wharf; pronounced *key*] — key

quite — quiet [not noisy]

rain — reign — rein [to control animals]

rap [strike; music] — wrap [enclose]

rational — rationale

ravage [damage] — ravish [fill with delight]

recant — recount

recoup [regain] — recuperate [recover from illness]

reek [stink] — wreak [cause harm]

relieve [*verb*] — relief [*noun*]

response [*noun*] — responds [*verb*]

ridden — written

riff [music] — rift [geology]

rise — rice

rite [ritual] — right — write

roll [*noun*: bread; *verb*: turn over] — role [part to play]

rote [repetition] — wrote

saw — so — sew

scene [location] — seen

seam [in clothes] — seem [appear]

senses — census [population count]

shed — shade

shone — shown

sit — set

soar — sore [hurt]

sole [single; fish] — soul [spirit]

sort [type or kind] — sought [looked for]

spayed [sterilized female animal] — spade [shovel]

straight [not crooked] — strait [narrow water passage]

striped [e.g., a zebra] — stripped [uncovered]

suite [rooms or music] — suit — sweet

super — supper [meal]

sympathies [*noun*] — sympathize [*verb*]

tale [story] — tail

than — then

there — their — they're

thing — think

this — these

urban [in cities] — urbane [sophisticated]

vanish [disappear] — varnish

vein [to carry blood] — vain

veracity [truthfulness] — voracity [hunger]

viscous — vicious

vortex [whirlpool] — vertex [highest point, angular point]

waist [your middle] — waste

wait — weight [heaviness]

waive [give up] — wave

wants — once

weak [not strong] — week

weather [sunny, wet, etc.] — whether [or not]

wedding — weeding

were — where — we're

wet — whet [sharpen]

who's — whose

wholly [completely] — holy [sacred]

winch — wench

woman — women

yoke [for animals] — yolk [of an egg]

Mondegreens and Eggcorns

A **mondegreen** is a misheard lyric, saying, catchphrase, or slogan. The word was coined by the Scottish writer Sylvia Wright in a 1954 article in *Harper's Magazine*. There she wrote that, as a child, she had misinterpreted the lyrics of a line of a Scottish ballad "They hae slain the Earl o' Moray and laid him on the green." She had thought it went, "They hae slain the Earl o' Moray and Lady Mondegreen." A closely related term is **eggcorn**: this was coined to refer to mishearings that retain their original meaning; that term's etymology is that it's an eggcorn for the seed of the oak tree.

Sometimes mondegreens become so prevalent that they replace the originals. For example, the line **Four calling birds** in "The Twelve Days of Christmas" was originally **Four colley birds** (**colley** is regional English meaning *black*). Word etymologies show a surprisingly large number of the sort of mondegreens called reanalysis: **An apron** was originally **a napron; an umpire** was **a noumpere; an adder** was **a nadder, a notch** was **an otch,** a newt was **an ewt,** etc.

You should watch out for mondegreens and eggcorns, especially when you're quoting song lyrics or catchphrases. If there's any doubt about an interpretation you have that seems odd, try googling the source.

Of course I can't make a list of what might be the more likely mondegreens and eggcorns. What I'll do is provide a list of a few, for your amusement. See if you can figure out what the correct phrase was. In the style of magazine quizzes, I'll put the answers upside-down at the bottom.

1. Holy imbecile, tender and mild.
2. Round John Virgin
3. Bells on cocktails ring, making spareribs bright.
4. Olive, the other reindeer
5. Jose, can you see
6. A girl with colitis goes by.
7. Gladly, the cross-eyed bear
8. beckon call
9. ex-patriot
10. a bad wrap
11. ad homonym
12. cuddle-fish
13. on tender hooks
14. escape goat
15. blessing in the skies
16. wet one's appetite
17. for all intensive purposes
18. hack-kneed platitudes
19. Pullet Surprise
20. a bowl in a china shop
21. old-timers' disease
22. tow the line
23. self of steam
24. have another think coming
25. pass mustard
26. test your metal
27. a doggy-dog world
28. neck in neck
29. baited breath

1. Holy infant, so tender and mild., 2. Round yon Virgin, 3. Bells on bobtails ring, making spirits bright., 4. All of the other reindeer, 5. Oh say can you see, 6. A girl with kaleidoscope eyes. (Beatles), 7. Gladly the Cross I'd Bear. (Hymn), 8. beck and call, 9. expatriate, 10. a bad rap, 11. ad hominem, 12. cuttle-fish, 13. on tenterhooks, 14. scapegoat, 15. blessing in disguise. 16. whet one's appetite, 17. for all intents and purposes, 18. hackneyed platitudes, 19. Pulitzer Prize, 20. a bull in a china shop, 21. Alzheimer's disease, 22. toe the line, 23. self-esteem, 24. have another thing coming, 25. pass muster, 26. test your mettle, 27. a dog-eat-dog world, 28. neck and neck, 29. bated breath

PART IV: GRAMMAR

Verb Forms

The basic tenses are present, past, and future. For the verb **to run**, here's how they work:

	Past	Present	Future
first-person singular	I ran	I run	I will run
first-person plural	we ran	we run	we will run
second-person singular	you ran	you run	you will run
second-person plural	you ran	you run	you will run
third-person singular	he/she/it ran	he/she/it runs	he/she/it will run
third-person plural	they ran	they run	they will run

Years ago, students used to be taught this rule about the future tense: for the first person, singular and plural, ordinarily use **shall**, but use **will** when the sentence expresses determination or intention about the future:

I/we shall begin classes next Thursday.

I/we will make sure he never does that again. (= intention/determination)

And, just to make things more complicated, the opposite way for second and third persons:

You will enjoy that movie.

You shall regret what you did today (= intention/determination)

He/she/it/they will be here later.

He/she/it/they shall never come here again. (= intention/determination)

If you've never heard this rule, sorry to have bothered you: it's now firmly dead. The word **shall** is on its way to disappearance: used five times more often in 1820 than in 2000, and still in decline. Just forget about **shall**.[1]

The Continuous Tenses

How to use the continuous form of verbs presents a good deal of difficulty for English learners, and no wonder. The rules are complicated and hard to apply. Native speakers can just hear, most of the time, which forms of verbs to use, but not always. We'll look at some of the rules, but the best thing to do, if you're having trouble with these, is to pay more attention to the examples that follow, and to how they're used in everyday talk and writing.

The continuous tenses of verbs are, as the name indicates, used to refer to some action or state that was, is, or will be continuing at the time indicated. You'll get the idea from these examples:

Simple Verbs	Continuous Verbs
The car rolled slowly down the hill.	The car was rolling slowly before he put the hand brake on.
I read the book yesterday	I was reading the book yesterday when the doorbell rang.
I know what you want.	I am cooking dinner right now.
I will phone you tomorrow.	I will be sleeping when the results are announced.
The TV program will have ended before we have to leave.	The TV program will have been running for an hour before we have to leave.

The continuous forms of these sorts of verbs are not common, because they often refer to an action or state that is simply true at a time, but is not seen as a continuing process:

Feeling: care, desire, dislike, envy, fear, hate, hope, like, loathe, love, mind, need, prefer, regret, trust, want, wish

Sensing: appear, hear, notice, see, seem, smell, sound, taste

Communicating: agree, astonish, deny, disagree, impress, mean, please, promise, refuse, satisfy, surprise

---

1 Except in set phrases like **Shall we go?** and when singing "We shall overcome." This sentence obviously expresses determination; but according to the old rule, that should be **We will overcome**. Oh well.

Thinking: believe, comprehend, doubt, expect, feel that (meaning think that), forget, hope, imagine, know, mean, realize, recognize, remember, suppose, think, understand

Other: belong, concern, contain, consist of, cost, depend on, deserve, exist, fit, have, hold, include, involve, lack, matter, owe, own, possess, resemble

👎 I am seeing the keys I couldn't find earlier.

👎 I am hearing the knock on the door.

👎 He is not understanding what I meant.

👎 Melissa was not believing what he said.

👎 You are knowing the pythagorean theorem.

👎 Tony will be comprehending her absence when he finds out that she was ill.

👎 My words were not meaning that I didn't like it.

👎 Mike had been doubting that the recipe would turn out well, but then it did.

👎 Megan is supposing that there is a good school near here.

👎 I am wishing I could come along. .

👎 We are preferring to wait here.

👎 I am hating Brussels sprouts.

Note that some verbs have one meaning that has a continuous form, and a different meaning that does not. This is because one meaning refers to an ongoing action, and the other refers to a state of affairs that's true at a time, but is not thought of as a continuing process. Compare the different meanings here:

☑ I am thinking of writing a novel. (considering)

👎 I am thinking that this answer is correct. (believing)

☑ He was tasting the stew while cooking it. (if she did it several times)

👎 This stew is tasting too salty.

☑ They are having lunch. (eating)

👎 I am having a new car. (owning)

☑ Ryan was missing his dog. (remembering with longing)

👎 Ryan was missing the bus. (arriving too late)

☑ I'd love to, but I am seeing somebody now. (dating)

👎 I am seeing somebody coming. (visually perceiving)

☑ She's looking for an apartment. (searching for)

👎 That is looking good to eat. (appearing to be)

157

English teachers complain about the McDonald's slogan **I'm loving it**, on the grounds that love is a verb that doesn't often occur in the continuous forms:

🖘 **I'm loving apple pie.**

☑ **I love apple pie.**

Of course, advertising slogans often employ distorted language to attract attention to themselves:

🖘 **Dare greatly** — slogan for Cadillac

but **love** can sometimes be used correctly in the continuous form, when what's going on is not a permanent or semi-permanent state, but a state going on over a particular finite time — such as eating at McDonald's (the more finite the better). So the slogan can be interpreted to mean

☑ **I'm loving it, here eating at McDonald's.**

The Perfect Tenses

The perfect tenses of verbs are so called because one of the strict meanings, based on its Latin roots, of the word **perfect** is *finished*. These tenses are used to refer to some action or state that that was, is, or will be completed at the time indicated. You'll get the idea from these examples:

The past perfect:
   When I had finished breakfast, I left the house.

Two actions are mentioned here: leaving the house, in the past, and finishing breakfast, which happened earlier than that. The sequence of before-the-past + past is indicated by using the past perfect and the simple past verbs. It would still be clear what the sequence was here because of the normal assumptions we'd make about the story, but consider this:

   When Sara telephoned, Jonathan remembered what she said.

We'd assume, reading this one, that what Jonathan remembered was what Sara said during the call. But compare

   When Sara telephoned, Jonathan remembered what she had said.

Now it's clear from the use of the past perfect here (**had said**) that what Jonathan remembered was what Sara said *before* the call.

   Sam went out when Natalie arrived.

158

This seems to make the two things simultaneous, or one a consequence of the other. Compare

Sam had gone out when Natalie arrived.

This use of the past perfect makes it clear that Sam left, *and then* Natalie arrived some time after.

The future perfect:

When you visit tomorrow, I will have cleaned up.

compare:

When you arrive tomorrow, I will clean up.

The use of the future perfect in the first clearly puts the cleaning before the future arrival. (So you can relax about that.) The second moves the action of cleaning *after* the arrival, almost as a consequence.

The present perfect:

The past and future perfect indicate a time before a past or future event; similarly, the present perfect indicates a time before a present time. Compare

I'm hungry.
I have been hungry.

The use of the present perfect in the second sentence points at being hungry before the present. Maybe it means that the speaker was hungry for a while before now, and is still; maybe it means that the speaker was hungry for a while in the past. But what's the difference between the present perfect and the simple past?

I have been hungry.
I was hungry.

Here are some more pairs of present perfect and simple past. Is there a difference in meaning?

I have lived in Halifax.
I lived in Halifax.

She has gone to the supermarket twice this week.
She went to the supermarket twice this week.

Haley has just finished her lunch.
Haley just finished her lunch.

Eliza has been to Paris.
Eliza was in Paris.

Sometimes maybe a difference is detectable. For example, if you are asked about living in Halifax, you will answer using the present perfect if you're still living there:

I have lived in Halifax for 23 years.

but with the simple past if you don't live there any more:

I lived in Halifax for 23 years.

The Subjunctive

This is another special form, called a mood, of verbs. Readers who have learned traditional grammar will expect to see the subjunctive in certain places, but it is dying among modern users, who might not even have heard of the term; but a good writer uses the subjunctive correctly. It's possible to get along without it, and some people won't notice. But now that you've come this far, why not try to master it?

Subjunctive verbs, broadly speaking, express the unreality of what's spoken about. They can be used to indicate that the situation didn't (or won't) occur:

☑ **If I *had been* at that party, I would have told him to stop drinking right then.** (In this and the following examples, the subjunctive verb is in italics.)

☑ **I don't have $10, but if I *had* it, I would pay for the pizza.**

☞ **I don't have $10, but if I have it, I'll pay for the pizza.** (The mistake is that this is in the indicative, not the subjunctive.)

or about hypotheticals:

☑ **Suppose Hitler *had won* World War II; what language would we be speaking now?**

☑ **If I *could snap* my fingers and be there in an instant, I would go to that wedding in Bermuda.**

☑ **If I *left* the party right now, would the hosts be upset?**

☑ **If I *were* you, I wouldn't reply to that email.**

or to express wishes:

☑ **wish I *were* in Dixie.**

✊ **wish I was in Dixie.** (Indicative)

or to express a suggestion, a demand, a proposal, or a preference; or to give advice:

☑ **It's necessary that you *get* that book back to the library today.**

☑ **I'd prefer that you *didn't* come with me.**

☑ **Julia insists that he *stay*; Nicole insists that he go.**

☑ **Alex was surprised by the request that he come over immediately.**

160

☑ I suggest that he *forget* all about it.

☑ My teacher recommended that I *drop* the course.

☑ I insist that you *phone* your mom right now.

☑ Melissa demanded that Fred *be* included in the group.

or to express urgency or importance:

☑ It's important that she *remember* this appointment.

☑ It's best that she not be *invited*.

☑ My boss insisted that I *be promoted* this time.

But if the speaker doesn't want to indicate any of these feelings, the subjunctive is not used. The first sentence of each pair uses indicative verbs (= not subjunctive). The second uses subjunctives:

☑ If I leave right now, will the hosts be upset?

☑ If I *left* right now, would the hosts be upset? (More doubt speaker is going to leave)

☑ If the library has that book, you'll find it in their web catalog.

☑ If the library *had* that book, you'd find it in their web catalog. (Sounds like the speaker doesn't think the library has it.)

☑ If New Year's Day comes on a Saturday or Sunday next year, we will have Monday off. (Neutral about truth or falsity)

☑ If New Year's Day *came* on a Saturday or Sunday next year, we would have Monday off. (Speaker doesn't think it will.)

☑ Suppose Kaitlyn mailed it last Tuesday; then it will be in the mailbox now.

☑ Suppose Kaitlyn mailed it last Tuesday; then it would be in the mailbox now. (More doubt)

☑ If I'm elected, I'll see that you get a job.

☑ If I *were* elected, I would see that you got a job. (More doubt)

Notice that in **if**-constructions, the subjunctive must be used in the if-clauses, but the conditional form of the verb (using **would** or **could**) is used in the other (main) clause:

☑ If I *were to go* to the movie this weekend, you *could go* with me.

In English there is no difference between the subjunctive and normal, or indicative, form of the verb

☑ It's important that you *forget* all about it.

except for the present-tense third-person singular, which drops the **-s** or **-es** so that it looks and sounds like the present tense for everything else:

☑ It's important that he *forget* all about it.

161

and for the verb **to be**. The subjunctive mood of the verb **to be** is **be** in the present tense and **were** in the past tense, regardless of what the subject is.

☑ He requires that everyone *be* on time.

☑ I wish she *were* there yesterday.

Sometimes **could, should,** or **would** plus verb forms are ways of expressing the same subjunctive mood:

☑ I wish he *were* more prompt.

☑ I wish he *would be* more prompt.

But this cannot happen in the past tense.

🖓 I wish he would have been more prompt.

🖓 If he would have been more prompt, we would have made it on time.

☑ I wish he *had been* more prompt.

☑ If he *had been* more prompt, we would have made it on time.

Sequence of Tenses in Indirect Speech

Direct speech reports the very words someone used; indirect speech reports the upshot of what they said. For example, if Brianna said "I am hungry," yesterday, then you could report this with a direct quotation:

Yesterday, Brianna said, "I am hungry."

or with indirect speech:

Yesterday, Brianna said that she was hungry.

Notice the change: in the direct quotation, the present tense verb **am** is used; in indirect, it changes to the past tense **was**, to match the tense of the main verb **said**.

Why there is this change in the tense of the verb should make sense on the basis of the discussion of time-sequences above, in the section on the perfect tense. In this case, Brianna was talking yesterday about being hungry then; so she put her sentence into the present tense. But today, when we report the substance (not the very words) of what she said, we say that what she was talking about was having been hungry then, so we put the verb in the past tense.

In general, then, when what's said is indirectly reported (not directly quoted), tenses move one step back in time. When the past words mentioned something to happen in the (then) future, a conditional verb is used in the reporting sentence instead. Here's a table that summarizes the possibilities:

"I *am* hungry," she said. (Simple present)

She said that she *was* hungry. (Simple past)

"I *am* fixing lunch," she reported. (Present continuous)

She reported that she *was fixing* lunch. (Past continuous)

"I *ate* breakfast early," she explained. (Simple past)
She explained that she *had eaten* breakfast early. (Past perfect)

"I *have eaten* only one meal today," she told me. (Present perfect)
She told me that she *had eaten* only one meal that day. (Past perfect)

"I *had* just *put* in the toast when you phoned," she explained. (Past perfect)
She explained that she *had* just *put* in the toast when I phoned. (Past perfect)

She said, "I *have been trying* to remember that all morning." (Present perfect continuous)
She said that she *had been trying* to remember that all morning. (Past perfect continuous)

"I *was trying* to remember it last night too," she added. (Past continuous)
She added that she *had been trying* to remember it the previous night too. (Past perfect continuous)

"I *will see* you next month," she said. (Future)
She said that she *would see* me next month. (Present conditional)

She said, "*I'll be* feeling better then." (Future continuous)
She said that she *would be* feeling better then. (Conditional continuous)

But in the following cases, there is no tense change from the quoted verb to the reporting sentence:

1) The verb in the reporting sentence is in a present tense. (You can use this to report what was said when it was said a short time ago.)
Bill says, "I *am* hungry."
Bill says he *is* hungry.

Anna says, "I *am* looking forward to seeing Kaia tomorrow."
Anna says she *is* looking forward to seeing Kaia tomorrow.

2) The reporting verb is in the past tense, but what was reported is still true, or a general truth:
Larry said, "I *am* a pretty good skater."
Larry said that he *is* a pretty good skater.

Our physics teacher told us, "Systemic entropy always *increases*."
Our physics teacher told us that systemic entropy always *increases*.

In other words, roughly speaking, a tense change is not appropriate when the statement being reported is as true now as it was when it was uttered, and especially if the person reporting the words agrees that they are still true.

These verbs in the direct quotation do not change in reported speech: **might, could, would, should, ought to:**

Leslie said, "I *might* **get a job in England next year."**
Leslie told me that she *might* **get a job in England next year.**

Arnold warned us, "You *should* **be careful about the icy road."**
Arnold warned us that we *should* **be careful about the icy road.**

Active and Passive Voice

Sentences using a verb in the active voice basically say *X does Y.* The passive-voice version changes that around into *Y is done by X.*

Some examples:

Active	Passive
The author discusses this in chapter 12.	This is discussed by the author in chapter 12.
Our shipping department will calculate postage.	Postage will be calculated by our shipping department.
In a serious earthquake, collapsing buildings kill people.	People are killed by collapsing buildings in a serious earthquake.
Our van will deliver your furniture on Thursday.	Your furniture will be delivered by our van on Thursday.
My mechanic suggested that I get those brakes fixed.	It was suggested by my mechanic that I get those brakes fixed.
Somebody broke this dish.	This dish was broken by somebody.

Another form of passive construction just leaves out the agent, the *X* that does *Y,* and says, in effect, merely, *Y is done.* This is what's sometimes called the *impersonal passive voice.*

Active	Passive
This is discussed in chapter 12.	(The author?) discusses this in chapter 12.
Postage will be calculated.	(The shipping department?) will calculate postage.
People are killed in a serious earthquake.	In a serious earthquake, (falling buildings?) kill people.
Your furniture will be delivered on Thursday.	(Our van?) will deliver your furniture on Thursday.

It was suggested that I get those brakes fixed.	(My mechanic?) suggested I get those brakes fixed.
This dish was broken.	(Somebody?) broke this dish.

If you have a grammar-checker on your word processor, it might be smart enough to find passive constructions in what you write, and stupid enough to suggest that you change each one to active. The idea that passive-voice sentences are an error, or an automatic sign of bad writing, is another superstition. Passive-voice constructions are *often* inferior to their active-voice transformations, but not *always*: anyway, they should not be used very frequently in any piece of writing. Here's why:

+ When it mentions an agent, a passive-voice sentence it is usually wordier than the corresponding active sentence: **X was done by Y**, rather than **Y did X**. Remember this basic rule of good writing: when two sentences say the same thing, the shorter one is almost always better.
+ A passive-voice sentence inverts the normal word-order in a sentence, so it's a little bit more difficult to read. Putting a large number of passive-voice sentences into something you're writing will cause reader fatigue. Remember this other basic rule of good writing: be kind to your readers. Even if you don't like them, writing that's easier on them will be more effective.

But the impersonal passive voice, which leaves out mention of the doer altogether, is sometimes shorter than the active form, and not more difficult to read:

Julia kicked Mike. (active)
Mike was kicked by Julia. (passive)
Mike was kicked. (impersonal passive)

Sometimes, pompous writers, afraid that short direct sentences won't sound sufficiently official or smart, dress the impersonal passive up with padding:

☹ **What happened was, Mike was kicked.**
☹☹ **What transpired was the following: Mike was kicked.**

The unpadded impersonal passive gains its advantages of directness and brevity at a cost: it provides less information. Who or what did it? Sometimes this construction is used on purpose to hide the identity of the doer, and distract the audience from assigning responsibility. (Have you ever told the person you're living with "The dish got broken"?) Corporate and military talk, and especially political talk, is full of this: things *happen*, rather than being *done by someone*. This is not merely a writing error — it's sleazy. It's a *moral* error.

165

Mistakes were made in terms of comments — Nixon's press secretary Ziegler on lies he told about Watergate.

Serious mistakes were made. — Then-president Regan, about the Iran/Contra scandal.

Mistakes were made — Then V.P. George Bush about Iran/Contra.

Mistakes were made — Henry Kissinger about allegations of war crimes.

Mistakes were made.... — Cardinal George Pell to an enquiry into alleged sexual abuses by priests.

Mistakes were made here.... — President Clinton, about Democratic fundraising scandals.

Yes of course mistakes were made.... — Former British PM David Cameron about UK middle-east policy.

There were mistakes made ... — Candidate Jeb Bush about his Iraq policies.

Journalist Tristin Hopper (in the Canadian *National Post*) reports that a search of Canadian federal parliamentary transcripts revealed nearly 100 **mistakes were made** over the last 20 years.

So why isn't a passive construction always undesirable? The impersonal passive voice may be justified when you want to hide the identity of *X*, or when that identity is unknown, or unimportant. And sometimes a passive construction just sounds better. The first item in this pair, with two passive constructions, is a little shorter and not clearly inferior to the second:

This cart is provided for your convenience, and must be returned here immediately after use.

The management has provided this cart for your convenience. You must return it here immediately after use.

The first item in the following pair is clearer and more direct:

Your water will be turned off briefly tomorrow morning to allow plumbing repairs.

The repair staff will turn your water off briefly tomorrow to allow plumbing repairs.

Who is the agent in the following impersonal passives? In neither case can we assign agency.

☑ **The old songs are loved.**

☹ **Everyone loves the old songs.** (not exactly)

☹ **People** (as opposed to animals?) **love the old songs.**

☑ **The store was robbed.**

☹ **Somebody robbed the store.**

Lastly, it's sometimes considered good form in science writing to make your prose impersonal; thus:

It is demonstrated that the presence of hemoglobular neophrasticin is a causal factor in hiccups.

166

is preferred to

I demonstrate that the presence of hemoglobular neophrasticin is a causal factor in hiccups.

The idea here is that the impersonal form carries the suggestion of objectivity. That's strange, isn't it? Trying to make it seem like what's written is a fact of nature rather than a human product? Nobody will be fooled into thinking that your writing wasn't written by a human. I don't particularly like impersonal writing (are you surprised to hear this?), but if that's what they insist on, then you should oblige.

Note, however, that this lack of **I** in writing is no longer considered preferable in many other sorts of writing, especially in the humanities. This allows you to avoid the impersonal passive, and, equally importantly, avoid the silly phrase **the present author**, or the royal/editorial plural **we**,[2] when you're talking about yourself. Just say **I**. Similarly, it's often permissible to address the reader as **you**. You've noticed that in this book I'm not avoiding **I** or **you**.

Subject-Verb Agreement

A singular subject takes a singular verb. A plural subject takes a plural verb. We were looking above at errors that stemmed from uncertainty about whether particular subjects were singular or plural. But now we turn to errors in agreement when the singular/plural status of the subject is clear.

Problems in subject/verb agreement rarely arise in SWE or IEE in simple sentences:

☞ **They goes to the store now.**
☞ **This bus run down Spring Garden Road.**

But problems are more common in sentences such as this:

☞ **The state of Afghanistan's roads reflect the chaotic situation.**
☑ **The state of Afghanistan's roads reflects the chaotic situation.**

Here the proximity of the plural noun **roads** and the verb **reflect** makes it seem that **roads** is the subject; but the subject is, in fact, the singular noun **state**. The prepositional phrase (consisting of a preposition like **in**, **of**, **under**, **at**, etc. plus the following words) does not influence the verb. Leaving out the prepositional phrase **of Afghanistan's roads** puts the real subject next to the verb: **The state ... reflect**, making the mistake obvious. Some more examples of this sort of thing:

☞ **The use of mobile phones and other electronic devices are prohibited.**
☑ **The use ... is prohibited.**

---

2 This sort of phrase isn't even standard anymore if you're the Queen of England, and anyway you're probably not. If you are, then it's an honour that you're reading my book, Your Majesty.

🖐 **As the statement by Belgium's Prime Minister about his country's deficit and unem-ployment problems indicate, many nations are in the same shape, or worse.**

☑ **As the statement ... indicates** (The subject is the singular noun statement, so the verb must be *indicates* rather than *indicate*.)

🖐 **Courses offered range from the history of the Greek and Roman world to the 20th cen-tury, and covers Britain, Europe, North America, Africa, and the Far East.** — History Dept. Prospectus, Birkbeck College, University of London

☑ **Courses offered range ... and cover**

Words in parentheses (brackets) do not influence the verb. Thus:

☑☹ **Elvis (and his entourage) always arrives late.**

Similarly:

☑☹ **Elvis — and his entourage — always arrives late.**

Sorry — these sound very odd. As always, you should try to make your writing smooth and natural, not merely grammatically correct. So these sentences should be rewritten. Without the parentheses, the subject is plural:

☑ **Elvis and his entourage always arrive late.**

coupled with, together with, and **accompanied by** Similarly, sentences take a singular verb when a singular noun subject is followed by phrases beginning with these words. You can see this if you leave out these phrases:

🖐 **Strong wind, coupled with heavy rain, are hitting Atlantic Canada.**

☑ **Strong wind ... is hitting Atlantic Canada.**

🖐 **Shiraz, together with smoky gouda, were served to the guests.**

☑ **Shiraz ... was served to the guests.**

🖐 **James, accompanied by his two sisters, are arriving later.**

☑ **James ... is arriving later.**

Collective Nouns

A collective noun is the name of a group of people or things that is sometimes considered as a single thing — the whole group — rather than a plurality of people or things. When this is the case, the collective noun takes a singular verb. But when the verb refers to actions that are done by the individual people or things that make up the group, then the verb should be plural.

Consider these examples involving the collective noun **council.**

council Is this singular or plural? See if you can sort out correct/incorrect in the following:

☑ **The council meets in September.**
👎 **The council meet in September.**
👎 **The council is at each other's throats.**
☑ **The council are each other's throats.**

It's the council as a unit that meets in September — so singular; but it's each of the members of the council that are at each other's throats — so plural.

How about this one:

👎 **Sadly, the intended audience — men — isn't reading** — headline, the *Toronto Globe and Mail.*

The subject here is clearly **audience**, but the emphasis here (made even clearer by **men**) is on the individuals that make up the group, not the aggregate. It's individual members of the audience (particular men) who aren't reading, not the audience as a whole. So this is better:

☑ **Sadly, the intended audience — men — aren't reading.**

Compare:

☑ **The intended audience — unmarried women — has grown.**

There are lots of collective nouns. A very small sample:

board	family	herd	percentage
bulk	flock	host	pile
bunch	flood	jury	press
committee	generation	majority	proportion
company	government	mass	stack
couple	group	minority	staff
crew	half	multitude	team
department	handful	pack	variety
faculty	heap	panel	

To amuse yourself (if you're easily amused) you might try thinking up a sentence for some of these examples in which the word is singular and another in which it's plural.

Here are some more cases that work the same way:

five peanuts Is this singular or plural? It certainly looks like it's plural:

☑ **Five peanuts were rolling around on the floor during the party.**

But this kind of expression also has a singular use (rejected by my grammar-checker) when what's being talked about is not the individual things in question, but rather the quantity that they together constitute:

☑ Five peanuts is what the Chinese recipe called for.

☑ Two teaspoons of salt contains double the maximum daily intake of sodium.

☑ Fifty dollars is more than I can afford.

none This presents problems. Older grammar books, reasoning that **none** means *no one*, will insist that this is singular, so in answer to the question **Where are the students?** they will accept **None is here** and **None of the students is here** but reject **None are here** and **None of the students are here**. But modern grammarians recommend that you take a look at the noun of which there is said to be none. If it's singular, then **none of** takes a singular verb:

☑ None of the coleslaw was eaten.

☜ None of the coleslaw were eaten.

But things get slightly more difficult when that noun is plural. In that case, none will usually be counted as plural, though Sticklers will object, and using a singular verb will sound very stilted:

⚠ None of the outfielders were at practise.

🎓 None of the outfielders was at practice.

Sometimes there's no corresponding noun in the sentence:

? None was missing.

? None were missing.

In that case, what is being talked about will probably be made clear by the context. If that indicates that what's being said is that none of the hardware was missing, then use the singular verb.

☑ None was missing.

If it indicates that what's being said is that none of the potato chips were missing, then use (with caution) the plural verb:

⚠ None were missing.

all This works the same way.

☑ All of the whisky is gone.

☑ All of the marbles are back in the box.

a lot So does this.

☑ A lot of people were there.

☑ A lot of the lawn has not been mowed.

(But see the entry for allot/alot/a lot regarding the use of **a lot**)

more And this.

- ☑ **Want some more cake? More is in the refrigerator.**
- ☑ **Want some more grapes? More are in the refrigerator.**

Other Agreement Problems

there is/there are The real subject of sentences beginning with these phrases follows the verb. So:

- ☑ **There is turkey in the fridge if you want it.**
- ☑ **There are seven people in the waiting room.**

There's, the contraction of **there is**, is often mistakenly used with a plural (following) subject:

- 👎 **There's seven people in the waiting room.**

what Which of these is correct?

- ? **What got Mr. Trudeau into his present predicament was his ludicrous efforts to deny what every intelligent person knows.** — Margaret Wente in the *Toronto Globe and Mail*
- ? **What got Mr. Trudeau into his present predicament were his ludicrous efforts....**

The grammar of sentences like these, starting with **what**, can be very puzzling. They often contain two verbs, and the singular/plural question sometimes isn't clear for either:

In this sentence, it's clear that **is** (singular) is correct both times:

- ☑ **What is upsetting is Caleb's complaint.**

But what should we say about these?

- ? **What is upsetting is Caleb's complaints.**
- ? **What is upsetting are Caleb's complaints.**
- ? **What are upsetting are Caleb's complaints.**

Various authorities offer complicated rules for dealing with cases like these, and they disagree with each other. The best bet here is to paraphrase:

- ☑ **The thing that's upsetting is Caleb's complaining.**
- ☑ **The things that are upsetting are Caleb's complaints.**

Here's an example of the same sort of problem:

- ? **A large part of what's causing these children to die are unsafe conditions.** — CBC Radio News

Is this an inverted sentence, with **unsafe conditions** as the subject?

- ? **Unsafe conditions are a large part....**

171

Or should this be understood the way it's presented, with **a large part** as the subject? In that case, it should be

☑ **A large part … is unsafe conditions.**

The answer here, again, is, who knows? People might object to either. If you're worried, rephrase.

☑ **Unsafe conditions make up a large part of what's causing these children to die.**

[X] and [Y] as a subject in a sentence normally takes a plural verb:

☑ **Logan and Lauren are arriving late.**

But when it's clear that the sentence is talking about one thing, then the verb should be singular:

☑ **The largest country, and the one containing the furthest-north city, is Russia.**

☑ **Bacon and eggs is my favourite breakfast.**

Both of these are acceptable, but the second is perhaps more natural:

☑ **Seven and five are twelve.**

☑ **Seven and five is twelve.**

either … or The verb agrees with the second of the things mentioned:

🕮 **Either Hanna or her children is going to be here.**

⚠ **Either Hanna or her children are going to be here.**

☑ **Either Hanna's children or Hanna is going to be here.**

🕮 **Either Hanna's children or Hanna are going to be here.**

(Old grammar books got this wrong, specifying that the verb after **either … or** is always singular. That's why there's a ⚠ on that sentence above.)

However, both of these sound terrible:

☹ **Either Hanna or I is going to be here.**

☹ **Either Hanna or I am going to be here.**

The best thing to do here is to rewrite:

☑ **Either Hanna or I will be here.**

neither/nor This works the same way as **either … or**, discussed just above.

🕮 **Neither Hanna nor her children is going to be here.**

⚠ **Neither Hanna nor her children are going to be here.**

☑ **Neither Hanna's children nor Hanna is going to be here.**

🕮 **Neither Hanna's children nor Hanna are going to be here.**

both a positive and a negative subject Then the verb agrees with the positive subject. (This is logical, because it, not the other thing, is the real subject.)

- ☑ **Bad weather, not labour demands, is responsible for the high food prices.**
- ☑ **Not bad weather, but labour demands, are responsible for the high food prices.**
- ☑ **Labour demands, not bad weather, are responsible for the high food prices.**

one of takes a singular verb.

- ☑ **One of them has the key.**
- ☑ **One of the books is missing.**

But compare:

- ☑ **He is one of those people who have the key.**
- ☑ **That is one of the things that have me worried.**

In both of these, there is a plural subject for have: **people** and **things**. (People have the key; and he is one of this group: people who have the key.) (Things have me worried, and this is one of that group: things that have me worried.)

But

- ☑ **He is the only one of those people who has the key.**
- ☑ **That is the only one of the things that has me worried.**

In both of these, the subject of the verb is singular: **who** (referring to **he**), and **that** (referring to **thing**). (He — the only one — has the key; That — the only thing — has me worried.)

This is really complicated, and if these distinctions concerning **one of** don't make a lot of sense to you, don't worry. Usage here is quite variable, and the rules above are not often strictly enforced.

a number of is plural; **the number of** is singular:

- ⚠ **A number of books are missing.**
- ☑ **The number of missing books is uncertain.**

There's an old rule that **a number of** is singular, because **number** is singular, and the object of the preposition **of** is not the subject that will determine the number of the verb. This is a superstition, but, as always, ⚠.

anyone/anybody/no one/nobody/each/every/either/neither All are singular:

- ☑ **Anyone who had a ticket was allowed in.**
- ☞ **Anyone who had a ticket were allowed in.**

these/those kind/kinds of

These kinds of sentences are mistakes:

📖 **Ms. Gokool said those kind of figures could inform the work of...** — the *Toronto Globe and Mail.*

📖 **Some people still do things by hand. Saskathesan restaurateurs are those kind of people.** — the *Toronto Globe and Mail*

📖 **These Kind of Attacks Can Happen Anywhere in the World** — Barack Obama, misquoted in a headline in CNSNews.com website. (What he really said was "These kinds of attacks...")

These/those applies to **kind**, not the plural noun that follows **kind**. So it should be **that/this kind** or **those/these kinds**. And **kind of** goes with a singular following noun, **kinds of** with a plural. Here's what I mean:

☑ **those kinds of things**
☑ **these kinds of things**
☑ **that kind of thing**
☑ **this kind of thing**

The following sentence contains what probably is an error:

? Several of the men brought their wife to the picnic.

This appears to indicate an extraordinary case of bigamy, implying that one woman came to the picnic who was married to several men. But this:

? Several of the men brought their wives to the picnic.

suggests the opposite sort of bigamy: each of them has several wives.

This is one of those cases in which the logical resources of English are not fully up to the job of disambiguation. Of course, a reasonable person hearing either sentence in the usual sort of situation (e.g., it's not a picnic for old-style Mormons) would correctly assume that no variety of bigamy is implied.

Comparative and Superlative

When comparing two things, use the comparative form of adjective (ending in **-er**), or **more**. When comparing three or more things, use the superlative form of adjective (ending in **-est**), or **most**.

📖 **Supremely rational self-interest tells only half the story, and not even the most important half.** — *Extreme Trust: Turning Proactive Honesty and Flawless Execution into Long-Term Profits*, by Don Peppers and Martha Rogers, Ph.D. (About this use of **Ph.D.**, see the section Citing and Quoting Authorities, below.)

☑ **... the more important half.**

☞ **Jill Daugherty, 34, was in graduate school and working as a geological engineer in Kingston when the youngest of her two children developed a brain tumour at the age of 2½.** — the *Toronto Globe and Mail*

☑ **... the younger of her two children....**

☞ **Critics of the new system say it encourages corruption as bureaucrats who control the currency can offer access to the better of the three rates.**
— "FACTBOX: Venezuela's bolivar currency devaluation," Reuters.com

☑ **... the best of the three rates.**

Split Infinitives

Infinitives are made out of verbs by putting **to** in front of them: **to see, to be, to love, to lead**, and so on. This is a way of turning a verb into a noun.

Splitting an infinitive is inserting one or more words between the **to** and the verb: **to clearly see, to always be, to passionately love....** Generations of students have been told that *infinitives must never be split.*

> Nobody is sure exactly where this rule came from. Sometimes it's guessed that Victorian grammar pundits created this rule, based on their view that infinitives were never split in Latin, which, they supposed, was the only perfectly logical language. This is doubly silly. Even if Latin were more logical, there would be no reason to inflict its rules on English; anyway, you can't split an infinitive in Latin, because infinitives are one word in that language: **to see** = *videre*; **to be** = *esse*; **to love** = *amare*.

But that doesn't mean that you should go ahead and split your infinitives all over the place. There are two reasons not to:

+ Sometimes what you write (or say) will be read (or heard) by people who had that rule drummed into them and will recoil in horror at your split infinitive, deciding that you're badly educated or linguistically incompetent. Never mind if they're right or not; it's a good idea to not give them this impression.

+ Split infinitives sometimes sound bad even to people who have never been taught that rule, or who have decided it is invalid. Maybe this is the result of their having read and heard generations of writers/speakers who believed the rule and kept their infinitives unsplit. Maybe an unsplit infinitive is just more graceful than a split one. See what you think by comparing the following:

☹? **He always tried to clearly see his duty.**
☑ **He always tried to see his duty clearly.**

☹? She hated to always be the worst hockey player in her gym class.

☑ She hated always to be the worst hockey player in her gym class.

Maybe there's a difference in meaning between the second two sentences. The first sentence seems to say that it would have been okay if she was the worst player only some of the time — it's that it was *always* that she hated. The second could be saying that what she hated was being the worst player (and she always hated this). Do you detect a difference in meaning in the other examples?

☹? To passionately hate is destructive.

☑ To hate passionately is destructive.

Well, maybe. But how about these:

☹? Children are sometimes taught to thoroughly chew their food.

☹? Children are sometimes taught thoroughly to chew their food.

☹? Children are sometimes taught to chew their food thoroughly.

☹? To boldly go where no man has gone before.

☹? Boldly to go where no man has gone before.

☹? To go boldly where no man has gone before.

You may tend to prefer the split versions of these. And there are some sentences with split infinitives that seem natural and graceful to some people, maybe even superior to their alternatives:

⚠ I can't manage to really like kale.

⚠ My dad's trying to better understand what's happening in my life.

⚠ The contract has a provision allowing us to voluntarily add to our pension plan.

⚠ I think you ought to carefully read that letter.

This one:

⚠ He was forced to figuratively eat his words.

doesn't really mean the same as any of these:

He was forced figuratively to eat his words.

He was forced to eat his words figuratively.

He was figuratively forced to eat his words.

It's often hard to say why some of these split-infinitive sentences seem good and others seem bad. But consider these:

⚠ She expected the new ad campaign to more than double her company's sales.

? She expected the new ad campaign to result in more than double her company's current sales.

? She expected the new ad campaign would more than double her company's current sales.

There's no way that **more than** can simply be moved outside the infinitive. The reason here is that the name of the action that she expects here is **more than doubling**. There's nothing particularly wrong with the second or third sentences; they're just replacements for what didn't need replacing. The reason that the first sentence gets a ⚠ rather than a ✓ is just that readers who learned that old no-split-infinitives rule might object.

This one, however, is clearly terrible:

👎 **Yo, I'm afraid to not be a teen-ager in two years. No one takes you seriously as an adult.** — software developer Isaiah Turner, quoted in *The New Yorker.*

If you trust you ear on these things, and are not worried about the reactions of old-school critics in your audience, go ahead and use the good split infinitives.

Like vs. As

The preposition **like** has perfectly familiar and acceptable uses:

✓ **Nathan, like Natalie, always arrives late.**
✓ **This book is very much like her previous ones.**
✓ **The boat sank like a stone.**

But the following are mistakes in formal English, though they are frequently heard in informal spoken English:

✊ **I want to be good in algebra like my older brother was.**
✊ **It's like he wanted me to fail.**
✊ **The boat sank like it had been torpedoed.**

What's gone wrong here is that **like** introduces a clause. That means that what it introduces is not the name of a person or thing, but something that could stand on its own, as a whole sentence.

A conjunction is a word that can introduce a clause. An old rule says that **like** cannot be a conjunction. What should be substituted is a genuine conjunction: **as, as if,** or **as though.**

✓ **I want to be good in algebra as my older brother was.**
✓ **It's as if he wanted me to fail.**
✓ **The boat sank as though it had been torpedoed.**

The increased use of **like** as a conjunction (and the frequent awkwardness of its replacement with **as, as if,** or **as though**) has made some people think that it's time to throw away the old rule and accept it into formal writing. But Sticklers will get peeved at this use. You'd better avoid it. Except in this sentence:

✓ **Tut-tut, it looks like rain.** — A.A. Milne, *Winnie-the-Pooh*

Like is actually a conjunction here. The sentence doesn't say that something resembles rain. It really says *it looks like it's going to rain*; the verb is omitted, but understood. But nobody with any sense would object to the grammar here.

> "Winston tastes good, like a cigarette should" is one of the most famous advertising slogans of all time. You don't see a full verb in what follows **like**, but it's understood that what's being said here is short for **like a cigarette should taste**, so this uses **like** as a conjunction.
>
> When the slogan appeared in 1954, it was immediately the object of widespread, highly publicized scorn from the grammar-conscious. Ogden Nash published a poem in *The New Yorker* about it, including the line "*Like* goes Madison Avenue, *like so* goes the nation."" Walter Cronkite refused to say it on TV. On an episode of *The Beverly Hillbillies*, sponsored by Winston, Jed said "Winston tastes good…" and Granny added "Like a cigarette had ought-a!" The tobacco company asked, "What do you want, good grammar or good taste?" and cried all the way to the bank about the criticism; all that publicity made Winston the #2-, then the #1-selling cigarette in the US.

The Order of Adjectives

In the section called "A Surprising Note on Rules" above, there was a discussion of the fact that we follow rules of language very often with no idea of what those rules are; they have to be discovered by linguists. Here's a striking example of that.

If English is your first language, or you're very competent at English as a second language, it will be clear to you there's something wrong with this sentence:

🗫 Abagail owns a green Cape-Cod small cozy bungalow.

What's wrong is the order of those adjectives **green**, **Cape-Cod**, **small**, and **cozy**. Let's shuffle them around and see what happens:

🗫 Abagail owns a Cape-Cod small cozy green bungalow.

🗫 Abagail owns a small Cape-Cod green cozy bungalow.

☑ Abagail owns a cozy small green Cape-Cod bungalow.

Now consider this one:

🗫 When we arrived, tiny retriever gorgeous black three puppies greeted us.

Here's the right order:

☑ When we arrived, three gorgeous tiny black retriever puppies greeted us.

The two following sentences have adjectives in the right order. You might try shuffling them, to see how this makes things wrong.

☑ Worn-out big ancient brown leather running shoes were in the closet.

☑ Sam bought two amazing huge square Persian carpets.

What's going on here is a rule about the order of adjectives: from beginning to end they must be put in this order:

1. Quantity or number
2. Quality or opinion
3. Size
4. Age
5. Shape
6. Colour
7. Proper adjective (often nationality, other place of origin)
8. Material
9. Purpose or qualifier

1. Quantity or number		three		two
2. Quality or opinion	cozy	gorgeous	worn-out	amazing
3. Size	small	tiny	big	huge
4. Age*			ancient	
5. Shape*				square
6. Colour	green	black	brown	
7. Proper adjective	Cape-cod			Persian
8. Material			leather	
9. Purpose or qualifier		retriever	running	
10. Noun	bungalow	puppies	shoes	carpets

*when there are both sorts of adjective, the order here may be transposed.

Imagine trying to learn this rule by memorizing these categories and order, and calculating how this applies every time you want to write or speak a sentence with two or more adjectives in a row. You couldn't do it. Amazingly, however, children learn how to apply this rule very successfully at an early age, when they still have trouble figuring out which way of putting on their underwear is backwards. If you can't hear the proper order, don't try learning the rule. Just listen a lot.

Danglers and Misplacements

The part of the following sentence before the comma describes **the committee**:

> **Having taken into account the various reports, the committee decided to delay the project for a year.**

In this sentence, the first two words describe **the dog**:

> **Barking continuously, the dog frantically looked for the squirrel.**

179

In this one, **running up the tree** describes **the squirrel:**
> **The dog barked at the squirrel running up the tree.**

There are two sorts of errors involving descriptions like this, both frequently seen and easily avoided. They are *danglers* and *misplacements*. Compare the last sample sentence above with this one:

🖐 **Running up the tree, the dog barked at the squirrel.**

In this one, **running up the tree** appears to describe **the dog.** So it seems to say that the dog was barking while (extraordinarily) running up the tree. The descriptive phrase is misplaced.

In this sentence (as in many others examples we will look at) readers can be trusted to figure out what was meant; nevertheless, good writing technique tries to save readers from confusion, even when the confusion is momentary and slight. The way to make it clear which noun is described by the descriptive phrase is to put the phrase closer to the noun it's meant to describe.

🖐 **Wrapped in Santa-Claus paper, I put the gift under the Christmas tree.**

☑ **I put the gift, wrapped in Santa-Claus paper, under the Christmas tree.**

It's **the gift**, not **I**, that's wrapped.

🖐 **I saw an alligator driving down a Florida highway.**

☑ **Driving down a Florida highway, I saw an alligator.**

Alligators aren't allowed to drive, even in Florida.

The second sort of error, maybe more common, is a descriptive phrase describing nothing mentioned in the sentence:

☑ **Re-reading *Catcher in the Rye*, it's amazing how little Salinger's work ages.**

In that sentence, what or who is doing the re-reading? The descriptive phrase is a *dangler*, attached to nothing. The sentence should be changed to give the descriptive phrase its anchor — a noun representing what is being described, underlined in these examples:

☑ **Re-reading *Catcher in the Rye*, I was amazed at how little Salinger's work ages.**

or

☑ **Re-reading *Catcher in the Rye*, you are amazed how little Salinger's work ages.**

Or the sentence can be completely rewritten:

☑ **It became clear to me, while re-reading *Catcher in the Rye*, how amazingly little Salinger's work has aged.**

This mistake is most often found when the main sentence starts with **It is**, or is in the passive voice. The obvious way to fix this is to change the main sentence into the active voice, supplying the subject for the phrase to modify.

180

👎 After prolonged stirring, it was determined that the precipitate had dissolved.

☑ After prolonged stirring, we determined that the precipitate had dissolved.

☑ After prolonged stirring, the precipitate had dissolved.

Or just rewrite:

👎 Applying this algorithm to the problem, it is immediately clear what the solution is.

☑ Applying this algorithm to the problem immediately makes the solution clear.

In the following, the anchor noun is similarly missing, and the descriptive phrase appears to apply to the wrong noun:

👎 Turning over while fast asleep, my pillow got tossed to the floor. (*The pillow was not asleep.*)

☑ Turning over while fast asleep, I tossed my pillow to the floor.

👎 Leaving the room, the lights must be turned off.

☑ When you leave the room you must turn off the lights.

👎 Walking around the field, wild strawberries were seen everywhere.

👎 Wild strawberries were seen everywhere, walking around the field.

☑ Wild strawberries could be seen everywhere in the field.

☑ When I walked around the field, I could see wild strawberries everywhere.

👎 Born in 1955, the Second World War meant little to him.

☑ Born in 1955, he had little understanding of the Second World War.

👎 With her 90th birthday on the horizon, Globe writer shines a spotlight on Sonya Bata.
— headline, the *Toronto Globe and Mail* (Bata, not the *Globe* writer, is almost 90.)[3]

☑ With her 90th birthday on the horizon, Sonya Bata speaks to Globe writer.

Avoiding dangling descriptive phrases altogether is good policy, but some usage experts now judge that some danglers have been used for so long, and are so familiar, that they will bother nobody except Sticklers.

Acceptable danglers may start, for example, with these words: **according to, assuming, considering, regarding, respecting, speaking of, taking into account,** or **turning for a moment.** (But grammar purists will still consider them mistakes.) Notice in the examples below, however, that fixing this by inserting a noun for the phrase to refer to produces a slightly wordier sentence; the rewriting, given after this is in each case, eliminating that modifying phrase altogether, is better.

---

3 Strangely, the house style of the *Toronto Globe and Mail* avoids italics in titles of newspapers, books, plays, etc. See section on italics for proper use.

Steven Pinker writes:

> Considering how often these forms turn up in edited prose and how readily they are accepted even by careful readers, two conclusions are possible: either dangling modifiers are a particularly insidious grammatical error for which writers must develop sensitive radar, or they are not grammatical errors at all.... The second conclusion is the right one. (— "10 'Grammar Rules' it's OK to Break [Sometimes]." The UK *Guardian* website.)

He later points out what you probably missed: that his sentence beginning with **Considering** has a dangler.

⚠ Considering all the above-mentioned studies, the evidence shows conclusively that smoking can cause cancer.

☹ Considering all the above-mentioned studies, we conclude that smoking causes cancer.

☑ These studies show conclusively that smoking can cause cancer.

⚠ Considered from a cost point of view, TitanoPharmCorp could not really afford to purchase Iatrogenerica America.

☹ Considered from the point of view of cost, the purchase of TitanoPharmCorp was not a wise move by Iatrogenerica America.

☑ TitanoPharmCorp could not really afford to buy Iatrogenerica America.

⚠ Talking about terrible actors, Sylvester Stallone deserves the anti-Oscar for lifetime disachievement.

⚠ Nutritionally speaking, it's better to substitute partly skimmed milk for whole.

⚠ Regarding the proposal I sent, have you any comments?

⚠ According to the rule book, the batter was out.

Some people feel that writing which is filled with modifying phrases and passive constructions sounds more important; but readers are annoyed, not impressed, by this. Rewrite!

☹ Another significant characteristic having a significant impact on animal populations is the extreme diurnal temperature range on the desert surface. (*Can a characteristic have an impact? A small point is here buried in a morass of meaningless abstraction.*)

☑ The extreme diurnal temperature range on the desert surface also strongly affects animal populations.

☹ Referring generally to the social stratification systems of the city as a whole, we can see clearly that types of accommodation, varying throughout in accordance with income levels and other socio-economic factors, display a degree of diversity.

☑ **In this city rich people and poor people live in different neighbourhoods, and in different sorts of houses.** (*Duh! The obviousness of the point here was hidden behind all that blahblah.*)

When you cut out the padding in this way, you may discover that what you say is not weighty and important, but in fact trivial or meaningless. Don't be discouraged; this happens to many good writers. Just make sure to edit what you write.

More unacceptable danglers and misplacements:

☞ **While reaching toward the top shelf, a book fell on her head.**
☑ **While reaching toward the top shelf, she was hit on the head by a falling book.**
☑ **A book fell on her head while she was reaching toward the top shelf.**

☞ **Without knowing her telephone number, it was impossible for me to reach her.**
☑ **Not knowing her telephone number, I found it impossible to reach her.**

☞ **On behalf of City Council and the people of Windsor, it gives me great pleasure to welcome you to our city.**
☑ **On behalf of City Council and the people of Windsor, I am pleased to welcome you to our city.**

☞ **Parents find surprise goodbye note written by 6-year old son after his death.** — headline, the *Toronto Globe and Mail*[4]
☑ **After his death, parents find surprise goodbye note written by 6-year old son.**

☞ **One morning I shot an elephant in my pajamas. How he got into my pajamas, I'll never know.** — Groucho Marx, *Animal Crackers*
☑☹ **One morning, in my pajamas, I shot an elephant.**

☑ **When completely cooked, you should let the stew cool uncovered.**
☑ **When completely cooked, the stew should be left to cool uncovered.**
☑ **When it is completely cooked, you should leave the stew to cool uncovered.**

☞ **My cousin went hunting for a rabbit with a shotgun.**
☑ **My cousin went hunting with a shotgun for a rabbit.**

☞ **The union local representing guards and other correctional officers alleges that, unlike other jails, sprinklers and alarms at Toronto South have been placed within easy reach of aspiring vandals.** — the *Toronto Globe and Mail*
☑ **... unlike those in other jails ...**

☞ **Filled with half-a-kilo of cocaine, Spanish police couldn't resist tweeting a photo of Mr. Big's unusual excess baggage....** — the *Toronto Globe and Mail*
☑ **Spanish police couldn't resist tweeting a photo of Mr. Big's unusual excess baggage — filled with half a kilo of cocaine — ....** (*Note also here that there shouldn't be hyphens in half-a-kilo.*)

---

4 This mistake was corrected in the *Globe* column mentioned in a footnote in the section on word usage.

The misplacement of **only** is a very common error.

🗣 I have only seen sparrows in my back yard this year.

☑ I have seen only sparrows in my back yard this year.

Can you see why the first sentence says that the only thing that you've done to the sparrows is see them? (I.e., you've not shot at them, or photographed them, etc.) Take care what you do with that word **only**. Another frequently misplaced word is **even**:

🗣 **We are at the very beginning stages of even discussing this subject.** — Sean Spicer, White House spokesman

The Supposedly Dangling Infinitive

Remember that an infinitive is a verb form with **to** in front of it: **to eat, to run, to be**. These can also introduce a modifying phrase.

☑ **To receive a complimentary copy, you should return the business reply card before June 30.**

There's nothing wrong with this sentence. The infinitive phrase **To receive a complimentary copy** attaches properly to the subject-verb combination **you should return** supplied right after it. Now consider:

☑ **To receive a complimentary copy, return the business reply card before June 30.**

This is okay also. The subject of the main sentence is **you**, not written but understood.

But now look at this one:

? **To receive a complimentary copy, the business reply card should be mailed before June 30.**

Now the actor of the action has disappeared because of the passive voice; it's not even **you** understood. This is especially common in scientific writing, where (as previously mentioned) an impersonal style is sometimes preferred, so this grammatically fine sentence

☑ **To determine the source of the infection, we tested water samples from surrounding wells.**

has to be replaced by this dangling one:

? **To determine the source of the infection, water samples from surrounding wells were tested.**

Some authorities consider this an unacceptable dangler, but sentences with this sort of structure are so common and so well understood that other authorities (sometimes grudgingly) find it acceptable. If the expectations of scientific style demand it, go ahead and write dangler-sentences. Here are two dangler-sentences (about other matters) taken from the authoritative *Scientific Style and Format: the CSE Manual for Authors, Editors, and Publishers* (7th edition, 2006):

> **To avoid potential confusion about the meaning of the comma, the following style is recommended.**

> **To facilitate prompt binding of the issues of a volume, the title page, the volume table of contents, ..., are usually published as the end pages of the last issue of the volume.**

But if dangler **to**-sentences aren't required in the type of writing you're doing, you should avoid them, because they are often awkward and ugly sentences, and Sticklers might find them grammatically unacceptable. Rewrite supplying the missing subject-verb combination:

⚠☹ **To conclude this essay, the French Revolution was a product of many interacting causes. (The French Revolution concluded no essays.)**

☹ **To conclude this essay, let me say that the French Revolution was a product of many causes.** (Writers do not need to tell readers that the essay is concluding; that white space at the bottom gives this secret away. A little word such as **then**, set off by commas, will suffice to signal that this is a summing-up.)

☑ **The explanations given for the French Revolution, then, are not mutually exclusive; the Revolution was a product of many interacting causes.**

☑ **To appreciate the full significance of the Meech Lake Accord, a range of factors needs to be considered.**

⚠☹ **To appreciate the full significance of the Meech Lake Accord, we need to consider many things.**

☹ **The Meech Lake Accord was important in many ways.**

Gerunds and the Possessive Case

Consider these two sentences:

☑ **I hate that man singing off-key.**

☑ **I hate that man's singing off-key.**

They are both grammatically correct (though the first one would benefit if **who is** were inserted between **man** and **singing**); but they mean different things. The first sentence means that you hate the *man*. The second sentence means that you hate the *singing*. Which do you want to say?

Another example of the same:

☑ **Fran laughing is delightful.** (*What's delightful is Fran, when she's laughing.*)

☑ **Fran's laughing is delightful.** (*What's delightful is that laughing, when done by Fran.*)

The subject of the first sentence is **Fran**, and of the second, **laughing**.

Now consider these two sentences:

🖫 Installing the wrong washer increases the risk of a faucet leaking.

☑ Installing the wrong washer increases the risk of a faucet's leaking.

These sentences have different objects of the preposition **of**: in the first, it's **faucet**; in the second it's **leaking**. Of what is the risk increased? Not of a faucet; of leaking. The second one alone is a correct way of saying what's obviously intended here. But this sort of mistake is very familiar.

Singing, laughing, and **leaking** all are gerunds — nouns made out of verbs. Here are other examples of that mistake,[5] and of its fix using a gerund and a possessive:

🖫 I appreciate you helping out with my computer.

☑ I appreciate your helping out with my computer.

🖫 Granny breaking a bone is what we are all afraid of.

☑ Granny's breaking a bone is what we are all afraid of.

🖫 Improvement depends on the patient taking the proper dose of this medication.

☑ Improvement depends on the patient's taking the proper dose of this medication.

I've reluctantly awarded 🖫 to the first of each of these pairs. They really do violate an old grammar rule, but almost everyone talks this way. Many people would think that the 🖫 sentences above sound right, and that the ☑ versions sound wrong or at least a bit odd. Maybe this is another case in which an old grammar rule is fading away, and those 🖫 sentences should have been marked ⚠ instead. Well, again, you should judge just how Stickley the audience to your writing will be.

Notice here that there are two correct versions, and one incorrect:

☑ My imitating her singing was what made her angry.

☑ I, imitating her singing, was what made her angry.

🖫 Me imitating her singing was what made her angry.

The subject of the first sentence is **imitating** (imitating made her angry); of the second it's **I** (I made her angry), and **imitating** is a verb (participle) here, not a noun (gerund). Was it the imitation that made her angry, or was it I? Either way, it makes sense. But the subject of the third has to be **Me** (**Me … made her angry**). Mistake.

Ending Sentences with Prepositions

Traditionally, it was considered a mistake to end a sentence with a preposition, or in general to detach a preposition from its object. Thus:

---

5   In case you're interested, the official name of this mistake is the *fused participle*.

✊ Vancouver is the only city I want to live in.

☑ Vancouver is the only city in which I want to live.

I suspect that this is another one of those absurd grammar rules invented for a crazy reason — in this case that Latin didn't disconnect prepositions from their objects[6] — and that had no prior foundation in good English writing. Well, as usual, Sticklers will insist on the traditional rules, crazy or not, so you should probably obey this one in the most formal writing. Maybe the ✊ in the sentence above should have been a ⚠. But where some slight informality is tolerated, it's permissible to end a sentence with a preposition when that reads more naturally.

☑ Where do you come from?

☹ From where do you come?

☑ Ugh, what did you step in?

☹ Ugh, in what did you step?

What's often the case when this seems proper is that there's a two-word verb phrase: **step in, come from.** Other examples:

☑ All that noise is too much to put up with.

☹ All that noise is too much with which to put up.

☹☹ All that noise is too much up with which to put.

☑ A good teaching job is hard to come by.

☹☹ A good teaching job is something by which it is hard to come.

☑ You should try to cheer up.

The Cases of Pronouns

One weird thing about pronouns in English, unlike nouns, is that they have *nominative* (or *subjective*) and *objective* cases.

	NOMINATIVE	OBJECTIVE
first-person singular	I	me
first-person plural	we	us
second-person singular	you	you
second-person plural	you	you
third-person singular	he	him
	she	her
	it	it
third-person plural	they	them

---

6 The rule against splitting infinitives—see the discussion of this above—is another.

What this means is that the pronouns have different forms depending on how they are used in the sentence. You'll see what I mean in the examples. We'll start with the first-person pronoun, **I** (nominative) and **me** (objective).

The nominative case is used for the subject of a sentence:

☑ **I went to the store.**

And inside clauses in which it is the subject:

☑ **This is the book that I recommended.**

☑ **He is older than I am.**

A rarer, and more questionable, use of the nominative is in uses such as these:

☑ **It is I who broke that dish.**

☑ **He is older than I.**

Back to those, and other questionable uses, in a moment.

These are uses for the objective case:

☑ **That movie amused me.** (**me** is the direct object of the verb: objective case)

☑ **Grace gave me her old books.** (**me** is the indirect object of the verb: objective case)

☑ **Katherine sent emails to me.** (**me** is the object of the preposition: objective case)

The mistaken use of **me** in the subject of a simple sentence, for example,

☞ **Me and Jayden are going to the mall.**

is almost never encountered in IEE or SWE. It's more common for people to say **I** where **me** is correct, in cases such as these:

☞ **That's a matter between Taylor and I.** (object of preposition **between**; should be **me.**)

☞ **Our boss gave Austin and I the day off.** (indirect object of verb **gave**; should be **me.**)

☞ **That teacher hates Harper and I.** (direct object of verb **hates**; should be **me.**)

I suspect that speakers are afraid of the word **me**, having been corrected when using it as subject.

Fear of **me** is probably also the reason that people incorrectly substitute **myself**:

☞ **That's a matter between Taylor and myself.**

☞ **Our boss gave Austin and myself the day off.**

☞ **That teacher hates Harper and myself.**

Using **me** as the subject of a sentence (**Me and Aiden are going ...**) might be called *undercorrection*: the speaker isn't aware of the rules of educated speech, or isn't paying attention to them, or is using another dialect. But the use of **I** in place of **me** is often rather *overcorrection*: the speaker is aware of the uneducated use of **me**, and is trying to avoid it, but isn't quite sure how to use it correctly. The use of **myself** in this way is similarly overcorrection.

When you knock at a door, and someone inside says, **Who is it?**, saying **It is I** would be correct, according to the standard grammatical rules. But that sounds pedantic, strange, and artificial. Educated people would say **It's me**, and grammar experts who are not slavishly tied to the old rules find this entirely acceptable, at least in spoken informal use. But be careful: in formal written English, a Stickler might object.

He is older than me is a similar problem. It's officially a mistake, because **am** is understood as following the pronoun. **He is older than me (am)** makes that mistake clear. It should be **He is older than I (am)**. But **He is older than me** is almost always acceptable — in informal English anyway.

And another similar situation arises with uses of the pronoun **who**. Its objective case is **whom**, so these are correct, according to the traditional rules:

☑ **Who liked that movie?** (**Who** is the subject, so it's in the nominative case.)

☑ **Whom did that movie amuse?** (**Whom** is direct object of verb: objective case.)

☑ **To whom did Taylor recommend that movie?** (**Whom** is object of preposition: objective case.)

Like the other pronouns, this one sometimes appears in the nominative case when the objective case is called for:

⚠ **Who did that movie amuse?**

⚠ **Who did Taylor recommend that movie to?**

But this sort of official error is so widely heard that it's considered acceptable in IEE, though it might be objected to in written form. Unlike **me**, **him**, **her**, and **us**, the objective pronoun form **whom** sounds stuffy and pedantic. You're very unlikely to hear **Whom were you talking to?** or even worse, **To whom were you talking?** except maybe in the lounge of the English Department, where people might also say, **Oh, indeed; but that notwithstanding, one might presume to think....**

Whom has been dying for a century. Here's its chart:

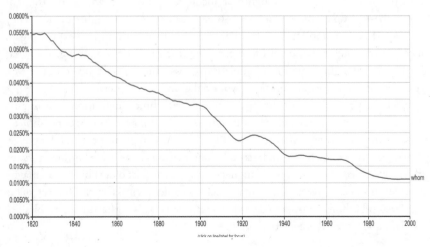
(click on line/label for focus)

And, again, there are cases of overcorrection: when speakers are afraid that they're saying **who** when **whom** is required; so you might hear:

🖙 That person, whom I realized had to be her brother, was here again today.

but this is correct:

☑ That person, who I realized had to be her brother, was here again today.

think:

☑ ... who (I realized) had to be her brother ...

Sentences and Fragments

One of the first things kids are taught about grammar is the rule that whole sentences are okay and incomplete sentences are not. Well, what's the difference? A whole sentence is a collection of words that expresses a complete thought. Incomplete sentences — sentence fragments — express incomplete thoughts. Let's see if this information is of any use. Check out the thoughts connected with the following bits of language, and see whether they're complete or not:

1. **Of course!**
2. **What?**
3. **Never.**
4. **The shorter the better.**
5. **A liar and a cheat.**
6. **Not one minute sooner.**
7. **This is not it.**
8. **In case of fire, break glass, open door, pull handle down.**

Did you detect complete thoughts or incomplete thoughts when you thought about these? I don't know whether 1–6 express complete thoughts or not. They are, in a sense, incomplete, but the item with the strongest claim on expressing an incomplete thought is 7; until I find out what it is that isn't something, and what it isn't, the thought remains incomplete, I guess. But 7 would be accepted as a complete sentence by everyone, even your old grammar teacher.

Well, maybe we can get further with a more technical definition: if it doesn't have a subject and a verb, then it's incomplete. By this test, 1–6 are incomplete, despite the fact that sentences just like them are regular parts of language, constantly used and always understood. Sentence 8 is, likewise, a familiar and apparently well-constructed bit of language, despite the lack of a subject. (So maybe all that's needed is a verb? Grammar teachers sometimes assert the subject **you** is "understood" though not stated in 8. So why can't we say that unstated bits are "understood" in all these sentences?)

But in IEE, 1–6 can all be fully acceptable, provided that they're in the right context. (They would not be acceptable in formal written English.)

Here are some larger contexts into which I'll insert these sentences, so you can see that they're all natural things we'd say.

- ✊ **"Would you like to see some photos of my grandchildren?" "Of course!"**
- ✊ **"I hope you're interested in [mumble mumble]." "What?"**
- ✊ **I'll never forgive my ex-wife for what she put me through during the divorce. Never.**
- ✊ **Short sentences are better than long ones. The shorter the better.**
- ✊ **I stopped visiting Uncle Fred when I discovered that he's a liar. A liar and a cheat.**
- ✊ **You'll turn on the TV when you've finished your homework. Not one minute sooner.**
- ✊ **The literary world was hoping for the equal of _To Kill a Mockingbird_. This is not it.**

Notice how the prior sentence makes the following one make perfect sense.

The formula mentioning complete thoughts may have some point to it: that when you encounter the sentence fragments all by themselves, their specific meaning isn't clear to you. But that isn't relevant, because in real life (as opposed to grammar books) their meaning is filled out by the surrounding context. Item 7, above, is clearly a complete sentence, but the thought it expresses is supplied only by its surrounding context.

> You should note that this phenomenon is not restricted to sentence fragments. It's widespread in all of language. Consider this little linguistic object:
>
> **I like chocolate too.**
>
> Another uncontestably complete sentence, but notice how what it means is filled in by context, and how different contexts make different meanings:
>
> **My daughter likes chocolate. I like chocolate too.**
> **I like vanilla ice cream. I like chocolate too.**
> **I sell chocolate in my little shop. I like chocolate too.**

Nonsense can result when the appropriate sort of context is lacking:

- 🤜 **And it isn't here.** (_This wouldn't make sense if it were the first sentence of a book._)
- ✊ **It was the fifth of September. But it was cloudy all morning.** (_But?_)
- 🤜 **Most of the planets have more than one moon. Later.**
- 🤜 **My father was fond of golf. Next year is a leap year. When we got in the car Wyoming was rectangular. She and the others drove to the university.**

The first paragraph of this well-written newspaper article contains nothing but sentence fragments:

A world unclear about the future of American diplomatic and trade policy. A country unsure of the future of health care. A capital uneasy about the next chief executive. A Congress unsettled about its new role. A series of unforeseeable obstacles — like the weekend quarrel over whether the new president had legitimacy — ahead.

Amid all of these uncertainties, only one thing is clear...

—"As Trump Inauguration Looms, Tension, Uncertainty Dominate," by David Shribman, the *Toronto Globe and Mail*

Beginning Sentences with Conjunctions

The idea that one should never begin a sentence with a conjunction — words such as **and, or, but, when, because, if, so, yet, for, nor, in case, once, unless, until** — has followed a familiar pattern: originally a rule dreamed up by order-loving grammarian, but widely ignored by good writers, then deemed a superstition that we should forget about. But in this case, things are more complicated.

Sometimes, when correctly attached to relevance-giving contexts, sentences beginning with some conjunctions are acceptable. Consider these sentences (and fragments) out of context:

And you should refrigerate it once it has cooled.

Or I'll phone you if the meeting ends earlier.

But the world wasn't ready for such a revolutionary view.

However, in context, they can all make perfect sense:

When it's cooked, let the stew sit without cover off the burner. And you should refrigerate it once it has cooled.

I'll meet you outside at 3:00. Or I'll phone you if the meeting ends earlier.

Eighteenth-century scientists and philosophers proposed the idea of the natural evolution of life forms. But the world wasn't ready for such a revolutionary view.

But sometimes beginning a sentence with a conjunction is more questionable. Consider:

Broiling meat at a high temperature keeps it juicy. Because it seals the surface.

I want to see you today. After you're finished with your class. Because I have something to tell you.

The difference here is that we've got a different type of conjunction. These conjunctions — all of the *coordinating conjunctions* — are fine for starting sentences (in the right context):

and	for	nor	yet
but	or	so	

But these — a partial list of the subordinating conjunctions — are different.

after	because	if	that	when	whether
although	before	if only	though	where	which
as	even if	rather than	unless	whereas	while
as if	even though	since	until	wherever	

Coordinating conjunctions connect two clauses of equal importance — independent clauses. They might be separated into two sentences without the conjunction, leaving the meaning substantially intact. Compare

I'll meet you outside at 3:00, or I'll phone you if the meeting ends earlier.

I'll meet you outside at 3:00. I'll phone you if the meeting ends earlier.

But when two clauses are connected by a subordinating conjunction, one is subordinate — depends on, is of less importance than — the other. Removing the conjunction and making the clauses into separate sentences makes a significant difference. Compare:

Fred went to see the house where he had grown up.

Fred went to see the house. He had grown up.

I wanted to see you today, after you're finished with your class.

I wanted to see you today. You're finished with your class.

This distinction — between coordinating and subordinating conjunctions — makes a difference for use. Let's look first at coordinating conjunctions.

Sentences starting with coordinating conjunctions tend to make things more staccato, less flowing; this may be a valuable stylistic tool. It makes for shorter sentences, and may increase readability. They are a very useful tool, even in serious formal writing. The tendency in all writing has been very much toward shorter sentences; you will become acutely aware of this if you struggle through the multiple-clause writing typical of nineteenth- or eighteenth-century English.

But be careful. First, as usual, Sticklers will object to violations of the old rules they learned in school. As always, you should know your audience. Even though there's a good case for their acceptability, it wouldn't be much trouble for you to be on the safe side, and combine two sentences into a form that will bother nobody:

⚠ **Eighteenth-century scientists and philosophers had already proposed the idea of the natural evolution of life forms. But the world wasn't ready for such a revolutionary view.**

☑ **Eighteenth-century scientists and philosophers had already proposed the idea of the natural evolution of life forms, but the world wasn't ready for such a revolutionary view.**

193

WRITING WRONGS: COMMON ERRORS IN ENGLISH

Second, when this produces very short sentences, the effect may be one you don't want. To see this, compare these two:

Spiny anteaters lay eggs. But nevertheless they are mammals.
Spiny anteaters lay eggs, but nevertheless they are mammals.

The first one produces a pause after the first sentence, and then adds the second as a sort of blunt surprise. It has an emphatic rhythm. It's punchier than the second, which is smoother, with a more uniform flow. Can you hear the difference? There's the same contrast here:

The literary world was hoping for the equal of *To Kill a Mockingbird*. This is not it.
The literary world was hoping for the equal of *To Kill a Mockingbird*, but this newly released novel is not it.

Dramatic effects like this are only rarely — maybe never — appropriate in formal writing. They're useful and fully acceptable in more informal writing, for example, fiction, poetry, newspaper opinion pieces and editorials, and ads. They can certainly be overdone in any context; frequent use will be tedious. Save this sort of construction for the occasions where it will stand out and make a difference.

An extremely successful use of sentences starting with conjunctions is the King James version of Genesis. Here's the way it starts:

In the beginning God created the heaven and the earth.
And the earth was without form, and void; and darkness [was] upon the face of the deep.
And the Spirit of God moved upon the face of the waters.
And God said, Let there be light: and there was light.
And God saw the light, that [it was] good: and God divided the light from the darkness.
And God called the light Day, and the darkness he called Night.
And the evening and the morning were the first day.

The overwhelming majority of the rest of the sentences in Genesis start with **And.**

You are not writing the Bible. Do not attempt this at home, kids.

Third: Coordinating conjunctions *coordinate*. They shouldn't start a sentence that doesn't coordinate appropriately with the previous one.

☞ **The Spiral Nebula in Andromeda is visible to the naked eye. But there are over 25,000 species of roundworms.**

☞ **Last night's ballgame was won by St. Louis, 8–5. So Magellan did not survive the round-the-world trip of his ship.**

This is of course also true when the two are combined as clauses of one sentence:

👎 **The Spiral Nebula in Andromeda is visible to the naked eye, but there are over 25,000 species of roundworms.**

But sentences starting with subordinating conjunctions act much more like sentence fragments. They're extremely informal, and they introduce intense choppiness into your writing. Compare:

☑ **I want to see you. After you're finished with your class. Because I have something to tell you.**

☑ **After you're finished with your class, I want to see you, because I have something to tell you.**

This dramatic choppy effect, more extreme than that produced by short sentences beginning with coordinating conjunctions, is never appropriate in formal contexts, and should be used, if at all, only very sparingly otherwise. And, like sentence fragments, they're very easy to overuse.

👎 **The picnic will take place on Saturday. Unless it's raining.**

👎 **Broiling meat at a high temperature keeps it juicy. Because it seals the surface.**

Note, however, that connecting them to make one sentence (in either order) is acceptable:

☑ **Broiling meat at a high temperature keeps it juicy, because it seals the surface.**

☑ **Because it seals the surface, broiling meat at a high temperature keeps it juicy.**

(The second example shows again that the rule "Never start a sentence with a conjunction" is too simple.)

Run-on Sentences

The illegitimate combination of what should be two sentences is called a run-on sentence.

👎 **Early last Thursday we were walking in the woods it was a bright and clear morning.**

👎 **Getting things ready, please don't turn off your PC.**

👎 **The threat from radical Islamic terrorism is very real, just look at what is happening in Europe and the Middle-East.** — Donald Trump tweet (Note also mistaken hyphen in *Middle-East*)

In informal contexts, and when the two combined sentences are very short, it's permissible.

✊ **Lil's here, Bill isn't.**

Often the best thing to do with an unacceptable run-on sentence is to separate it into two:

195

WRITING WRONGS: COMMON ERRORS IN ENGLISH

☑ Early last Thursday we were walking in the woods. It was a bright and clear morning.

☑ Getting things ready. Please don't turn off your PC.

Another good fix is to separate the two clauses with a semicolon:

☑ Early last Thursday we were walking in the woods; it was a bright and clear morning.

☑ Getting things ready; please don't turn off your PC.

And another good fix is to separate the two clauses with a conjunction:

☑ It was raining and I was getting soaked.

☑ It was raining but my umbrella was keeping me dry.

☑ You can have fries with that or you can have a salad.

☑ I was soaking wet because it was raining.

☑ I'm going to the party even if you stay home.

A comma preceding the conjunction is optional, but useful when the clauses are long. When the clauses contain commas, use a semicolon as a stronger separator:

☑ It was raining, and I was getting soaked.

☑ It was raining, but my umbrella was keeping me dry.

☑ You can have fries with that, or you can have a salad.

☞ In early 1942, the Germans were advancing on all fronts, in Africa, Russia, and Europe and it appeared that the allied cause was lost.

☑ In early 1942, the Germans were advancing on all fronts, in Africa, Russia, and Europe; and it appeared that the allied cause was lost.

Connecting three clauses with these words produces a punchy effect and is acceptable when the clauses are short:

☑ It's raining, and I'm cold, and I'm hungry too.

☑ Johnny joined up and Jimmy was there and George got a sergeant's rating.

Don't give your right name, the army don't care, and the life is so fascinating. — Bertolt Brecht, "The Army Song" from *Threepenny Opera*

But if you connect three longer clauses with these words, it's sometimes better to group two of them, separating the third with a semicolon, which is stronger punctuation:

☹ It was raining, and I was getting soaked, but there was no bus coming.

☹ It was raining, but my umbrella was keeping me dry and the bus was coming soon.

☑ It was raining, and I was getting soaked; but there was no bus coming.

☑ It was raining; but my umbrella was keeping me dry, and the bus was coming soon.

☹ You can have fries with that, or you can have a salad, or you can just have your hamburger alone.

☑ You can have fries with that, or you can have a salad; or you can just have your hamburger alone.

As we have seen, two sentences may be joined by inserting connectives like **and, or, yet,** or **but** in between. But these will not work as connectives: **hence, however, otherwise, therefore,** or **then,** with or without a comma preceding:

🖛 With the exception of identical twins, no two people have exactly the same genetic makeup hence it is impossible for two non-twins to look exactly the same.

🖛 With the exception of identical twins, no two people have exactly the same genetic makeup, hence it is impossible for two non-twins to look exactly the same.

🖛 During the rainy season more water flows over Victoria Falls than over any other falls in the world, whereas several other falls are higher than Victoria.

🖛 You had better leave now otherwise we will call the police.

Inserting a semicolon, or splitting into two sentences, will work:

☑ With the exception of identical twins no two people have exactly the same genetic makeup; hence it is impossible for two non-twins to look exactly the same.

☑ During the rainy season more water flows over Victoria Falls than over any other falls in the world. However several other falls are higher than Victoria.

☑ You had better leave now. Otherwise we will call the police.

Punctuation

The Comma ,

Here are the occasions when a comma is required:

1. A list of more than two.

> I bought apples and oranges.
> I bought apples, oranges, and grapefruit.

Believe it or not, there's a long-standing and bitter controversy over the necessity of the comma following the next-to-last item on a list, the one preceding **and** or **or**. Some authorities are adamantly in favour of omitting it:

> I bought apples, oranges and grapefruit.

And some are ferociously in favour of putting it in:

> I bought apples, oranges, and grapefruit.

Are you willing to go to the barricades for one side or the other?[7] The main argument for leaving it out is that it saves space. (Really? It saves about 1 mm. Gimme a break.) The main argument for putting it in is that it occasionally prevents ambiguity of the sort that these examples exhibit:

---

7   If you want to get involved in this argument, you should know that a comma in that position is called the Oxford (or serial) comma.

WRITING WRONGS: COMMON ERRORS IN ENGLISH

🖐 **This book is dedicated to my parents, Ayn Rand and God.** (This makes it sound like the writers' parents were Ayn Rand and God. That's probably not what was meant.)

☑ **This book is dedicated to my parents, Ayn Rand, and God.**

🖐 **Lucy's Christmas purchases included a pair of gloves, a book, and an iPad and a chewy toy for her cat.** (Lucy's cat certainly deserves an iPad, but again, that's probably not what's meant.)

☑ **Lucy's Christmas purchases included a pair of gloves, a book, and an iPad, and a chewy toy for her dog.**

🖐 **Men, women and their money** (This *Toronto Globe and Mail* headline suggests that the article will be about men, on the one hand, and women and their money on the other. It was really about both genders and their respective approaches to money.)

☑ **Men, women, and their money**

Sometimes a comma helps when there's a long-winded and complicated list of two:

☹ **Every time I think about our summer in Paris I remember the fresh juicy peaches and plums we bought in the local street-market and the walks along the riverbank and the Champs-Élysées at dusk.**

☑ **Every time I think about our summer in Paris I remember the fresh juicy peaches and plums we bought in the local street-market, and the walks along the riverbank, and the Champs-Élysées at dusk.**

2. In between clauses:

As mentioned above:

☑ **I didn't expect Sheila to be home so early, but when I came in, there she was.**

except when the clauses are very short, where the comma is optional:

☑ **I'm ready and so is he.**

Note that when the clauses have a subject in common, a comma would be incorrect:

☑ **Leonard spent the night in a motel in San Diego and visited the zoo the next morning.**

In longer or more complicated sentences, omitting this comma can produce difficulty for the reader:

🖐 **Because of the work that we had done before we were ready to hand in the assignment.**

It looks like a sentence fragment, but its grammar is made clear by putting in the comma:

☑ **Because of the work that we had done before, we were ready to hand in the assignment.**

3. After introductions to a sentence, and around parenthetical remarks:

☑ Despite not knowing the language, I got along fine in Budapest.
☑ If Pat reads her email, she'll know that we're going to try to get to see her during our visit.
☑ I'm not sure, however, whether I'll be able to make it to the meeting.
☑ My brother, the guy you met earlier, wants your email address.

Be careful to include the second comma when this material comes in the middle of a sentence:

🖒 I'm not sure, however whether I'll be able to make it to the meeting.
🖒 My brother, the guy you met earlier wants your email address.

Again, when introductory material is very short, the comma can be omitted:
☑ I'm pretty tired. Moreover I'm fed up with the whole thing.

4. Sometimes between a list of adjectives:

Here:
☑ a larger, wider garage

but not here:
🖒 a boring, planning meeting
☑ a boring planning meeting

The difference is subtle. Here are two good tests to indicate when a comma is needed:

* When you can turn the phrase into something that makes equally good sense by reversing the order of the adjectives, then a comma is needed:
    a larger, wider garage → **a wider, larger garage** (So a comma is necessary)
    a boring planning meeting → **a planning boring meeting** (So omit the comma)

* When you can insert **and** between the two adjectives and get something that is equally acceptable, then a comma is needed:
☑ **a larger, wider garage** → **a wider and larger garage** (So a comma is necessary)
☑ **a boring planning meeting** → **a boring and planning meeting** (So omit the comma)

5. After a direct quotation:

There's a difference between US and UK usage here. In the US, double quotation marks are used, and the comma goes inside the final one. In the UK, single quotation marks are used, and the comma goes outside the final one.
☑ US: "I'm ready for anything," he said.
☑ UK: 'I'm ready for anything', he said.

For more about quoting, see the section on quotation marks, below.

6.   Adding information that's not essential.

Notice the slight difference between these two sentences:

Kaia's sister, Anna, is two years older than she is.
Kaia's sister Anna is two years older than she is.

The first suggests that Kaia has only one sister, whose name, parenthetically added, is Anna. The second suggests that Kaia probably has more than one other sister, and specifies that it is Anna who is being talked about.

Another example:

All my friends, who live in Halifax, will be invited.
My friends who live in Halifax will be invited.

Putting commas around **who live in Halifax** shows it is not part of the essential identification of the people being talked about. It happens that the speaker's friends all live in Halifax. But the second specifies that is those friends *who live in Halifax* (not anywhere else) who are being invited. It's part of the essential identification of the subject here.

A clause necessary for identification, restricting things or people to a sub-group, is called a *restrictive clause*. A clause that just provides by-the-way information is called a *non-restrictive* clause.

Here's how to distinguish between a restrictive clause and a non-restrictive one: if you can delete the clause, or put it into parentheses, without changing the essential meaning of the sentence, then it's non-restrictive.

So if these don't change the essential meaning you were trying to express,

All my friends will be invited.
All my friends (who live in Halifax) will be invited.

then the clause is not part of the essential identification; it's a non-restrictive clause and should be set off with commas.

But suppose that's essential information: you're inviting those of your friends who live in Halifax. Then leaving that bit out, or putting it into parentheses, changes the meaning. It's a restrictive clause, and does not get surrounded by commas.

A few more examples:

☑ **Philadelphia, where I was born, has grown considerably since then.**
☞ **Philadelphia where I was born has grown considerably since then.** (It's not necessary to identify which Philadelphia is being talked about as the one where the writer was born.)
☞ **The town, where I was born, has grown considerably since then.**
☑ **The town where I was born has grown considerably since then.** (Here it is essential; otherwise the sentence doesn't specify which town.)

We've been looking at clauses beginning with **who** and **where**. But now consider clauses beginning with **which** and **that**.

☑ **The cars I've owned, which have been Fords, have lasted well.**

☑ **The cars I've owned that have been Fords have lasted well.**

The commas tell you that the clause in the first sentence is non-restrictive — not essential to identifying what is being talked about; it just offers the information that all the speaker's cars have been Fords. But the second restricts the subject matter to those cars that were Fords.

The use of **which** to begin the non-restrictive clause, and of **that** to begin the restrictive clause, is not accidental. A long-standing, controversial, and often-ignored rule tells us to use **which** for non-essential, and **that** for essential identifying clauses. Doing this, as well as using commas properly, will give readers information about what you intended to communicate.

Is this **which/that** distinction just another old, useless superstition, one that belongs on the grammar trash heap? As usual, in formal writing you should obey even old, possibly moribund, and widely ignored grammar rules, in case a Stickler will read your writing. It's a difficult rule to apply,[8] and it's redundant, because the commas, used well, are sufficient. However, even though it's redundant, it will sometimes make for clearer unambiguous communication. If you want to write really well, it's a rule you should pay attention to.

Problems with **that**, **which**, **who**, and **whose** can often be avoided, and your writing similarly improved as well, by rephrasing and eliminating clauses starting with these words, making things shorter and therefore better. (Remember the mantra I gave you earlier? "SHORTER, BETTER." Repeat that 100 times.).

Notice how things are improved by this sort of rephrasing:

☹ **The ending, which comes as a surprise to most readers, is profoundly unsettling.**

☑ **The ending is both surprising and unsettling.**

☹ **The 2012 campaign, which had been carefully planned, was an enormous success.**

☑ **The carefully planned 2012 campaign was an enormous success.**

☹ **The surplus that we project for 2017 will probably be exceeded in 2018.**

☑ **The projected 2017 surplus will probably be exceeded in 2018.**

☹ **Eisenhower hired as his personal driver a woman who turned into a long-term friend.**

☑ **Eisenhower and his driver became long-term friends.**

Writers sometimes add a comma when they feel a sentence is getting long, regardless of whether one is needed or is appropriate. In general, it's not a good practice to put a comma just anywhere in a sentence where you'd naturally pause briefly, or take a breath. A frequent error is to insert one between subject and verb:

---

8   When the manuscript for my first book was returned to me by the copy-editor, every **which** was crossed out, and replaced with **that**, and every **that** replaced with **which**.

☞ **The ever-increasing gravitational pull of the global economy, is drawing almost every area of the earth into its orbit.**

☑ **The ever-increasing gravitational pull of the global economy is drawing almost every area of the earth into its orbit.**

The Question Mark ?

A common mistake in use of the question mark is using it in the indirect reporting of a question:

☞ **She asked me whether the quiz is scheduled for Friday?**

☑ **She asked me whether the quiz is scheduled for Friday.**

☑ **She asked me, "Is the quiz scheduled for Friday?"**

☑ **Did she ask you whether the quiz is scheduled for Friday?**

When a sentence includes a direct quotation, or a name of a publication, or a parenthetical remark, there are special (and sometimes odd-seeming) rules for the placement of question marks. See sections on these topics.

The Exclamation Mark !

This is for giving extremely strong emphasis to a statement:

☑ **Watch out!**

But this sort of thing occurs with any frequency only when somebody is quoted. Otherwise, sentences almost never need that sort of emphasis; so almost all uses are inappropriate. Exclamation marks should never appear in formal writing, but in informal writing (especially in email and tweeting), they should be used very sparingly. If you're older than 12,

This is the cutest cat ever!!!!!!!!!!!!!!!!!!

is really too much. A great deal of what you're saying might be extremely exciting, but remember that there are diminishing returns here: if exclamation marks occur often, they will cease to communicate urgency or emphasis, just as shouting all the time would. Overuse kills credibility. People will think maybe you should relax a bit, or will ask you if everything is alright.

> Of the 745 tweets sent out by Donald Trump during the first 139 days of 2017, 53% included an exclamation mark. Yuge!
>
> An especially inappropriate use of that punctuation occurred in a condolence tweet Trump sent:
>
> "Terrible tragedy in Tennessee. Melania and I send our condolences!"

On a typewriter (remember them?), the only way to make an exclamation mark was to type an apostrophe, backspace, and type a period under it. This pain-in-the-neck procedure discouraged the use of the exclamation mark, so it was a feature, not a bug, of that ancient technology.

The Semicolon ;

This has a variety of uses.

1. Linking closely related ideas.

A period might be used instead, but the semicolon signals to the reader the close relationship between the two ideas. In the following example the second sentence reinforces the statement of the first; a semicolon is thus appropriate, although a period is also correct:

- ☑ **This book is both exciting and profound. It is one of the best books I have read.**
- ☑ **This book is both exciting and profound; it is one of the best books I have read.**

Similarly, in the following example the second sentence gives evidence supporting the statement made in the first sentence. Again, a semicolon is appropriate:

- ☑ **The team is not as good as it used to be. It has lost four of its past five games.**
- ☑ **The team is not as good as it used to be; it has lost four of its last five games.**

2. Linking things in a list with punctuation inside them.

- ☑ **The following were told to report to the coach after practice: Jackson, Form 2B; Marshall, Form 3A; Gladys, Form 1B.**

The semicolon is a stronger punctuation than the comma. Consider:

> **We're thinking of setting up offices in London, and Paris, or Rome.**

This sentence doesn't make any clear sense. Different things may have been intended here.

- ☑ **We're thinking of setting up offices in London; or Paris and Rome.**

But this one clarifies things. It says that there are two possibilities being considered: London alone, or Paris and Rome both.

- ☑ **We're thinking of setting up offices in London or Paris; and Rome.**

This one similarly clarifies things. What's under consideration here is Rome plus one of the other two cities.

Got it? (But neither sentence makes it easy on the reader. There are longer, clearer ways of saying these things.)

Another example of this sort:

☞ **The law firms involved were Gornisht, Helfen, Moe, Larry, and Curly, and Itchy and Scratchy.** (You can't tell, but the firms are (1) Gornisht, Helfen; (2) Moe, Larry, and Curly; (3) Itchy and Scratchy.)

☑ **The law firms involved were Gornisht, Helfen; Moe, Larry, and Curly; and Itchy and Scratchy.**

Finally: as we noticed above, two clauses that could be independent sentences can be joined together by one of these words: **and, but, nor, or, so, yet, for,** with a comma preceding that word (or without if the clauses are short).

I like to go to the zoo, and I like to go to the movies too.

Bill Clinton's autobiography is interesting, but it's way too long.

I'll drive you to the airport or Sally will.

But when two clauses that could be independent sentences are joined together by one of these conjunctions: **accordingly, again, also, besides, consequently, finally, furthermore, hence, however, incidentally, indeed, likewise, moreover, namely, nevertheless, nonetheless, otherwise, similarly, still, that is, then, therefore, thus,** a semicolon must precede that word.

I'll be spending late Thursday afternoon at the dentist; accordingly, I'll have to miss book club that day.

Tarquin will be a post-doctoral fellow; that is, he'll be paid for a year of research with minimal teaching duties.

The Colon :

The most common uses of the colon are the following:

+ in headings or titles, to announce that more is to follow, or that the writer is about to list a series of things;
+ to introduce a quotation;
+ between two clauses, to indicate that the second one provides an explanation, or a definition, or a description of what was stated in the first.

Here are some examples:

☑ **UNQUIET UNION: A Study of the Federation of Rhodesia and Nyasaland.**

☑ **In the last four weeks he has visited five countries: Mexico, Venezuela, Panama, Haiti, and Belize.**

☑ **The theory of the Communists may be summed up in a single phrase: abolition of private property.**

☑ **Economists call this "stagflation": inflation coupled with economic stagnation (slow growth, unemployment).**

At least one side of a colon must be a complete sentence, whereas both sides of a semicolon (except in a list) must be. Mistakes in using a colon include the following:

+ Insertion between a verb or a preposition and its list of objects:

👎 In the last few weeks I baked: cookies, banana bread, and apple pie.

✓ ... I baked cookies, banana bread, and apple pie.

+ After the conjunction **that**:

👎 My teacher always told me that: nice girls don't chew gum, and it's always a good idea to be a little bit early.

✓ My teacher always told me that nice girls don't chew gum, and....

+ After an introductory word such as **for example, including, such as,** or **that is**

👎 I've always been fond of Szechuan dishes, such as: kung pao chicken, twice-cooked pork, and mapo tofu.

✓ ... Szechuan dishes such as kung pao chicken....

The Hyphen -

When two words function as a single unit of meaning, they come in several forms:

+ Always combined into one: **teaspoon, screwdriver, watchband, bookshelf, shipbuilder.**
+ Always separated into two words: **school bus, computer printer, steering wheel, health care.**
+ Always hyphenated: **baby-sitter, ex-marine, accident-free.**

How do you know which form is right?

👎 This Russian connection non-sense is merely an attempt to cover-up the many mistakes made in Hillary Clinton's losing campaign. — Donald Trump tweet.

✓ This Russian connection nonsense is merely an attempt to cover up....

Sometimes the two-word form presents ambiguities that are avoided by hyphenating. (The first ambiguity is spelled out for you in parentheses; see if you can find the others.)

👎 **an old furniture store** (is this an old store, or an antique store?)

✓ **an old-furniture store** (oh, okay)

👎 **a violent weather conference**

✓ **a violent-weather conference**

👎 **The worst paid job**

✓ **The worst-paid job**

👎 A stained glass window
☑ A stained-glass window

👎 A high school teacher
☑ A high-school teacher

Well, this last example may not really be ambiguous, because one way of understanding it is so (ahem!) unlikely, and the other way is rather automatic, given the very familiar coupling of **high** and **school**.

In many cases, two or three forms show up correctly. Sometimes this is a matter of how that form is functioning in a sentence. A frequent example of this is the compound adjective. When it comes before the noun it modifies, it's hyphenated; but it's separated into two words otherwise.

☑ This is a tax-free bond.
☑ This bond is tax free.

☑ I prefer a hand-operated coffee grinder to a manual one.
☑ My coffee grinder is hand operated.

☑ This is only a short-term plan.
☑ No change is planned for the short term.

☑ It's an open-ended question.
☑ That question is open ended.

Another relevant distinction is between compound nouns and the corresponding compound adjectives.

☑ They took a half-hour break.
☑ A half hour is allowed for the break.

☑ It's a fifth-storey apartment.
☑ The apartment is on the fifth storey.

☑ A fifteenth-century manuscript.
☑ A manuscript from the fifteenth century.

But sometimes there is one form considered correct, and this is a rather arbitrary matter.

> **checkbook** but **reference book**
> **cross-section** but **cross reference**
> **vice president** but **vice-consul**
> **six and one-half** but **six and one twenty-fifth**

When in doubt, check a good dictionary.

The Dashes – —

First I want you to look very closely at these three lines: - , – , — . Can you see that they're all different lengths? This is something most people don't notice. The first one is the hyphen, the one we've just been talking about. The next, larger two are dashes. The smaller one is called an *en-dash*, and the larger one is called an *em-dash*. The reason they got these names is because in many typefaces, the smaller dash is about the width of the character **n**, and the wider one is about the width of the character **m**. In the late stone age, when people still used typewriters, they made no distinction between the en-dash and the em-dash, both of which were usually typed with two hyphens in a row, with or without spaces before and after. Sometimes people just used a hyphen for all three. Now your computer can produce all three of them, and it's time you learned the difference.

The en-dash has some very restricted uses. It's most frequently used to mean *between the two items connected.*

The Second Boer War (1899–1902) is also known as the South African War.

The article is found in Volume XXIV of *Button Collecting Today*, pp. 593–602.

The November–March period is the low season for Alaskan cruises.

The Toronto–Montréal train trip takes about five hours.

The Ali–Frazier match in 1971 was called "The Fight of the Century."

Em-dashes are often used in much the same way as parentheses or a pair of commas, to set off an idea within a sentence.

Peterborough (home of Broadview Press) is a pleasant city of 81,000.

Peterborough — home of Broadview Press — is a pleasant city of 81,000.

A dash may also be used in place of a colon to set off a word or phrase at the end of a sentence, or as an alternative to parentheses when you want a passage to stand out more strongly:

He fainted when he heard how much he had won: one million dollars.

He fainted when he heard how much he had won — one million dollars.

Except when an em-dash sets off something at the end of a sentence, as in the example just above, em-dashes come in pairs. It's a good idea to restrict your use of them to one pair per sentence; otherwise things can get confusing. Used sparingly in a passage of prose, they can make things more vivid and less monotonous.

Parentheses ( )

Parentheses are used to set off an interruption in the middle of a sentence, or to make a point that is not part of the main flow of the sentence. They are frequently used to give examples, or to express something in other words using the abbreviation **i.e.** For example,

> **Several world leaders of the 1980s (Deng in China, Reagan in the US, etc.) were very old men.**

A parenthetical remark of this sort is used properly when it's removable from the sentence without any loss of sense or resulting grammatical problem. You can tell by this test that there's an error in these examples:

☞ **Elvis (and his entourage) were three hours late.**

☞ **Elvis were three hours late.**

☑ **Elvis (and his entourage) was three hours late.** (Yes, I know this sounds strange. See the discussion of this in the section on Subject-Verb Agreement, above.)

Parenthetical remarks are easily overused. If you find that your writing has more than one per page, consider deleting some. Here's a good rule to keep in mind, and to break just once in a while: if what you say in parentheses is important, put it into a non-parenthetical sentence of its own, or use commas or em-dashes instead. If it's not important, leave it out.

There are also a variety of minor uses for parentheses:

+ Citation (proper form for this kind of use is discussed in detail in Part VII):

☑ **And of course electricity had application way beyond simply providing lighting (Bryson, 2010, p. 132).**

+ Explanation of abbreviation:

☑ **This was decided in secret, inside the PMO (Prime Minister's Office).**

+ Birth and death dates.

☑ **The inventor of the ballpoint pen was John Jacob Loud (1844–1916).**

Be careful about using final punctuation:

☑ **I'm looking for peanut butter (and jelly).**

The parenthetical remark here is inside the main sentence, so the period ending the sentence goes outside the second parenthesis.

☑ **Is there any peanut butter left (or jelly)?**

Again the remark is inside the sentence, which is a question, so its question mark goes outside the second parenthesis.

☑ **I made myself a grilled peanut butter and banana sandwich (how delicious is that?).**

Here the parenthetical remark is a question, so it gets its own question mark.

☑ **I'm looking for the peanut butter. (And for the jelly.)**

Here the parenthetical remark is a separate sentence, with its own punctuation inside the parentheses.

Square Brackets [ ]

Square brackets are used for:

+ Parentheses within parentheses:

☑ **The CEO met with heads of all the divisions (Marketing, Shipping, Development [the head of this division arrived late], and Communications.)**

☑ **I've been collecting Chinese pottery (from the Song [960–1279] and Yuan [1279–1368] dynasties [but I'm not interested in the Ming dynasty (1368–1644)]).** (Get all that? The parentheses, square and round, are all correct, though there are less confusing ways of writing this information.)

+ Inside direct quotations, to show that the inserted explanatory words are not part of what was said:

☑ **Lentricchia claims that "in reading James's Preface [to *What Maisie Knew*] one is struck as much by what is omitted as by what is revealed."**

☑ **And, of course, she finished her thank-you speech for the award with "I couldn't have done all this without the help of [several people you've never heard of], and God."**

The Apostrophe '

Okay, PAY ATTENTION. This may be the most important part of the book. Why? Because misuse of the apostrophe is extremely common, and people who know how to use it will take apostrophe mistakes in your writing to be a sure sign that you're an uneducated slob. Really. This mistake attracts disdain more than any other. The fact that misuse is widespread doesn't make it any better.

It's very easy to avoid the most common apostrophe errors. Much simpler than some of the other things we've been talking about so far. SO PAY ATTENTION, okay? Sorry for yelling.

The two common uses for the apostrophe are for possessives and for contractions.

To make a singular noun possessive add an apostrophe and an **s: Saturn's rings; Trump's hair; New York's skyline; the manuscript's only error.**

There's some disagreement among grammar experts about what to do with singular nouns already ending in **s** or an **s-** or **z-** sound. But let's keep it simple: just add an apostrophe and an **s. Gladys's dog; the duchess's picnic; Katz's secret; Halifax's harbour; the wilderness's appeal; Descartes's Meditations.**[9]

For plural terms ending in **s**, just add an apostrophe: **My friends' dogs; cars' mufflers; his parents' rules.** For plural terms not ending in s such as **mice** and **men**, add an apostrophe and an **s: mice's holes, men's rooms.**

---

9 Some authorities rule that proper names from the Bible or antiquity that end in an s or z sound are an exception; they just add an apostrophe: **Jesus', Moses', Aristophanes', Socrates'.**

🖐 **Italy's Foreign Minister tapped to be the countries' next PM.** — the *Toronto Globe and Mail*

Countries' is the correct possessive form for the plural word **countries**.
☑ **The two countries' flags were flying at the border.**

But Italy is just one country. The plural of country is country's.
☑ **Italy's Foreign Minister tapped to be the country's next PM.**

BUT, and this is important, possessive pronouns just add **s**, no apostrophe: **its**, **theirs, ours, yours**. (**It's** is not the possessive form of **it**: the word is instead a contraction of **it is**. See below about contractions).
🖐 **The dog is looking for it's bone.**
☑ **The dog is looking for its bone.**
☑ **Their pizza has arrived.**
🖐 **The pizza which has just arrived is their's.**
☑ **The pizza which has just arrived is theirs.**
🖐 **It will be he's and I's responsibility ... to secure the nation....** — George W. Bush, in a nominating speech

By the way: both of these are correct:
☑ **For months, this sketch has been a preoccupation of Cameron Thomas's.** — the *Toronto Globe and Mail* [10]
☑ **... a preoccupation of Cameron Thomas.**

The **of** is sufficient to indicate possession.
    Here's another context in which the apostrophe is optional
☑ **The Cleveland Indians' logo**
☑ **The Cleveland Indians logo**

In the first phrase, the logo is said to be possessed by the team — thus the possessive. But in the second case, Cleveland Indians is used as an adjective. Compare: **at the Thursday meeting, at Thursday's meeting; the basement's door, the basement door.**

    IMPORTANT!: Despite what you see often, for example, in hand-lettered signs, the apostrophe is not merely a decoration to be inserted before any old **s**. In particular, plurals are almost never formed by adding **'s**:
🖐 **The boy's were out walking their dog's.**
☑ **The boys were out walking their dogs.**

Almost never. Some authorities very *very* reluctantly authorize the addition of **'s** to make a plural of an acronym, initialism, number, or letter, but it's much better just to add s when that won't make for trouble:

---

10 A fine point of grammar pointed out by the *Globe's* Public Editor.

☹ The GNP's of these twelve countries add up to half that of the US.
☑ The GNPs....

☹ The 1960's were the era of sex, drugs, and rock 'n' roll.
☑ The 1960s were the era of sex, drugs, and rock 'n' roll.

☹ In the European style, he writes a little crossbar through his 7's.
☑ In the European style, he writes a little crossbar through his 7s.

But in the following examples, those apostrophes to form plurals seem unavoidable, because of the confusing unreadability where they're left out:

☹ Mind your p's and q's.
☹☹ Mind your ps and qs.

☹ A list of do's and don't's
☹☹ A list of dos and don'ts

☹ I filed these with the a's and o's.
☹☹ I filed these with the as and os.

The second main use of the apostrophe is inside contractions, to show where something has been left out: **don't** (= **do not**); **can't** (= **cannot**); **I'll** (= **I will**); **he's** (= **he is/has**). Did you notice that double contraction inside **rock 'n' roll**, above? (= **rock and roll**).

It's easy to tell when you have a contraction: try replacing it with what it may be a contraction of:

I don't care what people say.
I do not care what people say.

The fact that the second is equivalent to the first shows that **don't** is a contraction, needing an apostrophe where the second **o** is left out of **do not**. This technique is useful where there's likely to be confusion. Are these correct?

I love they're dog.
You're dog is barking.
The dog has lost it's bone.

The apostrophes show that those words are contractions: **they're** contracts **they are; you're** contracts **you are; it's** contracts **it is/has**. Replacements of the contractions with the longer form yields these nonsense sentences:

I love they are dog.
You are dog is barking.
The dog has lost it is bone.

211

So we know that all three contractions are incorrect. What should have been in their place is **their, your,** and **its.**

They're/their, you're/your, and **it's/its** are the most widespread confusions. Here are some others.

☑ **There's a bat in the attic!** (contraction of **there is**)

☑ **The cat on the mat is <u>theirs</u>.**

☑ **<u>There</u> are some strange things going on.**

☑ **<u>We're</u> all going to see that movie tomorrow.** (contraction of **we are**)

☑ **<u>Were</u> you there yesterday?**

☑ **<u>Whose</u> car is that?**

☑ **<u>Who's</u> in that car?** (contraction of **who is**)

A word about acceptability of contractions. They used to be forbidden in formal writing. My first book manuscript (1987) came back from the copy-editor with every contraction crossed out and replaced by the expanded two-word version. Well, perhaps publishers were stuffier in those days. Perhaps they felt that contractions made things sound offhand and casual, inappropriate sounds for the output of a distinguished academic press, where solemnity was more in order. But nowadays, objections are much less frequent. Contractions make things sound more relaxed and natural and direct, less pompous and mannered. But again: know your audience. You might be faced with an old-school publisher or a journal that insists on formality (apparently more common in the sciences than in the humanities), or a reader who's offended. I didn't give all those sentences above with contractions in them a ⚠, but be aware.

Quotation Marks "

The main use of quotation marks is to show that the words are reported exactly as they were originally spoken or written. (Making changes in what's quoted, indicated by ellipses or material in brackets, is discussed below.)

For shorter quotations (maybe 50 words or fewer[11]), quotations are integrated into the text.

☑ **US Swimmer Ryan Lochte, commenting on his lie about having been the victim of a post-Olympics robbery, said, "I over-exaggerated that story."** (Do you like that term **over-exaggerated**? See section on Euphemisms below.)

---

11 The three major comprehensive style manuals give different advice about the length limit for "short" quotations, and some other minor disagreements. If strict adherence to one of these styles is required, see details in Part VI of this book.

The **US** notation above and below means that we're talking about the quotation-mark conventions that apply in the US (and Canada). There are differences, mentioned below, in the UK (and other English-speaking countries).

Longer quotations are normally printed in blocks indented left and right, and sometimes single spaced (if the main text is spaced wider), or in a smaller font. Do not put quotation marks before and after these.

In the example above, note the comma before the quotation's start, and the final punctuation — the period — inside the second quotation mark.

The same placement for a quotation that's a question:

☑ US She asked, "Where are you going?"

unless it's what's outside the quotation marks that's the question

☑ US Did he say, "I'm skipping class today"?

When the sentence continues after the quotation of a question, the question mark takes the place of the normal (US) comma,

☑ US "Where are you going?" she asked.

and (I knew you'd ask about this!) when the quoted material and the surrounding sentence are both questions, use only one question mark, inside the final quotation mark.

☑ US Did she ask, "Where are you going?"

But other punctuation goes outside the second quotation mark.

☑ US She said, "I'm skipping class today"; then she drove happily off to the beach.

☑ US He emphasized "the three chief weapons of the Spanish Inquisition": fear, surprise, and ruthless efficiency.

In the UK, the usual procedure is to use single-quotes (inverted commas) instead, and to place the final punctuation outside them:

☑ UK Swimmer Ryan Lochte, commenting on his lie about having been the victim of a post-Olympics robbery, said, 'I over-exaggerated that story'.

Quotations inside quotations use the alternative marks: single in the US, double in the UK:

☑ US According to Clinton's Press Secretary, "when the President said, 'I never inhaled,' he meant it."

☑ UK According to Clinton's Press Secretary, 'when the President said, "I never inhaled", he meant it'.

A different sort of use: Words that are being *mentioned*, rather than *used* to convey meaning, may be set off by quotation marks, single quotation marks, or italics:

The words "except" and "accept" are sometimes confused.

The words 'except' and 'accept' are sometimes confused.

The words *except* and *accept* are sometimes confused.

(Notice that this book sets these off by putting them in bold face type.)

Quotation marks are sometimes used to indicate that the writer does not endorse what's inside a word or a brief phrase. This means, in effect, *only so-called*, suggesting that what's inside is euphemistic, ironic, or false. These are sometimes called "scare quotes":

After a violent workout the weightlifters would each consume a "snack" of a steak sandwich, a half-dozen eggs, several pieces of bread and butter, and a quart of tomato juice.

My last "camping" trip, in an RV with a bathroom, a microwave, and air-conditioning, was actually enjoyable.

What are they doing in this sign? (photograph on the Internet):

STOP!
WASH YOUR
HANDS Before
Touching "A"
Puppy! "You"
Can-Pass-Germs
from Puppy-To-Puppy!

Because quotation marks may be used to convey the sense *supposed* or *so-called* (see above), other use sometimes creates unintentionally ludicrous effects.

"FRESH" "FRUIT"

I preferred to read this, my favourite hand-lettered supermarket sign, as implying that the stuff being sold was not really fresh, and was only supposedly fruit.

Here, however, is an intentional use:

Ivanka Trump has "written" a "book" — cover-line for column, the *Toronto Globe and Mail*

Compare the following two versions of the same report. The first one uses quotation marks to report what was said. The second uses them to express the writer's skepticism about the claim, and to hint that Yeltsin was actually drunk:

President Yeltsin appeared to stagger as he left the plane. "The President is feeling tired and emotional," his Press Secretary later reported.

A "tired and emotional" President Yeltsin appeared to stagger as he left the plane.

Do not, please, use quotation marks to be cute, or to indicate a pun or a slangy or informal word. These uses are annoying and tacky.

Signs sometimes use quotation marks for emphasis, or for some other purpose (who knows what).

Another important use of quotation marks is to surround names of:

- magazine and journal articles
- book chapters
- poems (except for long ones)
- short stories
- songs
- episodes of a TV series
- nicknames **(Tony "The Squid" Calamari)**

The Ellipsis ...

Those three dots are used to mark the place where something is left out of a direct quotation. You're allowed to leave things out when it's irrelevant to the reason you're putting the quotation in, or repetitious. This is a kindness to your readers. Suppose you're interested in quoting a historical authority who says:

During the seventeenth century, the Dutch, French, Spanish, Portuguese, English, and others, all struggled to maintain and extend colonies and trading-posts in distant corners of the globe.

But if you're writing about the Dutch only, then you'd want to condense this quotation to:

During the seventeenth century, the Dutch ... struggled to maintain and extend colonies and trading-posts in distant corners of the globe.

(Remember that these words have to be attributed to the authority who said them. Don't forget the footnote or parenthetical reference.)

It's wrong to use this sort of ellipsis to remove words that change the meaning, even in small ways. If Morty Schmidlap, movie reviewer for the *Rapid City Republican-Chronicle*, writes

This movie is really really terrible, far worse than any of Botticelli's earlier products; those were never great, but they were okay.

Then it's clearly immoral for the movie's ad agency to use the following in their advertising:

"This movie is really really ... great." — Schmidlap, *Rapid City Republican-Chronicle*

The use of ellipses to make a speaker sound bad by changing the meaning of a quotation is known colloquially in some journalistic circles as "dowdification," named after *New York Times* journalist Maureen Dowd, who has occasionally been guilty of this. In 2003, for example, Dowd wrote

"Al Qaeda is on the run," President Bush said last week. "That group of terrorists who attacked our country is slowly but surely being decimated.... They're not a problem anymore."

But what Bush said was rather different, and somewhat more likely to be true:

Al Qaeda is on the run. That group of terrorists who attacked our country is slowly, but surely being decimated. Right now, about half of all the top al Qaeda operatives are either jailed or dead. In either case, they're not a problem anymore.

An ellipsis is three dots, never more or less. But when you do this on a word-processor, it might take over and replace it with a single-character ellipsis. It has a space before and after.

Exactly how to use an ellipsis in direct quotations is discussed in detail below, in the beginning of Part VII.

A different, increasing, and very informal use of the ellipsis (without following period) is to indicate a trailing off of thought, or hesitation, or uncertainty:

After that argument, I wondered whether ... But then, could I face her when ... ? Well, what I mean, I guess, is ...

The Chicago Manual of Style advises that this use, suggesting "faltering or fragmented speech accompanied by confusion, insecurity, distress, or uncertainty," is appropriate in fiction, but hardly ever in expository prose. If you're confused, insecure, etc., about what you're writing, think more about what you want to say. Or at least try to cover up your insecurity.

The ellipsis is also seen in eighteen-year-olds' prose as a substitute for other punctuation:

So then I'm like walking down the hall ... and she's like what are you doing here ...
and I'm like this is my y'know spare period ... but she was like pissed off anyways ...

And sometimes it's used to create what the author thinks would be a dramatic pause:

> **Then, thirty years after dropping my wedding ring into the river, I cut open a fish and ... there it was!**

Of course all this is inappropriate in formal writing; be careful about using it elsewhere. A little goes a long way, maybe too long.

Italics

Publications[12]

Italics are used for names of:
+ books, newspapers, journals, and magazines
+ plays
+ long musical pieces
+ movies
+ television and radio programs
+ artworks
+ famous speeches
+ long poems
+ pamphlets
+ vehicles (ships, spacecraft, specially named trains)
+ sounds reproduced as words (**Fido's *grrrrr* indicated that the mail had arrived.**)
+ blogs

HOWEVER:

When a musical piece is named by type, number, and/or key (e.g., **Beethoven's Symphony No. 3, Bach's Violin Concerto in E Major**), no italics or quotation marks are needed.

No italics for titles of long sacred works (**the Bible, the Qu'ran**), or for titles of books of the Bible (**Genesis**), or sections of it (**The Sermon on the Mount**).

Newspaper names need italics. Official titles of newspapers only sometimes begin with **The**, and only sometimes include a place name. But a simplified way of referring to all of them is preferred. Here's one among several generally accepted systems:[13]

An initial **The** may be omitted, or included, no italics or capital, when things sound better. **The New York Times** is its official name, but:

☑ **I read it in the *New York Times*.**

---

12 Very detailed instructions for citation are given for the three main styles in Part VII of this book.
13 This one is from the latest *Chicago Manual of Style*.

Daily News and **The Independent** are their official names, but the place of publication should be added, italicized.

- ☑ I read it in the *New York Daily News*.
- ☑ I read it in the *UK Independent*.

Add an additional state or province name, abbreviated and in parentheses, if the location is less well known or ambiguous. **The Citizen Record** and **The Times** are their official names, but:

- ☑ I read it in the *Amherst (NS) Citizen-Record*.
- ☑ I read it in the *Ottawa (IL) Times*.

Adding a city name is not necessary when the newspaper is national or well known:

- ☑ I read it in *USA Today*.
- ☑ I read it in the *Wall Street Journal*.

Note that names of standalone single-episode TV shows are italicized, as are names of TV series, but names of episodes of series are enclosed in quotation marks.

- ☑ *Super Bowl XXIV*
- ☑ *Seinfeld*
- ☑ *Seinfeld*, Season 6, Episode 2, "The Big Salad."

When an exclamation mark or question mark is part of a title, that mark is italicized. If that ends a sentence, don't add a period.

- ☑ I enjoyed *Who's Afraid of Virginia Woolf?* (Question mark in italics)
- ☑ Do you have a copy of *The Grapes of Wrath*? (Question mark not in italics)

Non-English Words

Non-English words or phrases that have not been adopted into English should be italicized. Words that have been thoroughly anglicized, for example **bon voyage** and **mozzarella**, are not italicized. There will, of course, be cases in which it's not clear whether a word has become sufficiently English; a good test is to look it up in an English dictionary. Do not italicize long passages in another language; treat them as quotations instead. And do not italicize proper names.

Emphasis

You should use italics this way only sparingly, if at all. Sometimes writers italicize every word that they would emphasize if they were teachers speaking the text before a big audience of slow students. This is very tiresome. Don't do it.

An alternative way to emphasize words is to put them in boldface. Underlining is the equivalent of italicizing, which was not possible in handwriting or typewriting.

But now that your computer can produce italics, use that instead (unless for a separate way of setting off words, as in this book).

As mentioned above, you can use either italics or quotation marks when you are talking about a word, not using it:

👎 St Catharines is often misspelled

☑ *St Catharines* is often misspelled.

☑ 'St Catharines' is often misspelled.

☑ "St Catharines" is often misspelled.

Capitalization

There are a few simple rules for capitalization. Beyond that, everything gets murky.

Here are the simple ones:

+ Capitalize the first word of a sentence.
+ Capitalize the word I.
+ Capitalize proper names. Do not capitalize common nouns.

Here's a list comparing proper names and common nouns:

PROPER	COMMON
June	summer
Parliament of Canada	in parliament
Mother (used as a name)	my mother
Remembrance Day	in remembrance
Memorial Day	as a memorial
National Gallery	a gallery
Director	a director
Professor	a professor
the Restoration (historical period in England)	a restoration (the event of restoring something)
the Middle Ages (historical period)	middle age (period of life)
God	a god
Catholic (member of that church)	catholic (meaning universal)
Liberal (member of that party)	a liberal (holding those ideals)
Democrat (member of that party)	a democrat (holding those ideals)

Simple, right? Well, in most cases, yes; but sometimes things are not clear.

Suppose you're writing material for the website of Chattahoochee Valley Community College (Go Pirates!). It's clear that all four words are in the institution's proper name, so all four initial letters are capitals. But what about when the word **college** appears in the text like this:

? The College provides parking spaces for students in the east and west designated parking lots.

? The college will have a [Halloween] scary-themed chili and dessert cook-off beginning at 11:30 p.m.

Is the second word of that sentence a part of its proper name, so capitalized? Or is it a common noun, so lower case? The answer is, well, who knows. The actual website of that college deals with this problem by capitalizing the word in the first sentence above, but not capitalizing it in the second.

But here are some additional guidelines for particular cases:

When a word that's not ordinarily a proper name (e.g., **river**) is part of a proper name, it's capitalized:

☑ The Chattahoochee River forms half of the Alabama/Georgia border.

But where separated in a sentence from the rest of the name, it is not:

☑ Where Florida meets the southwest corner of Georgia, the Chattahoochee and Flint rivers converge to form Lake Seminole,

Capitalize days of the week (**Monday**), months (**July**), Holidays (**Labour Day**), eras (**the Scottish Enlightenment**), but not seasons (**summer**) or centuries (**the eighteenth century**).

Capitalize adjectives incorporating proper names (**Newtonian physics**), except where those names have lost contact with their adjectival meaning (**french fries**).

Capitalize the first word of a sentence even when it is a name that begins with a lower case letter:

☑ Rachel owns an iPod.
☑ IPods are ubiquitous.

See below regarding sentences beginning with numerals.

Names of academic subjects (**biology, philosophy**) are not capitalized (unless they are names of languages). Capitalize major words, not articles, short prepositions, or conjunctions, in the titles of books, articles, stories, poems, films, and so on.

✍ Robert Boardman discusses *The Bridge On The River Kwai* extensively in his book.

☑ Robert Boardman discusses *The Bridge on the River Kwai* extensively in his book.

Numerals

Should a figure be given using numerals, or written out?

? The building is 72 storeys tall.

? The building is seventy-two storeys tall.

220

There are two common ways of handling this:

1. Numbers of one or two words should be written out. Use figures for all other numbers.

2. Numbers of ten and below should be written out. Use figures for all other numbers.

But the first rule is ambiguous: is **twenty-four** one word or two? Anyway, you can take your choice here. You can also find other proposals. It doesn't really matter what rule you choose, as long as you're consistent.

Different systems for dealing with numbers all agree, however, that sentences should not begin with numerals. Either write out the numeral or rewrite the sentence.

🖐 **61% of eligible unregistered voters couldn't register because they didn't update their address.**

☑ **Sixty-one percent of eligible unregistered voters couldn't register because they didn't update their address.**

☑ **In the 2016 election, 61% of eligible unregistered voters couldn't register because they didn't update their address.**

But don't get ridiculous:

🖐 **Sixty-five million seven hundred forty-six thousand, five hundred forty-four people voted for Hillary Clinton, according to the count at December 11.**

If you want the number to be that exact, put it in numeral form in the middle of a sentence:

☑ **According to December 11 recount, 65,746,544 people voted for Hillary Clinton.**

However, it's normally better to approximate very large numbers; don't be afraid to combine numerals and words, substituting words for rows of zeroes, like this:

☑ **According to the December 11 recount, more than 65.7 million people voted for Hillary Clinton.**

Note that numerals are always used for dates and years; but write out numbers of centuries:

☑ **December 11, 2016 (or 11 December 2016)**

☑ **The twenty-first century**

Use numerals for scores:

☑ **The most lopsided game in college football history occurred in 1916 when Georgia Tech beat Cumberland 222–0.**

PART V: STYLE

Redundancy

When we speak or write, we tend to think of the words not one at a time, but rather in groups — modules — that get plugged in. These modules often contain redundancies, repeating the same thing, saying what doesn't need to be said over again.[1] So instead of saying **it's a necessity** we tend to say **it's an absolute necessity.** Instead of **appears to be** we tend to say **appears on the surface to be.** (What other sort of necessity or of appearance is there?) That sort of writing happens when you write with your brain turned down to simmer. It's sloppy, and it's annoying to the reader. It weakens your prose. Deletion of the unnecessary parts almost invariably results in more pleasing, stronger, and more convincing writing.

I'll give you a list of many of the very common overstuffed word modules you might find yourself using. In each case, the redundant, unnecessary part has been crossed out with strikethrough ~~like this~~. You'll notice that the crossed-out part can almost always be removed from a sentence without the slightest loss of meaning.

Here's how I suggest you use this list. Obviously, it will be impossible for you to look up every word module in something you're writing to see if it's on the list. What you should do instead is read this list, imagining sentences containing each module, and noticing how no meaning is lost and writing is improved when the struck-through portion is deleted. Doing this can make you aware of the production of overstuffed modules when you write and when you revise.

In many cases, these word modules come in different, related versions. For example:

~~advance~~ notice
~~advance~~ planning
~~advance~~ warning

---

1   Notice the redundancies in that sentence?

To save space, and because the advice is the same in all three cases, they have been combined into one item:

~~advance~~ (notice/planning/warning)

This means that you should choose one of the items separated by slashes inside the parentheses.

$20 million dollars *OR* $20 million ~~dollars~~

~~12~~ (midnight/noon)

3 am ~~in the morning~~

~~absolute~~ necessity

~~absolutely~~ (essential/nothing)

~~actual~~ (earnings/results)

(~~actual/true~~) fact

~~added~~ (bonus/plus)

~~adequate~~ enough *OR* adequate ~~enough~~

~~a distance of~~ 5 kilometers

admit ~~to~~

~~advance~~ (notice/planning/warning)

(advance/proceed) ~~forward~~

a few ~~short~~ years

after ~~the conclusion of~~

age/aged 75 ~~years old~~ *OR* age/aged 75 years old

aid ~~and abet~~

~~all-time~~ record

~~a myriad of~~

answer ~~back~~

~~any and~~ all *OR* any ~~and all~~

anything ~~at all~~

~~apparent~~ paradox

appears ~~on the surface~~ to be

~~approximately~~ about *OR* approximately ~~about~~

~~as far as~~ this essay ~~is concerned, it~~ will deal with

~~as~~ per

~~as to~~ whether

~~at a~~ later ~~date~~

(attach/assemble/associate/aggregate/ blend/bond/collaborate/collect/connect/ consolidate /combine/congregate/ connect/conspire/cooperate/couple/ gather/ join/meld/merge/mingle/mix / pool/share) ~~together~~

~~a total of~~ twelve people

~~audible~~ gasp

~~bare~~ naked

~~basic~~ (necessity/fundamental/essential)

because ~~of the following reasons~~

before leaving ~~the aircraft~~, please check ~~around your immediate seating area~~ for any ~~personal~~ belongings ~~you might have brought on board~~.

~~begin to~~ notice

(big/large/small) ~~in size~~

biography ~~of his life~~

(boarding/decision-making/evacuation/ healing/planning/rehabilitation) ~~process~~

both (alike/equal/together) *OR* both ~~(alike/ equal/together)~~

~~both~~ share

~~brief~~ (summary/moment)

~~broad~~ generalization

but nevertheless *OR* but ~~nevertheless~~

by ~~means of~~

can ~~be able to~~ do it *OR* can be able to do it

cancel ~~out~~

cannot help ~~but~~

(~~careful/close~~) scrutiny; ~~closely~~ scrutinize

cause of ... is ~~due to~~

close ~~down~~

~~closed~~ fist

~~co~~equal

~~common~~ bond

~~complete~~ (stranger/opposite/details/
shutdown)

~~completely/totally/absolutely/entirely/all
the more/partially~~ (full/empty/devoid/
effectual/superfluous/complete/
unanimous/essential/necessary/
fixed /free/off/positive/transformed/
surrounded/legal/perfect/true/engulf/
destroy/eliminate/fill/ finish/unique)

~~conclusive~~ proof

consensus ~~of opinion~~

consider ~~as~~

conspire ~~together~~

consult ~~with~~ someone

continue ~~on~~

~~co-~~(partner/conspirator/equal)

~~coveted~~ honor

(~~customary/usual~~) habit

cut ~~back~~

cut into ~~two~~ halves

(~~dead/deadly~~) serious

depreciate ~~in value~~

~~diametrically~~ opposed

disappear ~~from sight~~

discuss ~~about~~ something

divide ~~up~~

~~do~~ (damage/harm) ~~to~~

(doubtless/much/thus/first/second ...)~~ly~~

during ~~the course of~~

each ~~and every~~ OR ~~each and~~ every

~~early~~ beginnings

eliminate (~~altogether/entirely~~)

(emergency/crisis) ~~situation~~

end (product/result)

equal ~~to (each other/one another)~~

equally ~~as~~

every (~~last/single~~) (-one/person)

~~exact~~ same

~~exactly~~ (the same/identical/right)

fear ~~factor~~

~~fellow~~ colleagues

ferry~~boat~~

few ~~in number~~

fight ~~against~~

~~final~~ (conclusion/outcome/completion/result/
upshot)

first ~~and foremost~~ OR first ~~and~~ foremost

(~~first/originally/initially~~) conceived

~~first~~ priority

first time ~~ever~~

(first/second/third...)~~ly~~

focus ~~in~~ on

for ~~a combined total of twenty-four hours~~ a day

for ~~the purpose of~~

~~foreign~~ (imports/exports)

~~former~~ (alumnus/veteran)

~~fortuitous~~ (accident/coincidence)

~~free~~ gift

free ~~of charge~~

~~fresh~~ new OR fresh ~~new~~

~~fundamental~~ basis

~~future~~ (plans/prospects/outlook/potential/
forecast)

~~game~~ plan

~~general~~ (public/consensus)

harbinger ~~of things to come~~

hear ~~the sound of~~

he ~~is a man who~~

~~honest~~ truth

(hospital/prison/forest/university/etc.)
(~~setting/environment~~)

if ~~and when~~ OR if ~~and~~ when

if ~~at all~~ possible

~~important~~ essentials

I ~~myself~~

~~inadvertent~~ error

~~in a place~~ where

225

in ~~actual~~ fact

in any way~~, shape, or form~~

~~in~~ between

in close ~~proximity~~ to

~~in conjunction~~ with

~~increasingly~~ more *OR* increasingly ~~more~~

~~inner~~ (feelings/core)

~~in order~~ to

in some ~~size, shape, or~~ form

(inside/outside) ~~of~~ something

intensity ~~level~~

interact ~~with each other~~

investigate (~~about/into~~)

I pictured ~~in my mind~~

is ~~a~~ strange ~~one~~

is ~~located~~ in

I thought ~~to myself~~

I was unaware ~~of the fact~~ that

~~jam~~ packed

join ~~up with~~

~~joint~~ cooperation

(large ~~size~~/large-~~sized~~/large ~~in size~~) (*OR* medium... *OR* small...)

(large/small/grow) ~~in size~~

(lift/heat/open/hurry/divide/end/join) ~~up~~

linger ~~on~~

~~literally~~ true

(longer/shorter) ~~in length~~

lose ~~out~~

lower something ~~down~~

~~mainly~~ focuses on

~~manual~~ dexterity

many ~~different~~ (kinds/ways)

~~mass~~ exodus

(mean/seek) ~~for~~

~~mental~~ attitude

~~minute~~ detail

~~money-back~~ refund

~~most~~ especially

mutual advantage ~~of both~~

~~mutual~~ (agreement/exchange/cooperation)

near ~~to~~ something

~~new~~ (innovation/recruit/initiative)

none ~~at all~~

~~novel~~ innovation

(off/outside/inside) ~~of~~

~~old~~ adage

~~on a~~ (daily/regular) ~~basis~~

~~one and~~ the same

~~ongoing~~ commitment

on ~~the face of the~~ earth

~~outer~~ rim

~~over-~~exaggerating

~~pair of~~ twins

~~particular~~ interest

(~~past/prior~~) (history/memories/experiences/ records/achievements/precedents/track record)

pause ~~for a moment~~

~~personal~~ (opinion/friend/favourite/visit/ belongings)

~~personally~~ meet

~~personally,~~ I think

pervade ~~throughout~~

pick ~~and choose~~ *OR* pick ~~and~~ choose

~~place of~~ abode

plan (~~ahead/in advance~~)

~~please~~ RSVP

~~point in~~ time

~~polar~~ opposites

~~positive~~ (endorsement/improvement)

~~possibly~~ might

postpone ~~until later~~

~~potential~~ hazard

~~pre-~~(plan/record/condition)

proceed ~~forward~~

protest ~~against~~

~~qualified~~ expert

rate ~~of speed~~

razed ~~to the ground~~

reason ~~why~~

(reconsider/repeat/return/reiterate) ~~again~~

red *etc.* ~~in colour~~

re-elected ~~for another term~~

(refer/relate/revert/retreat/return/respond/
repeat/regress) ~~back~~ to

related ~~to one another~~

repeat ~~again~~

~~right~~ now

risk ~~factor~~

(round/square/triangular) ~~in shape~~

same ~~identical~~ *OR* ~~same~~ identical

~~school~~teacher

~~self-~~confessed

~~separate~~ pieces

~~sequential~~ order

~~serious~~ crisis

share ~~in common~~

shooting ~~incident~~

short ~~length of~~ time

(short/tall) ~~in height~~

(shower/thunderstorm) ~~activity~~

shrug ~~one's shoulders~~

~~single~~ most

~~so as~~ to

sooner ~~rather than later~~

~~specific~~ details

~~still~~ continues to

stressed ~~out~~

subject ~~matter~~

(such as/for example) *A, B, C* ~~etc.~~

(~~sum/combined/final~~) total

summarize ~~briefly~~

surrounded ~~on all sides~~

~~surrounding~~ circumstances

~~temper~~ tantrum

~~temporary~~ reprieve

~~terrible~~ tragedy

the estimated departure ~~time is now
scheduled for~~ 11:35

the future ~~to come~~

the last and ~~final boarding call~~

~~the month of~~ April

~~theoretically~~ possible

~~the question as to~~ whether

there is no doubt ~~but that~~

this ~~is a subject which~~ is

throughout the ~~entire~~

~~time~~ period

~~to be in~~ need ~~of~~

~~total~~ (annihilation/abstinence)

(~~ultimate/overall~~) goal

(underneath/inside/off) ~~of~~

~~unexpected~~ (surprise/emergency)

~~unfilled~~ vacancy

unless ~~and until~~ *OR* ~~unless and~~ until

until ~~such time as~~

~~up~~ until

various ~~different~~

~~very~~ tragic

visible ~~to the eye~~

warn ~~in advance~~

weather ~~conditions~~

whether ~~or not~~

while ~~at the same time~~

whole ~~entire/whole~~ entire

~~wide~~ (range/variety)

win ~~a victory~~

~~with a view~~ to

~~workable~~ solution

Acronyms frequently produce redundancy, when the last letter in the acronym stands for the word following it. For example: **ATM** is an acronym for **Automatic Teller Machine**, so an ATM machine is an Automatic Teller Machine machine. These redundancies are frequent and acceptable in speech, but probably best avoided in careful writing.

227

Other examples:

ABS system = Antilock Braking System system
AIDS syndrome = Acquired Immune Deficiency Syndrome syndrome
ATV vehicle = All Terrain Vehicle vehicle
CNN news network = Cable News Network news network
HIV virus = Human Immunodeficiency Virus virus
LCD display = Liquid Crystal Display display
NATO organization = North Atlantic Treaty Organization organization
OPEC countries = Organization of the Petroleum Exporting Countries countries
PC computer = Personal Computer computer
PDF format = Portable Document Format format
PIN number = Personal Identification Number number
SCUBA apparatus = Self-Contained Underwater Breathing Apparatus apparatus
SUV vehicle = Sports Utility Vehicle vehicle
UPC code = Universal Product Code code

Filler

A number of people, y'know, load up their talk, I mean, with, like, bits of, um, basically, like meaningless time-wasters, y'know? This might serve the purpose of stalling, when they're trying to give their brains time to catch up to their mouths. But that's not necessary in writing; you can write as slowly as your brain speed requires; but bad writing is often loaded with little space-wasting fillers that really should have been left out. Useless fillers are just as harmful to your writing as redundant word modules.

The list below gives common phrases that are very likely to show up uselessly in writing. As above, look through this list and imagine each bit puffing out a sentence. Then be aware of avoiding this sort of thing when you write or revise.

Note that many of these phrases have legitimate uses. They're a problem when they're just inserted uselessly.

actually	as (you/we) all know	I might add that
aforementioned	basically	in a manner of speaking
after all was said and done	by and large	in a very real sense
all things considered	by definition	in actual fact
as a matter of fact	by the same token	in actuality
as a whole	fact of the matter	in essence
as far as I'm concerned	for all intents and purposes	in fact
as regards	(from/according to) my point	in itself
as stated earlier	of view	in my opinion
as the case may be	honestly	in nature

in reality	it has come to my attention	needless to say
interestingly enough	that	obviously
in terms of	it is (clear/evident/apparent/	on the subject of
in the final analysis	crucial/important/	quite clearly
in their own right	interesting) to note that	that being said
it appears	it seems as though	the point I'm trying to make
it can be seen that	it should be (noted/pointed	what I mean to say is
it goes to show that	out) that	when you get right down
	more or less	to it

Overblown Language

This section is like the previous one on bloated language. There, the emphasis was on expressions that were redundant and that should be made shorter by deletion. Here, we again have expressions that are too big and complicated, but these can't be fixed by deletion; instead, writing is improved by substituting another expression that is shorter, clearer, and more direct.

Simplicity and brevity were not always so important. Here's a typical sample of writing from an 1867 issue of the *Toronto Globe*:

> It is deeply to be deplored that men who had earned the admiration of the people of British America by long years of able and patriotic public service, should allow the passing disappointment of the hour to betray them into the unseemly attitude they now hold.[2]

By the standards of the day, that was good writing, but it's far too complex and pompous-sounding for our taste. But this is not completely a matter of arbitrary fashion. Good writing nowadays is much kinder to the reader than that elaborate old-fashioned stuff. Of course, this is true partially because we have become used to the new sparse style, so we labour over the earlier style to an extent that readers in 1867 wouldn't have.

Nobody's tempted now to write in that nineteenth-century style, but that does not mean that everyone writes clearly and simply. Overblown expression these days comes in various forms, but it's often the result of the writer's desire to impress — yet it has the opposite effect. Pompous overblown language just annoys. What will really impress readers is writing that uses ordinary words, and brief, clear, and direct expression.

---

2 The *Globe* was criticizing Joseph Howe, former premier of Nova Scotia, who opposed his province's entry into the new union of provinces that would be Canada.

229

Here are some examples of overblown language.

> **Please** be advised that commencing Monday, August 29th 2016, Atlantic Ventilation will be cleaning all unit exhaust vent lines. Work will commence at 8:30 am each morning and is expected to take one week to complete. Cleaning will be completed from the balcony access panels. Entry will be required with the Superintendent through each unit. This job is weather permitting and should rain disrupt the cleaning during the week, it may be necessary to carry the cleaning into the following week. We ask for your assistance to ensure access is granted through the unit to the patio. Cleaners will commence on the 12th floor and work their way down. — posted notice from a condominium management

Here's my rewrite:

> **Beginning** Monday, August 29th, Atlantic Ventilation will be cleaning exhaust vent lines in all apartments. The work is expected to take a week, but longer if there are rain delays. They'll be working from the 12th floor down, beginning at 8:30 a.m. each day. Cleaning will be done through the vent panels on the balcony, so please allow the workers and the building superintendent to get there through your apartment.

This replaces 111 words with 70, and it sounds like it's written by a human being, not a corporation.

The next sample was written by a spokesperson for Niagara (Ontario) Catholic School District Board. After five of their elementary schools almost simultaneously cancelled a previously booked presentation of a play advocating tolerance for kids who are troubled about their gender identity, all claiming last-minute discovery of scheduling conflicts, the *Toronto Globe and Mail* newspaper asked whether this reflected a board policy. Here's the email reply:

> **As** a fully inclusive and supportive Catholic Board for all students and staff, decisions regarding offering presentations to students from community members are made upon individual consideration and review. We will continue to follow our process when presentations are offered to be delivered within our school communities.[3]

This is bureaucratic talk designed *not* to communicate.

Overblown language is verbose, repetitive, woolly, pompous, overly abstract, or vague. Often it simply results from the use of fancy words where plain ones would do. Here is a table listing overblown words and phrases and better, simpler replacements.

Note: In some cases there are subtle meaning differences between the verbose items in the left column and the plain item in the right. Then this replacement might be a bad idea. Also: a desirable feature of good writing is variety (and a

---

3   Did you notice the dangler in this splendid example of bureaucratic blather?

certain level of educated diction). So you'll need to consider whether a simplification would eliminate overblown language or just make what you write dull and repetitious.

a (bigger/greater/higher/larger) degree of	more
accede to	agree to, allow
accommodation(s)	room
accompany	go with
accorded	given
acquiesce	agree
acts of a hostile (character/nature)	hostile acts
address [*verb*]	deal with? talk about?
a decreased number of	fewer
adjacent to	next to
advantageous	helpful, useful
adversely impact on	hurt, set back
advise	tell
afford an opportunity	allow, let
alleviate	ease
a (large/small) number of	(many/few)
all of a sudden	suddenly
almost never	seldom
along the lines of in the nature of much the same as	like
annex [*verb*] append	attach
answer in the (affirmative/negative)	answer (yes/no)
any and all	any? all?
a number of	some
appear	look, seem
apprise	tell
approximately in the neighborhood of	about
are deserving of	deserve
are in (agreement/agreeance)	agree

arrive	come
as a consequence of due to the effects of (due to/in light of/in view of/owing to/on account of/ considering) the fact that for the reason that on the grounds that	since, because (of)
as a means of	to
ascertain	find out
as of late of late	lately
as regards concerning in connection with in regard to in relation to in respect of pertaining to regarding relating to with reference to with regard to with respect to	about
aspect component element portion	part
(a/the) majority of	most
at the conclusion of subsequent to	after
at the earliest possible date forthwith in a timely manner in the (near/not-too-distant) future sooner rather than later with a minimum of delay without further delay	now, quickly, soon, as soon as possible
at the end of the day	someday? finally? everything considered?

at the same time that during such time as during the (period/time) that (during/in the course of) for the duration of in the course of	while
at present at this moment in time at this particular point in time at the present time	now
attain	reach
attired	dressed
basic fundamentals	basics
bestow	give
brings to mind	recalls? suggests?
buy-in	commitment, agreement
came to a realization	realized
capability	ability
capable of being	can be
cast [verb]	throw
cease cease and desist desist	stop, end
challenge concern issue situation	problem
circumvent	avoid
cognoscenti	experts, authorities
commence inaugurate initiate institute [verb]	begin
complete finalize	finish
complimentary continental breakfast	free muffins and coffee
conceal	hide

conceptualization	idea
conduct an investigation into	investigate
constitutes	is, makes up
cutting-edge state-of-the-art	latest
deem	consider, judge, think, treat as
delineate	describe
demise decease pass pass on	die, death
depart	go, leave
depend upon	depend on
(de-/em-)plane	get (off/on)
(regardless of/notwithstanding/irrespective of) the fact that	although, even though, despite
detain	hold
dialogue [*verb*]	discuss
disburse	pay
discontinue	stoop
discover	find
disseminate	spread
donate	give
effect modifications	change
effectuate	carry out
elucidate	explain, make clear
emolument	pay
employ (an instrument) utilize	use
make an effort/attempt endeavour [*verb*]	try
enumerate	count
envisage	expect, imagine
eventuate (in)	happen, result (in)
evince	show

exhibit	show
exhibits a tendency has a tendency	tends
expedite	hasten
expeditiously	quickly
expend	spend
expiration, expiry	end
extend to	give to
fabricate	make, make up
facilitate	help
fail to comply with	violate
feedback	opinion, reaction
fetid	stinky
few and far between	rare
finalize	complete
focus on	discuss? keep in mind? consider? think about?
for the purpose of	to
gainful employment	paid work
gain entry into	enter
give an indication of	indicate
give consideration to take into consideration	consider
going forward on a go-forward basis	from now on
has a requirement for	needs
has the (ability/opportunity/capability/ capacity) to is able to is capable of is in the position to	can
have a negative attitude	be critical? pessimistic?
have a (wish/hope/expectation/understanding)	(wish/hope/expect/understand)
have the responsibility for	must
head up	lead

235

heads-up	warning, latest information
henceforth	from now on
hitherto	until now
hold a belief	believe
hold in abeyance	wait, postpone
if it should (happen/transpire) that in the (event/eventuality) that under the circumstances in which	if
imbibe	drink
impacts on	has an effect on
implement [*verb*]	put into effect
in a positive fashion	approvingly
in a situation in which on the occasion of under circumstances in which	when
in all likelihood in all probability it is likely that	probably
in an ad-hoc way on an ad-hoc basis	ad hoc
in any way, shape, or form	at all
inception	beginning
in close proximity to in the vicinity of	near
indicate	say, show
individual	person
in every instance at all times	always
in excess of	more than
in lieu of	instead of
innumerable	many
input	comments, response
inquire request [*verb*] solicit	ask (for)

in short supply	scarce
(in spite/regardless of the fact) that	although
interface [*verb*]	interact
interrogate	question
in the (affirmative/negative)	yes/no
in the event of	if
in the majority of cases	usually, most
in this day and age	today, now, these days
in three days' time	in three days
intimate [*verb*]	suggest
is aware of the fact that	knows that
is scared of	fears
it goes without saying that	obviously
it is incumbent upon me to	I (must/should)
it is only a matter of time before	eventually
it would appear	it (appears/seems)
last but not least	finally
liaise with	meet with? work with? discuss with?
looking to	hoping to? expecting to?
luncheon	lunch
made out of	made from? made of?
make (an arrangement/a plan/a decision/an inquiry/an acquisition/an attempt)	(arrange/plan/decide/ask/get/try)
manifested	shown
manner	way
marginal	small
necessitate	require
not later than	by
occasion [*verb*]	cause
on a (case by case/regular/day-to-day) basis	(individually/regularly/daily)
on numerous occasions	often
on the face of the earth	anywhere
on the part of	by
opt for	choose

optics	look [*noun*]
options	choices
over and over again time and time again	repeatedly
paradigm (in non-technical use)	model? pattern? structure? formula? point of view?
parameters (in non-technical use)	limits or measures of a system
peruse	read
place [*verb*]	put
point the finger at	blame
portion	part
possess	own, have
predominant	main
present [*verb*]	give
presently	soon? or now?
preserve retain	keep
previous to prior to	before
prior	earlier
proceed	go (ahead)
provides (guidance/leadership/help) for	(guides/leads/helps)
purchase	buy
relate	tell
remain	stay
remainder	rest
remove	take away, haul off
rethink	review, reconsider
share this with you	tell you this
subsequently	later, afterward
subsequent to that time	after that
sufficient	enough
summon	send for, call
synergy	the improvement resulting from working together

take issue with	disagree with, challenge
terminate	end
the fact of the matter is that	in fact
the fact that I had arrived	my arrival
thereafter	then
the thought process	thinking
transmit	send
transpire	happen
utilize	use
valid	true
viable	practical, workable
virtually	almost
visualize	imagine, predict
whereas	since
with the exception of	except for

(If you have studied Latin, you might notice that the left-hand column above contains many words with Latin roots, with corresponding right-hand-column words of Anglo-Saxon origin. This is no coincidence. Words derived from Anglo-Saxon are almost always more emphatic, clearer, shorter, and more concrete and direct than their Latinate equivalents.)

The Thesaurus

Back when there were books, a thesaurus was one that gave, for each word listed, a large number of synonyms or closely related terms. So you could look up a word like **dig** and find: "delve, spade, mine, excavate, channel, deepen, till" and on and on. With the use of this reference work, you could turn a very ordinary sentence like **The cat sat on the mat** into the much fancier **The feline was situated atop the floor covering**. You know already that this is not a good idea. A thesaurus in book form, however, was extremely useful: rip out all the pages, crumple them up, and use them for starting a charcoal fire. Unfortunately, however, the printed-paper thesaurus has been replaced by a computer app that's probably lurking in a corner of your word processor. This is not useful for starting fires.

Biased or Insulting Language

Worries and Motives

The obvious principle for writers — indeed, for everyone — is to avoid unnecessary offence or insult. But authors react to this in different ways.

Authors who intentionally use what is claimed to be insulting language do not necessarily do so from sexism or racism or insensitivity to the feelings of the disabled. Instead, they may be insisting on a right to free expression, or refusing to use what are sometimes awkward or distracting or downright ridiculous "politically correct" substitutions for such language. In doing so, they of course run the risk of creating genuine offence, but they might consider this not to be *unnecessary* offence. When they intentionally raise such political issues while writing about something else, they distract readers from the point of their writing, but sometimes they regard such distraction as valuable, because it will inject the political issues they want to raise into writing on other topics.

These attitudes shouldn't be summarily brushed off. There is considerable value in unrestricted free expression. And it's clear that some of the judgements that particular bits of language are offensive (or might be) are the result of oversensitivity. Support groups and social workers and university committees keep imagining new insults in old words, and sometimes they almost talk their clients/students into thinking or pretending that these words hurt. It's also clear that some of the suggested replacements result in distorted and peculiar writing. And one might reasonably ask about some of the condemned terms whether their presence in writing actually produces any harm, and whether any harm is cancelled or counteracted by their replacements. Even the most sincere and enthusiastic enemy of sexism and racism must answer this question: will removal of the nasty bits of language actually *result* in any political change?

Ostentatiously leaving offensive bits of language in writing raises distracting political issues, but so does replacing them by awkward and unconventional euphemisms. Some of those advocating this language reform intentionally seek these distortions, because they also want to remind readers of the political issues involved here. But there is another point to consider. A replacement may produce disruptive side-effects at first, but these tend to disappear with continuing use. Obvious examples of this are the replacement of the supposedly sexist term **chairman** by the gender-neutral term **chair**; and the introduction of the title **Ms**. At first, both seemed unnecessary to some people, absurd to others, and awkward to many; and the words distractingly screamed their political point to everyone. But by now they have become normal, accepted, even unnoticed.

Anyway, there is a third point of view about all this. Many authors want to avoid language that genuinely insults or shows bias but are doubtful about some of

240

the latest hypersensitive additions to the taboo lists. And they're also interested in avoiding the linguistic messes that result from some substitutions. They'd rather avoid distracting and irrelevant political gestures one way or the other. So they want to sort out what's genuinely offensive from what's not, and to find ways that won't trash their writing to avoid the former.

There are, of course, unquestionably insulting, politically retrograde, nasty bits of English that ought to be avoided: **spic, wop, nigger, kike, homo, fag, dyke, retard**…. There's no problem recognizing them, and except when discussing awful language, or when putting words into the mouth of fictional bigots, these offensive epithets must be avoided. That's easy to do.

There are many less-awful terms that are now fairly widely considered offensive, but it's hard to identify them. They're not always identified as such in dictionaries. You can easily find lists of all sorts of supposedly objectionable expressions on the internet, but these lists will often be either collections of obviously awful, nasty slang expressions (and there are hundreds of them), or attempts to include just about anything that anybody has found objectionable, often absurdly. A third possibility is that a list is a satire, concocted by an enemy of "political correctness" including piles of bizarre and ridiculous items.

You should avoid the obviously horrible, of course, and ignore as well the suggestions that are the result of absurd oversensitivity to insult and absurd undersensitivity to language. Identifying what's in between is the problem.

But here's an important point. If it seems that some term is felt to be genuinely objectionable by a significant number of people, it's better to avoid or replace it, however you feel about it.

In addition to the necessity of avoiding offence, there's a very good pragmatic reason why you should be aware of, and be careful to avoid, what's considered biased or offensive speech: speech codes are taken very seriously these days by corporations and government, and especially by universities, and violations can result in re-education or dismissal or litigation or punishment. Whatever your views on any of the issues above, for your own good you had better be careful.

It's obvious that the issue of bias in language provides problems for writers. So what to do about it?

Replacement

Consider first words with **man** (or **men**) or other gender indicators inside them. Replacement can sometimes be made smoothly, in a way that grinds no political axes and creates no attention-getting terminological absurdities. Here is a list of some of them, with the smooth replacement for each in the right column:

bellboy	bellhop
chairman	chair
fireman	firefighter
foreman	manager, supervisor
freshman	first-year student
garbage man	garbage collector
infantryman	foot soldier
mailman, postman	letter carrier, mail carrier
mankind	humans
policeman	police officer
stewardess	flight attendant
weatherman	weather reporter
workman	worker

And, of course, **man** meaning *human*. The crew of the Starship *Enterprise* was quite slow on this matter. As late as the twenty-third century, their catchphrase was still **To boldly go where no man has gone before**. But during the twenty-fourth century, they smartened up and replaced it, smoothly, with **To boldly go where no one has gone before**.[4]

But questions can be raised about how well other proposed replacements work. These don't seem to work well at all:

alderman	councillor
businessman	business person, entrepreneur
cave man	cave dweller
con-man	con-artist
draftsman	drafter
fisherman	fisher
gunman	shooter
headmaster	principal
housewife	housekeeper, homemaker
longshoreman	ship loader, stevedore
man-hours	work hours
manmade	handmade, human-made, constructed, simulated
middleman	intermediary
night watchman	night guard, night watch
repairman	repairer
unsportsmanlike	unsporting
waitress	waitperson, server
weatherman	weather forecaster

---

4   *Star Trek*, original series (1960s), and revival (1980s and 1990s), respectively. See section above for discussion of this split infinitive.

Some of these replacements seem very awkward and will call attention to themselves when used. Others seem inexact.

Alderman and **headmaster** are often official titles. Until the councils and schools change these, it will continue to be necessary to use these words in many contexts.

Businessperson is a very awkward replacement for **businessman**; using that term will trip up some readers, and will likely introduce gender-bias issues that will distract readers from the point of your writing. **Entrepreneur** is quite different in meaning.

Cavemen are cave-dwellers, but there's a robust stereotype expressed by the word **caveman**, and a metaphorical derivative, neither of which are captured by **cave-dweller**. (Of course, maybe you want to be respectful of our very early long dead human ancestors, and avoid this stereotype, but that's another matter.)

Fisher has a long way to go before it comfortably replaces **fisherman**.

Gunman refers to a person who is armed with a gun, or expert in its use, or a person who uses it in a crime without necessarily shooting it; so **shooter** is often a poor substitute. (In addition, it suggests, as **gunman** does not, a basketball player who aims to score, or a piece in a marble-game.)

Weather forecaster is an imperfect substitute for **weatherman**, because the person on TV who reads the weather forecast is usually just another TV talker, not a real meteorologist.

And the following **man** words don't have any very obvious smooth replacements: **backwoodsman, layman, sportsman, handyman, watchman, pitchman, highwayman, craftsman, layman, statesman, bagman, baseman, brinksmanship, grantsmanship, horsemanship, marksmanship, salesmanship, workmanship, penmanship, everyman, bogeyman, superman, snowman, manslaughter, manpower, manhunt, manhole, man-handle, man-eater, man o' war, straw man argument, man-in-the-street, man-in-the-moon, manned spaceflight.**

Between the smooth and problematic, there are many suggested replacements that some people will find awkward or inexact, while others will find them smooth and precise. Here's a list of some of these:

actress	actor
cleaning lady, maid	cleaner, house worker
clergyman	minister, member of the clergy
congressman	representative
mankind	humankind, people, humanity, humans
manly	self-confident, courageous, straightforward
salesman	salesperson, sales agent, sales associate, sales representative, member of the sales force
spokesman	spokesperson, representative

243

gendered pronouns he, his, him, she, hers, her. Simple replacement strategies for these are often not terribly satisfactory. One widely tried response is to substitute **he or she, his or her, him or her.** This produces a somewhat lumpy sentence, and in some cases a real monstrosity:

☹ **Everyone at the meeting is interested in explaining his point of view even though he can see that it bores his colleagues.**

☹☹ **Everyone at the meeting is interested in explaining his or her point of view even though he or she can see it bores his or her colleagues.**

A second strategy is to replace all such pronouns with female ones, or to alternate male pronouns with female. Some people will not find this jarring. Here's an example that might bother everyone:

☞ **At the high school reunion, everyone talked about her teachers. When somebody mentioned his old gym teacher, everyone tried to think of her name. She finally came up with it, and everyone who remembered him had a story to tell about her.**

Another strategy is to use **their** or some related word as the relative pronoun for a singular subject:

✍☹ **Everyone at the meeting is interested in explaining their point of view even though they can see it bores their colleagues.**

☞ **Only one person introduced themself.** (*not a word*)

☞ **Only one person introduced theirself.** (*not a word*)

Peculiarly, in the first sentence the subject **everyone** takes a singular verb **is**, but (traditionally) plural pronouns, **they, their.** Does this sort of use show that **they** and **their** are mutating, and can now be taken as singular as well? Not really. Look at this typical example:

✍☹ **You can't make assumptions that a student did not have enough support or that they were not doing well academically.** — Dr. Brenda Whiteside, Guelph University Associate Vice-President of Student Affairs, quoted in the *Toronto Globe and Mail*

Here, **they** refers back to the singular noun phrase **a student**, but it takes the plural verb **were**. While this kind of thing gets around sexism, there doesn't seem to be any way to understand it that is grammatically coherent. It will seem annoyingly ungrammatical to Sticklers for sure, but to many other readers/hearers as well. On the other hand, this usage is becoming more frequently adopted and more frequently accepted. Maybe it's time everyone tried to get used to it?

For further discussion of this problem, see the entry their/them/they/theirselves/them selves/themselves/themself in the dictionary, "Meanings, Uses, and Idioms," above.

Other Problems

The following table lists a number of sometimes-condemned terms referring to physical or mental problems, diseases, or disabilities, with their sometimes-suggested replacements. You may find objections to some of these terms to be absurd or oversensitive, or their suggested replacements unsatisfactory for a variety of reasons. But replacements such as these are often officially required in official writing for certain disciplines or for certain audiences. Find out!

deaf	hearing-impaired (*although this also has been criticized*)
is confined to a wheelchair is wheelchair-bound	uses a wheelchair is a wheelchair-user
the mentally retarded retardation mentally deficient	person with developmental delay person with cognitive disability
birth defect	congenital disability
is able-bodied	does not have a disability is non-disabled
drug abuser	drug user/misuser
mentally ill person	person diagnosed with a psychiatric disorder
(afflicted with/stricken with/suffers from/victim of) muscular dystrophy (*etc.*)	has muscular dystrophy (*etc.*)
blind	*restrict* blind *to total loss of sight; otherwise, substitute* (limited/low) vision, visually impaired
the disabled person	the person, who has a disability,
epileptic fit	epileptic seizure
dwarf midget	person with short stature little person person with dwarfism
alcoholic	person with alcoholism

And, of course, there have been replacement suggestions that are widely viewed as absurdly euphemistic and non-communicative. Is the suggestion that instead of saying **a fat person** we say **a person of size** serious, or a parody intended to trivialize the whole issue?

A routinely used description is found in this headline from the *Toronto Globe and Mail*:

245

- ☹ **School board says it acted to keep students safe from special-needs pupil with behavioural issues**

and the story below it talks about this pupil in the same terms. Do you understand what sort of child they're talking about, and why others needed to be kept safe? We can appreciate the newspaper's desire to be respectful, but this sort of language does not communicate much information.

The word **gay** has been widely accepted as a replacement for **homosexual**, but, because this is supposed to be too narrow in its scope, the acronym **LGBT** (**Lesbian, Gay, Bisexual, Transsexual**) has achieved substantial currency. But recently this too has sometimes been deemed inadequate for the variety of sexual categories that should be recognized, and one suggested replacement is **LGBTTIQQ2S: Lesbian, Gay, Bisexual, Transsexual, Transgendered, Intersex, Queer, Questioning, and Two-Spirited.** We will see if this term proves too ungainly to achieve general use.

The Workaround

I emphasize again: *it's most important that writers avoid language with a genuine potential to offend someone.* But in some cases smooth substitution is not available, and suggested replacements would be distracting and awkward. Some writers are not out to make a political point and are thus wary of oversensitive or awkward or distracting replacements, which raise partisan issues. For them, in these cases, the best policy would be to work around these difficulties — to rephrase, rather than merely replace. This sentence is widely found insulting:

- ☹ **Jordan has a birth defect but his twin sister is normal.**

But it's not improved by a recommended substitution:

- ☹☹ **Jordan is differently abled congenitally but his twin sister is enabled.**

However, it can be fixed by rewriting:

- ☑ **Jordan was born with a disability but his twin sister was not.**

Similarly:

- ☹ **Arnold worked summers as a longshoreman.**
- ☑ **Arnold worked summers loading and unloading ships.**

- ☹ **I spent all day at home waiting for the repairman.**
- ☑ **I spent all day at home waiting for the plumber.**

Rewriting can also often provide a satisfactory solution to the gendered pronoun problem. Pronouns are gendered only in the singular, so a sentence acceptable to everyone makes the noun that is the reference of the pronoun plural:

- ☹ **Everyone at the meeting is interested in explaining his point of view even though he can see that it bores his colleagues.**

246

☑ **All the people at the meeting are interested in explaining their points of view even though they can see that they bore their colleagues.**

☹ **Problems arise when a person's ambitions conflict with his actual prospects.**

☑ **Problems arise when people's ambitions conflict with their actual prospects.**

Well, that's the good news. But the bad news is that this nifty solution is sometimes not easily accomplished. Some sentences with singular subjects and relative pronouns are not convertible to plural; for example, this sentence:

☹ **Somebody has left the headlights on in his car.**

is not convertible to:

☹ **Some people have left the headlights on in their car.**

But rewriting can still smoothly avoid this problem:

☑ **The headlights have been left on in somebody's car.**

See if you find this smoother and more natural than

? **Somebody has left the headlights on in their car.**

Other sorts of smooth rewrites:

☹ **A bad writer overuses his thesaurus.**

☑ **A bad writer overuses the thesaurus.**

☹ **If one does all the exercises regularly, he'll increase his leg muscle strength.**

☑ **If you do all the exercises regularly, you'll increase your leg muscle strength.**

☹ **Each teacher hopes to discover the best way for him to communicate to students.**

☑ **Each teacher hopes to discover the best way to communicate to students.**

Euphemisms

Euphemisms are meant to be softer and nicer than the words they replace—indirect ways of avoiding the unpleasant or unmentionable.

Sometimes they are used to make something awful seem okay. There are plenty of examples of this from politics, for example when the US agencies involved called their torture of prisoners **enhanced interrogation**. Euphemism is also used for (less horrible) public relations by corporations. After a United Airlines passenger who had a ticket and an assigned seat was punched and dragged off the plane by his feet when it turned out that the airline needed to bump him off the plane to get its staff to the plane's destination, and social media displayed videos of the incident and photos of the man bleeding at the mouth, the airline's CEO Oscar Munoz said, "I apologize for having to re-accommodate these customers."[5]

---

5   We looked at some examples of bureaucrat-speak in the section on overblown language. Here's what else Munoz had to say: "We are also reaching out to this passenger to talk directly to him and further address and resolve this situation."

247

"I want to apologize for my behavior last weekend for not being more careful and candid in how I described the events." — US Olympic swimmer Ryan Lochte, offering an apology for lying to police about a post-game non-existent armed robbery.

* * *

Third Official:	Well, most things we do for pleasure nowadays are taxed, except one.
Politician:	What do you mean?
Third Official:	Well, er, smoking's been taxed, drinking's been taxed but not … thingy.
Politician:	Good Lord, you're not suggesting we should tax … thingy?
First Official:	Poo poo's?
Third Official:	No, no, no – thingy.
Second Official:	Number ones?
Third Official:	No, thingy.
Politician:	Thingy!
Second Official:	Ah thingy. Well it'll certainly make chartered accountancy a much more interesting job.

— *Monty Python's Flying Circus* TV series, episode 15.

The emphasis in this book has been on honest, simple, and direct language, and using euphemisms runs counter to this. Of course there will be occasions when the direct alternative to a euphemism would unnecessarily shock or offend, so euphemisms surely have their place. But when there's no real need to tiptoe around things, euphemisms make language smudgy, prissy, and cowardly — sometimes even dishonest. You can judge when they're useful and when they are not.

One problem with using euphemisms is that they have a limited life-span. When new, they seem not to have the unpleasant flavour of what they name, but this does not last; so a new euphemism is then necessary; and so on. Examples:

What was called, a long time ago, **the deadhouse** was renamed, in succession, **the morgue, the mortuary, the mortician's, the funeral parlour**; it's now known as **the funeral home**, but be careful: that name will be replaced soon.

Toilet, itself a euphemism,[6] was replaced with **bathroom** or **washroom** or **restroom**. So if you're in need of a euphemism, make sure that you don't use an outdated one. Another thing to be aware of is that they vary by locality.

---

6   The earliest use of this term to refer to the place for urination and defecation recorded by the OED was in 1886, and for the appliance in that room for that purpose, 1894. Prior to this **toilet** meant a place for, or the process of, washing and dressing. Notice how the later euphemisms also talk about washing (or resting).

An anecdote illustrates locality variation: My British-born wife was met with a moment's hesitation when she asked, in a hotel lobby in Arizona, to be directed to the washroom; but then she was shown to the room containing the hotel's washers and dryers.

Another illustrates euphemism unclarity. A few years ago, both my parents were inmates in an old-age/nursing home, which I privately called **Euphemism City** because nothing was called by its real name there. My sister and I went to the dining room where our father was assigned a seat. The woman who always sat at his table was gone. When we asked what happened to her, the server replied, "She's gone to another place." We have no idea whether this meant that she died or was merely transferred to another dining room.

The euphemisms on the list below are mostly from informal language, but slang euphemisms, of which there are uncountably many, are not included. Other examples of euphemism can be found in the section on biased language.

EUPHEMISM	MORE DIRECT
abattoir	slaughterhouse
adult beverage	beer liquor wine
adult (entertainment/materials)	pornography
after-death care provider bereavement counsellor funeral director	undertaker
a little thin on top	bald
alternative truth disinformation misrepresentation	lie
armed intervention	war
bathroom lavatory (men's/women's) room rest room washroom	toilet
bathroom tissue	toilet paper
beauty spot	mole, wart, pimple

249

being involuntarily separated	
laid off	
let go	
offered (a career change/an early retirement opportunity/a career or employee transition)	fired
personnel realignment	
staff is being re-engineered	
surplus reduction in personnel	
workforce imbalance correction	
between jobs	unemployed
caretaker custodian	janitor
chemical dependency	drug addiction
collateral damage	accidental death (combat)
correctional facility	jail
cremains	ashes (from cremation)
departed no longer with us passed passed (away/on)	died
detainee	prisoner
do away with oneself	commit suicide
down there private parts	genitals
economically depressed neighborhood substandard housing area	slum
educator	teacher
enhanced interrogation	torture
escort sex worker	prostitute
ethnic cleansing	genocide
executive/administrative assistant	secretary
expecting in the family way	pregnant
expectorate	spit
family planning	contraception

gaming	gambling
hooking up making love sleeping with	having sexual intercourse
indisposed unwell	ill
inebriated intoxicated	drunk
memorial park remembrance park	graveyard cemetery
misappropriate	steal
monthlies the curse	menstruation
negative medical outcome	death (under medical care)
perspire	sweat
pregnancy termination	abortion
pre-owned vehicle	used car
put down put to sleep	euthanized (of a pet)
relocation center	prison camp
sanitary landfill	garbage dump
senior citizen golden ager	old person
substance abuser	drug addict
undocumented workers	illegal aliens

The euphemism **dried plums** was introduced in the US after over a year's negotiations between what was then called the California Prune Board and the Department of Food Labeling, a division of the Federal Department of Agriculture. The Prune Board's motivation was apparently that the word **prune** was associated with constipation, and occurred in related jokes. This is not the only food that has had an official name change. Here are some more:

OLD NAME	NEW NAME
Chinese gooseberry	kiwi fruit
Patagonian toothfish	Chilean sea bass
horse mackerel	tuna
dolphin-fish (*not the mammal*)	mahi-mahi
slimehead	orange roughy
goosefish	monkfish
pollock	Boston bluefish
wolffish	ocean catfish
dogfish (*a species of shark*)	rock salmon
rockfish	red snapper
mud crab	peekytoe crab
sea snail	abalone
rapeseed oil	canola oil
niger seed	Nyjer® seed*
Sugar Frosted Flakes	Frosted Flakes
Sugar Smacks	Honey Smacks
Super Sugar Crisp	Golden Crisp

*This spelling replacement was made because of the frequent unfortunate mispronunciation of the name.

During the eighteenth and nineteenth centuries, it was considered improper in some circles to refer directly to some body parts, so euphemisms were necessary for talk about turkeys. Careful speakers used the terms **drumstick** or **lower joint** instead of **leg**. Replacements for **thigh** were **upper joint** or **dark meat,** and for **breast**, **white meat**.

The food-names **pork**, **mutton**, **veal**, and **beef** derive from French and may have been euphemistic replacements for the animal names. (Nobody polite asks, at table, for some more **pig-meat**.) Or perhaps the use of these words arose because, in Norman times, rich fancy people in England spoke, and ordered their food in, French.

Jargon, Good and Evil

Good Jargon

Jargon is specialized language used by a particular group or profession. It can produce comprehension problems for newcomers to the group, or for outsiders, but it often serves a purpose. It can provide shortcuts for frequently referred-to complicated concepts, for which there is no exact term in regular English, and which it would be a waste of time and effort to spell out whenever that concept was referred to. In this way, jargon (unlike redundant and bloated language) can make what you write shorter and clearer.

When you're writing for a specialized field, you, of course, must make sure that you have used their jargon words correctly. You might also want to introduce a new jargon word in what you write, or to use an existing word with a new technical sense. You must make sure that this new bit of specialized language is helpful in the ways jargon can be, and that you define it very carefully at the first use.

Evil Jargon

Highly specialized jargon can result in prose that, one suspects, nobody understands:

> If such a sublime cyborg would insinuate the future as post-Fordist subject, his palpably masochistic locations as ecstatic agent of the sublime superstate need to be decoded as the "now-all-but-unreadable DNA" of a fast deindustrializing Detroit, just as his Robocop-like strategy of carceral negotiation and street control remains the tirelessly American one of inflicting regeneration through violence upon the racially heteroglossic wilds and others of the inner city. — Rob Wilson, "Cyborg America: Policing the Social Sublime in *Robocop* and *Robocop2*"

or that's just flabby:

> This change will allow us to better leverage our talent base in an area where developmental roles are under way and strategically focuses us toward the upcoming Business System transition where Systems literacy and accuracy will be essential to maintain and to further improve service levels to our customer base going forward. — from "Examples of Bad Writing," Westvalley.edu website. Source not provided.

A frequent misuse of jargon is to impress readers: when writers try to demonstrate how importantly professional or official their writing is, or how intellectual, or

253

how knowledgeable about a specialized field they are, or how profound their ideas are. This rarely has its intended effect. It's more likely to make the reader annoyed.

The production of mush-mouthed semi-formal boiler-plate language globules requires little or no thought, and it therefore suggests a not-overly-bright author. Here's a couple of real-life examples:

> The optics of berating someone who speaks out upon feeling victimized are deeply concerning, and do little to advance the dialogue on gender-based violence and gender equality. What we need is an environment that em-powers all individuals to stand their ground, not a fear-based culture that dangles the threat of public flogging in the face of anyone who feels they have been violated. Regardless of how minor this particular infraction may appear to outsiders, or how partisan in nature they decide to paint MP Ruth Ellen Brosseau's intent, what matters is that this MP felt that her rights were infringed upon. To truly advance the dialogue on gender-based violence and equality, this needs to be enough. — Rebecca Wagner, Letter to the Editor, the *Toronto Globe and Mail*

> Reach Out is a synergistic effort to advance learning opportunities of CSU students and Colorado's historically under served secondary students by providing a platform for educational outreach while directly supporting and simultaneously advancing university strategic goals in the areas of outreach, diversity, and curricular innovation. — Website of Access Center, Colorado State University

Especially annoying is the use of trendy buzzwords — indicators (writers hope) of how plugged-in they are to the latest intellectual/political trends and groovy[7] language.

Here's a list of some current (or somewhat passé) jargonistic words. In most cases, they are easily replaceable by ordinary words, and should be replaced. In some cases, however, they may stand for and abbreviate a complicated concept (e.g., **paradigm**, **holistic**, **closure**, **synergy**); but when used as trendy buzzwords, it's often unclear exactly what they're supposed to mean.

(There's some overlap between this list and the list of overblown language and its replacements, above).

---

7 **Groovy** suddenly became a trendy word in 1971, and then usage quickly faded almost to zero. That's one problem with trendy words. If you're not careful to abandon them before their short life-span ends, you'll be marked as hopelessly ungroovy.

access (verb)

across-the-board

address an issue (= talk about? deal with? a
   problem?)

adversely impact on (= hurt, set back)

advance the dialogue

afford an opportunity (= allow, let)

at the end of the day

at this point in time (= now)

basically

been there, done that

blueprint (= plan)

bottom line (= final total)

buy-in (noun, = commitment, agreement)

buzzword (currently fashionable word)

cautiously optimistic

challenge (= problem)

closure

comfort level

community

conceptualize

constructive

conversation ("starting a conversation about")

cool

cost-effective (= worth the cost)

cutting edge (= up-to-date)

deal with

dialogue (verb)

disconnect (noun)

diversity

downside (= the bad results)

downsize (= reduce the size of)

du jour (= currently fashionable)

ecology (= environment)

effort (verb, as in "We're efforting that.")

empower; empowerment

enhance

environment

epicentre (= centre)

escalate (= to intensify)

eventuate (= result)

exit strategy

exposure (= liability)

facilitate (= ease, help, make possible)

facilitator

factor

feedback (= opinion, reaction)

framework

gravitas (= appropriately serious manner)

grow ("grow the business") (=expand? increase?
   broaden?)

guesstimate (estimate that's just a guess)

heads-up

holistic

identify with ("I can identify with you.")

impact (verb = affect)

impact (noun = effect), impactful

implement

in the final analysis

incent (verb = to provide incentive)

indicate (= say)

individual (= person)

interface with

issue (= problem)

-IZE words (e.g., incentivize)

leverage (verb, = magnify, multiply, augment, or
   increase)

liaise with (= meet with, work with, discuss with)

lifestyle

matrix

meaningful

methodology

mindfulness

multitask (do several things more or less
   simultaneously)

need-to-know basis

network (verb)

no-brainer (= easy decision)

nurture

office (verb, as in "the smarter way to office")

on the cusp

on-task

on the same page as

opt for (= choose)

optics

optimal

-oriented (e.g., result-oriented)

outside the box

overly

paradigm (= model? pattern? structure? formula? accepted point of view?)

paradigm shift

parameter (= limit, boundary)

point in time

politically correct (or P.C.)

prioritize (= put into order of importance)

proactive

pushing the envelope

quality time

quantum leap (= revolutionary step)

reach out

reality check

relate ("I can relate to that.")

resonate ("Does that resonate with you?")

rethink (= review, reconsider)

scenario

sea change (= [big?] change)

sector, public/private (= government/business)

share this with you (= tell you this)

situation, (no-lose, no-win, win-win, lose-lose)

specificity

stakeholders

state of the art (= latest development)

synergy (= an improved effect of working together, cooperation)

to effect modifications (to make changes)

transparent / transparency

unpack ("Let me unpack that statement.")

upside (= the good results)

user-friendly

utilize (= use)

venue (= the place for an event)

viable (= practical, workable)

vibrant

visualize (= see, predict)

wake-up call

wellness

-WISE words (e.g., money-wise, weather-wise)

world-class

worst-case scenario

Excessive Abstraction

Some subjects demand abstract thought and writing, but it's always best to keep things as concrete as possible. Explain things. Give examples.

Read as much of the following real book excerpt as you can bear. Notice how the problem here is not jargon: almost every word is ordinary. It's the fog of over-the-top abstraction (plus sentences that are absurdly long and complex), resulting in a comprehensibility score of zero.

Total presence breaks on the univocal predication of the exterior absolute the absolute existent (of that of which it is not possible to univocally predi-cate an outside, while the equivocal predication of the outside of the absolute exterior is possible of that of which the reality so predicated is not the reality, viz., of the dark/of the self, the identity of which is not outside the abso-lute identity of the outside, which is to say that the equivocal predication of identity is possible of the self-identity which is not identity, while identity is univocally predicated of the limit to the darkness, of the limit of the reality of the self). This is the real exteriority of the absolute outside: the reality of the absolutely unconditioned absolute outside univocally predicated of the dark: the light univocally predicated of the darkness: the shining of the light univocally predicated of the limit of the darkness: actuality univocally predicated of the other of self-identity: existence univocally predicated of the absolutely unconditioned other of the self. — D.G. Leahy, *Foundation: Matter the Body Itself*[8]

Well, that's about the worst there could be. Your writing is way better. But reducing abstraction will improve most people's writing. Here are some examples:

☹ **The 1903 law provided an authorization of this kind of action.**

☑ **The 1903 law authorized this kind of action.**

☹ **Cessation of that sort of atmospheric pollution produced by the factory arrived that summer.**

☑ **In the summer, the factory ceased polluting the atmosphere.**

Metaphors and Similes

A metaphor is a comparison using words that do not apply literally. When you say that somebody's all steamed up, you're comparing that person's anger to a boiling pot of water; of course there's no literal steam there. A related figure of speech is the simile, which makes the comparison with the words **like** or **as**, for example, **blind as a bat; cute as a kitten.**

These figures of speech are sometimes useful in livening up prose. Saying that someone is **blowing his own horn** is a bit more colourful than its literal translation: **telling people how good and successful he is.** But there are dangers in using them. Many metaphors are so frequently used that they no longer add any pizzazz. Saying, for example, that someone has **missed the boat** adds no more than saying that somebody is mistaken. Instead of relying on the old clichés, you might try thinking up some fresh comparisons. This is hard to do. Here are a few samples of tired metaphors and more lively replacements:

TIRED	MORE LIVELY
paved the way	blazed a path
hotbed	cauldron
nipping something in the bud	digging up the seedlings

8   No joke: this is a real excerpt from a real book published by a real academic press (Albany: State University of New York Press, 1996, 238–39). Thanks to Dennis Dutton for providing this unbeatable example, which can be found on the website for his *Philosophy and Literature* Bad Writing Contest (1998). Want more of this quotation (haha)? It's in the Contest website: http://www.denisdutton.com/bad_writing.htm.

257

There are thousands of conventional — tired — metaphors and similes. Here's a list of a small number of them.

800 lb gorilla
a breeze (easy)
acid test
albatross
all steamed up
anger bottled up inside
apple of my eye
barking up the wrong tree
batten down the hatches
belling the cat
better half
birds of a feather
bite the bullet
bitter end
black-and-white dualism
blank cheque
blanket of bullets
blanket of snow
blind as a bat
blow one's own horn
boiling mad
bootstrapping
brass ring
bread and circuses
broken heart
bubbly personality
bucket brigade
busy as a bee
cabin fever
catch-22 (logic)
character assassination
cherry picking (fallacy)
chicken or the egg
China syndrome
coarse manner of speech
cold feet
colourful remark
consumed by love
couch potato

crossing the Rubicon
crossroads (choices)
cultural mosaic
dark horse
deep dark secret
different tack
difficult to swallow
digest the news/information
domino effect
early bird
elephant in the room
endless night
evening of one's life
eyes were saucers
fade off to sleep
fatted calf
feel blue
few bad apples
figurehead
flogging a dead horse
fog of war
food for thought
fork in the road
gentle as a lamb
give a wide berth
glowing review
Gordian knot
grassroots
Greek to me
grey area
ground zero
hand over fist
hard and fast
head was spinning
heart of gold
heart of stone
heartbroken
high and dry
Hobson's choice

Holy Grail
hotbed of unrest
hue and cry
in a nutshell
inflamed temper
jumping for joy
keep your eyes peeled
kicked the bucket
know the ropes
lame duck
landslide victory
late bloomer
left high and dry
light in a sea of darkness
light of my life
loose cannon
love is war
melting pot
miss the boat
monkey see, monkey do
moral compass
mother lode
muckraking
mudslinging
music to my ears
musical chairs
my memory is a little cloudy
night owl
night was falling
nip in the bud
no-win situation
opening up new horizons
paved the way for
peace of mind
pink elephants
plain sailing
point of no return
poison pill
pole position

pork barrel legislation
pull your socks up
puppet government
Pyrrhic victory
quiet as a mouse
rainbow of flavours
raining cats and dogs
riding a wave of support
riding coattails
rollercoaster of emotions
rolling in dough
Rosetta Stone
sacred cow
sacrificial lamb
sea of sadness
shady character
shake a leg
shining example
ship of state
shooting the messenger
shot across the bows

show someone the ropes
silver bullet
simmer down
sleep tight
slippery as an eel
smart as a fox
smell of fear
smoking gun
snake oil
soapbox
something to chew on
son of a gun
spiritual seeking
stalking horse
standing on the shoulders
    of giants
stench of failure
strong as an ox
sunset clause
survival of the fittest
sweet smell of success

swims like a fish
teaching grandmother to
    suck eggs
the apple of my eye
three sheets to the wind
throw caution to the winds
time is money
to the bitter end
tunnel vision
walk the plank
walks like a duck
war chest
weathering a storm
wedge issue
wheels of justice
whipping boy
white elephant
wise as an owl
witch hunt
work has dried up
yin and yang

Mixed Metaphors

Mixed metaphors are incongruous combinations of two metaphors. They arise when people talk or write in clichés, not thinking about the literal meanings of their words. It's important to avoid them. Examples:

- If we bite the bullet we have to be careful not to throw the baby out with the bathwater.
- We will leave no stone unturned as we search for an avenue through which this issue may be resolved.
- Step up to the plate and lay your cards on the table.
- Get all our ducks on the same page.
- Iron out the remaining bottlenecks.
- The man on the street has trouble keeping his head above water.
- He's out on a limb because his colleagues pulled the rug out from under him.
- That isn't rocket surgery.
- Her saucer-eyes narrow to a gimlet stare and she lets Mr. Clarke have it with both barrels. — Quoted from the Bulwer Lytton Fiction Contest in Dennis Simanaitis's blog
- I knew enough to realize that the alligators were in the swamp and that it was time to circle the wagons. — Rush Limbaugh (reportedly)

259

+ As Putin rears his head and comes into the airspace of the United States of America, where do they go? Alaska. — Gov. Sarah Palin

Parallel Construction

When there are two or more linguistic items with a similar function, they should have a similar form. For example, when there are two or more things talked about in a sentence, they should all be referred to with nouns, or all with verbs, without mixing the grammatical forms. Do you know what I'm talking about? Well, the mistake of failure of parallel construction is difficult to explain, but it's easier to see in examples. Here are some.

🖢 **Madison likes reading, hiking, and to ride her bike.**
☑ **Madison likes reading, hiking, and bike riding.**
☑ **Madison likes to read, to hike, and to ride her bike.**

🖢 **We operate in 15 countries today and growing.** — newspaper ad from Freshii fast-food chain
☑ **We operate in 15 countries today, and that number that is growing.**

🖢 **The day was both cold and it was windy.**
☑ **The day was both cold and windy.**

🖢 **The parts of speech studied in fifth grade include the verb, the noun, and prepositions.**
☑ **The parts of speech studied in fifth grade include the verb, the noun, and the preposition.**

🖢 **This is not a movie just for children but adults.**
☑ **This is a movie not just for children, but also for adults.**

🖢 **Oranges are great because they're delicious, inexpensive, and they are full of vitamin C.**
☑ **Oranges are great because they're delicious, inexpensive, and full of vitamin C.**

🖢 **I would rather play cards than to go fishing.**
☑ **I would rather play cards than go fishing.**

🖢 **Samantha hates not only to go to bed early but also waking up late.**
☑ **Samantha hates not only to go to bed early but also to wake up late.**
☑ **Samantha hates not only going to bed early but also waking up late.**

🖢 **The engine in the Ford is bigger than the Chevvy.**
☑ **The engine in the Ford is bigger than the engine in the Chevvy.**

👎 **The teen attacker has fetal alcohol spectrum disorder, a low IQ and suffers from post-traumatic stress disorder stemming from sexual abuse inflicted on him as a child, the court has heard.** — the *Toronto Globe and Mail*

☑ **The teen attacker has fetal alcohol spectrum disorder, a low IQ, and post-traumatic stress disorder stemming from sexual abuse inflicted on him as a child, the court has heard.**

Sometimes parallel constructions simply make things more effective. Consider this splendid rhetoric:

> But, in a larger sense, we can not dedicate — we can not consecrate — we can not hallow — this ground. ... The world will little note, nor long remember what we say here, but it can never forget what they did here. It is for us the living, rather, to be dedicated here to the unfinished work which they who fought here have thus far so nobly advanced. It is rather for us to be here dedicated to the great task remaining before us — that from these honored dead we take increased devotion to that cause for which they gave the last full measure of devotion — that we here highly resolve that these dead shall not have died in vain — that this nation, under God, shall have a new birth of freedom — and that government of the people, by the people, for the people, shall not perish from the earth. — Lincoln's Gettysburg Address

Now compare this awful plodding rewrite, without all those parallel constructions. There's nothing wrong here. It's just that all the oomph is gone.

> But, in a larger sense, we can not dedicate, consecrate or hallow this ground. ... The world will little note or remember for long what we say here, but it can never forget what those men accomplished on this battlefield. It is for us the living, rather, to be dedicated here to the unfinished work which they who fought here have thus far so nobly advanced. We should instead be dedicated to the great task remaining before us, and from these honored dead we take increased commitment to that cause for which they gave the last full measure of devotion. So we should here highly resolve that these dead shall not have died in vain; and make sure that this nation, under God, has a new birth of freedom; and also that government of, by, and for the people shall not perish from the earth.

Of course, you don't need to be told that Lincoln's majestic rhetorical style,[9] while immensely effective in the context, is not exactly appropriate when you're making

---

9 Consider **to that cause for which they gave the last full measure of devotion**. As discussed in the section on ending sentences with prepositions, avoiding this sometimes leads to over-formality. The occasion of this speech, however, required the maximum formality, and **to that cause which they gave the last full measure of devotion for** would have been (putting it mildly) no improvement.

a list for your car mechanic of what to repair, or when you're texting your BFF. As always, adjustment to where your words are aimed is of paramount relevance to what kind of language is appropriate.

Translation

If you ever need a translation in what you're writing — from another language into English, or from your English to another language, don't rely on the use of a bilingual dictionary, or, what amounts to the same thing, an online translation service. These are guaranteed to make a mess, because translation is not a simple matter of substituting a word in the original language for what the dictionary, or the computer program, finds is the most likely equivalent in the other language. Even if you've taken three years of the other language in school, you probably won't produce a good translation. Get a professional really bilingual person to do it.

You almost certainly can't judge how good a translation is into another language, but you can see what happens when inadequate translation tries to turn another language into English. Here, for example, is the helpful passage on the wrapper of some very good dried noodles I bought, made in China, and probably labelled in English with the help of a dictionary or online translator:

> This product uses the noodles which wheat flour traditional process precision work becomes, is the modern life fast boils the good food, boils, to fry, the hot pot, the dry mix to be possible.

I'm not making fun of them — I understand their problem. The point is that our attempts at translation can sound just that way to them. The moral is this: if it's important, get a professional.

You'll need to be careful even when getting a professional translation. Here are some excerpts from an advertising email I received from a Hong Kong company that specializes in Chinese-English translation:

> Our highly qualified and experienced freelance translators with their translation experience ranges from five to over twenty five years in relevant fields to assure our translation quality. Our clients regularly appreciate our high-quality work and dependability. … We manage all projects closely from start to finish and keep you regularly informed on its progress. We aim at delivering within the time limit. We always ensure the consistency of the translation and the quality of the finished project.

PART VI: OVERALL FORM; THE WRITING PROCESS

Short and Long Sentences

Have a look at this sentence:

> We were informed of your government's new initiative to link young people about to graduate from post-secondary education with small businesses who need skilled employment candidates by a teacher from Saskatchewan who is a member of our team of educators that is championing the inclusion of health literacy into high-school curricula. — Example from http://scottswrittenwords. blogspot.ca/2012/01/writing-tips-dont-overload-your.html

Got that all? No? There's too much packed in here. This should have been presented in several shorter sentences, with appropriate connection.

Here's another one:

> However, when a police officer has committed a serious crime of violence by breaking the law, which the officer is sworn to uphold, it is the duty of the court to firmly denounce that conduct in an effort to repair and to affirm the trust that must exist between the community and the police to whom we entrust the use of lethal weapons within the limits prescribed by the criminal law. — Excerpt from a written decision by Ontario Superior Court Justice Edward Then, quoted in the *Toronto Globe and Mail*

But short sentences are not always better. Consider this:

Hartford was once known as an industrial center. It was the home of several manufacturers. They made firearms, typewriters, bicycles, and even cars. — This and its replacement below are from "The Guide to Grammar and Writing," a website sponsored by the Capital Community College Foundation.

Too many short choppy sentences. Compare its replacement:

Once known as an industrial center, Hartford was the home of manufacturers of firearms, typewriters, bicycles, and even cars.

Greening

Almost everything almost everybody writes is too long. What I mean is that each paragraph could be considerably condensed without losing any of its content. Sentences could be shorter; repetition and digression could be removed.

Shorter is better for several reasons. The main reason, of course, is that it's easier on readers, who will have a tendency to doze off if your writing is too wordy and diffuse. A reader who is bored and frustrated by overwriting will not be eager to understand what you have to say, or to believe it. When your points are right there, clear and brief, instead of being buried under piles of bloated verbiage, it will be much easier to take, better understood, and more effective. But there's another reason why making your writing shorter will make it better: when you edit a draft for concision, you'll have to sort out what's necessary from what's not, you'll get clearer on what you really wanted to say, and you'll make sure you say it, and not a bunch of other things.

But the early writing training most of us got had just the opposite effect. Remember when you had a school assignment to write, say, 1000 words on The Causes of World War I, and the best you could come up with was eight or ten sentences? Then these had to be expanded with fluff to come close to the assigned length, so you wrote:

What are, or were, the many and varied causes of World War I, that great war (often called The Great War because it was so great) that caused so much warfare and death and destruction all over Europe? This is a very important question, a question that historians the world over, here and elsewhere, have often debated at length, and will continue to debate for as long as there is awareness of that great and horrible war that caused all that death and destruction.... [*84 words. 916 to go.*]

Your teacher was annoyed, not fooled, by this.

Your writing is not that bad anymore. I can tell from here. But it's probably still bloated. So what should you do? When you have written a draft of something, put it away for a little while, then come back and green it. Read through it, thinking

264

constantly: is there a way that I could say this more briefly? If yes, do it. It will almost certainly bring about a significant reduction in blather in your writing, and a significant increase in quality as well.

Sometimes writers report that they were trained to write much better by an early job in which they were forced to condense their own, or others', writing. Here's what two of the best contemporary non-fiction writers have to say about this.

Nora Ephron writes:

> [Another] advantage to all those years in the newspaper business is that I learned to write short. Much too short probably, but as vices go, that's far better than much too long. Nothing in the [*New York*] *Post* ran over fifteen hundred words: six hundred words was more like it. And the lack of space forced me to select, to throw out everything but the quote I liked best, the story that seemed most telling. — "Preface to the 1980 Edition," *Wallflower at the Orgy*

Calvin Trillin worked when he was young as a copy-editor for *Time Magazine*. One of the editors' jobs was to cut down submitted stories, which were often several times too large for the space the magazine had allotted for them. Editors used a green pencil to cross out what could be eliminated, so they called this job *greening*.

> The instructions were expressed as how many lines had to be greened — "Green seven" or "Green twelve".... I was surprised that what I had thought of as a tightly constructed seventy-line story — a story so tightly constructed that it had resisted the inclusion of that maddening leftover fact — was unharmed, or even improved, by greening ten per cent of it. The greening I did in Time Edit convinced me that just about any piece I write could be improved if, when it was supposedly ready to hand in, I looked in the mirror and said sternly to myself "Green fourteen" or "Green eight." — "This Story Just Won't Write," *The New Yorker*

Planning Overall Structure

Sometimes it's said that the first thing you should do when writing an extended piece is to make an outline. This may be the right way to proceed, if you know the structure of what you're going to write before you begin. But very often you don't. Maybe you don't know where your writing is going to go; or maybe you have some ideas about it, but things change as you write. It's not necessary that you start with the structure of your writing in mind. The important thing is to start writing, however full or partial, organized or incoherent, adequate or inadequate your ideas are.

265

This is a very important fact about writing: *your best thinking happens while writing, not before.* You may think that you have your whole paper planned out, but when you start writing, it turns out that some of your ideas go nowhere; and others you hadn't thought of earlier turn up and become an important part of the paper. Frequently you may change your mind entirely about central points. This is normal; don't be afraid of it.

Because pre-writing planning is so often of limited worth, and because you're going to follow my advice and begin to write when you haven't a clue what you're going to say, your first draft will be a mess: disorganized, imprecise, full of false starts, repetition, and even self-contradiction. That's fine. Put it away for a few hours or a day, if your deadline isn't looming, and come back and read what you've written, and then rewrite it. At this point you can begin to figure out a good structure for what you have to say, move things around, and delete irrelevancies and false starts. So here comes the second very important fact about writing: *first drafts are never any good.* Writing gets good only after several rewrites.

Here's another reason this procedure is useful. When you start doing something and run into problems, instead of grinding away until you make some progress, the best strategy by far is to do something completely different for a while. When you're not consciously thinking about your earlier task, unconscious parts of your brain are still working on it. Later, when you resume the task, you may well find that new approaches and better solutions come easily. This is a free gift from your unconscious brain: work that you aren't aware of, that took place while you abandoned that essay that was giving you trouble, and you were doing something utterly different, like drinking a beer or watching trash TV, or having a nap or a run around the block. This really works. Try it. (But note: to use this technique, you'll have to start working on your writing well before the deadline for completing it. Is there a chance you'll do this?)

Here's something else you may have heard is necessary in good writing: it starts with a statement of the overall point, and finishes with another summary of what has been written. In other words: you're supposed to say what you're going to say, then say it, then say what you've said. This may be good advice for beginning writers, since it will force them to think about the overall meaning and structure of their writing; but doing this mechanically is often just needlessly repetitive. You don't want to make your readers scream with boredom. I trust you to think about overall matters without being forced to write those overall opening and closing bits. You can make the overall structure clear without them. In any case, even if you do want to begin what you're writing with a summary, it may not be a good idea to start writing with that beginning, for the reasons noted above: it may be that you don't know where you're going when you start writing, or you change your mind as you go on. Your opening and closing summaries can be supplied, if necessary, later on.

It's absolutely essential that your finished product have a clear and sensible structure. What this means is that material on the same topic should be all together, and topics should be arranged in a rational order.

So what is a sensible structure? There's no simple answer to that question, no general formula for structuring. What sort of structure you should aim at depends on what sort of writing you're doing, and on what sort of contents you produce. But I can give you some general hints about basic structures. You may be able to adapt one of these, or at least looking these over may give you an idea of what you should be aiming at.

- Sequential: When telling a story, it may make the most sense to relate incidents in the order in which they occurred.
- Spatial: When describing a scene, you might move from left to right, or from bottom to top, or from near to far, or from big to small. Just as long as there's some sort of system.
- Importance: When you have several things to say, you might arrange them with the most important ones first — or last.
- Comparison: When comparing two things or two situations, you may begin with similarities, then move on to differences.
- Cause and effect: When your point is to argue for the causes of something, you may want to distinguish several causal factors, which are together responsible. Keep details of each factor together.
- Argument for and against: Start with a statement of the question you'll be examining. Then explain one or more answers you'll be rejecting (perhaps by identifying, or quoting, authorities who give this answer); then provide your arguments against that answer. Then state what you think is the right answer, and give arguments for it.

Signposting

I mentioned above that the ritual mechanical say-what-you're-going-to-say is often not really a good idea, but what *is* necessary is making the reader aware of the structure of your ideas, and where individual parts stand in that structure. There are several tools for doing this effectively and without driving your readers to strong drink.

First, think about the relationship of small-scale ideas, within a sentence, or between sentences or groups of them. Are these ideas opposed to each other, or two different ways of saying the same thing? Is the second an example of the first? Is it an argument for the earlier claim? Is it another in a list? Connecting words and phrases make relationships like these clear. Your writing should make liberal use of them.

267

THESE WORDS JOIN IDEAS THAT ARE IN SOME WAY OPPOSED TO EACH OTHER:

although	nevertheless
but	though
despite	whereas
even if	while
however	yet
in spite of	

THESE JOIN LINKED OR SUPPORTING IDEAS:

also	indeed
and	moreover
as well	not only ... but also
further furthermore	similarly
in addition	: [colon]
in fact	; [semicolon]

THESE INTRODUCE CAUSES OR REASONS:

as	for
as a result of	on account of
because	since
due to	

THESE INTRODUCE RESULTS OR CONCLUSIONS:

and so	it follows that
as a result	so
consequently	therefore
hence	thus
in conclusion	to sum up
in consequence	these findings indicate that

THESE EXPRESS PURPOSE:

in order to	so that
so as to	

THESE INTRODUCE EXAMPLES:

for example	such as
for instance	: [colon]
in that	

268

THESE INDICATE ALTERNATIVES:

either ... or	or
if only	otherwise
in that case	rather than
instead	unless
instead of	whether ... or
neither ... nor	

THESE ARE USED TO MAKE COMPARISONS:

by comparison	on the one hand ... on the other hand
in contrast	for one thing ... for another

OTHER JOINING WORDS AND PHRASES:

above/below	in that
as illustrated above/below	in the event of
as mentioned	in the light of
as shown in the diagram	in this respect/in some respects
as we can see/we can see that	second/in the second place
assuming that	to begin with
first/in the first place	whereby
in other words	

And in a work more than a few pages long, it's often very useful to insert topic headings.

Paragraphing

There are no strict rules about where and how often to start new paragraphs. Sometimes a subtle point in an argument will require a paragraph of almost an entire page to elaborate; occasionally a single sentence can form an effective paragraph. Yet separating ideas into paragraphs remains an important aid to the processes of both reading and writing.

A single paragraph should contain a coherent blob of thought, with the contents containing a single idea, distinct from the ideas of the paragraphs before or after. Well, that doesn't tell you very much, does it? Anyway, try to aim at paragraphs usually consisting of more than one or two sentences, and fewer than eight or ten. You'll see internet pages on which every sentence is a new paragraph: that's definitely too many. Or on which there is no paragraphing. Bad form also. Here are some more particular hints about when to start a new paragraph:

In Narration:

+ when the story changes direction.
+ when there is a gap in time in the story.
+ when you switch from quoting one speaker to quoting another.

In Description:

+ when you switch from describing something to describing something else.

In Persuasion or Argument:

+ when a new topic is introduced.
+ when there is a change in direction of the argument.

When Changing From One Mode To Another:

+ The "modes" here, commonly combined in writing, are description, narration, and argument.

---

alphabetical order You learned all there is to know about this in grade 3 or so, right? Nope. You might be surprised to find out that there are two conflicting "theories" that disagree on ordering multi-word entries. The letter-by-letter theory ignores spaces and hyphens; the word-by-word theory sorts by the first word of an entry term, then by the second. Both, however, stop at the first punctuation mark. An example makes this clear.

LETTER-BY-LETTER	WORD-BY WORD
a, one	a, one
all	all
all/both	all/both
allay	all books
all books	all of
allege	allay
all of	allege
allude/elude	allude/elude

Both ignore punctuation marks (including the slash **/**) and what follows them, except in case of ties. Thus **all/both** follows **all**, on both lists. Following **all/both** on the word-by-word list are the other items beginning with the word **all**, whereas the letter-by-letter list ignores the space between words, and considers the initial letters in the rest of the items as **alla**, **allb**, **alle**, **allo**, and **allu**.

Although you probably will never need to know this, both major style manuals (MLA and Chicago) advise that the letter-by-letter system is usually preferred. You'll find it used in the MEANINGS, USES, AND IDIOMS section of this book, and in the index. Would you have noticed if I hadn't told you?

270

Beginning writers are sometimes urged to begin each paragraph with a topic sentence saying what the subject of the paragraph is. This is another mechanical procedure that you may find helpful for producing coherent structure, but you'll hardly ever find this done by good writers, and doing it in a whole essay will make things very tedious for the reader. It's better just to bear in mind, when you're writing a paragraph, that each one should have a separate and coherent topic; and that it should be obvious to readers what the topic is, even if you don't start each paragraph with a statement of what it is.

It's also very important to ensure that paragraphs are connected to each other, either directly through the use of transitions or indirectly because of the obvious relationship between them.

Citing Sources

Footnotes serve two purposes: to add some material that is not sufficiently important to be included in the main text; or to give credit for something quoted or picked up from another source.

The first sort of footnote should probably be avoided, or minimized, anyway.[1] It's not a terrible mistake, but a lot of this distractingly interrupts the flow of the narrative in the main body of text.

One annoying thing scholars sometimes do is produce footnotes with long lists of books and articles relevant to the subject at hand. This kind of information may be helpful to readers, but if that's the case, an annotated and categorized bibliography of such material should be added at the end, instead. On the other hand, lists like this are sometimes created by authors just to show off the huge extent of their familiarity with the literature.[2] If the main purpose of what you're writing is to impress your graduate supervisor, or the marker of your senior paper, okay, try it. But most readers will probably be annoyed, not impressed.

But a footnote that cites the source of an idea or quotation performs an essential service. Citation and bibliography form is discussed in detail in Part VII, below.

Citing and Quoting Authorities

Who is an authority? This question has become increasingly difficult to answer.

---

1   As I haven't done in this book.
2   I used to know a professor who prided himself on his reading lists. He'd provide huge ones to students at the beginning of the term, demonstrating how comprehensive his knowledge of the literature was. No student paid any attention to these, but the professor believed (mistakenly) that this showed what a great teacher he was.

One reason for this is that the internet has taken over world civilization, and you can get plenty of articles by googling just about anything. For example, Nelson Goodman's "grue" paradox, a fairly obscure argument hidden in a remote corner of philosophy, returned an astounding 53,600 hits when I googled it. This embarrassment of riches produces two problems. First, if you're assigned to write about a subject, you're supposed to get some basic familiarity with what's been written about it. With 53,600 websites to consult, what in the world should you do? The second problem is that, as everyone who has googled any topic knows, a good deal of what's on the internet is

+ disguised commercial sites, designed to sell you something
+ the ravings of lunatics or crackpots
+ blather by uninformed people
+ fiction that pretends to be fact, created to discredit a political position or candidate, or just for the hell of it.

The trashification of the internet has shown an alarming increase in recent years. Some "authorities" will say anything they please (mostly on websites or social media), with no shred of logic or evidence but with the justification that we're in a "post-truth" society.

> "Sometimes we can disagree with the facts." — Sean Spicer, White House spokesman, defending his clearly false statements regarding the number of spectators at Trump's inauguration.

So what should you do? Well, there are some guidelines for searches for useful expert writing. Following them won't guarantee that you'll be able completely to avoid trash, but they'll make what you get much more likely to be reliable. Since you're probably an experienced internet surfer, you'll probably know the main rules-of-thumb already, but maybe there's a useful new idea in here:

+ Lots of spelling or grammar errors, or a general atmosphere of hysteria, are pretty good indications that you've hit on a crackpot. So is paranoiac conspiracy-theoretical talk, or a belligerent tone.
+ Academic status of the author, especially from a university whose name you recognize, is some indication of the reliability of what's written.
+ If what you've found was initially published on paper — in book form from a publisher you've heard of, or in a refereed journal — that's a fairly good indication of value. Sometimes internet-only journals are not refereed, or not reliably refereed, and what's in them can be worthless.
+ There are several universally respected websites, ones that are very careful about the reliability of what they print. For philosophy, nothing beats the online *Stanford Encyclopedia of Philosophy*. For medical information, you can

trust Medline.gov or MayoCline.com. To discover other comprehensive and trustworthy websites in the area you're writing about, ask your teacher, or go to a university library, where you'll find subject specialists able and eager to give you valuable hints for your online research.

+ Statistical data on all sorts of things can be obtained on the web from academic or government-sponsored sources. Don't trust statistical data somebody told you: often this sort of thing is just something somebody made up.

+ Newspapers (some of which still have websites you don't have to pay for) are mostly of very limited use these days, but these are still valuable sources of information: the *Guardian* (UK), the *New York Times*, the *Washington Post*, the *Wall Street Journal*. I'm talking about their news articles here, not their editorials or opinion pieces.

+ Wikipedia is sometimes reliable, but sometimes it's way off. There's really no way to tell when you're looking at a particular article. Consult it to get some clues about what the issues are, but don't count on what Wiki says to be good information.

+ It's a bad sign when authors of books or websites list their names beginning with **Dr.** or who follow it with **Ph.D.** or other degree abbreviations. Real authorities almost never flaunt their degree like this; it's a good sign the author is trying hard to impress, or maybe worse: that the degree is only honorary, · or a complete fake; or from an unaccredited institution or diploma mill, or bottom-of-the-barrel school; or in some academically questionable subject.

When to Cite Sources

It is very important to cite the source of every use of somebody else's words or ideas.

Well, not *every* use. You needn't give attribution for what can be considered *common knowledge*. What does that mean? Something is common knowledge when most people, educated people anyway, would know it, or if it's widely known within some discipline. This includes things you might have to look up, like the fact that William Henry Harrison was the ninth President of the US, or that most metals require 6.2 cal. of heat in order to raise the temperature of 1 gram-atomic mass of the metal by 1°C. (They tell me that this is common knowledge among chemists.) Ideas like this are not the product of any one person. Interpretations or theories, on the other hand, unless they are widely accepted, are not common knowledge and should be attributed to their source.

Factual matter that's not common knowledge can be included as a direct quotation from the authority in question, or in a paraphrase in your own words of what the authority said. Don't overdo direct quotation; it's often better to paraphrase, unless there's something amusing or interesting or important or controversial about the words the authority used.

Sometimes advice-to-writers websites tell you that when you're arguing for something in your writing, something you thought of all by yourself, it would be a good idea anyway to include a list of publications which argue more or less for the same thing. This, it's said, will make your point more plausible to readers, when they find out that you're not the only crackpot that made that claim. Might this lend credibility to your writing? Maybe.

Depending on the discipline, some writing is treated as authoritative, but other writing is more controversial. When you are including mention of the latter, it's to introduce the point, not to support it. You'll have to add what you can of your own support.

Why is attribution to their authors of every quotation or idea you got from them necessary? One reason is this. Suppose you write:

> Zachary Schmidlap claims that Jane Austen's novel *Dudes and Dudesses* should best be interpreted as [blah blah blah]. But I disagree. I believe that [blah blah blah].

Your readers might want to look at the article by Schmidlap to see what his full arguments are, whether you've got them right, whether he's made a good case, etc. In that case, you provide a service to these readers by giving details of where Schmidlap's article is, so they can get hold of it and read it for themselves.

But here comes a much more compelling reason:

Plagiarism

This is a very important point, so I'll shout, using all capital letters: THE USE OF SOMEBODY ELSE'S WORDS OR IDEAS WITHOUT ATTRIBUTION IS PLAGIARISM, AND IT IS LIKELY TO GET YOU INTO ACADEMIC OR EVEN LEGAL TROUBLE.

Now that I have your attention, here are the finer details.

These are the usual ways of committing plagiarism:

+ It isn't difficult to find "paper-mills" on the internet that will sell you finished academic papers on a variety of topics. Some of these papers are not terrible.
+ It's very easy to find a discussion of anything on the internet, and to copy and paste it into your writing.
+ In your research, you may have copied verbatim somebody's writing into your notes, and then later transferred that to your paper, without crediting the source.

+ Even if it's in your own words, an idea or fact or other bit you got from somebody else must be given proper attribution (unless it's common knowledge).

Buying a paper from a paper-mill, or copying something from the internet without
attribution, is cheating. Including words or ideas somebody else came up with is
theft. Providing a footnote to the originators of quotations or ideas constitutes payment for what they have done and makes your use legitimate, not theft. (Isn't that
amazing? Where else can you get such valuable stuff for such a trivial payment?)

The last two types of plagiarism are sometimes done by accident, when you
forget that what's in your preliminary notes was actually someone else's words or
idea. But legally speaking, plagiarism doesn't require intent. This is why it's important to keep very good notes in preparation for writing: keep track of when
something is in somebody else's words, or is somebody else's idea, and of the details
of the source. Morally speaking, this sort of accidental plagiarism isn't as bad as
the intentional kind, but it's still bad. You really should have been more careful. It's
important.

Cheating and theft are things that are abhorrent to you, of course, but maybe
you have, *ahem!*, a friend without your moral scruples who would benefit from
the following considerations: PLAGIARISM WILL BE CAUGHT AND
PUNISHED. The people who grade your academic papers will be exquisitely
tuned to the signs of plagiarism. They're used to your writing style or to what they
expect writers at your level should produce, and they will be able to detect the
undisguisable traces of somebody else's writing in what you hand in. And there
are surprisingly effective internet tools for detecting plagiarism. Getting caught
plagiarizing can wreck your academic or professional career. Don't do it, please.

PART VII: SOURCE MATERIAL AND CITATION

How to Insert Source Material

There are three main ways of working source material into a paper: summaries, paraphrases, and direct quotations. In order to avoid plagiarism, care must be taken with all three kinds of borrowing, both in the way they are handled and in their referencing. In what follows, a passage from page 102 of Terrence W. Deacon's book *The Symbolic Species: The Co-Evolution of Language and the Brain* (New York: Norton, 1997) serves as the source for a sample summary, paraphrase, and quotation. The examples feature the APA style of in-text parenthetical citations, but the requirements for presenting the source material are the same for all academic referencing systems.

Original source:

> Over the last few decades language researchers seem to have reached a consensus that language is an innate ability, and that only a significant contribution from innate knowledge can explain our ability to learn such a complex communication system. Without question, children enter the world predisposed to learn human languages. All normal children, raised in normal social environments, inevitably learn their local language, whereas other species, even when raised and taught in this same environment, do not. This demonstrates that human brains come into the world specially equipped for this function.

Summarizing and Paraphrasing

A summary is a short account of a longer passage or whole work; a paraphrase is a short account of a short passage. An honest and competent summary or paraphrase must not only represent the source accurately but also use your original wording and include a citation. It is a common misconception that only quotations need to be acknowledged as borrowings in the body of an essay; but without a citation, even a fairly worded summary or paraphrase is an act of plagiarism. The first example below is faulty on two counts: it borrows wording (underlined) from the source, and it has no parenthetical reference.

> **Researchers** agree that language learning is **innate, and that only innate knowledge can explain** how we are able **to learn** a **system** of **communication** that is so **complex**. **Normal children raised in normal** ways will always **learn their local language, whereas other species do not, even when taught** human language and exposed to the **same environment**.

The next example avoids the wording of the source passage, and a parenthetical citation notes the author and date (but note that no page number is provided, as APA does not require these in citations of summarized material); the full reference to the source would be listed at the end of the paper.

> ☑ There is now wide agreement among linguists that the ease with which human children acquire their native tongues, under the conditions of a normal childhood, demonstrates an inborn capacity for language that is not shared by any other animals, not even those who are reared in comparable ways and given human language training (Deacon, 1997).

Simply substituting synonyms for the words and phrases of the source, however, is not enough to avoid plagiarism. Even with its original wording, the next example also fails but for a very different reason: it follows the original's sentence structure, as illustrated in the interpolated copy below it.

> Recently, linguists appear to have come to an agreement that speaking is an in-born skill, and that nothing but a substantial input from in-born cognition can account for the human capacity to acquire such a complicated means of expression (Deacon, 1997).

> **Recently** (*over the last few decades*)**, linguists** (*language researchers*) **appear to have come to an agreement** (*seem to have reached a consensus*) **that speaking is an in-born skill** (*that language is an innate ability*)**, and that nothing but a substantial input** (*and that only a significant contribution*) **from in-born cognition** (*from innate knowledge*) **can account for the human capacity** (*can explain our ability*) **to acquire such a complicated means of expression** (*to learn such a complex communication system*) **(Deacon, 1997).**

What follows is a good paraphrase of the passage's opening sentence; this paraphrase captures the sense of the original without echoing the details and shape of its language.

☑ **Linguists now broadly agree that children are born with the ability to learn language; in fact, the human capacity to acquire such a difficult skill cannot easily be accounted for in any other way (Deacon, 1997).**

Quoting Directly

Unlike paraphrases and summaries, direct quotations must use the exact wording of the original. Because they involve importing outside words, quotations pose unique challenges. Quote too frequently, and you risk making your readers wonder why they are not reading your sources instead of your paper. Your essay should present something you want to say — informed and supported by properly documented sources, but forming a contribution that is yours alone. To that end, use secondary material to help you build a strong framework for your work, not to replace it. Quote sparingly, therefore; use your sources' exact wording only when it is important or particularly memorable.

To avoid misrepresenting your sources, be sure to quote accurately; to avoid plagiarism, take care to indicate quotations as quotations, and cite them properly. If you use the author's name in a signal phrase, follow it with the date in parentheses. For all direct quotations, you must also include the page number (or paragraph number for a nonpaginated online source) of the original in your citation, as in the following examples.

Below are two problematic quotations. The first does not show which words come directly from the source.

👎 **Deacon (1997) maintained that children enter the world predisposed to learn human languages (p. 102).**

The second quotation fails to identify the source at all.

👎 **Many linguists have argued that "children enter the world predisposed to learn human languages."**

The next example corrects both problems by naming the source and indicating clearly which words come directly from it.

☑ **Deacon (1997) maintained that "children enter the world predisposed to learn human languages" (p. 102).**

Formatting Quotations

There are two ways to signal an exact borrowing: by enclosing it in double quotation marks and by indenting it as a block of text. Which you should choose depends on the length and genre of the quotation and on the style guide you are following.

Short Quotations

What counts as a short quotation differs among the various reference guides. In MLA style, "short" means up to four lines; in APA, up to forty words; and in Chicago Style, up to one hundred words. All the guides agree, however, that short quotations must be enclosed in double quotation marks, as in the examples below.

Short quotation, full sentence:

> **According** to Deacon (1997), linguists agree that a human child's capacity to acquire language is inborn: "Without question, children enter the world predisposed to learn human languages" (p. 102).

Short quotation, partial sentence:

> **According** to Deacon (1997), linguists agree that human "children enter the world predisposed to learn human languages" (p. 102).

Long Quotations

In APA style, longer quotations of forty words or more should be double-spaced and indented, as a block, about one-half inch from the left margin. Do not include quotation marks; the indentation indicates that the words come exactly from the source. Note that indented quotations are often introduced with a full sentence followed by a colon. The page number appears after the closing period of the indented quotation.

> **Deacon** (1997) maintained that human beings are born with a unique cognitive capacity:

> > Without question, children enter the world predisposed to learn human languages. All normal children, raised in normal social environments, inevitably learn their local language, whereas other species, even when raised and taught in this same environment, do not. This demonstrates that human brains come into the world specially equipped for this function. (p. 102)

Quotations within Quotations

You may sometimes find, within the original passage you wish to quote, words already enclosed in double quotation marks. If your quotation is short, enclose it all in double quotation marks, and use single quotation marks for the embedded quotation.

> **Deacon (1997) was firm in maintaining that human language differs from other communication systems in kind rather than degree: "Of no other natural form of communication is it legitimate to say that 'language is a more complicated version of that'" (p. 44).**

If your quotation is long, keep the double quotation marks of the original. Note as well that in the example below, the source's use of italics (*simple*) is also faithfully reproduced.

> **Deacon (1997) was firm in maintaining that human language differs from other communication systems in kind rather than degree:**
>
> > **Of no other natural form of communication is it legitimate to say that "language is a more complicated version of that." It is just as misleading to call other species' communication systems *simple* languages as it is to call them languages. In addition to asserting that a Procrustean mapping of one to the other is possible, the analogy ignores the sophistication and power of animals' non-linguistic communication, whose capabilities may also be without language parallels. (p. 44)**

Adding to or Deleting from a Quotation

While it is important to use the original's exact wording in a quotation, it is allowable to modify a quotation somewhat, as long as the changes are clearly indicated and do not distort the meaning of the original.

Sometimes it's useful to add emphasis to a quotation, so that readers pay special attention to a word or several. You can do this by putting what you want to emphasize in italics, but you must indicate that the italics are yours, not the original author's.

Using italics to add emphasis to part of a quotation

A frequent way of doing this is:

> **Yet our experience of its naturalness, its matter-of-factness, belies its *alien nature* in the grander scheme of things. (p. 44, emphasis added)**

281

APA style wants this in square brackets immediately following the added emphasis:

> **Yet our experience of its naturalness, its matter-of-factness, belies its *alien nature* [emphasis added] in the grander scheme of things. (p. 44)**

There was a word in italics in the quotation beginning with **Of no other natural form**, at the end of the previous section. That emphasis was in the original quotation, not added. When this is the case, you can note [emphasis in original].

You may want to add to a quotation in order to clarify what would otherwise be puzzling or ambiguous to someone who does not know its context; put whatever you add in square brackets.

Using square brackets to add to a quotation

> **Deacon (1997) concluded that children are born "specially equipped for this [language] function" (p. 102).**

If you would like to streamline a quotation by omitting anything unnecessary to your point, insert an ellipsis (three spaced dots) to show that you've left material out.

Using an ellipsis to delete from a quotation

> **Deacon argued that it is "misleading to call other species' communication systems … languages" (p. 102).**

When the quotation looks like a complete sentence but is actually part of a longer sentence, you should provide an ellipsis to show that there is more to the original than you are using.

> **Deacon (1997) concluded that "… children enter the world predisposed to learn human languages" (p. 102).**

When the omitted material runs over a sentence boundary or constitutes a whole sentence or more, insert a period plus an ellipsis.

> **Deacon (1997) claimed that human children are born with a unique ability to acquire their native language: "Without question, children enter the world predisposed to learn human languages…. [H]uman brains come into the world specially equipped for this function" (p. 102).**

Be sparing in modifying quotations; it is all right to have one or two altered quotations in a paper, but if you find yourself changing quotations often, or adding to and omitting from one quotation more than once, reconsider quoting at all. A paraphrase or summary is very often a more effective choice.

Integrating Quotations

Quotations must be worked smoothly and grammatically into your sentences and paragraphs. Always, of course, mark quotations as such, but for the purpose of integrating them into your writing, treat them otherwise as if they were your own words. The boundary between what you say and what your source says should be grammatically seamless.

- Deacon (1997) pointed out, "whereas other species, even when raised and taught in this same environment, do not" (p. 102).
- ☑ According to Deacon (1997), while human children brought up under normal conditions acquire the language they are exposed to, "other species, even when raised and taught in this same environment, do not" (p. 102).

Avoiding "dumped" quotations

Integrating quotations well also means providing a context for them. Don't merely drop them into your paper or string them together like beads on a necklace; make sure to introduce them by noting where the material comes from and how it connects to whatever point you are making.

- For many years, linguists have studied how human children acquire language. "Without question, children enter the world predisposed to learn human language" (Deacon, 1997, p. 102).
- ☑ Most linguists studying how human children acquire language have come to share the conclusion articulated by Deacon (1997): "Without question, children enter the world predisposed to learn human language" (p. 102).
- "Without question, children enter the world predisposed to learn human language" (Deacon, 1997, p. 102). "There is ... something special about human brains that enables us to do with ease what no other species can do even minimally without intense effort and remarkably insightful training" (Deacon, 1997, p. 103).
- ☑ Deacon (1997) based his claim that we "enter the world predisposed to learn human language" on the fact that very young humans can "do with ease what no other species can do even minimally without intense effort and remarkably insightful training" (pp. 102–103).

Signal Phrases

To leave no doubt in your readers' minds about which parts of your essay are yours and which come from elsewhere, identify the sources of your summaries, paraphrases, and quotations with signal phrases, as in the following examples.

283

As Carter and Rosenthal (2011) demonstrated …

According to Ming, Bartlett, and Koch (2014), …

In his latest article McGann (2015) advanced the view that …

As Beyerstein (2000) observed, …

Kendal and Ahmadi (1998) have suggested that …

Freschi (2004) was not alone in rejecting these claims, arguing that …

Cabral, Chernovsky, and Morgan (2015) emphasized this point in their recent
   research: …

Sayeed (2003) has maintained that …

In a landmark study, Mtele (1992) concluded that …

In her later work, however, Hardy (2005) overturned previous results, suggesting that
   …

In order to help establish your paper's credibility, you may also find it useful at times to include in a signal phrase information that shows why readers should take the source seriously, as in the following example:

In this insightful and compassionate work, clinical neurologist Oliver Sacks (1985) described …

Here, the signal phrase mentions the author's professional credentials; it also points out the importance of his book, which is appropriate to do in the case of a work as famous as Sacks's *The Man Who Mistook His Wife for a Hat.*

Below is a fuller list of words and expressions that may be useful in the crafting of signal phrases:

according to _____,	confirm	intimate
acknowledge	contend	note
add	declare	observe
admit	demonstrate	point out
advance	deny	put it
agree	dispute	reason
allow	emphasize	refute
argue	endorse	reject
assert	find	report
attest	grant	respond
believe	illustrate	suggest
claim	imply	take issue with
comment	in the view of _____,	think
compare	in the words of _____	write
conclude	insist	

MLA Style

"MLA style" refers to the referencing guidelines of the Modern Language Association, which are favoured by many disciplines in the humanities. The main components of the MLA system are in-text author–page number citations for the body of an essay, and a bibliography giving publication details — the list of "Works Cited" — at the end of it.

This section outlines the key points of MLA style. Consult the *MLA Handbook* (8th edition, 2016) if you have questions not answered here; you may also find answers at the website of the MLA (www.mla.org), where updates and answers to frequently asked questions are posted.

About In-Text Citations

in-text citations: Under the MLA system a quotation or specific reference to another work is followed by a parenthetical page reference:

> **Bonnycastle refers to "the true and lively spirit of opposition" with which Marxist literary criticism invigorates the discipline (204).**

The work is then listed under "Works Cited" at the end of the essay:

> **Bonnycastle, Stephen. *In Search of Authority: An Introductory Guide to Literary Theory*. 3rd ed., Broadview Press, 2007.**

(See below for information about the "Works Cited" list.)

no signal phrase (or author not named in signal phrase): If the context does not make it clear who the author is, that information must be added to the in-text citation. Note that no comma separates the name of the author from the page number.

> **Even in recent years some have continued to believe that Marxist literary criticism invigorates the discipline with a "true and lively spirit of opposition" (Bonnycastle 204).**

placing of in-text citations: Place in-text citations at the ends of clauses or sentences in order to keep disruption of your writing to a minimum. The citation comes before the period or comma in the surrounding sentence. (If the quotation ends with punctuation other than a period or comma, then this should precede the end of the quotation, and a period or comma should still follow the in-text citation.)

> **Ricks refuted this point early on (16), but the claim has continued to be made in recent years.**
>
> **In "The Windhover," on the other hand, Hopkins bubbles over; "the mastery of the thing!" (8), he enthuses when he thinks of a bird, exclaiming shortly thereafter, "O my chevalier!" (10).**

When a cited quotation is set off from the text, however, the in-text citation should be placed after the concluding punctuation.

> **Muriel Jaeger draws on the following anecdote in discussing the resistance of many wealthy Victorians to the idea of widespread education for the poor:**
>
>> **In a mischievous mood, Henry Brougham once told [some well-off acquaintances who were] showing perturbation about the likely results of educating the "lower orders" that they could maintain their superiority by working harder themselves. (105)**

in-text citation when text is in parentheses: If an in-text citation occurs within text in parentheses, square brackets are used for the reference.

> **The development of a mass literary culture (or a "print culture," to use Williams's expression [88]) took several hundred years in Britain.**

page number unavailable: Many web sources lack page numbers. If your source has no page or section numbers, no number should be given in your citation. Do not count paragraphs yourself, as the version you are using may differ from others.

> **In a recent Web posting a leading critic has clearly implied that he finds such an approach objectionable (Bhabha).**

If the source gives explicit paragraph or section numbers, as many websites do, cite the appropriate abbreviation, followed by the number.

> **Early in the novel, Austen makes clear that the "business" of Mrs. Bennet's life is "to get her daughters married" (ch. 1).**
>
> **In "The American Scholar" Emerson asserts that America's "long apprenticeship to the learning of other lands" is drawing to a close (par. 7).**

Note that (as is not the case with page numbers), MLA style requires a comma between author and paragraph or section numbers in a citation.

> **Early in the novel, Mrs. Bennet makes it clear that her sole business in life is "to get her daughters married" (Austen, ch. 1).**

one page or less: If a source is one page long or less, it is advisable to still provide the page number (though MLA does not require this).

> **In his *Chicago Tribune* review, Bosley calls the novel's prose "excruciating" (1).**

multiple authors: If there are two authors, both authors should be named either in the signal phrase or in the in-text citation, connected by *and*.

> **Chambliss and Best argue that the importance of this novel is primarily historical (233).**

> **Two distinguished scholars have recently argued that the importance of this novel is primarily historical (Chambliss and Best 233).**

If there are three or more authors, include only the first author's name in the in-text citation, followed by *et al.*, short for the Latin *et alii*, meaning *and others*.

> **Meaning is not simply there in the text, but in the complex relationships between the text, the reader, and the Medieval world (Black et al. xxxvi).**

corporate author: The relevant organization or the title of the piece should be included in the in-text citation if neither is included in the body of your text; make sure enough information is provided for readers to find the correct entry in your Works Cited list. Shorten a long title to avoid awkwardness, but take care that the shortened version begins with the same word as the corresponding entry in "Works Cited" so that readers can move easily from the citation to the bibliographic information. For example, *Comparative Indo-European Linguistics: An Introduction* should be shortened to *Comparative Indo-European* rather than *Indo-European Linguistics*. The first two examples below cite unsigned newspaper or encyclopedia articles; the last is a corporate author in-text citation.

> **As *The New York Times* reported in one of its several December 2 articles on the Florida recount, Vice-President Gore looked tired and strained as he answered questions ("Gore Press Conference" A16).**

> **In the 1990s Sao Paulo began to rapidly overtake Mexico City as the world's most polluted city ("Air Pollution" 21).**

> **There are a number of organizations mandated "to foster the production and enjoyment of the arts in Canada" (Canada Council for the Arts 2).**

more than one work by the same author cited: If you include more than one work by the same author in your list of Works Cited, you must make clear which work is being cited each time. This may be done either by mentioning the work in a signal phrase or by including in the citation a short version of the title.

> **In *The House of Mirth*, for example, Wharton writes of love as keeping Lily and Selden "from atrophy and extinction" (282).**

> **Wharton sees love as possessing the power to keep humans "from atrophy and extinction" (*House of Mirth* 282).**

> Love, as we learn from the experience of Lily and Selden, possesses the power to keep humans "from atrophy and extinction" (Wharton, *House of Mirth* 282).

multi-volume works: Note, by number, the volume you are referring to, followed by a colon and a space, before noting the page number. Use the abbreviation "vol." when citing an entire volume.

> Towards the end of *In Darkest Africa* Stanley refers to the Victoria Falls (2: 387).

> In contrast with those of the medieval period, Renaissance artworks show an increasing concern with depicting the material world and less and less of an interest in metaphysical symbolism (Hauser, vol. 2).

two or more authors with the same last name: If the Works Cited list includes two or more authors with the same last name, the in-text citation should supply both first initials and last names, or, if the first initials are also the same, the full first and last names:

> One of the leading economists of the time advocated wage and price controls (Harry Johnston 197).

> One of the leading economists of the time advocated wage and price controls (H. Johnston 197).

indirect quotations: When an original source is not available but is referred to by another source, the in-text citation includes *qtd. in* (an abbreviation of *quoted in*) and a reference to the second source. In the example below, Casewell is quoted by Bouvier; the in-text citation directs readers to an entry in Works Cited for the Bouvier work.

> Casewell considers Lambert's position to be "outrageously arrogant" (qtd. in Bouvier 59).

short poems: For short poems, cite line numbers rather than page numbers.

> In "Dover Beach" Arnold hears the pebbles in the waves bring the "eternal note of sadness in" (line 14).

If you are citing the same poem repeatedly, use just the numbers for subsequent references.

> The world, in Arnold's view, has "really neither joy, nor love, nor light" (33).

longer poems: For longer poems with parts, cite the part (or section, or "book") as well as the line (where available). Use Arabic numerals, and use a period for separation.

In "Ode: Intimations of Immortality" Wordsworth calls human birth "but a sleep and a forgetting" (5.1).

novels or short stories: When a work of prose fiction has chapters or numbered divisions the citation should include first the page number, and then book, chapter, and section numbers as applicable. (These can be very useful in helping readers of a different edition to locate the passage you are citing.) Arabic numerals should be used. A semicolon should be used to separate the page number from the other information.

When Joseph and Fanny are by themselves, they immediately express their affection for each other, or, as Fielding puts it, "solace themselves" with "amorous discourse" (151; ch. 26).

In *Tender Is the Night* Dick's ambition does not quite crowd out the desire for love: "He wanted to be loved too, if he could fit it in" (133; bk. 2, ch. 4).

plays: Almost all plays are divided into acts and/or scenes. For plays that do not include line numbering throughout, cite the page number in the edition you have been using, followed by act and/or scene numbers as applicable:

As Angie and Joyce begin drinking together Angie pronounces the occasion "better than Christmas" (72; act 3).

Near the conclusion of Inchbald's *Wives as They Were* Bronzely declares that he has been "made to think with reverence on the matrimonial compact" (62; act 5, sc. 4).

For plays written entirely or largely in verse, where line numbers are typically provided throughout, you should omit the reference to page number in the citation. Instead, cite the act, scene, and line numbers, using Arabic numerals. For a Shakespeare play, if the title isn't clear from the introduction to a quotation, an abbreviation of the title may also be used. The in-text citation below is for Shakespeare's *The Merchant of Venice*, Act 2, Scene 3, lines 2–4:

Jessica clearly has some fondness for Launcelot: "Our house is hell, and thou, a merry devil, / Dost rob it of some taste of tediousness. / But fare thee well; there is a ducat for thee" (*MV* 2.3.2–4).

works without page numbers: If you are citing literary texts where you have consulted editions from other sources (on the web or in an e-book, for instance), the principles are exactly the same, except that you need not cite page numbers. For example, if the online Gutenberg edition of Fielding's *Joseph Andrews* were being cited, the citation would be as follows:

> When Joseph and Fanny are by themselves, they immediately express their affection for each other, or, as Fielding puts it, "solace themselves" with "amorous discourse" (ch. 26).

Students should be cautioned that online editions of literary texts are often unreliable. Typically there are far more typos and other errors in online versions of literary texts than there are in print versions, and such things as the layout of poems are also frequently incorrect. It is often possible to exercise judgement about such matters, however. If, for example, you are not required to base your essay on a particular copy of a Thomas Hardy poem but may find your own, you will be far better off using the text you will find on the Representative Poetry Online site run out of the University of Toronto, for example, than you will using a text you might find on a "World's Finest Love Poems" site.

sacred texts: The Bible and other sacred texts that are available in many editions should be cited in a way that enables the reader to check the reference in any edition. For the Bible, book, chapter, and verse should all be cited, using periods for separation. The reference below is to Genesis, chapter 2, verse 1.

> According to the Judeo-Christian story of creation, at the end of the sixth day "the heavens and the earth were finished" (Gen. 2.1).

works in an anthology or book of readings: In the in-text citation for a work in an anthology, use the name of the author of the work, not that of the editor of the anthology. The page number, however, should be that found in the anthology. The following citation refers to an article by Frederic W. Gleach in an anthology edited by Jennifer Brown and Elizabeth Vibert.

> One of the essays in Brown and Vibert's collection argues that we should rethink the Pocahontas myth (Gleach 48).

In your list of Works Cited, this work should be alphabetized under Gleach, the author of the piece you have consulted, not under Brown. If you cite another work by a different author from the same anthology or book of readings, that should appear as a separate entry in your list of Works Cited — again, alphabetized under the author's name.

tweets: Cite tweets by giving the author's name in your text rather than in an in-text citation.

> Jack Welch quickly lost credibility when he tweeted that the US Bureau of Labor had manipulated monthly unemployment rate statistics in order to boost the post-debate Obama campaign: "Unbelievable job numbers..these Chicago guys will do anything..can't debate so change numbers."

About Works Cited

MLA Core Elements

The Works Cited list in MLA style is an alphabetized list at the end of the essay (or article or book). The entire list, like the main part of the essay, should be double-spaced throughout, and each entry should be given a hanging indent: the first line is flush with the left-hand margin, and each subsequent line is indented one tab space.

The Works Cited list should include information about all the sources you have cited. Do not include works that you consulted but did not cite in the body of your text.

MLA style provides a set of citation guidelines that the writer follows and adapts, regardless of whether the source being cited is print, digital, audio, visual, or any other form of media. All sources share what the MLA call "Core Elements," and these, listed in order, create the citation for all your entries: Author, Title of Source, Title of Container (larger whole), Other Contributors, Version, Number, Publisher, Publication Date, and Location. Each element is followed by the punctuation marks shown in the table below, unless it is the last element, which should always close with a period. (There are a few exceptions to this rule, which are outlined below.) Most sources don't have all the elements (some don't have an author, for example, or a version, or a location); if you find that this is the case, omit the element and move on to the next.

The table can function as a guide when creating citations. Once you have found all the publication details for your source, place them in order and punctuate according to the table, leaving out any elements for which you don't have information.

1. Author.
2. Title of source.
3. Title of container,
4. Other contributors,
5. Version,
6. Number,
7. Publisher,
8. Publication Date,
9. Location.

In the sections below, you will discover how to identify the core elements of MLA style and how to use them across media. For a list of examples, please see pages 68 to 84.

Author

This element begins your citation. For a **single author,** list the author's last name first, followed by a comma, and then the author's first name or initials (use whatever appears on the work's title page or copyright page), followed by a period. (Note that the abbreviation UP below is the standard MLA abbreviation for *University Press.*)

> Graham, Jorie. *From the New World*. Ecco, 2015.
> McKerlie, Dennis. *Justice between the Young and the Old*. Oxford UP, 2013.

If a source has **two authors,** the first author's name should appear with the last name first, followed by a comma and *and.* Note also that the authors' names should appear in the order they are listed; sometimes this is not alphabetical.

> Rectenwald, Michael, and Lisa Carl. *Academic Writing, Real World Topics*. Broadview Press, 2015.

If there are **three or more authors,** include only the first author's name, reversed, followed by a comma and *et al.* (the abbreviation of the Latin *et alii*, meaning *and others*).

> Blais, Andre, et al. *Anatomy of a Liberal Victory*. Broadview Press, 2002.

Sources that are **edited** rather than authored are usually cited in a similar way; add "editor" or "editors" after the name(s) and before the title.

> Renker, Elizabeth, editor. *Poems: A Concise Anthology*. Broadview Press, 2016.

When referring to an edited version of a work written by another author or authors, list the editor(s) after the title, in the Other Contributors element.

> Trollope, Anthony. *The Eustace Diamonds*. 1873. Edited by Stephen Gill and John Sutherland, Penguin, 1986.

Authors can be organizations, institutions, associations, or government agencies ("corporate authors"). If a work has been issued by a **corporate author** and no author is identified, the entry should be listed by the name of the organization that produced it.

> Ontario, Ministry of Natural Resources. *Achieving Balance: Ontario's Long-Term Energy Plan*. Queen's Printer for Ontario, 2016, www.energy.gov.on.ca/en/ltep/achieving-balance-ontarios-long-term-energy-plan. Accessed 10 May 2016.

If the work is published by the same organization that is the corporate author, skip the author element and list only the publisher. The citation will begin with the source title.

2014 Annual Report. Broadview Press, 2015.

"History of the Arms and Great Seal of the Commonwealth of Massachusetts." Commonwealth of Massachusetts, www.sec.state.ma.us/pre/presea/sealhis. htm. Accessed 9 May 2016.

"Our Mandate." Art Gallery of Ontario, www.ago.net/mandate. Accessed 10 May 2016.

Works with an **anonymous author** should be alphabetized by title, omitting the author element.

Sir Gawain and the Green Knight. Edited by Paul Battles, Broadview Press, 2012.

Works under a **pseudonym** should appear with the pseudonym in place of the author's name. Online usernames are copied out exactly as they appear on the screen.

@newyorker. "With the resignation of Turkey's Prime Minister, the country's President now stands alone and unchallenged." *Twitter*, 6 May 2016, twitter. com/NewYorker/status/ 728676985254379520.

Note that the author element is flexible. If you are discussing the work of a film director, for example, the director's name should be placed in the author element, with a descriptor.

Hitchcock, Alfred, director. *The Lady Vanishes.* United Artists, 1938.

If, on the other hand, you are discussing film editing, you would place the film editor in the author element. In this case, you might also include Hitchcock's name in the "Other Contributors" element.

Dearing, R.E., film editor. *The Lady Vanishes*, directed by Alfred Hitchcock, United Artists, 1938.

If no single contributor's work is of particular importance in your discussion of a film or television source, omit the author element altogether.

"The Buys." *The Wire*, created by David Simon and Ed Burns, directed by Peter Medak, season 1, episode 3, HBO, 16 June 2002, disc 1.

If you are citing a **translated source** and the translation itself is the focus of your work, the translator or translators can be placed in the author element.

Lodge, Kirsten, translator. *Notes from the Underground.* By Fyodor Dostoevsky, edited by Kirsten Lodge, Broadview Press, 2014.

When the work itself is the focus, as is usually the case, the author should remain in the author element, and the translator moved to the "other contributors" element:

> Dostoevsky, Fyodor. *Notes from the Underground*. Translated and edited by Kirsten Lodge, Broadview Press, 2014.

This principle holds true across media and elements. Adapt the MLA structure to create citations that are clear, most relevant to your work, and most useful to your reader.

Title of Source

The title of your source follows the author element. Copy the title as you find it in the source, but with MLA-standard capitalization and punctuation. Capitalize the first word, the last word, and all key words, but not articles, prepositions, coordinating conjunctions, or the *to* in infinitives.

> Carson, Anne. *The Albertine Workout*. New Directions, 2014.

If there is a **subtitle**, include it after the main title, following a colon.

> Bök, Christian. *The Xenotext: Book 1*. Coach House Books, 2015.

Your title gives the reader information about the source. Italicized titles indicate that the source is a complete, independent whole. A title enclosed in quotation marks tells the reader that the source is part of a larger work.

A **book** is an independent whole, so the title is italicized.

> Wordsworth, William. *Poems, in Two Volumes*. Edited by Richard Matlak, Broadview Press, 2016.

Other examples include **long poems** (*In Memoriam*), **magazines** (*The New Yorker*), **newspapers** (*The Guardian*), **journals** (*The American Poetry Review*), **websites** (*The Camelot Project*), **films** (*Memento*), **television shows** (*The X-Files*), and **compact discs** or **record albums** (*Dark Side of the Moon*).

A **poem**, **short story**, or **essay** within a larger collection is placed in quotation marks.

> Wordsworth, William. "The Solitary Reaper." *Poems, in Two Volumes*, edited by Richard Matlak, Broadview Press, 2016, p. 153.

Other examples include **chapters in books** ("The Autist Artist" in *The Man Who Mistook His Wife for a Hat and Other Clinical Tales*), **encyclopedia articles** ("Existentialism"), **essays in books or journals** ("Salvation in the Garden: Daoism and Ecology" in *Daoism and Ecology: Ways within a Cosmic Landscape*), **short stories** ("Young Goodman Brown"), **short poems** ("Daddy"), **pages on websites** ("The Fisher King" from *The Camelot Project*), **episodes of television shows** ("Small Potatoes" from *The X-Files*), and **songs** ("Eclipse" from *Dark Side of the Moon*). Put the titles of **public lectures** in double quotation marks as well ("Walls in *The Epic of Gilgamesh*").

These formatting rules apply across media forms. A website is placed in italics; a posting on the website is placed in quotation marks.

> **Stein, Sadie. "Casting the Runes."** *The Daily: The Paris Review Blog*, 9 Oct. 2015, www.theparisreview.org/ blog/2015/10/09/casting-the-runes/.

If the title of a stand-alone work contains the title of a work that is not independent, the latter is put in double quotation marks, and the entire title is put in italics ("*Self-Reliance" and Other Essays*). If the title of a stand-alone work appears within the title of another independent work, MLA recommends that the latter be put in italics and the former not (*Chaucer's* House of Fame: *The Poetics of Skeptical Fideism*). If the title of a non-independent work is embedded in another title of the same kind, put the inner title into single quotation marks and the outer title in double quotation marks ("The Drama of Donne's 'The Indifferent'").

When a stand-alone work appears in a **collection**, the work's title remains in italics.

> **James, Henry.** *The American. Henry James: Novels 1871-1880*, edited by William T. Stafford, Library of America, 1983.

Title of Container

Very often your source is found within a larger context, such as an **anthology, periodical, newspaper, digital platform**, or **website**. When this is the case, the larger whole is called the "container." For an article in a newspaper, for example, the article is the "source" and the newspaper is the "container." For a song in an **album**, the song is the "source" and the album is the "container."

The title of the container is usually italicized and followed by a comma.

> **Gladwell, Malcolm. "The Art of Failure: Why Some People Choke and Others Panic."** *The New Yorker*, 21 Aug. 2000, www.newyorker.com/magazine/2000/08/21/the-art-of-failure. Accessed 18 Feb. 2013.

The container can be a website; a book that is a collection of stories, poems, plays, or essays; a magazine; a journal; an album; or a database.

When doing research, particularly online, one often comes across nested containers, in which, for example, an article is found in a collection of essays, which is itself found in a database. All containers are recorded in the citation, so your reader knows exactly how to find your source. Add more container elements as needed. Additional containers should follow the period at the end of the information given for the preceding container (usually after the date or location element).

It can be helpful to see this process charted out. Notice that the publication information for the container follows that of the source.

Here is an example of an **article from a periodical**, accessed from an online database.

1. Author.	Sohmer, Steve.
2. Title of source.	"12 June 1599: Opening Day at Shakespeare's Globe."
CONTAINER 1:	
3. Title of container,	*Early Modern Literary Studies: A Journal of Sixteenth- and Seventeenth-Century English Literature,*
4. Other contributors,	
5. Version,	
6. Number,	vol. 3, no.1,
7. Publisher,	
8. Publication Date,	1997.
9. Location.	
CONTAINER 2:	
3. Title of container,	*ProQuest,*
4. Other contributors,	
5. Version,	
6. Number,	
7. Publisher,	
8. Publication Date,	
9. Location.	www.extra.shu.ac.uk/emls/emlshome.html.

Citation as It Would Appear in Works Cited List:

Sohmer, Steve. "12 June 1599: Opening Day at Shakespeare's Globe." *Early Modern Literary Studies: A Journal of Sixteenth- and Seventeenth-Century English Literature*, vol. 3, no.1, 1997. *ProQuest*, www.extra.shu.ac.uk/emls/emlshome. html.

The next example is an **e-book version** of Jane Austen's *Emma*, accessed from a publisher's website. The novel is self-contained, so no title of a container is given until the digital platform information is recorded in the second container.

1. Author.	Austen, Jane.
2. Title of source.	*Emma.*
CONTAINER 1:	
3. Title of container,	
4. Other contributors,	Edited by Kristen Flieger Samuelian,
5. Version,	
6. Number,	
7. Publisher,	
8. Publication Date,	2004.
9. Location.	

CONTAINER 2:	
3. Title of container,	*Broadview Press,*
4. Other contributors,	
5. Version,	
6. Number,	
7. Publisher,	
8. Publication Date,	
9. Location.	www.broadviewpress.com/ product/ emma/#tab-description.

Citation as It Would Appear in Works Cited List:

Austen, Jane. *Emma*. Edited by Kristen Flieger Samuelian, 2004. *Broadview Press*, www.broadviewpress.com/product/emma/#tab-description. Accessed 5 Feb. 2016.

The elements are recorded sequentially to create your citation. Notice that any elements that don't apply to this source are left out. Any element that is the same for both containers (in this case, the publisher) is recorded in the last (here the second) container; however, the location of this e-book (the website) contains the name of the publisher, so in this case the publisher field is left empty. This removes the need to repeat information in the citation.

Here is an example citation of a **performance in a television series**, accessed on Netflix.

1. Author.	Spacey, Kevin, performer.
2. Title of source.	"Chapter 5."
CONTAINER 1:	
3. Title of container,	House of Cards,
4. Other contributors,	directed by Joel Schumacher,
5. Version,	
6. Number,	season 1, episode 5,
7. Publisher,	
8. Publication Date,	2013.
9. Location.	
CONTAINER 2:	
3. Title of container,	Netflix,
4. Other contributors,	
5. Version,	
6. Number,	
7. Publisher,	
8. Publication Date,	
9. Location.	www.netflix.com/search/house?jbv=70178217&jbp=0 &jbr=021.

Citation as It Would Appear in Works Cited List:

Spacey, Kevin, performer. "Chapter 5." *House of Cards*, **directed by Joel Schu-macher, season 1, episode 5, 2013.** *Netflix*, **www.netflix.com/search/house?jbv= 70178217&jbp=0&jbr=021.**

Notice that in this case Netflix produced the show, so the publisher field is left empty in both containers. If the source had been an episode from a series produced by, for example, the BBC, you would include the BBC as publisher.

Tennant, David, performer. "Gridlock." *Dr. Who*, **directed by Richard Clark, series 3, episode 3, BBC, 2007.** *Netflix*, **www.netflix.com/search/dr%20who?jbv=70142441 &jbp=0&jbr=0.**

Other Contributors

There may be other key people who should be credited in your citation as contributors. This element follows the title of the source and the container (if there is one). The MLA recommends that you include the names of contributors who are important to your research, or if they help your reader to identify the source. Before each name, place a description of the role (do not abbreviate):

> adapted by
> directed by
> edited by
> illustrated by
> introduction by
> narrated by
> performance by
> translated by

If your listing of a contributor follows the source title, it is capitalized (following a period). If the contributor follows a container, it will be lower-case (following a comma).

Lao Tzu. *Tao Te Ching: A Book about the Way and the Power of the Way.* **Translated by Ursula K. Le Guin. Shambhala, 1997.**
James, Henry. *The American. Henry James: Novels 1871-1880*, **edited by William T. Stafford, Library of America, 1983.**

In the Other Contributors element, include the most relevant contributors not already mentioned in the author element. If you are writing about a television episode and a certain performance is one of the elements you discuss, for example, include the performer's name in the Other Contributors element, along with any other contributors you wish to include.

Medak, Peter, director. "The Buys." *The Wire*, created by David Simon and Ed Burns, performance by Dominic West, season 1, episode 3, HBO, 16 June 2002.

Note that the MLA guidelines are flexible; for this part of the citation especially, consider what your readers most need to know about your source and include that information. Note also that there is some flexibility in the author element; if a particular performance or other contribution is the major focus in your discussion of source, it can be cited in the author element instead.

Version

If your source is one of several editions, or if it is a revised version, record those details in this element of your citation, followed by a comma. The word "edition" is abbreviated in your citation (ed.).

Fowles, John. *The Magus*. Rev. ed., Jonathan Cape, 1977.

Shelley, Mary. *Frankenstein*. Edited by D.L. Macdonald and Kathleen Sherf, 3rd ed., Broadview Press, 2012.

You may also come across expanded editions, revised editions, and updated editions, all of which can be noted in this element of your citation. Different media might use different terminology. For example in film you may find a director's cut, or in music an abridged version of a concerto: use the same principles as above, providing the relevant information in the Version element of your citation.

Coen, Ethan, and Joel Coen, directors. *Blood Simple*. Director's cut, Universal, 2001.

Number

If your source is part of a **multi-volume work**, or if it is part of a journal that is issued in numbers and/or volumes, include the volume information in this Number element of your citation.

If you are citing **two or more volumes** of a multi-volume work, the entry should note the total number of volumes. If you cite only one of the volumes, list it after the title.

Jeeves, Julie, editor. *A Reference Guide to Spanish Architecture*. 3 vols., Hackett, 2005.

Mercer, Bobby, editor. *A Reference Guide to French Architecture*. Vol. 1, Hackett, 2002.

Include the **volume and issue numbers** for journals. Use the abbreviations *vol.* for volume and *no.* for issue number.

Gregory, Elizabeth. "Marianne Moore's 'Blue Bug': A Dialogic Ode on Celebrity, Race, Gender, and Age." *Modernism/Modernity*, vol. 22, no. 4, 2015, pp. 759–86.

Some journals do not use volume numbers and give only an issue number.

Sanger, Richard. "Goodbye, Seamus." *Brick*, no. 93, Summer 2014, pp. 153–57.

The Number element is also where you record issue numbers for comic books, or the season and episode numbers for a television series.

Spacey, Kevin, performer. "Chapter 5." *House of Cards*, directed by Joel Schumacher, season 1, episode 5, 2013. *Netflix*, www.netflix.com/search/house?jbv=70178217&jbp=0&jbr=021.

Publisher

In this element of your citation, record the organization that produced the source, whether it be the publisher of a book, the organization running a website, or the studio producing a film. (In the case of a secondary container, include the organization that produced the container.) Do not abbreviate, except in the case of university presses, which may be abbreviated as *UP*. Note that places of publication are not included.

To find the publisher of a **book**, look on the title page or on the copyright page.

Dickens, Charles. *The Uncommercial Traveller*. Edited by Daniel Tyler, Oxford UP, 2015.
Rush, Rebecca. *Kelroy*. Edited by Betsy Klimasmith, Broadview Press, 2016.

For a **film** or **television series**, the studio or company that produced the show is recorded in the information on the back of a DVD or in the opening and closing credits.

Simon, David, creator. *The Wire*. HBO, 2002–2008.

For **websites**, the publisher's information can often be found in the copyright notice at the bottom of the page.

Bogan, Louise. "Women." 1922. *Representative Poetry Online*, edited by Ian Lancashire, University of Toronto, 2000.

A **blog network** may be cited as the publisher of the blogs it hosts.

Cairney, Paul, and Kathryn Oliver. "If scientists want to influence policymaking, they need to understand it." *Political Science*, The Guardian Science Blog Network, 27 Apr. 2016.

You may omit a publisher's name in the following kinds of publications:

- A periodical (journal, magazine, newspaper).
- A work published by its author or editor.
- A website whose title is essentially the same as the name of the publisher.
- A website not involved in producing the works it is making available (e.g., YouTube, JSTOR, ProQuest).

These are listed as containers, but not as publishers.

If **two or more publishers** are listed for your source, cite them both and separate them with a forward slash (/).

> Banting, Keith G., editor. *Thinking Outside the Box: Innovation in Policy Ideas*. School
> of Policy Studies, Queen's University / McGill–Queen's University Press, 2015.

Publication Date

In this element of your citation, record the date of publication for your source. For **books**, this date is found on the copyright page (and sometimes on the title page). If several editions are listed, use the date for the edition you have consulted.

> Stevenson, Robert Louis. *The Strange Case of Dr. Jekyll and Mr. Hyde*. Edited by
> Martin A. Danahay, 3rd ed., Broadview Press, 2015.

Online sources almost always have a date posted, and this is the date you should record in this element.

> Heller, Nathan. "The Big Uneasy: What's Roiling the Liberal-Arts Campus?"
> *The New Yorker*, 30 May 2016, www.newyorker.com/magazine/2016/05/30/
> the-new-activism-of-liberal-arts-colleges.

A source may be associated with **more than one publication date**. An article online may have been previously published in print, or an article printed in a book may have been published previously in a periodical. In this case, the MLA recommends that you record the date that is most relevant to your use of the source. If you consulted the online version of an article, for example, ignore the date of print publication and cite the online publication date.

For books, we record the year of publication. For other sources, whether to include a year, month, and day depends on your source and the context in which you are using it. If you are citing an **episode from a television series**, for example, it is usually enough to record the year it aired.

> Medak, Peter, director. "The Buys." *The Wire*, created by David Simon and Ed Burns,
> season 1, episode 3, HBO, 2002.

If, however, the context surrounding the episode is being discussed in your work, you should be more specific about the date:

> Medak, Peter, director. "The Buys." *The Wire*, created by David Simon and Ed Burns, season 1, episode 3, HBO, 16 June 2002.

For a **video posted on a website**, include the date on which the video was posted. In the example below, the posting date should be included in the second container, which records the details for the digital platform. The date the video was released is included in the publication details for the source.

> Gleeson, Thomas, director. *Home*. Screen Innovation Production, 2012. *Vimeo*, uploaded by Thomas Gleeson, 31 Jan. 2013, www.vimeo.com/58630796.

If you are citing a **comment posted on a web page**, and the time the content was posted is indicated, include the time in your entry.

> Evan. Comment on "Another Impasse on Gun Bills, Another Win for Hyperpolitics." *The New York Times*, 21 June 2016, 9:02 a.m., www.nytimes.com/2016/06/22/us/politics/washington-congress-gun-control.html.

Larger projects are created over a longer span of time. If you are documenting a web project as a whole, include the full range of years during which it was developed.

> Secord, James A. et al., editors. *Darwin Correspondence Project*. 1974–2016, www.darwinproject.ac.uk/.

The dates of publication for **periodicals** vary. Include in full the information provided by the copyright page, whether it be indicated by season, year, month, week, or day.

> Sanger, Richard. "Goodbye, Seamus." *Brick*, no. 93, Summer 2014, pp. 153–57.
>
> Trousdale, Rachel. "'Humor Saves Steps': Laughter and Humanity in Marianne Moore." *Journal of Modern Literature*, vol. 35, no. 3, 2012, pp. 121–38. *JSTOR*, www.jstor.org/stable/10.2979/jmodelite.35.3.121.

Location

The content of the Location element varies considerably between print, digital, and other sources.

For **print sources** within a periodical or anthology, record a page number (preceded by p.) or a range of page numbers (preceded by pp.).

> Gregory, Elizabeth. "Marianne Moore's 'Blue Bug': A Dialogic Ode on Celebrity, Race, Gender, and Age." *Modernism/Modernity*, vol. 22, no. 4, 2015, pp. 759–86.
>
> Walcott, Derek. "The Sea Is History." *The Broadview Anthology of Poetry*, edited by Herbert Rosengarten and Amanda Goldrick Jones, Broadview Press, 1992, p. 757.

> Wills, Garry. "A Masterpiece on the Rise of Christianity." Review of *Through the Eye of a Needle: Wealth, The Fall of Rome, and the Making of Christianity in the West, 350–550 AD*, by Peter Brown. *New York Review of Books*, 11 Oct. 2012, pp. 43–45.

An **online work** is located by its URL, or web address. When copying the URL into your citation, remove the *http://*; this means that usually the URL will begin with *www*. If you need to break a URL over two or more lines, do not insert any hyphens at the break point; instead, when possible, break after a colon or slash or before other marks of punctuation.

> Trousdale, Rachel. "'Humor Saves Steps': Laughter and Humanity in Marianne Moore." *Journal of Modern Literature*, vol. 35, no. 3, 2012, pp. 121–38. *JSTOR*, www.jstor.org/stable/10.2979/jmodelite.35.3.121.

Some publishers assign DOIs (Digital Object Identifiers) to their online publications, and these, when available, are preferable to URLs, as they do not change when the source moves (whereas URLs do). If your source has no DOI but offers a "stable" URL, choose that one to include in your citation. The publisher in this case has agreed not to change the URL.

> Yearling, R. "*Hamlet* and the Limits of Narrative." *Essays in Criticism: A Quarterly Journal of Literary Criticism*, vol. 65, no. 4, 2015, pp. 368–82. *Proquest*, doi:dx.doi.org/10.1093/escrit/cgv022.

We find a **television episode** on a DVD by its disc number. Place the disc number in the Location element.

> "The Buys." *The Wire*, created by David Simon and Ed Burns, directed by Peter Medak, season 1, episode 3, HBO, 2002, disc 1.

For a **work of art** that you have seen in person, cite the name of the institution and city where you saw it in the Location element. Leave out the name of the city if the city name is part of the institution name (e.g., The Art Institute of Chicago).

> Sargent, John Singer. *Henry James*. 1913. National Portrait Gallery, London.

Some **archived sources** have a different system for locating objects in the archive. Where this is the case, include the code or number in the Location element.

> Blake, William. *The Marriage of Heaven and Hell*. 1790–1793. The Fitzwilliam Museum, Cambridge, 123-1950. Illuminated printed book.

If you are citing a **live performance** or **lecture**, name the location and the city. Omit the city name if it is part of the location name.

Royal Winnipeg Ballet. *The Princess and the Goblin*. Directed and choreographed by Twyla Tharp, performances by Paloma Herrera and Dmitri Dovgoselets, 17 Oct. 2012, Centennial Concert Hall, Winnipeg.

Optional Elements

You may include any of the following elements in your citation if you think they are helpful to your reader.

Date of Original Publication

If your source has been republished, it may give your reader some important context if you include the date of original publication. If you do so, place the date immediately after the source title and close with a period.

Trollope, Anthony. *The Eustace Diamonds*. 1873. Edited by Stephen Gill and John Sutherland, Penguin, 1986.

City of Publication

Including the city of publication is not very useful these days, so the MLA has decided to remove this element from citations. There are two situations, however, where you may wish to include the city. If the book was published before 1900, the city of publication is associated more closely with the source than is the publisher. For these books, you may substitute the city of publication for the publisher.

Dickens, Charles. *Our Mutual Friend*. Vol. 1, New York, 1800.

Some publishers release more than one version of a text in different countries (a British and an American edition, for example). In you are reading an unexpected version of a text, or the version you are reading has historical significance, place the name of the city in front of the publisher.

Lawrence, D.H. *Lady Chatterley's Lover*. London, Penguin, 1960.

Books in a Series

If your source is a book in a series, you may add the series name in roman (i.e., without italics) at the end of your citation, preceded by a period.

Shakespeare, William. *As You Like It*. Edited by David Bevington, Broadview Press, 2012. Broadview Internet Shakespeare Editions.

Unexpected Type of Work

If your source needs further explanation, place a descriptive term (e-mail, transcript, broadcast, street performance, talk, address) at the end of the citation, preceded by a period.

> Rosenheim, Jeff. "Diane Arbus." Art Gallery of Ontario, 6 May 2016, Toronto. Lecture.

Date of Access

It is optional to include a date of access for your online citations, but it can be a good idea, particularly if the source does not have a date of publication.

> Crawford, Isabella Valancy. "The Canoe." *Representative Poetry Online*, edited by Ian Lancashire, Web Development Group, Information Technology Services, University of Toronto Libraries, www.tspace.library.utoronto.ca/html/1807/4350/poem596.html. Accessed 24 Nov. 2015.

Examples

The following are examples of MLA-style citations for sources across various media. While these examples can offer useful guidance, remember that the MLA guidelines may be adapted to suit the details of the sources you are documenting, as well as the context in which you are using them.

single author:

> Graham, Jorie. *From the New World*. Ecco, 2015.
>
> Malory, Thomas. *Le Morte D'Arthur: Selections*. Edited by Maureen Okun, Broadview Press, 2014.

two authors:

> Auden, W.H., and Louis MacNiece. *Letters from Iceland*. Faber & Faber, 2002.
>
> Rectenwald, Michael, and Lisa Carl. *Academic Writing, Real World Topics*. Broadview Press, 2015.

three or more authors:

> Blais, Andre, et al. *Anatomy of a Liberal Victory*. Broadview Press, 2002.
>
> Fromkin, Victoria, et al. *An Introduction to Language*. 4th Canadian ed., Nelson, 2010.

corporate author:

> *2014 Annual Report*. Broadview Press, 2015.

"History of the Arms and Great Seal of the Commonwealth of Massachusetts."
Commonwealth of Massachusetts, www.sec.state.ma.us/pre/presea/sealhis/
htm. Accessed 9 May 2016.

Ontario, Ministry of Natural Resources. *Achieving Balance: Ontario's Long-Term
Energy Plan*. Queen's Printer for Ontario, 2016, www.energy.gov.on.ca/en/ltep/
achieving-balance-ontarios-long-term-energy-plan. Accessed 10 May 2016.

works with an anonymous author: Works with an anonymous author should be alphabetized by title.

Beowulf. Edited and translated by R. M. Liuzza. 2nd ed., Broadview Press, 2012.

two or more works by the same author: The author's name should appear for the first
entry only; for subsequent entries substitute three hyphens for the name of the
author.

Menand, Louis. "Bad Comma: Lynne Truss's Strange Grammar." Review of *Eats,
Shoots and Leaves*, by Lynne Truss. *The New Yorker*, 28 June 2004, www.newy-
orker.com/magazine/2004/06/28/bad-comma. Accessed 18 Feb. 2013.

——. *The Metaphysical Club: A Story of Ideas in America*. Farrar, Straus and Giroux,
2001.

works under a pseudonym: These are given using the same formatting as author's
names. Online usernames are given as they appear.

@newyorker."With the resignation of Turkey's Prime Minister, the country's
President now stands alone and unchallenged." *Twitter*, 6 May 2016, twitter.
com/NewYorker/status/728676985254379520.

edited works:

Renker, Elizabeth, editor. *Poems: A Concise Anthology*. Broadview Press, 2016.

When referring to an edited version of a work written by another author or authors, list the editor(s) after the title.

Trollope, Anthony. *The Eustace Diamonds*. 1873. Edited by Stephen Gill and John
Sutherland, Penguin, 1986.

works in translation: The translator is normally listed in the Other Contributors
element of the citation.

Bolaño, Roberto. *By Night in Chile*. Translated by Chris Andrews, New Directions,
2003.

If your work focuses on the translation itself, you may list the translator in the
author element, moving the author to the Other Contributors element.

Andrews, Chris, translator. *By Night in Chile*. By Roberto Bolaño, New Directions, 2003.

selections from anthologies or collections of readings: A selection from a collection of readings or an anthology should begin with the name of the author of the selection. If they are available, be sure to add the selection's inclusive page numbers after the anthology's publication date.

Crawford, Isabella Valancy. "The Canoe." *Representative Poetry Online*, edited by Ian Lancashire, U of Toronto, 1997, www.rpo.library.utoronto.ca/poems/canoe. Accessed 20 Apr. 2015.

Gleach, Frederic W. "Controlled Speculation: Interpreting the Saga of Pocahontas and Captain John Smith." *Reading Beyond Words: Contexts for Native History*, edited by Jennifer S. H. Brown and Elizabeth Vibert, Broadview Press, 1996, pp. 21–42.

Mahfouz, Naguib. "*Half a Day*." The Picador Book of African Stories, edited by Stephen Gray, Picador, 2001, pp. 3–6.

cross-references for works from the same collection or anthology: It can be more efficient to create a full entry for the collection or anthology, and then to list each cited item in its own entry. Position the entries in the Works Cited list alphabetically, as you normally would, and use a short form for the collection or anthology, as in the following example:

Brown, Jennifer S. H., and Elizabeth Vibert, editors. *Reading Beyond Words: Contexts for Native History*. Broadview Press, 1996.

Cruikshank, Julie. "Discovery of Gold on the Klondike: Perspectives from Oral Tradition." Brown and Vibert, pp. 433–59.

Gleach, Frederic W. "Controlled Speculation: Interpreting the Saga of Pocahontas and Captain John Smith." Brown and Vibert, pp. 21–42.

multi-volume works: If you are citing one or more of the volumes, list them after the title. The entry may note the total number of volumes at the end of the citation (this is optional).

Mercer, Bobby, editor. *A Reference Guide to French Architecture*. Vol. 1, Hackett, 2002. 3 vols.

Jeeves, Julie, editor. *A Reference Guide to Spanish Architecture*. 3 vols., Hackett, 2005.

different editions: The edition should be specified whenever it is not the first edition. Include whatever the title page indicates about the particular edition, and use abbreviations (e.g., rev. ed. for revised edition, 2nd ed. for second edition, and so on).

Fowles, John. *The Magus*. Rev. ed., Jonathan Cape, 1977.

Shelley, Mary. *Frankenstein*. 1818. Edited by Lorne Macdonald and Kathleen Scherf, 2nd ed., Broadview Press, 1999.

The Bible. Authorized King James Version, Oxford UP, 2008.

republished sources: When a source was previously published in a different form, you may include information about the prior publication. This is an optional element; include this information at your discretion, if you feel it would give your reader important context for the source.

MacMillan, Margaret. "Hubris." *History's People: Personalities and the Past, Massey Lectures*, CBC Radio, 3 Nov. 2015, www.cbc.ca/radio/ideas/history-s-people-personalities-the-pastlecture-2-1.3301571. Podcast. Originally delivered at the Arts and Culture Centre, St. John's, NL, 25 Sept. 2015, 7:00 p.m. Lecture.

reference work entries: List by the author of the entry, if known; otherwise, list by the entry itself. The citation of a well-known reference work (because such works are frequently updated) should not have full publication details; provide the edition number, date, and location only. Don't include page numbers for works that arrange their entries alphabetically.

"Artificial." *Oxford English Dictionary*. 2nd ed., 1989. Fowler, H.W. "Unique." The King's English, 2nd ed., 1908. *Bartleby.com*, bartleby.com/116/108.html#2. Accessed 5 Mar. 2016.

Marsh, James. "Canoe, Birchbark." *The Canadian Encyclopedia*, 2000 ed., McClelland & Stewart, 1999.

works with a title in the title: A title that is usually italicized should remain italicized when it appears within quotation marks:

Yearling, R. "*Hamlet* and the Limits of Narrative." *Essays in Criticism: A Quarterly Journal of Literary Criticism*, vol. 65, no. 4, 2015, pp. 368–82. *Proquest*, doi:dx. doi.org/10.1093/escrit/cgv022

Titles that are in quotation marks that appear within other titles in quotation marks are enclosed by single quotation marks:

Bettelheim, Bruno. "'The Goose Girl': Achieving Autonomy." *The Uses of Enchantment: The Meaning and Importance of Fairy Tales*, Vintage-Random House, 1989, pp. 136–43.

An italicized title that is included within another italicized title is neither italicized nor placed in quotation marks. It appears in roman:

Morelli, Stefan. *Stoppard's* Arcadia *and Modern Drama*. Ashgate, 2004.

If a title normally enclosed in quotation marks appears in an italicized title, keep the quotation marks:

> Wimsatt, C.W. *"Fern Hill" and British Poetry in the 1950s*. ECW, 2004.

material from prefaces, introductions, etc.: If you refer to something from a work's preface, introduction, or foreword, the reference under Works Cited should begin with the name of the author of that preface, introduction, or foreword. Add inclusive page numbers after the date of publication.

> Warkentin, Germaine. Introduction. *Set in Authority*, by Sara Jeannette Duncan, Broadview Press, 1996, pp. 9–51.

magazine articles: The title of the article should appear in quotation marks, the title of the magazine in italics. If no author is identified, the title of the article should appear first. If the magazine is published monthly or every two months, give the date as month and year. For magazines published weekly or every two weeks, give the date as day, month, and year. Abbreviate the names of months (except for May, June, and July).

> MacRitchie, Lynn. "Ofili's Glittering Icons." *Art in America*, Jan. 2000, pp. 44–56.
>
> "Greens in Pinstriped Suits." *The Economist*, 21 May 2016, www.economist.com/news/business/21699141-climate-conscious-shareholders-are-putting-big-oil-spot-greens-pinstriped-suits.

If you accessed the article online yourself, you may include the date of access, though it is an optional element. If the website is hosted by a body other than the magazine itself, include it as a second container with its accompanying publication details.

> Gladwell, Malcolm. "The Art of Failure: Why Some People Choke and Others Panic." *The New Yorker*, 21 Aug. 2000, www.newyorker.com/magazine/2000/08/21/the-art-of-failure. Accessed 18 Feb. 2013.
>
> Kreimer, Julian. "Mernet Larsen." *Art in America*, vol. 104, no. 4, 2016, pp. 115–16. *Academic Search Complete*, www.search.ebscohost.com/login.aspx?direct=true&db=a9hAN=114088897&site=ehost-live. Accessed 4 Nov. 2015.

newspaper articles: The basic principles to follow with newspaper articles or editorials are the same as with magazine articles (see above). Note, however, that when the newspaper's sections are paginated separately, section as well as page numbers are often required. If an article is not printed on consecutive pages, include only the first page number followed by a plus sign. In the following reference the article begins on page 3 of the first section:

> Yakabuski, Konrad. "Many Looking for Meaning in Vice-Presidential Debate." *The Globe and Mail*, 12 Oct. 2012, p. A3+.

If you are citing an online version of a newspaper article you should include the date you accessed the site. The site name, if it is different from the container title, should also be included.

> Kaplan, Thomas. "Bernie Sanders Wins Oregon; Hillary Clinton Declares Victory in Kentucky." *The New York Times*, 17 May 2016, www.nytimes.com/ 2016/05/18/ us/politics/bernie-sanders-oregon-results.html. Accessed 17 May 2016.

journal articles: The basic principles are the same as with magazine articles, but entries for journal articles include the volume and issue numbers.

> Roy, Indrani. "Irony and Derision in Congreve's *The Way of the World*." *PMLA*, vol. 120, no. 6, 2005, pp. 60–72.

If you are citing an online version of a journal article you should include the date you accessed the site, as well as any additional containers and their publication details (databases, for example).

> Sohmer, Steve. "12 June 1599: Opening Day at Shakespeare's Globe." *Early Modern Literary Studies: A Journal of Sixteenth- and Seventeenth-Century English Literature*, vol. 3, no. 1, 1997. *ProQuest*, www.extra.shu.ac.uk/emls/emlshome. html. Accessed 18 May 2016.

book reviews: The name of the reviewer (if it has been provided) should come first, followed by the title of the review (if there is one), and the information on the book itself.

> Leiter, Brian, and Michael Weisberg. "Do You Only Have a Brain? On Thomas Nagel." Review of *Why the Materialist Neo-Darwinian Conception of Nature Is Almost Certainly False*, by Thomas Nagel, *The Nation*, 22 Oct. 2012, www.thenation. com/article/do-you-only-have-brain-thomas-nagel/. Accessed 22 Oct. 2012.
> Wills, Garry. "A Masterpiece on the Rise of Christianity." Review of *Through the Eye of a Needle: Wealth, The Fall of Rome, and the Making of Christianity in the West, 350–550 AD*, by Peter Brown, *New York Review of Books*, 11 Oct. 2012, pp. 43–45.

periodical publications in online databases:

> Hill, Katherine C. "Virginia Woolf and Leslie Stephen: History and Literary Revolution." PMLA, vol. 96, no. 3, 1981, pp. 351–62. *JSTOR*, www.jstor.org/ stable/461911. Accessed 6 Oct. 2012.

illustrated books: Include the illustrator's name as well as the author's name.

> Juster, Norman. *The Phantom Tollbooth.* Illustrated by Jules Feiffer, Yearling-Random House, 1961.

graphic narratives: In many graphic narratives, both the illustrations and the text are created by one person; these kinds of works should be documented as in the first example below. Use the second example's format for works whose text is by one person and illustrations by another.

> Leavitt, Sarah. *Tangles: A Story about Alzheimer's, My Mother, and Me.* Freehand Books, 2010.
> Pekar, Harvey. *Ego and Hubris: The Michael Malice Story.* Art by Gary Dumm, Ballantine-Random House, 2006.

films or television episodes: These entries may be tailored to the context in which you are citing the work. If you are discussing the work of a director, for example, place the director's name in the Author element:

> Zeitlin, Behn, director. *Beasts of the Southern Wild.* Performances by Quvenzhané Wallis and Dwight Henry, Fox Searchlight, 2012.
> Medak, Peter, director. "The Buys." *The Wire,* created by David Simon and Ed Burns, season 1, episode 3, HBO, 16 June 2002.

If you are discussing a particular performance, place the actor's name in the Author element.

> Moss, Elizabeth, performer. "A Little Kiss." *Mad Men,* directed by Jennifer Getzinger, AMC, 25 Mar. 2012.
> Spacey, Kevin, performer. "Chapter 5." *House of Cards,* directed by Joel Schumacher, season 1, episode 5. Netflix, www.netflix.com/search/house?jbv=70178217&jbp=0&jbr=021.

online videos: If your source is a video on a website, cite, if you can, who uploaded the video, and the date on which the video was posted.

> Gleeson, Thomas, director. "Home." Screen Innovation Production Fund, 2012. *Vimeo,* uploaded by Thomas Gleeson, 31 Jan. 2013, www.vimeo.com/58630796.

radio broadcasts:

> "Glenn Gould Special." *The Sunday Edition,* narrated by Robert Harris and Michael Enright, CBC Radio One, 23 Sept. 2012.

podcasts:

> "Too Old to Be Governable Too Young to Die Edition." *Slate's Culture Gabfest*, narrated by Stephen Metcalf, Julia Turner, and Laura Miller, 18 May 2016, www.slate.com/articles/podcasts/culturegabfest/2016/05/. Accessed 18 May 2016.

recorded music:

> Williams, Lucinda. "Real Love." *Little Honey*, Lost Highway, 2008.

live performances: If you are citing a live performance or lecture, include the physical location and the city where the performance or lecture was delivered, as well as the date. Omit the city name if it is part of the location name. Include other information about the performance — the names of the director, the conductor, and/or lead performers, for instance — where such information is relevant. If your work focuses on the contribution of a performance's director, for example, cite that person in the Author element. Other important contributors follow the title in the Other Contributors element.

> Bedford, Brian, director. *The Importance of Being Earnest*, by Oscar Wilde. Performances by Brian Bedford, Santino Fontana, David Furr, Charlotte Parry, and Sarah Topham, Roundabout Theatre Company, American Airlines Theatre, New York. 3 July 2011.
> MacMillan, Margaret. "Hubris." *History's People: Personalities and the Past*, Arts and Culture Centre, St. John's, NL, 25 Sept. 2015, 7:00 p.m. Massey Lecture.

works of visual art: When citing a physical object you have experienced, such as a work of art, provide in the Location element the name of the institution and city where you experienced it. Leave out the name of the city if the city name is part of the institution name (e.g., Art Institute of Chicago).

> Housser, Yvonne McKague. *Cobalt*. 1931. National Gallery of Canada, Ottawa.
> Sargent, John Singer. *Henry James*. 1913. National Portrait Gallery, London.

If you access a work of art online or in a book, you should include full information about the website or volume you consulted.

> Colquhoun, Ithell. *Scylla*. 1938. Tate Gallery, London. *Tate Women Artists*, by Alicia Foster, Tate, 2004, p. 85.
> Giotto di Bondone. *Lamentation*. 1304–06. Capella Scrovegni, Padua, *Web Gallery of Art*, www.wga.hu/frames-e.html?/html/g/giotto/. Accessed 29 Jan. 2013.

interviews: Begin all entries for interviews with the name of the person being interviewed, and if there is a title for the interview, include it (in quotation marks if it is part of another work, or in italics if it has been published by itself). If there is no title, or if the title does not make clear that the work is an interview, write Interview, and give the name of the interviewer, if known. Finish with whatever publication information is appropriate. If you conducted the interview yourself, give the name of the person you interviewed, the medium (Personal interview, Telephone interview), and the date.

Erdrich, Louise. Interview by Bill Moyers, *Bill Moyers Journal*, PBS, 9 Apr. 2010, www.pbs.org/moyers/journal/04092010/watch2.html. Accessed 16 Jan. 2013.

Nelson, Willie. "The Silver-Headed Stranger." Interview by Andrew Goldman, *New York Times Magazine*, 16 Dec. 2012, p. 12.

Rosengarten, Herbert. Personal interview, 21 Jan. 2013.

online projects: In the case of large projects, cite the full range of years during which the project has been developed:

Secord, James A. et al., editors. *Darwin Correspondence Project*. 1974–2016, www.darwinproject.ac.uk/.

Willett, Perry, editor. *Victorian Women Writers Project*. Indiana University Digital Library Program, 1995–2016, webapp1.dlib.indiana.edu/vwwp/welcome.do. Accessed 26 Nov. 2012.

e-books: E-books should be documented according to the same principles as other digital media. Make sure to add a Container element citing the digital platform from which the e-book has been accessed or downloaded.

Austen, Jane. *Pride and Prejudice*. 1813. *Project Gutenberg*, 2008, www.gutenberg.org/files/1342/1342-h/1342-h.htm. Accessed 20 Feb. 2016.

Emerson, Ralph Waldo. *The American Scholar*. 1837. *American Transcendentalism Web*, ed. Ann Woodlief, Virginia Commonwealth U, 1999, www.transcendentalism-legacy.tamu.edu/authors/emerson/essays/amscholar.html. Accessed 16 Mar. 2013.

Herman, Jonathan R. *I and Tao: Martin Buber's Encounter with Chuang Tzu*. State U of New York P, 1996. *Google Books*, books.google.ca/books?id=I1U10Ei8ob0C. Downloaded 30 May 2015.

Shakespeare, William. *As You Like It*. Edited by David Bevington, Broadview Press, 2012. *Broadview Press*, www.broadviewpress.com/product/as-you-like-it/#tab-description. Downloaded 3 Mar. 2016.

information databases:

Gaston, Craig. "Consumption-related greenhouse gas emissions in Canada, the United States and China." *Statistics Canada*, 8 Dec. 2011, www.statcan.gc.ca/pub/16-002-x/2011004/part-partie4-eng.htm. Accessed 17 Apr. 2016.

entry in a wiki: Wikis are online sites that can be added to and edited by any site user; as such, they may be subject to frequent changes made by any number of authors and editors. Do not, therefore, provide any authors' names. Start with the entry's title; then give the name of the wiki, the site publisher, the date of the entry's last update, the medium, and the date you accessed the site.

> "William Caxton." *Wikipedia*. Wikimedia Foundation, 20 Oct. 2012, www. en.wikipedia.org/wiki/William_Caxton. Accessed 26 Oct. 2012.

blog post: Include the title of the posting as your source title, the blog title as the first container, and the name of the blog host as a publisher.

> LePan, Don. "Reading and Writing and Work." *Animals, Rising Stories, Etc.*, Blogspot, 21 May 2016, www.donlepan.blogspot.ca. Accessed 24 May 2016.

e-mail message: Use the subject as the title and place it within quotation marks.

> Milton, Frank. "Thoughts on Animal Rights." Received by the author, 15 Jan. 2013.

If it is not clear from the context of your work that the source being cited is an e-mail, you may wish to add an optional element to the end of your citation that indicates the type of work.

> Stuart, Jennifer. "My Experience of the Attack." Received by the author, 17 May 2016. E-mail.

tweet: Copy the full, unchanged text of the tweet in the title element and enclose it in quotation marks. The username is included as the Author element.

> @newyorker. "With the resignation of Turkey's Prime Minister, the country's President now stands alone and unchallenged." *Twitter*, 6 May 2016, twitter. com/ NewYorker/status/728676985254379520.

comment posted on a web page: Usernames are given in full, unchanged. If the comment is anonymous, skip the author element. If the comment does not have its own title, provide instead a description of the comment that includes the title of the work being commented on (e.g., Comment on "Clinton Aims for Decisive Victory"). If it is available, include the exact time of posting in the Publication Date element.

> Evan. Comment on "Another Impasse on Gun Bills, Another Win for Hyperpolitics." The *New York Times*, 21 June 2016, 9:02 a.m., www.nytimes.com/2016/06/22/ us/politics/washington-congress-gun-control.html.

Among the details to notice in this referencing system:

+ MLA style focuses on the process of documentation, not the prescriptive following of specific guidelines (though consistent formatting according to MLA principles is still vital to communicate clearly with your reader).
+ To create a citation, list the relevant elements in the order prescribed by MLA (see the table on page 291). Any elements that don't apply to a given source are left out (placeholders for unknown information like n.d. ["no date"] are not required).
+ Follow the punctuation guidelines in the table on page 291. Any elements recorded after a period should be capitalized; elements following a comma should be lower-case.
+ Your citation should give your reader a map to your exact source. If you are documenting an article found in a periodical, for example, which was itself found in a database, you should include the publication details of both "containers" (periodical and database) as part of your citation. See the "Title of Container" section above for details.
+ Terms such as *editor, edited by, translator, translated by*, and *review* are not abbreviated.
+ If there are three or more authors or editors, only the first name is given, reversed, followed by *et al.*
+ Citations for journals include abbreviations for volume and issue ("vol. 40, no. 3").
+ Give the publisher's name in full, but drop business words such as "Company." For university presses, use the abbreviations *U, P,* and *UP.*
+ City names are not required as part of the publication details.
+ The date of access for an online source is optional.
+ Page numbers are preceded by p. for a single page reference, or pp. for a range of pages.
+ Include the URL (with *http:* removed) or the DOI in the location element for digital sources. Do not surround the address with angle brackets and do conclude with a period.
+ You do not have to identify the media type of your source, unless it is required for clarity.

Chicago Style

About Chicago Style

The University of Chicago's massively comprehensive *Chicago Manual of Style* (16th edition, 2010), provides full information on two documentation systems: an author-date system of citation that is similar to APA style, and a traditional foot- or endnoting system. The latter, which this book refers to as Chicago Style, and which is often used in the history and philosophy disciplines, is outlined below.

In the pages that follow, information about electronic sources has been presented in an integrated fashion, with information about referencing hard copies of print sources presented alongside information about referencing online versions. General guidelines covering entries for online sources are as follows. Begin each note and bibliography entry for an electronic source as you would for a non-electronic source, including all relevant publication information that the source makes available. Then provide either the website's URL, followed by the usual end punctuation for the note or entry, or, if available, the source's digital object identifier (DOI): a string of numbers, letters, and punctuation, beginning with 10, usually located on the first or copyright page. If both a URL and DOI are available, provide only the latter; DOIs are preferred because they are stable links to sources, whereas URLs are often not permanent. If you need to break a URL or DOI over two or more lines, do not insert any hyphens at the break point; instead, break after a colon or double slash or before other marks of punctuation. Except when there is no publication or modification date available, Chicago Style does not require the addition of access dates for online material, but your instructors may wish you to include them. If so, put them after the URL or DOI, after the word *accessed*.

notes: The basic principle of Chicago Style is to create a note each time one cites a source. The note can appear at the foot of the page on which the citation is made, or it can be part of a separate list, titled *Notes*, situated at the end of the essay and before the bibliography. For both foot- and endnotes, a superscript number in the text points to the relevant note:

> **Bonnycastle refers to "the true and lively spirit of opposition" with which Marxist literary criticism invigorates the discipline.[1]**

The superscript number [1] here is linked to the information provided where the same number appears at either the foot of the page or in the list of notes at the end of the main text of the paper:

> **1. Stephen Bonnycastle, *In Search of Authority: An Introductory Guide to Literary Theory*, 3rd ed. (Peterborough, ON: Broadview Press, 2007), 204.**

Notice that the author's name is in the normal order, elements of the note are separated by commas, publication information is in parentheses, and the first line of the note is indented. The note ends with a page number for the citation.

In addition, all works cited, as well as works that have been consulted but are not cited in the body of your essay, must be included in an alphabetically arranged list, titled *Bibliography*, that appears at the end of the essay. The entry there would in this case be as follows:

Bonnycastle, Stephen. *In Search of Authority: An Introductory Guide to Literary Theory*. 3rd ed. Peterborough, ON: Broadview Press, 2007.

In the entry in the bibliography, notice that the author's name is inverted, elements of the entry are separated by periods, no parentheses are placed around the publication information. Also, the entry is given a hanging indent: the first line is flush with the left-hand margin, and subsequent lines are indented. Notice as well that the province or state of publication is included in both notes and bibliography entries if the city of publication is not widely known.

In the various examples that follow, note formats and bibliography entry formats for each kind of source are shown together.

titles: italics/quotation marks: Notice in the above example that both the title and the subtitle are in italics. Titles of short works (such as articles, poems, and short stories) should be put in quotation marks. In all titles key words should be capitalized. For more details, see section 2 of the chapter on MLA documentation above.

multiple references to the same work: For later references to an already-cited source, use the author's last name, title (in shortened form if it is over four words long), and page number only.

1. Bonnycastle, *In Search of Authority*, 28.

If successive references are to the same work, use ibid. (an abbreviation of the Latin *ibidem*, meaning *in the same place*) instead of repeating information that appears in the previous note.

1. Sean Carver, "The Economic Foundations for Unrest in East Timor, 1970–1995," *Journal of Economic History* 21, no. 2 (2011): 103.

2. Ibid., 109.

3. Ibid., 111.

4. Jennifer Riley, "East Timor in the Pre-Independence Years," *Asian History Online* 11, no. 4 (2012): par. 18, http://www.aho.ubc.edu/prs/text-only/issue.45/16.3jr.txt.

5. Ibid., par. 24.

Carver, Sean. "The Economic Foundations for Unrest in East Timor, 1970–1995." *Journal of Economic History* 21, no. 2 (2011): 100–121.

WRITING WRONGS: COMMON ERRORS IN ENGLISH

> Riley, Jennifer. "East Timor in the Pre-Independence Years." *Asian History Online*
>   11, no. 4 (2012). http://www.aho.ubc.edu/prs/text-only/issue.45/16.3jr.txt.

page number or date unavailable: If an internet document cited is in PDF, the page numbers are stable and may be cited in the same way that one would the pages of a printed book or journal article. Many internet page numbers are unstable, however, and many more lack page numbers. Instead, provide a section number, paragraph number, or other identifier if available.

> 2. Hanif Bhabha, "Family Life in 1840s Virginia," *Southern History Web Archives*
>   45, no. 3 (2013): par. 14. http://shweb.ut.edu/history/american.nineteenthc/bhab-
>   ha.html (accessed March 3, 2009).

> Bhabha, Hanif. "Family Life in 1840s Virginia." *Southern History Web Archives* 45,
>   no. 3 (2013). http://shweb.ut.edu/history/american.nineteenthc/bhabha.html.

If you are citing longer texts from electronic versions, and counting paragraph numbers is impracticable, chapter references may be more appropriate. For example, if the online Gutenberg edition of Darwin's *On the Origin of Species* were being cited, the citation would be as follows:

Darwin refers to the core of his theory as an "ineluctable principle."[2]

> 2. Charles Darwin, *On the Origin of Species* (1856; Project Gutenberg, 2001),
>   chap. 26, http://www.gutenberg.darwin.origin.frrp.ch26.html.

> Darwin, Charles. *On the Origin of Species*. 1856. Project Gutenberg, 2001. http://
>   www.gutenberg.darwin.origin.frrp.ch26.html.

Students should be cautioned that online editions of older or classic works are often unreliable; typically there are far more typos and other errors in online versions of literary texts than there are in print versions.

When there is no date for a source, include n. d., as in the first example below. When there is no date for an online source, include your access date.

> 1. Thomas Gray, *Gray's Letters*, vol. 1 (London: John Sharpe, n. d.), 60.
> 2. Don LePan, *Skyscraper Art*, http://www.donlepan.com/Skyscraper_Art.html
>   (accessed February 10, 2013).

> Gray, Thomas. *Gray's Letters*. Vol. 1. London: John Sharpe, n. d.
> LePan, Don. *Skyscraper Art*. http://www.donlepan.com/Skyscraper_Art.html (ac-
>   cessed February 10, 2013).

two or more dates for a work: Note that in the Darwin example above both the date of the original publication and the date of the modern edition are provided. If you are citing work in a form that has been revised by the author, however, you should cite the date of the revised publication, not the original.

1. Eric Foner, *Free Soil, Free Labor, Free Men: A Study of Antebellum America*, rev. ed. (New York: Oxford University Press, 1999), 178.

Foner, Eric. *Free Soil, Free Labor, Free Men: A Study of Antebellum America*. Rev. ed. New York: Oxford University Press, 1999.

two or three authors: If there are two or three authors, they should be identified as follows in the footnote and in the Bibliography. Pay attention to where commas do and do not appear, and note that in the Bibliography entry, only the first author's name is inverted. Put the names of the authors in the order in which they appear in the work itself.

4. Eric Alderman and Mark Green, *Tony Blair and the Rise of New Labour* (London: Cassell, 2002), 180.

Alderman, Eric, and Mark Green. *Tony Blair and the Rise of New Labour*. London: Cassell, 2002.

four or more authors: In the footnote name only the first author, and use the phrase *et al.*, an abbreviation of the Latin *et alii*, meaning *and others*. In the bibliography name all authors, as below:

11. Victoria Fromkin et al., *An Introduction to Language*, 4th Canadian ed. (Toronto: Nelson, 2010), 113.

Fromkin, Victoria, Robert Rodman, Nina Hyams, and Kirsten M. Hummel. *An Introduction to Language*. 4th Canadian ed. Toronto: Nelson, 2010.

author unknown/corporate author/government document: Identify by the corporate author if known, and otherwise by the title of the work. Unsigned newspaper articles or dictionary and encyclopedia entries are usually not listed in the bibliography. In notes, unsigned dictionary or encyclopedia entries are identified by the title of the reference work, e.g., *Columbia Encyclopedia*, and unsigned newspaper articles are listed by the title of the article in footnotes but by the title of the newspaper in the bibliography. Ignore initial articles (the, a, an) when alphabetizing.

6. *National Hockey League Guide, 1966–67* (Toronto: National Hockey League, 1966), 77.

7. "Argentina's President Calls on UK Prime Minister to Relinquish Control of Falkland Islands," *Vancouver Sun*, January 3, 2013, A9.

8. Broadview Press, "Questions and Answers about Book Pricing," Broadview Press, http://www.broadviewpress.com/bookpricing.asp?inc=bookpricing (accessed January 18, 2013).

9. Commonwealth of Massachusetts, *Records of the Transportation Inquiry, 2004* (Boston: Massachusetts Publishing Office, 2005), 488.

10. *Columbia Encyclopedia*, "Ecuador," http://bartleby.com.columbia.txt.acc. html (accessed February 4, 2013).

11. US Congress. House Committee on Ways and Means, Subcommittee on Trade, *Free Trade Area of the Americas: Hearings*, 105th Cong., 1st sess., July 22, 1997, Hearing Print 105–32, 160, http://www.waysandmeans.house.gov/hearings.asp (accessed January 22, 2013).

Following are the bibliography entries for the preceding notes (notice that, because unsigned newspaper articles and articles from well-known reference works are not usually included in Chicago Style bibliographies, the *Vancouver Sun* and *Columbia Encyclopedia* articles are not included):

Broadview Press. "Questions and Answers about Book Pricing." Broadview Press. http://www.broadviewpress.com/bookpricing.asp?inc=bookpricing (accessed January 18, 2013).

Commonwealth of Massachusetts. *Records of the Transportation Inquiry, 2004.* Boston: Massachusetts Publishing Office, 2005.

National Hockey League Guide, 1966–67. Toronto: National Hockey League, 1966.

US Congress. House Committee on Ways and Means. Subcommittee on Trade. *Free Trade Area of the Americas: Hearing before the Subcommittee on Trade.* 105th Cong., 1st sess., July 22, 1997. Hearing Print 105–32. http://www.waysand-means.house.gov/hearings.asp (accessed January 22, 2013).

works from a collection of readings or anthology: In the citation for a work in an anthology or collection of essays, use the name of the author of the work you are citing. If the work is reprinted in one source but was first published elsewhere, include the details of the original publication in the bibliography.

6. Eric Hobsbawm, "Peasant Land Occupations," in *Uncommon People: Resistance and Rebellion* (London: Weidenfeld & Nicolson, 1998), 167.

7. Frederic W. Gleach, "Controlled Speculation: Interpreting the Saga of Pocahontas and Captain John Smith," in *Reading Beyond Words: Contexts for Native History*, 2nd ed., ed. Jennifer Brown and Elizabeth Vibert (Peterborough, ON: Broadview Press, 2003), 43.

Gleach, Frederic W. "Controlled Speculation: Interpreting the Saga of Pocahontas and Captain John Smith." In *Reading Beyond Words: Contexts for Native History*, 2nd ed., edited by Jennifer Brown and Elizabeth Vibert, 39–74. Peterborough, ON: Broadview Press, 2003.

Hobsbawm, Eric. "Peasant Land Occupations." In *Uncommon People: Resistance and Rebellion*, 166–90. London: Weidenfeld & Nicolson, 1998. Originally published in *Past and Present* 62 (1974): 120–52.

indirect source: If you are citing a source from a reference other than the source itself, you should include information about both sources, supplying as much information as you are able to about the original source.

> In de Beauvoir's famous phrase, "one is not born a woman, one becomes one."[1]

> 1. Simone de Beauvoir, *The Second Sex* (London: Heinemann, 1966), 44, quoted in Ann Levey, "Feminist Philosophy Today," *Philosophy Now*, par. 8, http://www.ucalgary.ca.philosophy.nowsite675.html (accessed February 4, 2013).

> de Beauvoir, Simone. *The Second Sex.* London: Heinemann, 1966. Quoted in Ann Levey, "Feminist Philosophy Today," *Philosophy Now*, http://www.ucalgary.ca.philosophy.nowsite675.html (accessed February 4, 2013).

two or more works by the same author: After the first entry in the bibliography, use three hyphens for subsequent entries of works by the same author (rather than repeat the author's name). Entries for multiple works by the same author are normally arranged alphabetically by title.

> Menand, Louis. "Bad Comma: Lynne Truss's Strange Grammar." *The New Yorker*, June 28, 2004. http://www.newyorker.com/critics/books/?040628crbo_books1.
> ———. *The Metaphysical Club: A Story of Ideas in America.* New York: Knopf, 2002.

edited works: Entries for edited works include the abbreviation *ed.* or *eds.* Note that when *ed.* appears after a title, it means "edited by."

> 5. Brian Gross, ed., *New Approaches to Environmental Politics: A Survey* (New York: Duckworth, 2004), 177.
> 6. Mary Shelley, *Frankenstein*, 2nd ed., ed. Lorne Macdonald and Kathleen Scherf, Broadview Editions (1818; Peterborough, ON: Broadview Press, 2001), 89.

> Gross, Brian, ed. *New Approaches to Environmental Politics: A Survey.* New York: Duckworth, 2004.
> Shelley, Mary. *Frankenstein.* 2nd ed. Edited by Lorne Macdonald and Kathleen Scherf. Broadview Editions. Peterborough, ON: Broadview, 2001. First published in 1818.

translated works: The name of the translator follows the work's title. Notice that, in the example below, the work's author is unknown; begin with the author's name if it is known.

> 1. *Beowulf*, trans. R. M. Liuzza, 2nd ed. (Peterborough, ON: Broadview, 2012), 91.

> *Beowulf.* Translated by R. M. Liuzza. 2nd ed. Peterborough, ON: Broadview, 2012.

e-books: Electronic books come in several formats. The first of the two sample citations below is for a book found online; the second is for a book downloaded onto an e-reader.

    4. Mary Roberts Rinehart, *Tish* (1916; Project Gutenberg, 2005), chap. 2, http://www.gutenberg.org/catalog/world/readfile?fk_files=1452441.

    5. Lao Tzu, *Tao Te Ching: A Book about the Way and the Power of the Way*, trans. Ursula K. Le Guin (Boston: Shambhala, 2011), iBook Reader e-book, verse 12.

Lao Tzu. *Tao Te Ching: A Book about the Way and the Power of the Way*. Translated by Ursula K. Le Guin. Boston: Shambhala, 2011. iBook Reader e-book.

Rinehart, Mary Roberts. *Tish*. 1916. Project Gutenberg, 2005. http://www.gutenberg.org/catalog/world/readfile?fk_files=1452441.

magazine articles: The titles of articles appear in quotation marks. The page range should appear in the bibliography if it is known. (This will not always be possible if the source is an electronic version.) If no authorship is attributed, list the title of the article as the "author" in the footnote, and the magazine title as the "author" in the bibliography. Do not include page numbers for online articles.

    2. Alan Dyer, "The End of the World ... Again," *SkyNews*, November/December 2012, 38.

    3. "The Rise of the Yuan: Turning from Green to Red," *Economist*, October 20, 2012, 68.

    4. Wendell Steavenson, "Two Revolutions: Women in the New Egypt," *The New Yorker*, November 12, 2012, http://www.newyorker.com/reporting/2012/11/12/121112fa_fact_steavenson.

Dyer, Alan. "The End of the World ... Again." *SkyNews*, November/December 2012, 38–39.

Economist. "The Rise of the Yuan: Turning from Green to Red." October 20, 2012, 67–68.

Steavenson, Wendell. "Two Revolutions: Women in the New Egypt." *The New Yorker*, November 12, 2012. http://www.newyorker.com/reporting/2012/11/12/121112fa_fact_steavenson.

newspaper articles: The basic principles to follow with newspaper articles or editorials are the same as with magazine articles (see above). Give page numbers in the note if your source is a hard copy rather than an electronic version, but indicate section designation alone in the Bibliography entry.

    1. Konrad Yakabuski, "Many Looking for Meaning in Vice-Presidential Debate," *Globe and Mail* (Toronto), October 12, 2012, A3.

2. Claudia La Rocco, "Where Chekhov Meets Christopher Walken," *New York Times*, January 2, 2013, http://theater.nytimes.com/2013/01/03/theater/reviews/there-there-by-kristen-kosmas-at-the-chocolate-factory.html?ref=theater&_r=0.

La Rocco, Claudia. "Where Chekhov Meets Christopher Walken." *New York Times*, January 2, 2013, http://theater.nytimes.com/2013/01/03/theater/reviews/there-there-by-kristen-kosmas-at-the-chocolate-factory.html?ref=theater&_r=0.

Yakabuski, Konrad. "Many Looking for Meaning in Vice-Presidential Debate." *Globe and Mail* (Toronto), October 12, 2012, sec. A.

journal articles: The basic principles are the same as with magazine articles, but volume number, and issue number after *no.* (if the journal is published more than once a year), should be included as well as the date. Give page numbers where available. For online journal articles, provide the DOI, if available, rather than the URL.

1. Paul Barker, "The Impact of Class Size on the Classroom Behavior of Special Needs Students: A Longitudinal Study," *Educational Quarterly* 25, no. 4 (2004): 88.

2. Maciel Santos and Ana Guedes, "The Profitability of Slave Labor and the 'Time' Effect," *African Economic History* 36 (2008): 23.

3. Thomas Hurka, "Virtuous Act, Virtuous Dispositions," *Analysis* 66, no. 1 (2006): 72.

4. Ruth Groenhout, "The 'Brain Drain' Problem: Migrating Medical Professionals and Global Health Care," *International Journal of Feminist Approaches to Bioethics* 5, no. 1 (2012): 17, doi: 10.2979/intjfemappbio.5.1.1.

Barker, Paul. "The Impact of Class Size on the Classroom Behavior of Special Needs Students: A Longitudinal Study." *Educational Quarterly* 25, no. 4 (2004): 87–99.

Groenhout, Ruth. "The 'Brain Drain' Problem: Migrating Medical Professionals and Global Health Care." *International Journal of Feminist Approaches to Bioethics* 5, no. 1 (2012): 1–24, doi: 10.2979/intjfemappbio.5.1.1.

Hurka, Thomas. "Virtuous Act, Virtuous Dispositions." *Analysis* 66, no. 1 (2006): 69–76.

Santos, Maciel, and Ana Guedes. "The Profitability of Slave Labor and the 'Time' Effect." *African Economic History* 36 (2008): 1–26.

films and video recordings: Include the director's name, the city of production, the production company, and date. Add the medium of publication if the film is recorded on DVD or videocassette.

5. *Memento*, directed by Christopher Nolan (Universal City, CA: Summit Entertainment, 2000), DVD.

6. *Beasts of the Southern Wild*, directed by Behn Zeitlin (Los Angeles: Fox Searchlight Pictures, 2012).

Beasts of the Southern Wild. Directed by Behn Zeitlin. Los Angeles: Fox Searchlight Pictures, 2012.

Memento. Directed by Christopher Nolan. Universal City, CA: Summit Entertainment, 2000. DVD.

television broadcasts: Start with the title of the show; then give the episode number, broadcast date, and network. Include the names of the director and writer.

1. *Mad Men*, episodes no. 53–54, first broadcast March 25, 2012, by AMC, directed by Jennifer Getzinger and written by Matthew Weiner.

Mad Men. Episodes no. 53–54, first broadcast March 25, 2012, by AMC. Directed by Jennifer Getzinger and written by Matthew Weiner.

sound recordings: Include the original date of recording if it is different from the recording release date, as well as the recording number and medium.

1. Glenn Gould, performance of *Goldberg Variations*, by Johann Sebastian Bach, recorded 1981, CBS MK 37779, 1982, compact disc.

Gould, Glenn. Performance of *Goldberg Variations*. By Johann Sebastian Bach. Recorded 1981. CBS MK 37779, 1982, compact disc.

interviews and personal communications: Notes and bibliography entries begin with the name of the person interviewed. Only interviews that are broadcast, published, or available online appear in the bibliography.

7. Louise Erdrich, interview by Bill Moyers, *Bill Moyers Journal*, PBS, April 9, 2010.

8. Ursula K. Le Guin, "Beyond Elvish," interview by Patrick Cox, *The World*, podcast audio, December 13, 2012, http://www.theworld.org/2012/12/beyond-elvish/.

9. Willie Nelson, "The Silver-Headed Stranger," interview by Andrew Goldman, *New York Times Magazine*, December 16, 2012, 12.

10. Herbert Rosengarten, telephone interview by author, January 17, 2013.

Erdrich, Louise. Interview by Bill Moyers. *Bill Moyers Journal*. PBS, April 9, 2010.

Le Guin, Ursula K. "Beyond Elvish." Interview by Patrick Cox. *The World*. Podcast audio. December 13, 2012. http://www.theworld.org/2012/12/beyond-elvish/.

Nelson, Willie. "The Silver-Headed Stranger." Interview by Andrew Goldman. *New York Times Magazine*, December, 2012, 12.

book reviews: The name of the reviewer (if it has been provided) should come first, as shown below:

1. Brian Leiter and Michael Weisberg, "Do You Only Have a Brain? On Thomas Nagel," review of *Why the Materialist Neo-Darwinian Conception of Nature Is Almost*

Certainly False, by Thomas Nagel, *The Nation*, October 22, 2012, http://www.the-nation.com/article/170334/do-you-only-have-brain-thomas-nagel.

Leiter, Brian, and Michael Weisberg. "Do You Only Have a Brain? On Thomas Nagel." Review of *Why the Materialist Neo-Darwinian Conception of Nature Is Almost Certainly False*, by Thomas Nagel. *The Nation*, October 22, 2012. http://www.thenation.com/article/170334/do-you-only-have-brain-thomas-nagel.

blog posts: Begin with the author's name, if there is one.

1. Karen Ho, "What Will Gioni's Biennale Look Like?," *The Art History Newsletter*, July 20, 2012, http://arthistorynewsletter.com/.

Ho, Karen. "What Will Gioni's Biennale Look Like?" *The Art History Newsletter*. July 20, 2012. http://arthistorynewsletter.com/.

websites: Unless the website is a book or periodical, do not put the site's title in italics. If possible, indicate when the site was last updated; otherwise, include your date of access.

1. The Camelot Project. University of Rochester, last modified December 21, 2012, http://www.lib.rochester.edu/camelot/cphome.stm.

The Camelot Project. University of Rochester. Last modified December 21, 2012. http://www.lib.rochester.edu/camelot/cphome.stm.

online videos: Include the author and date of posting, if available, as well as the medium of the source.

1. Great Ape Trust, "Kanzi and Novel Sentences," YouTube video, January 9, 2009, http://www.youtube.com/watch?v=2Dhc2zePJFE.

Great Ape Trust. "Kanzi and Novel Sentences." YouTube video. January 9, 2009. http://www.youtube.com/watch?v=2Dhc2zePJFE.

tweets: As of this book's press time, Chicago Style recommends that a tweet be described fully in the essay's text, as in the first example below. Following that is, as an alternative, Chicago Style's suggested format for a Twitter feed note citation. There is as yet no guidance for formatting a bibliography entry for a tweet, but one would not go far wrong in following Chicago Style's general guidelines for web source entries; a suggested example is given in what follows.

Jack Welch (@jack_welch) quickly lost credibility when, on October 5, 2012 at 5:35 a.m., he tweeted that the US Bureau of Labor had manipulated monthly unemployment rate statistics in order to boost the post-debate Obama campaign: "Unbelievable jobs numbers ... these Chicago guys will do anything ... can't debate so change numbers."[1]

1. Jack Welch, Twitter post, October 5, 2012, 5:35 a.m., http://twitter.com/jack_welch.

Welch, Jack. Twitter post. October 5, 2012, 5:35 a.m. http://twitter.com/jack_welch.

APA Style

About In-Text Citations

in-text citation: The APA system emphasizes the date of publication, which must appear within an in-text citation. Whenever a quotation is given, the page number, preceded by the abbreviation *p.*, must also be provided:

> Bonnycastle (2007) refers to "the true and lively spirit of opposition" (p. 204) with which Marxist literary criticism invigorates the discipline.

It is common to mention in the body of your text the surnames of authors that you are citing, as is done in the example above. If author names are not mentioned in the body of the text, however, they must be provided within the in-text citation. In the example below, note the comma between the name and date of publication.

> One overview of literary theory (Bonnycastle, 2007) has praised "the true and lively spirit of opposition" (p. 204) with which Marxist literary criticism invigorates the discipline.

If the reference does not involve a quotation (as it commonly does not in social science papers), only the date need be given as an in-text citation, provided that the author's name appears in the signal phrase. For paraphrases, APA encourages, though does not require, a page number reference as well. The in-text citation in this case must immediately follow the author's name:

> Bonnycastle (2007) argues that the oppositional tone of Marxist literary criticism invigorates the discipline.

A citation such as this connects to a list of references at the end of the paper. In this case the entry under "References" at the end of the paper would be as follows:

> Bonnycastle, S. (2007). *In search of authority: A guide to literary theory* (3rd ed.). Peterborough, ON: Broadview Press.

Notice here that the date of publication is again foregrounded, appearing immediately after the author's name. Notice too that the formatting of titles differs from that of the MLA style; the details are in sections three and four, below.

no signal phrase (or author not named in signal phrase): If the context does not make it clear who the author is, that information must be added to the in-text citation. Note that commas separate the name of the author, the date, and the page number (where this is given):

> **Even in recent years some have continued to believe that Marxist literary criticism invigorates the discipline with a "true and lively spirit of opposition" (Bonnycastle, 2007, p. 4).**

titles of stand-alone works: Stand-alone works are those that are published on their own rather than as part of another work. The titles of stand-alone works (e.g., journals, magazines, newspapers, books, and reports) should be in italics. Writers in the social and behavioural sciences do not normally put the titles of works in the bodies of their papers, but if you do include the title of a stand-alone work, all major words and all words of four letters or more should be capitalized. For book and report titles in the References list, however, capitalize only the first word of the title and subtitle (if any), plus any proper nouns. Journal, magazine, and newspaper titles in the list of References are exceptions; for these, capitalize all major words.

titles of articles and chapters of books: The titles of these works, and anything else that is published as part of another work, are also not usually mentioned in the body of an essay, though if they are, they should be put in quotation marks, with all major words capitalized. In the References, however, titles of these works should not be put in quotation marks or italicized, and no words should be capitalized, with the exception of any proper nouns, and the first word in the title and the first in the subtitle, if any.

placing of in-text citations: When the author's name appears in a signal phrase, the in-text citation comes directly after the name. Otherwise, the citation follows the paraphrased or quoted material. If a quotation ends with punctuation other than a period or comma, then this should precede the end of the quotation, and a period or comma should still follow the parenthetical reference, if this is grammatically appropriate.

> **The claim has been convincingly refuted by Ricks (2010), but it nevertheless continues to be put forward (Dendel, 2013).**

> **One of Berra's favourite coaching tips was that "ninety per cent of the game is half mental" (Adelman, 2007, p. 98).**

> **Berra at one point said to his players, "You can observe a lot by watching!" (Adelman, 2007, p. 98).**

> **Garner (2011) associates statistics and pleasure.**

citations when text is in parentheses: If a parenthetical reference occurs within text in parentheses, commas are used to set off elements of the reference.

> **(See Figure 6.1 of Harrison, 2012, for data on transplant waiting lists.)**

electronic source — page number unavailable: If a web document cited is in PDF, the page numbers are stable and may be cited as one would the pages of a printed source. The page numbers of many web sources are unstable, however, and many more lack page numbers altogether. In such cases you should provide a section or paragraph number if a reference is needed. For paragraphs, use the abbreviation "para."

> **In a recent Web posting a leading theorist has clearly stated that he finds such an approach "thoroughly objectionable" (Bhabha, 2012, para. 7).**

> **Bhabha (2012) has clearly stated his opposition to this approach.**

> **Carter and Zhaba (2009) describe this approach as "more reliable than that adopted by Perkins" (Method section, para. 2).**

If you are citing longer texts from electronic versions, chapter references may be more appropriate. For example, if the online Gutenberg edition of Darwin's *On the Origin of Species* were being cited, the citation would be as follows:

> **Darwin refers to the core of his theory as an "ineluctable principle" (1856, Chapter 26).**

Notice that *chapter* is capitalized and not abbreviated.

Students should be cautioned that online editions of older or classic works are often unreliable; typically there are far more typos and other errors in such versions than there are in print versions. It is often possible to exercise judgement about such matters, however. If, for example, you are not required to base your essay on a particular edition of Darwin's *Origin of Species* but may find your own, you will be far better off using the text you will find on the reputable Project Gutenberg site than you will using a text you might find on a site such as "Manybooks.com."

two or more dates for a work: If you have consulted a reissue of a work (whether in printed or electronic form), you should provide both the original date of publication and the date of the re-issue (the date of the version you are using).

> **Emerson (1837/1909) asserted that America's "long apprenticeship to the learning of other lands" was "drawing to a close" (para. 1).**

The relevant entry in the list of references would look like this:

> **Emerson, R. W. (1909). *Essays and English traits*. New York, NY: P. F. Collier & Son. (Original work published 1837)**

If you are citing work in a form that has been revised by the author, however, you should cite the date of the revised publication, not the original.

> **In a preface to the latest edition of his classic work (2004), Watson discusses its genesis.**

multiple authors: If there are two or three authors, all authors should be named either in the signal phrase or in the in-text citation. Use **and** in the signal phrase but **&** in parentheses.

> **Chambliss and Best (2010) have argued that the nature of this research is practical as well as theoretical.**

> **Two distinguished scholars have argued that the nature of this research is practical as well as theoretical (Chambliss & Best, 2010).**

three to five authors: In the body of the text list the names of all authors the first time the work is referred to; for subsequent references use only the first author's name, followed by *et al.* (short for the Latin *et alii: and others*).

> **Chambliss, Best, Didby, and Jones (2011) have argued that the nature of this research is practical as well as theoretical.**

> **Four distinguished scholars have argued that the nature of this research is practical as well as theoretical (Chambliss, Best, Didby, & Jones, 2011).**

more than five authors: Use only the first author's name, followed by *et al.*

> **Chambliss et al. (2011) have argued that the nature of this research is practical as well as theoretical.**

> **Six distinguished scholars have argued that the nature of this research is practical as well as theoretical (Chambliss et al., 2011).**

corporate author: As you would with an individual human author, provide the name of a corporate author either in the body of your text or in a parenthetical citation. Recommended practice is to provide the full name of an organization on the first occasion, followed by an abbreviation, and then to use the abbreviation for subsequent references:

> **Blindness has decreased markedly but at an uneven pace since the late 1800s (National Institute for the Blind [NIB], 2002).**

author not given: If the author of the source is not given, it may be identified in the parenthetical reference by a short form of the title.

> **Confusion over voting reform is widespread ("Results of National Study," 2012).**

date not given: Some sources, particularly electronic ones, do not provide a date of publication. Where this is the case, use the abbreviation n.d. for no date.

> **Some still claim that evidence of global climate change is difficult to come by (Sanders, n.d.; Zimmerman, 2012).**

two or more works in the same citation: In this case, the works should appear in in-text citations in the same order they do in the list of references. If the works are by different authors, arrange the sources alphabetically by author's last name and separate the citations with a semicolon. If the works are by the same authors, arrange the sources by publication date. Add a, b, c, etc. after the year to distinguish works written by the same authors in the same year.

> **Various studies have established a psychological link between fear and sexual arousal (Aikens, Cox, & Bartlett, 1998; Looby & Cairns, 2008).**

> **Various studies appear to have established a psychological link between fear and sexual arousal (Looby & Cairns, 1999, 2002, 2005).**

> **Looby and Cairns (1999a, 1999b, 2002, 2005a, 2005b) have investigated extensively the link between fear and sexual arousal.**

two or more authors with the same last name: If the References list includes two or more authors with the same last name, the in-text citation should supply an initial:

> **One of the leading economists of the time advocated wage and price controls (H. Johnston, 1977).**

works in a collection of readings or anthology: In the in-text citation for a work in an anthology or collection of readings, use the name of the author of the work, not that of the editor of the anthology. If the work was first published in the collection you have consulted, there is only the one date to cite. But if the work is reprinted in that collection after having first been published elsewhere, cite the date of the original publication and the date of the collection you have consulted, separating these dates with a slash. The following citation refers to an article by Frederic W. Gleach that was first published in a collection of readings edited by Jennifer Brown and Elizabeth Vibert.

> **One of the essays in Brown and Vibert's collection argues that we should rethink the Pocahontas myth (Gleach, 1996).**

In your list of references, this work should be alphabetized under Gleach, the author of the piece you have consulted, not under Brown.

The next example is a lecture by Georg Simmel first published in 1903, which a student consulted in an edited collection by Roberta Garner that was published in 2001.

Simmel (1903/2001) argues that the "deepest problems of modern life derive from the claim of the individual to preserve the autonomy and individuality of his existence" (p. 141).

The reference list entry would look like this:

Simmel, G. (2001). The metropolis and mental life. In R. Garner (Ed.), *Social theory–Continuity and confrontation: A reader* (pp. 141–153). Peterborough, ON: Broadview Press. (Original work published in 1903)

As you can see, in your reference list these works are listed under the authors of the pieces (Gleach or Simmel), not under the compilers, editors, or translators of the collection (Brown & Vibert or Garner). If you cite another work by a different author from the same anthology or book of readings, that should appear as a separate entry in your list of references — again, alphabetized under the author's name.

indirect source: If you are citing a source from a reference other than the source itself, you should use the phrase "as cited in" in your in-text citation.

In de Beauvoir's famous phrase, "one is not born a woman, one becomes one" (as cited in Levey, 2001, para. 3).

In this case, the entry in your reference list would be for Levey, not de Beauvoir.

private and personal communications: Since the list of references should include only sources that your readers can access themselves, it should not include personal, private, and undocumented or unarchived communications, whether these are by telephone, written letter, e-mail, or other means. Cite these communications only in your text. Provide the initials and surname of the person you communicated with as well as the date of communication.

K. Montegna (personal communication, January 21, 2013) has expressed skepticism over this method's usefulness.

About References

The list of references in APA style is an alphabetized listing of sources that appears at the end of an essay, article, or book. Usually, it includes all the information necessary to identify and retrieve each of the sources you have cited, and only the works you have cited. In this case the list is entitled *References*. If the list includes all works you have consulted, regardless of whether or not you have cited them, it should be entitled *Bibliography*. The list of references should include only sources that can be accessed by your readers, and so it should not include private communication, such as private letters, memos, e-mail messages, and telephone or personal conversations. Those should be cited only in your text (see the section above).

Entries should be ordered alphabetically by author surname, or, if there is no known author, by title. The first line of each entry should be flush with the left-hand margin, with all subsequent lines indented about one half inch. Double-space throughout the list of references.

The basic format for all entries is author (if available), date (give n.d. if there is no date), title, and publication information. Remember that one function of the list of references is to provide the information your readers need if they wish to locate your sources for themselves; APA allows any "non-routine" information that could assist in identifying the sources to be added in square brackets to any entry (e.g., [Sunday business section], [Motion picture], [Interview with O. Sacks]).

In the References examples that follow, information about entries for electronic sources has been presented in an integrated fashion alongside information about referencing sources in other media, such as print, film, and so on. Whenever you are required to give a website URL that does not all fit on one line, do not insert a hyphen; break the URL before a slash or period (with the exception of the slashes in *http://*).

book with single author: For a work with one author the entry should begin with the last name, followed by a comma, and then the author's initials as applicable, followed by the date of publication in parentheses. Note that initials are generally used rather than first names, even when authors are identified by first name in the work itself. For publishers in North America, give the city and an abbreviation of the state or province of publication; give the city and country for works published elsewhere. Leave out abbreviations such as Inc. and Co. in publisher's names but keep Press and Books.

> Gee, J. P. (2012). *Social linguistics and literacies: Ideology in discourses* (4th ed.). London, England: Routledge.

two to seven authors: Last names should in all cases come first, followed by initials. Use commas to separate the authors' names, and use an ampersand rather than *and* before the last author. Note that the authors' names should appear in the order they are listed; sometimes this is not alphabetical.

> Eagles, M., Bickerton, J. P., & Gagnon, A. (1991). *The almanac of Canadian politics.* Peterborough, ON: Broadview Press.

more than seven authors: List the names of the first six authors, add an ellipsis, and then give the last author's name.

Newsome, M. R., Scheibel, R. S., Hanten, G., Chu, Z., Steinberg, J. L., Hunter, J. V. ... Levin, H. S. (2010). Brain activation while thinking about the self from another person's perspective after traumatic brain injury in adolescents. *Neuropsychology, 24*(2), 139–147.

corporate author: If a work has been issued by a government body, a corporation, or some other organization and no author is identified, the entry should be listed by the name of the group. If this group is also the work's publisher, write Author where the publisher's name would normally go.

Broadview Press. (2005). *Annual report.* Calgary, AB: Author.

Broadview Press. (n.d.). Questions and answers about book pricing. Broadview Press Web Site. Retrieved from www.broadviewpress.com/bookpricing. asp?inc=bookpricing

City of Toronto, City Planning Division. (2000, June). *Toronto at the crossroads: Shaping our future.* Toronto, ON: Author.

works with unknown author: Works with an unknown author should be alphabetized by title.

Columbia encyclopedia (6th ed.). (2001). New York, NY: Columbia University Press.

If you have referred to only one entry in an encyclopedia or dictionary, however, the entry in your list of references should be by the title of that entry (see below).

two or more works by the same author: The author's name should appear for all entries. Entries should be ordered by year of publication.

Menand, L. (2002). *The metaphysical club: A story of ideas in America.* New York, NY: Knopf.

Menand, L. (2004, June 28). Bad comma: Lynne Truss's strange grammar [Review of the book *Eats, shoots & leaves*]. *The New Yorker.* Retrieved from http://www. newyorker.com

If two or more cited works by the same author have been published in the same year, arrange these alphabetically and use letters to distinguish among them: (2011a), (2011b), and so on.

edited works: Entries for edited works include the abbreviation Ed. or Eds. The second example below is for a book with both an author and an editor; since the original work in this entry was published earlier than the present edition, that information is given in parentheses at the end.

Gross, B., Field, D., & Pinker, L. (Eds.). (2002). *New approaches to the history of psychoanalysis.* New York, NY: Duckworth.

Sapir, E. (1981). *Selected writings in language, culture, and personality*. D. G. Mandelbaum (Ed.). Berkeley, CA: University of California Press. (Original work published 1949)

works with an author and a translator: The translator's name, along with the designation Trans., is included in parentheses after the title; the original publication date is given in parentheses following the present edition's publication information.

Jung, C. G. (2006). *The undiscovered self* (R. F. C. Hull, Trans.). New York, NY: Signet. (Original work published 1959)

selections from anthologies or collections of readings: A selection from a collection of readings or an anthology should be listed as follows:

Gleach, F. W. (1996). Controlled speculation: Interpreting the saga of Pocahontas and Captain John Smith. In J. Brown & E. Vibert (Eds.), *Reading beyond words: Contexts for Native history* (pp. 21–42). Peterborough, ON: Broadview.

Rosengarten, H. (2002). Fleiss's nose and Freud's mind: A new perspective. In B. Gross, D. Field, & L. Pinker (Eds.), *New approaches to the history of psychoanalysis* (pp. 232–243). New York, NY: Duckworth.

Taylor, E. (1992). Biological consciousness and the experience of the transcendent: William James and American functional psychology. In R. H. Wozniak (Ed.), *Mind and body: René Descartes to William James*. Retrieved from http://serendip.brynmawr.edu/Mind/James.html

INDEX

From the Publisher

A name never says it all, but the word "Broadview" expresses a good deal of the philosophy behind our company. We are open to a broad range of academic approaches and political viewpoints. We pay attention to the broad impact book publishing and book printing has in the wider world; for some years now we have used 100% recycled paper for most titles. Our publishing program is internationally oriented and broad-ranging. Our individual titles often appeal to a broad readership too; many are of interest as much to general readers as to academics and students.

Founded in 1985, Broadview remains a fully independent company owned by its shareholders—not an imprint or subsidiary of a larger multinational.

For the most accurate information on our books (including information on pricing, editions, and formats) please visit our website at **www.broadviewpress.com**. Our print books and ebooks are also available for sale on our site.

broadview press
www.broadviewpress.com

The interior of this book is printed on 100% recycled paper.

PERMANENT   100%   BIO GAS®
                     E N E R G Y

Ancient
Forest
Friendly™